Man's Rage for Chaos

Man's Rage for Chaos

Man's Rage

biology, behavior,
by Morse

for Chaos
and the arts
Peckham

CHILTON BOOKS

a division of Chilton Company /
publishers / Philadelphia / New York

OTHER WORKS BY THE SAME AUTHOR

Beyond the Tragic Vision: The Quest for Identity in the Nineteenth
Century (1962)

Word, Meaning, Poem (with Seymour Chatman) (1961)

Humanistic Education for Business Executives (1960)

Charles Darwin's *The Origin of Species:* A Variorum Text (1959)

TO IRVIN L. CHILD

PREFACE

For thirty years I have been struggling with the crucial problem of this book, the relationship of the arts. I first encountered it in a meaningful and exciting form when I was studying English literature at the Princeton University Graduate School, and that was when I made my first primitive efforts to talk about Baroque painting and Seventeenth-Century English poetry in one terminology, using words I had learned from friends in the History of Art Department. My professors in the English Department were extremely discouraging; they regarded all such efforts with the utmost suspicion. They were, of course, right, but their reasons for their attitude were utterly inadequate, dictated, I felt then, and still feel, not by any genuine confrontation with the problem but by professional academic jealousy of all attempts to cross established scholarly boundaries. I was dashed, but not discouraged, and continued my speculations.

In 1957 I began to teach a course at the University of Pennsylvania on the relation of the arts to literature, and from that course the present book has emerged. The theory presented here has undergone development and modification for nearly a decade, and no doubt will continue to be modified. I am, however, sufficiently convinced of its soundness to offer the present account of it. Of its usefulness, I can only offer the testimony of my students, many of whom have asserted that other courses in the arts teach them adjectives, but that the theory presented here tells them how to go about perceiving and responding to painting, poetry, architecture, and music. Pragmatically, I feel, my approach is sound; whether it is theoretically sound the reader must decide for himself.

Although the central and crucial problem of the book is the relation of the arts, any theory of that relation must depend upon a general theory of art. The general failure to establish a theory of the relationship of the individual arts, and even the failure to make the study of the problem intellectually and academically professional, forced me, about ten years ago, to the conclusion that something was seriously wrong with the current notion of what art is. If our notion of art cannot explain how the arts are related, then something must be wrong with our notion of art. Consequently, it has been necessary for me to construct a general theory of art. The more I reflected, the more astonishing I found it that a couple of thousand people should sit quietly in a darkened auditorium while another hundred people made carefully predetermined sounds on a large variety of musical instruments. And the more astonishing I found it that every day, through the world, tens and tens of thousands of people visit museums, art galleries, public monuments, and churches, just to look at paintings and buildings. The expenditure of money, time, and energy involved seemed to me amazing, especially since for each individual and for the whole world so many real ills and troubles require attention. And when to the high arts I added the dozens and dozens and dozens of minor arts, when I thought of the vast expenditure of energy, thought, and time by middle-class American women on interior decoration alone, when I considered the truly staggering sums spent on organizing the materials and human energy necessary to produce floods of art throughout the history of man, it seemed to me that the only way to approach the matter was to consider artistic activity as a mode of biological adaptation. Shifting my attention from the work of art itself to artistic behavior and abandoning the distinction between good art and bad art, since on that subject there is no universal agreement whatever, I felt it would be useful to consider artistic behavior not to be some special kind of activity cut off from the rest of human behavior but to be as much of an adaptation of man to environment as any human activity. To me, the ultimate question about any kind of human behavior is a question about why any human being should trouble to do it. That is, what is its *function* in biological adaptation? Ultimately, this means that there is a physiological basis for artistic behavior, that creating works of art and looking at them serves some physiological need. I do not maintain that this is the only way of looking at human behavior, merely that it is the only way *to me,* and, furthermore, that it is the only way to gain something like scientific control over theories about art.

I have tried to eliminate any digressions from my line of argument, but since I have felt it necessary fairly often to analyze what makes a currently accepted idea unsatisfactory, and to anticipate objections and counterarguments, it has occurred to me that a brief outline of the course of my argument would be useful to some readers. *Chapter One,* then, presents the primary reason for thinking that the arts are related, analyzes a sample of current writing about the problem, and proposes an explanation of what is wrong with the current conception of art, the mistaken assumption that the drive to create art is the drive to create order. *Chapter Two* presents my reasons for shifting from the work of art to artistic behavior, and in an extension of sociological role-theory, proposes a definition of artistic behavior; the peculiarly *fashionable* character of such behavior is then analyzed, and the essence of such behavior is found in fashion, or, as I call it, non-functional stylistic dynamism. *Chapter Three* applies the game theory of behavior to art and locates the oddity of artistic behavior in what game-theory does not account for. To deal with this, a general theory of sign behavior is proposed and analyzed. *Chapter Four* examines the sign or semantic function of art, which has traditionally been called its "meaning" or "content." I show that this aspect has nothing to do with the essence of artistic behavior. So, in *Chapter Five,* I turn to the formal aspect and its oddities. First isolating the essence of artistic fashion in poetry, I derive from contemporary psychological research a theory of perception which explains the oddity of the formal aspect of art and its stylistic dynamism. I show that this theory is applicable to each of the arts. In *Chapter VI* I examine the stylistic history of each of four major arts as it developed in Europe from the early sixteenth century to the early nineteenth century, and propose a theory of how the arts are related. In *Chapter VII* I take up the problem of artistic value and, to conclude, propose a theory of the biological function of artistic behavior as a mode of adaptation of human organism to non-human environment.

For a long time I have hoped to find some physiological basis for my theory. In brief, my theory of the adaptational function of art amounts to this: On the basis of a phenomenal analysis of human behavior, it seems to me that a primary drive of human beings is towards order, that is, to perceive the environment as comprehensible and to make successful predictions about the future. I am convinced that to every situation a human being brings an orientation which is not derived from that situation but already exists in his perceptual powers before he comes to that situation. Such an orientation works only because it filters out from the situation any data which is not relevant to the needs of the moment. This orientation is the manifestation of the drive to order. However, the successful employment of the orientation means that much of the data of the situation is ignored or suppressed. But since an orientation does not prepare an individual to deal with a *particular* situation but only with a *category*, or *kind*, or *class* of situations, much of the suppressed data may very well be relevant. Moreover, every successful use of an orientation reinforces the tendency both to use it again and to do so without correcting it by relevant data. Thus arises the paradox of human behavior: the very drive to order which qualifies man to deal successfully with his environment disqualifies him when it is to his interest to correct his orientation. To use an old expression, the drive to order is also a drive to get stuck in the mud. There must, it seems to me, be some human activity which serves to break up orientations, to weaken and frustrate the tyrannous drive to order, to prepare the individual to observe what the orientation tells him is irrelevant, but what very well may be highly relevant. That activity, I believe, is the activity of artistic perception. Although I have not yet been able to find a sound physiological basis for my contention, I have not been too concerned. All of psychology is engaged in an effort to find a connection between the physiological level of human behavior and the phenomenal level, between what physiological research shows and what behavioral research shows. Not too much has been settled; indeed, almost no connection between behavior and brain activity has been unquestionably established. Recently, however, a most interesting theory has been proposed which, should it prove to be acceptable, would provide practically everything I need; and I have included, therefore, a brief discussion of that theory in an Appendix.

Rather than present a glossary, I have added an index of the special terms I have used. The trouble with a glossary is that its definitions are torn out of the context in which they appear. I have found that when I use the glossary of a terminologically novel book, I have to locate the original definition in the text anyway.

I should like to add here an expression of my gratitude to the following people, who read this book when it was a manuscript and gave me the benefit of their valuable criticism and suggestions: E. Anthony James, Ira Einhorn, Arthur H. Scouten, Mrs. Lee Friedman, and Robert Ockene. And my thanks are particularly due to Irvin L. Child, Professor of Psychology at Yale University, who encouraged me to keep trying when the first version of this book proved unacceptable to everyone involved, including myself.

Philadelphia, Pa.
March, 1965.

Note: Before going to press, I should like to call the reader's attention to an extremely valuable logical and empirical critique of the inadequacies of stimulus-response theory. It is *The Explanation of Behavior,* by Charles Taylor, Associate Professor of Philosophy, University of Montreal (London: Routledge & Kegan Paul; New York: The Humanities Press, 1965).

CONTENTS

FIVE: ART: THE FORMAL ASPECT *200*

SIX: THE RELATIONSHIP OF THE ARTS *255*

SEVEN: RAGE FOR CHAOS *308*

ILLUSTRATIONS

Plates

Figures in the Text

Man's Rage for Chaos

She was the single artificer of the world
In which she sang. And when she sang, the sea,
Whatever self it had, became the self
That was her song, for she was the maker.

. . . .

Oh! Blessed rage for order, pale Ramon,
The maker's rage to order words of the sea,
Words of the fragrant portals, dimly-starred,
And of ourselves and of our origins,
In ghostlier demarcations, keener sounds.

WALLACE STEVENS, *The Idea of Order at Key West**

We live in an old chaos of the sun,
Or old dependency of day and night,
Or island solitude, unsponsored, free,
Of that wide water, inescapable.

WALLACE STEVENS, *Sunday Morning**

"When *I* use a word," Humpty Dumpty said, in rather
a scornful tone, "it means just what I choose it to mean
—neither more nor less."

"The question is," said Alice, "whether you *can* make
words mean so many different things."

"The question is," said Humpty Dumpty, "which is to
be master—that's all."

LEWIS CARROLL, *Through the Looking-Glass*

---

* *The Collected Poems of Wallace Stevens*, by Wallace Stevens. Copyright Alfred A.
Knopf, Inc. Used by permission of Alfred A. Knopf, Inc.

1

ONE:
RAGE FOR ORDER

For twenty-five hundred years of Western culture, the question, "What is art?" has been under constant consideration. Within the past two hundred years a major branch of philosophy has emerged, aesthetics, devoted solely to the attempt to answer that question. Few intellectual enterprises have so utterly failed; and to-day, it is seriously wondered if the question, "What is art?" can be regarded as a meaningful philosophical question at all. This is a devastating conclusion; if it is widely accepted, there are bound to be extraordinary repercussions. By the standards of our culture, if a painter can no longer use the glamorous word "artist" to identify himself, his whole basis of self-valuation and public esteem is gone. So tremendous is the status of art in our times that it has become a substitute for religion, a revelation of the true meaning of human life.

It may be thought that the logical conundrums of philosophers have no impact on the general culture, but history tells us that this is not so. Sooner or later, ideas that devastate philosophy devastate everything else. For philosophy is and always has been devoted to one and only one question: "What are we talking about, if, indeed, we are talking about anything?" This question always ultimately means, "What aspect of human experience does a particular word locate and inform us about?" Such questions always turn out to be extraordinarily practical. For instance, when it was proposed that the Metropolitan Opera Company be excused from paying the Federal entertainment tax on the grounds that it was a cultural and artistic non-profit enterprise, more than one citizen of New York City insisted that opera is not art, but entertainment. And the same thing happened in Philadelphia when the city government gave a grant of several hundred thousand dollars to the Philadelphia Orchestra Society. "Orchestral music is not art; it is entertainment; public funds should not be used to support it." Such was the claim. Nevertheless, enormous public funds are devoted to various cultural enterprises because they support and exhibit "art." If no area of human experience can properly be called art, and if the word "art" actually gives us no information about anything, sooner or later the immense valuation our society grants to "art" will be weakened and destroyed. The reason for this threat is that this high valuation has been accomplished not in the name of paintings, or pieces of music, or poems, or buildings, but in the name of "art." The glamour of the *word* has made certain objects and cultural enterprises valuable, not the other way around. In the same way, it is the word "justice" that has given the law great dignity, not the just acts of judges, for this is a matter about which everyone is cynical. Judges are what they are, but "justice" never loses its value and its reference.

Yet it may be argued that just as the word "justice" entered human history because some way was needed to talk about what the word refers to, so the word "art" was essential for the same reason. People began to use an old word, which had meant merely "well-done," in a new way; it came to be evident, the argument continues, that paintings and musical compositions and poems and so on had something in common, and to refer to that common quality, the old word "art" was employed for a novel conception.

This is a telling argument, but a difficulty arises when an attempt is made to say what the various objects now called "works of art" do indeed have in common. If all the things we use this name for are really examples of art, surely they must have *something* in common. And if they do, just as surely it is not enough to call it "aesthetic quality" or, in the old-fashioned way, "beauty." For to employ such a strategy is merely to say that what works of art have in common is that we call them examples of "art." And that, of course, is to say nothing. To get around this problem, any number of philosophers and critics and laymen have set up rules for what should truly be called "art." But all these efforts have failed, and necessarily must fail, for the simple reason that someone else, with equal justification, always wants to include something that the proposed rules exclude. If "art" is to be a useful term, something in common to all works of art must be discovered, discovered empirically, by observation, not merely defined; for one definition is as good as another. If I want to include comic strips in the category "art," and also teakettles, no power on earth can stop me. When Picasso came along, any number of people wanted to deny to his paintings the accolade of "art," and there still are plenty of such people; probably they are in the majority.

Similarities between works of art must be found, therefore, if "art" is to have any meaning at all; and this means not merely similarities between two paintings but similarities between a painting and a poem and a work of architecture and a piece of sculpture and a musical composition. And these must be observable similarities, not definitional similarities. They must be similarities that anyone can see.

This is why the problem of the relationships among the arts is absolutely crucial to any notion of art. But it is also why that particular problem is minimized, ignored, swept under the rug, by aestheticians. For the unhappy fact is that no effort to establish the relationships among the arts has had any success whatever. It comes down to this: If the term "art" has any meaning at all, we ought to be able to establish and demonstrate the relationships of the arts. Any number of students of the arts and any number of aestheticians have triumphantly demonstrated that *all* attempts to establish such relationships have failed, but they seem to be happily unaware of what a curious light such triumphs shed on their own efforts to define "art," and to be blissfully unconscious of the fact that their victories are Pyrrhic. Actually, the utter failure to demonstrate the relationships among the arts seems to have been one of the principal motivations for those skeptical rebels among aestheticians who are beginning to deny that "art" has, as a term, any usefulness, validity, or legitimacy.

In discussing "art" there are two levels. One is the level of high abstraction: a cloud-cuckoo-land, some would call it. On this level it is possible to talk forever, and talk very beautifully and interestingly. The talk has been going on for twenty-five hundred years, and there seems to be no logical reason why it should not go on forever. Except that now, here and there, in Ohio, in Sweden, in Baltimore, in England, rebels are arising who are asking, "What *are* you talking about?" And they are not getting an answer. The other level is the one at which the inquirer asks, "What is the relation between this particular painting by Picasso and this particular symphony by Beethoven?" At this level, there have been daring spirits. But they have failed. Popular and semi-popular reviewers and critics and amateurs of the arts indulge in chit-chat about obviously false analogies among the arts. And otherwise there are embarrassment, silence, neglect, and avoidance. If there is no solution to this problem, aesthetics is finished. Indeed, there are aestheticians who say it is finished, though, to be sure, they go on talking about "art" anyway. But a concept which is so central to our culture, our society, and our economy, should not be tossed aside too lightly.

The issue, then, is clear, and the problem is crucial. If the word "art" has any meaning, there must be relationships among the arts. If no way of relating them can be found, then the word "art" means no more then it originally meant: "Something I like because I think it is well done." And this is, of course, one meaning constantly in use to-day, as in, "The engine of the Rolls-Royce is a real work of art." The necessary conclusion is that the extension of the meaning of "art" beyond this simple, original meaning has been illegitimate and should be abandoned. To be sure, everything in us cries out against such a conclusion. But these cries may come merely from our immersion in certain Western cultural conventions, not from our recognition of truth.

1. CULTURAL CONVERGENCE

Whenever a novel inquiry is begun, one can initially use only the ideas—that is, the conceptual instruments, the words—already available. It would do no good to deny at the outset of this inquiry the legitimacy of the term "art" as philosophy and philosophical aesthetics and the general culture have molded it. To do that would bar all further inquiry. One must begin with a practical question: "Has the use of the idea of 'art' led to the emergence of legitimate observations about the relationships of the arts and to the emergence of legitimate problems?" As we have seen, logical analysis tends to dissipate the problem in questions about the meaningfulness of the term. But the historical perspective makes the problem of the relationships of the arts seem real and important. For in the name of "art" there has been in the last few hundred years an immense effort devoted to the historical study of the various arts.

Earlier historical study of the arts was principally confined to explanatory notes on literary texts and, for the other arts, biographical anecdotes and observations on technique. Modern historical study, which began in the eighteenth century, involves the attempt to relate as richly as possible the work of art to the cultural milieu from which it emerged. The aim—a rather naive aim, to be sure—is to "account for the work," to explain its peculiarities by a somewhat simple-minded cause-and-effect thinking. Since both the *Aeneid* and *Paradise Lost* are normally classified as literary epics, why are they so different? The answer, it appeared, could be found in the different historical cultures in which they were created, and it soon became evident that explanations which accounted for differences between similar but historically distant works of literature could also account for differences between similar kinds of paintings and works of architecture. For example, the works of LeBrun and the works of Racine were different from those of other painters and dramatists because both were court-servants of Louis XIV; they were both responding to his demands for stateliness, splendor, nobility, and an ideal of true aristocracy.

Gradually there emerged a recognition of stylistic continuities within the history of each art and of major breaks between those continuities. Thus the notion of the "historical style" emerged and was established and became the principal object of inquiry for the historian of each of the arts. For the periods of continuity, merely for the convenience of discourse, it was necessary to have names, which in the study of English literature initially were taken from the names of reigning monarchs and from the number-titles of centuries. Since the historical-cultural study of literature developed earliest, its nomenclature is quite haphazard, and the historians of the other arts, heeding this casualness, attempted, and continue to attempt, to use more rigorously and exactly determined titles for their various stylistic continua. Some students of literature, only too aware of the deficiencies of their own stylistic nomenclature, turned to adopting some of those developed in art history. This practice began, in a very limited way, in the 1920's, and in conservative circles of literary scholarship is still regarded as daring, dangerous, or silly.

Nevertheless from all this puffing and spewing and scholarly pretension something of some slight validity seems to have emerged. Among investigators whose interest is in identifying historical continua of styles, there is a tendency to establish major stylistic breaks—the end of one stylistic continuum and the beginning of another—at about the same times. Among the investigators in various fields—literature, music, painting, architecture, sculpture, the decorative arts—there is a tendency to put the break between Mannerism and Baroque somewhere around 1600, between Baroque and Rococo somewhere around 1720, between Neo-Classicism and Romanticism (though here matters are very confused) somewhere towards the end of the eighteenth century. The most striking break of all, one on which not merely academic investigators are in agreement but all cultured Europeans and Americans, is the breakthrough into modern art in the first decade of this century. It is so easy to discern that in many instances—as with Picasso's "Les Demoiselles d'Avignon" (Plate XV) or the Fourth Movement of Schönberg's Second String Quartet—the exact work which marks the break is almost universally recognized and the exact time the break occurred is known, down to the month, or even the week.

It is easy to say that the empirical data here is properly located in the behavior of scholars, not in the existence of approximately simultaneous stylistic breaks, that the phenomenon is simply the consequence of taking over from one field and applying to another, categories the attributes of which include initial and terminal dates. It is depressingly easy to show that the language of humanistic scholars is unanalyzed and uncriticized to an extraordinary degree.[1] For examples the skeptic has only to adduce such instances as the classification of Pope as both Baroque and Rococo, of Donne as Mannerist and Baroque, and of the reclassification of Palestrina, long termed a Baroque composer, into the Mannerist category by Paul Henry Lang.[2] The identical reclassification of the Jesu church in Rome was felt at the time to be a great triumph in art history, one that made the boundaries between Mannerist and Baroque much firmer. This continuous categorial shuffling on the boundaries of stylistic continua has been going on a long time; there is no reason to think it will not continue to go on; and it is very damaging. Is a field of which the boundaries cannot be established much of a field? Is it a field at all? Is it merely an illusion?

---

[1] A devastating demonstration of precisely this point has been made in Robert E. Lane, *The Liberties of Wit: Humanism, Criticism, and the Civic Mind*, New Haven, 1961. Lane is a Professor of Political Science at Yale University.

[2] *Music in Western Civilization*, New York, 1941. This is a very thorough-going effort to use the stylistic categories of art history in structuring the stylistic history of music.

However, there is some reason to think that the position of the skeptic may be too extreme. If some categories produce illusions, others may do something more than that; they may enable us to make distinctions capable of being sustained by entirely different categories of perception and verbal behavior. Such distinctions may lead to successful prediction. The categories of Baroque and Mannerism, therefore, may not be empty categories but instrumentally valid. In this case the partial success of this kind of discourse about the interrelations of the arts is more impressive than the numerous failures. There may be disagreement about Donne and Pope, about Palestrina and Watteau, but among those who attempt to use this terminology at all there is considerable agreement about Milton, Bernini, Carissimi, and Corneille, who lie well within the field. Since this kind of study is young and admittedly still quite inexact, notions about Bernini which enable us to see otherwise disregarded qualities in Milton are as much as anyone needs to encourage him to pursue his investigations, to feel strongly that he is pursuing a real subject with instrumentally valid tools. In short, what has been done is at least impressive enough to convince us that a real problem is present and that it can be investigated with profit and to advantage, in spite of the meager and dubious results so far, which have very little scholarly and historical status—almost none among many responsible and serious scholars and critics. But then, irresponsibility towards conventional wisdom leads to great intellectual achievements as well as to crackpottery.

Still another reason to be suspicious of extreme skepticism is the one exceedingly unequivocal instance of stylistic discontinuity in modern cultural history, the shift into what is still called modern art or modern style, which occurred in architecture, painting, and music in 1907 and 1908, in poetry a little later, and in fiction a few years after that. Though there are continuities, the discontinuity is so striking that initially, even to Braque, "Les Filles d'Avignon" marked the death of a great talent. Braque's immediate response was to think of this new kind of painting in terms of Picasso's behavior. It is the obvious common sense way of responding, but it is not universally observed or even very common in stylistic studies. The evidence for stylistic change in art, of course, is in works of art themselves, laid out along a chronological scale. But this method of procedure traditionally has led to thinking about a stylistic series as something naturally structured in itself. Hence arise all kinds of speculations about the evolution of styles, and such thinking has led to a separation of art from all other kinds of artifacts, to a total repression of the simple and obvious fact that art is the consequence of behavior. For the spectator a work of art is the occasion for certain behavior; from the perspective of the artist, it is the consequence. A work of art is not a mountain or a tree. The connection between one work in a stylistic series and the next, even in the total work of a single artist, is not immediate but mediated by the behavior of the artist. The individual work is the result. Whatever the cause of the connection between one work of art and the next in a stylistic continuum, it is not to be located in works of art themselves. A stylistic continuum is not a self-contained process The only process is to be located in the artist, in the emergence not of novel configurations in works of art but in novel patterns of behavior in the artist. But when we are engaged in historical study, the behavior of the artist is inaccessible.

Nevertheless, in spite of this unfortunate truth, the fact of the matter can scarcely be ignored, for only when we suppress the tendency, so tempting and so illusory, to think of historical process as taking place "in" art, only when we turn our attention to the only place artistic process can take place, the behavior of artists, only then can we have any assurance of observing stylistic process as an empirically accessible phenomenon. Nor am I talking about that mysterious entity "creativity." Who is not creative? As soon as we abandon "creativity," which is something supposed to be an attribute of genius, and speak instead of "innovative behavior," it becomes obvious that everybody innovates, all the time. Such innovations become noticeable only when they are so gross in scale that they cannot be missed, or when they are offensive, or when they are highly valued because they solve a problem the culture faces, or when they occur in a situation in which innovation is valued. The fundamental source of innovation can be reduced to two factors: all behavior is patterned, and the patterns are responses to demands made upon the individual by his interaction with his environment.[3] One ultimate source of innovation, then, lies in the fact that the transmission of cultural patterns, since a communication process is involved, is always imperfect: as the communication engineers put it, there is always enough noise to make the communicated pattern fuzzy. Further, any new demand the environment makes upon the organism can only be met with a pattern the organism

---

[3] Here I depend upon H. G. Barnett, *Innovation: The Basis of Cultural Change*, New York, 1953. Barnett is a cultural anthropologist at the University of Oregon.

already has in his behavioral repertory. No matter how he may modify it by appropriate extemporizations—and they are often inappropriate—there is consequently always a gap between what the pattern can do and what the interaction with the environment demands. And this gap in turn leads to new adjustments, depending upon the flexibility of the organism. If the situation is one in which he can produce or innovate no instrumentally successful pattern of behavior, he will employ a completely inappropriate pattern: whether it is called psychosis or religious illumination depends upon the culture the organism is part of and upon its sanctions and behavioral status systems. His purpose is to reduce the tension elicited by the disorienting effect of a problem.

When one studies culture in the anthropological sense, therefore, one is engaged in studying patterns of human behavior and the attendant problems, transmission and innovation. Culture *is* patterns of behavior; and artifacts, including works of art, are merely the consequences or deposits of that behavior. Novel kinds of artifacts are consequences of novel kinds of behavioral patterns, again including works of art. Now, a most fascinating trait of human behavior—or culture— is cultural convergence. When the environment makes such a demand that the individual becomes aware of an insufficiency in the possibilities of his behavioral repertory, he feels disoriented and deprived. In short, a problem has emerged. To perceive and to identify a problem is the first step needed to overcome that sense of disorientation and deprivation. The environment, for example, may present an ambiguous situation, one which appears to call for two quite different and mutually exclusive patterns of behavior. The problem then emerges in the form of the necessity to make a decision as to which behavioral pattern to use; and this before the insufficiencies of the pattern chosen can be realized.

"Cultural convergence" refers to the phenomenon that different individuals in the same culture frequently arrive at the same solution to a problem, but quite independently of each other. They perceive the problem independently; and independently they arrive at the same solution. With the coming of the industrial revolution certain kinds of innovations became commercially valuable: hence the patent laws, which recognize two quite different kinds of innovation as well as the problem of cultural convergence. A "novel innovation" is the first of its kind; an "original innovation" is one independently arrived at but *after* the appearance of the first of its kind. In intellectual history one of the most famous examples of cultural convergence was Darwin's receipt of Wallace's theory of evolution, which was so like Darwin's that some of the phrases were identical. It is instructive of the nature of cultural convergence that some of Darwin's friends had warned him that precisely this would happen. The first thing Darwin did was to establish his priority at the next meeting of the Linnaean Society; Wallace, the younger man, deferred gracefully, accepting without question the grounds of priority, the legal grounds established by the patent laws.

Here are precisely the conditions needed to comprehend the phenomenon of the breakthrough of Western art into the Modern style. The Darwin-Wallace theory of evolution is a pattern of verbal behavior, a matter to be considered later. It was innovated precisely because both men saw the same problem; the gap between current theories of creation and the pertinent data, both living and fossilized. And both men arrived at almost identical results because both could innovate only with the patterns of verbal behavior already at hand, Malthusian population theory and Lyellian geology. Cultural convergence occurred because each could call upon only common cultural patterns; on this subject that is all there was. Hence also the almost immediate acceptance of the theory among the informed. In spite of highly publicized resistance, few theories have made their way so quickly among the competent. Yet one must wonder why more biologists had not come to the same conclusion, men with the same tradition and the same knowledge. Here, perhaps, is the emergence of genius, which appears to be a combination of high learning ability and of orientative flexibility.

When we separate a pattern of behavior from the situation in which it occurs, the more or less accepted term is "orientation." And we can make this separation because, and only because, we can see ourselves and others applying the same pattern of behavior to both minutely and strikingly different situations. The gap or insufficiency is a quantitative matter. Some people are better at problem perception than others; they can learn more readily the insufficiency of a given pattern and can more easily try a different one. This is not only a matter of intelligence but also of personality, words on which we hang above abysses of ignorance. Neurotics are individuals compulsively stuck with a given pattern of behavior in certain classes of situations; psychotics are individuals with an extremely narrow range of behavioral patterns no matter what the situation, a range which may narrow degeneratively until psychogenic death occurs. Nevertheless some neurotics and psychotics are highly intelligent. It is pertinent, moreover, that current psychiatric opinion judges that only persons with superior intelligence and a record of socially recognized achievement can truly profit from any psychotherapeutic method. Others can only be fixed into a pattern or patterns of behavior acceptable to themselves and to their social environment. Perhaps a neurotic or psychotic—the difference may be only of degree or of levels of dysorganization, as Karl Menninger has come to believe[4]—is one in whom, for whatever reason, a certain orientation has been so profoundly reinforced that in anything from a limited category of situation to all situations only that orientation can be called upon—or, more objectively—appears. The same effect, curiously, can be produced by brain lesions, and atherosclerosis in the brain can effect a tearing loose of all orientations from their customary situations so that they appear inappropriately and randomly.

We may speak, then, of learning ability and orientative flexibility as matters of intelligence and personality. These are not the same, for an individual may perceive a problem but be unable to free himself from an inappropriate patterned response. That is, some individuals may be aware of compulsions; if they were not, no individual, on his own, would seek out a psychiatrist. A highly flexible interaction of both factors in situations which the social environment highly values—or some segment of that environment—is responsible for the use of such ascriptions of high value as are transmitted by the words "genius" and "creativity." Hence a few people, long before Darwin, had perceived the species problem and had arrived at something very close to this theory, but only he, above all, and Wallace were able to do something with it. It is interesting that Wallace, in later years, being less of a genius than Darwin, was unable to endure the tension caused by the emergence of certain problems as evolutionary theory developed, particularly having to do with the brain size and capacity of primitive and civilized man, and turned to religious speculation. He reduced his tension, but he cannot be said to have contributed much to the solution of those problems, although he had contributed to their perception and location.

Now just as the Darwin-Wallace theory of evolution was a pattern of behavior, and just as their writing and publication were the arti-

---

[4] Karl Menninger, with Martin Mayman and Paul Pruyser, *The Vital Balance: The Process in Mental Health and Illness*, New York, 1963.

factual deposits of their behavior, so was the stylistic novelty of Wright, of Schönberg, of Picasso, of Stein, of Joyce. Putting aside for the moment not only the problem of the relationship of the arts but also the question of whether or not the various arts should even all be called "art" and even whether any two paintings, even by the same man, have *anything* in common, it cannot be doubted that all these artists thought of themselves, categorized themselves, by the word of a common cultural tradition, expected kinds of behavior of themselves which they saw as properly belonging to the same category of behavior, and innovated novelties in their particular artistic media at about the same time and when almost all were nearly of the same age. Each perceived a problem within the same cultural tradition, and each proceeded to the same solution. This is not to say that there is any identity embracing Gertrude Stein's poems and Picasso's cubist paintings. Although she thought so, there is no particular reason to believe her correct. But the solutions were identical in that each involved a thorough stylistic break in the continuity of their respective artistic styles such as European culture had never seen. It was as extraordinary an instance of cultural convergence as the Darwin-Wallace affair.

But, of course, what made the stylistic discontinuity they initiated so unequivocal and easy to locate was its revolutionary character, its extreme conspicuousness, its still highly controversial features. By contrast, all preceding European art appears to be a stylistic continuum. The extent of the stylistic revolution was unique, but from the conditions of the cultural field in which I have placed it, there is no reason to suppose that less obvious stylistic revolutions do not occur. When one faces the problem of grappling with the relationship of the arts, this particular cultural innovation is an irresistible *paradigm*:[5] to establish an instance of cultural convergence in artistic behavior is to make it possible to conceive of the probability that such a convergence has happened at other times in the history of artistic style; likewise, to establish an instance of clear discontinuity between two historically successive stylistic continua, is to make it possible to at least hypothesize the existence of similarly boundaried fields in stylistic history.

---

[5] "Paradigm" is a word which is spreading rapidly from technical philosophy of science to all the sciences and even to humanistic studies. It means "example," "pattern," "model," and is used when an instance is felt to be a perfect illustration of a theory, as in "science" is "the paradigm of true knowledge." (*Webster's New International Dictionary*, 3d ed.) It is particularly handy when the theory itself has not yet been constructed or is still unsatisfactory.

There appear to be good reasons, then, for thinking that the establishment of chronological simultaneity of stylistic boundaries in the various arts has a real basis. And, finally, there is reason for thinking, at least as an hypothesis, that the various kinds of artistic behavior are properly classified together on a basis other than mere expedient and illusory convention. In short, the problem of the relationship of the arts is a real problem, not a pseudo-problem, and the observable evidence for it is cultural convergence. Moreover, such a striking instance of stylistic convergence suggests that when we use the word "art" in its modern sense, we really are talking about something. If that is so, then it should be possible to find out what it might be.

But a question immediately arises: Why have the solutions to this problem been so unsatisfactory and so tentative? One possible answer is that the terms in which the questions are asked are themselves inadequate. Whenever a problem remains stubborn of solution over a long period of time, or when it yields only a little to enormous efforts, there is more than a possibility that the verbal instruments available are inappropriate. The late Paul Schrecker, Professor Emeritus of Philosophy at the University of Pennsylvania, once suggested to me that there may be relationships among the arts but that we lack an appropriate language with which to talk about them. Since the terms in which our question has been asked are the terms of traditional aesthetics and art criticism, the possibility arises that there is something seriously wrong with the current and dominant language of aesthetics.

2. A SAMPLE

It will be useful to begin with a sample of the kind of writing common in this field. It comes from *Milton, Mannerism, and Baroque*, by Roy Daniells.[6] Professor Daniells' book is an attempt to correct what he conceives to be the deficiencies and failures in the work of Professor Wylie Sypher, currently the best known writer in this field.[7] But Sypher's work is not taken seriously by scholars in the various arts which he deals with, nor by philosophical aestheticians. Daniells works in Sypher's tradition and with the same assumptions, in spite of his disagreement with him. Daniells' attempt in his Introduction to claim

---

[6] Toronto, 1963.
[7] Wylie Sypher, *Four Stages of Renaissance Style*, New York, 1952; *Rococo to Cubism in Art and Literature*, New York, 1960.

intellectual respectability for his enterprise is, I fear, whistling in the dark. He will meet no better reception than Sypher, or the great predecessor of both of them, Oswald Spengler. Both Daniells and Sypher are scholars of great learning, intelligence, and sensitivity. They do not really deserve the sneers with which specialists and aestheticians and other philosophers have dismissed them, for their assumptions are the very ones their opponents use, and indeed were derived from them. I have chosen to analyze certain passages from Daniells' book only because it is the most recent foray into this difficult field and because it is in many ways the best. I am not making a personal attack on Professor Daniells. I am interested only in exposing the assumptions responsible for what I believe to be unacceptable results. Professor Daniells can scarcely be blamed for holding those assumptions. They are the assumptions of the aestheticians, the philosophers, the critics, and the scholars who have the highest claim to attention and acceptance. They are our culture's central assumptions about art; nevertheless, I believe them to be wrong.

Discussing the difference between Renaissance and Baroque style, Daniells writes:

> It is probably possible to isolate one central motive leading to this vast and complex change in sensibility and creative urge. With a due regard for the fragile and tentative nature of all abstract terminology one would venture to assume that it is a desire for power, an intense desire to assert the predominance of the will . . . . What furnishes the connexion, it has been asked, between religious or political absolutism and stylistic coherence? It is not difficult to give a tentative answer . . . . Absolutism supposes omniscience, omnipotence, and omni-presence which compel subordination or provoke decorous resistance within the accepted modes . . . . We are gradually becoming aware that when Borromini or Cortona takes hold of a piece of undifferentiated space and turns it into a single unified field of force, vibrant with energies transmitted by new arrangements of columns, pilasters, cornice, and dome, new versions of nave, transept, and choir, this assertion of familiarity with the traditions of the faith, of power to express them with fresh logic and clarified rhetoric, of ability to seize the intellect and the emotions of the worshipper simultaneously—that this exhibition of sheer mastery is at least as explicit, as effective, and as intelligible as if he had written a book.[8]

These are stirring sentences, but reflection brings hesitations. When has there not been an intense desire to assert the predominance of the will? Was it more intense during the seventeenth century? How is it

---

[8] *Milton, Mannerism, and Baroque* by Roy Daniells, Toronto, 1963, pp. 54–56. Copyright University of Toronto Press. Used by permission of University of Toronto Press.

to be measured? Henry VIII certainly exhibited an intense desire to assert the predominance of the will, over wives and church alike, over the whole state; the emergent style in England during his lifetime was Mannerist. The fifteenth-century Medici certainly appear to have desired intensely to assert their wills over the political and economic and artistic life of Florence; during their regime the Renaissance style emerged. Hildebrand, Gregory VII, was the most masterful of all popes; the eleventh century saw the emergence of Romanesque. The American robber barons have no rivals in their desire to assert the predominance of their will over natural resources, labor, and government, and no rivals in their success; but their architects created in their mansions extraordinary syntheses of all the European styles, some with long axes and some as asymmetrical as the eighteenth-century English garden. The piratical J. P. Morgan's library is an exquisitely gracious piece of Late Enlightenment architectural design; yet cooperation with others is the central value of Enlightenment political and social thinking.

Further, did religious and political absolutism actually exist during the seventeenth century? W. H. Lewis has shown that the absolutism of Louis XIV was pretty much of an illusion.[9] His government had neither the social nor the economic techniques to assert the predominance of his will, and it is doubtful if he really wanted to. The same thing is true for the Popes. It may be said that such objections are not to the point. The desire was enough to be responsible for the style. But did Bernini submit himself so thoroughly to the wishes of the papacy that he became its pure architectural expression, with no mediation on his part? Actually, his design for the Louvre was rejected on the grounds that though it was a fine design it was dreadfully unfunctional. Further, there was no value in seventeenth-century political absolutism, whether desired or practiced, that cannot be traced back, unchanged, to far earlier periods.

Again, if "this exhibition of sheer mastery is at least as explicit, as effective, and as intelligible as if he had written a book," *how do we know*. What makes it so intelligible? The first part of the sentence from which this quotation comes can be applied equally well to any emergent style of European architecture. I confess I can imagine no work of art the elements of which have *not* been disposed by the will of the artist. For that matter, what are we talking about when we use the

---

[9] W. H. Lewis, *The Splendid Century*, New York, 1953.

word "will?" Contemporary philosophers and psychologists are alike in finding that they are much better off if they avoid that term. Further, Daniells remarks, "Finally, there is a change from absolute clarity, in which explicitness is the chief aim, to relative clarity, in which light and colour have their own life, and beauty is perceived in the very darkness which modifies form."[10] How is this consonant with "single unified field," "fresh logic," "clarified rhetoric," and "explicit mastery"? I should think that the "desire for power," the "desire to assert the predominance of the will," would result in an architecture so organized that everything would be completely lucid and all relations would be immediately obvious and clear. And Daniells does say this, but he also states that Baroque architecture has unorganized areas, mysterious areas, areas to which the observer cannot immediately orient himself; and throughout the book he implies the same things of painting and poetry. By his own account, Mannerism is far more lucid than Baroque.

This is a tangle, and there is little point in trying to straighten it out. Daniells is an exciting writer, but more by reason of rhetoric than compelling logic, of value terms than irresistible lucidity. It would be purposeless to dispute him; indeed it is almost impossible since, to dispute, one must have something more than an enchanting flow of rhetoric. His faults are those which he imputes to Sypher: "the effect is of a cross-country gallop."[11] Rather than dispute his conclusions, it is more useful to look for and question his assumptions.

The basic assumption emerges in this: "What furnishes the connexion, it has been asked, between religious or political absolutism and stylistic coherence?" Why should we think there is a connection? Neither the Baroque period nor the Rococo–Enlightenment–Neo-Classical period actually achieved absolutism; the Enlightenment not only did not desire it but desired something quite the opposite. Yet the arts were as stylistically coherent during the Enlightenment as during the reign of Baroque absolutism; if anything, they were far more coherent. Eighteenth-century Dublin is stylistically more coherent than seventeenth-century Rome, in which the stylistically rebellious Borromini struggled against the demands of the papacy with a behavioral quality quite other than decorum. Indeed, Douglas Haskell has shown that the political and cultural situation in Rome

---

[10] Daniells, p. 53.
[11] Daniells, p. 7.

was far more complicated than the simplistic notions of Daniells can possibly suggest.[12] But it is evident from the next sentence quoted, and from everything else in the book, that Daniells has something far more in mind than stylistic coherence, by which he means that all the arts, major and minor, serious and decorative, were obedient to the same stylistic principles. He means also that a particular desire or set of values necessarily is symbolized in a particular kind of style, that the seventeenth-century will-to-power has a one-to-one relation with Baroque style. Since, as we have seen, an artistic style is the deposit or evidence of a particular kind of patterned behavior, he really means that a particular orientation necessarily reveals itself in one, and only one, pattern of behavior. This is breath-taking. Paranoia, for example, reveals itself in innumerable patterns, even in the mask of sanity.

But perhaps this is pushing his position too far. Perhaps he means that such behavior is unique to artists. Some evidence for this is to be found in his introduction.

> In the academic world misgivings about the validity of a search for analogies between the arts die very slowly. Their departure should be hastened by certain successful efforts, which have brought real illumination. Such is Panofsky's analysis of parallels between Scholasticism and Gothic architecture. He establishes the intention of each, states the principles governing structures, produces convincing chronological parallels, and substantiates his argument by a wealth of reference to actual buildings.[13]

And he summarizes Panofsky's findings and arguments for another page. It is impossible, in art history, to call upon a name with greater authority than Panofsky's, and it is clear that in this passage Daniells proposes a justification for his subsequent procedures. But what, in fact, has Panofsky said?

For one thing he has said almost nothing about the other arts, nor about their relation. Daniells' assumption is that if what Panofsky says about architecture is true, then it must be true of the other arts; but if he is aware of this unexamined logical leap, he gives no indication. Further, all that Panofsky has asserted is that *some* of the decisions Gothic architects made were deduced from Scholasticism. But these decisions by no means account for *all* of the stylistic features of Gothic architecture. By accounting historically for *some* of the patterns of the

---

[12] Douglas Haskell, *Patrons and Painters: A Study in the Relations between Art and Society, in the Age of the Baroque*, New York, 1963.
[13] Daniells, p. 4.

behavior of Gothic architects, Panofsky has accounted for *some* of the defining attributes of the continuum of Gothic architectural style. That is all. He has not accounted for either the enormous variety of Gothic architecture, nor for its dynamism, nor, I believe, did he intend to. With the possible exception of *concordantia*, the reconciliation of opposites, he has said nothing about why Gothic architectural style continuously changed from building to building. Actually, Daniells could find the same kind of scholastic authority for certain decisions made by musicians and painters in Otto von Simson's *The Gothic Cathedral*[14] and Charles Bouleau's *The Painter's Secret Geometry*[15]; but these books likewise give only a static explanation for certain stylistic features.

Panofsky is an iconographer. Since the imagery of certain Romanesque, Gothic, Renaissance, Mannerist, and Baroque decorative schemes, like the windows of King's College Chapel in Cambridge or Tintoretto's canvases in the Scuola di San Rocco, was not only governed by theological conceptions but actually dictated by theologians, Panofsky proceeded on the hypothesis that certain non-figurative elements of Gothic architecture might likewise have been so determined. But the iconography is only part, and not the major part, of the total body of information conveyed by any of these vast decorations. For the very precise iconography of Gothic architectural structure, which Panofsky has successfully related to very precise propositions and a sharply defined body of documents, Daniells has substituted a vague pervasive spirit of the Baroque desire to assert the dominance of the will. He fancies that Panofsky's work is a paradigm for his own undertaking which he can safely follow; it is nothing of the sort.

Such a gross failure of the simplest kind of logic in a man so cultivated, so intelligent, so perceptive, and, for a literary scholar, so intellectually responsible as Daniells is astonishing. It is, I think, a true instance of *paralogism*, that is, an unconscious violation of logic. It occurs when an orientation is so dominant in a man that he misses the gap between his orientation and what he is actually saying, that is, the gap between his behavioral pattern and its logico-verbal environment; the result is that a problem is not perceived which should be perceived. The verbal behavior of schizophrenics is particularly rich in paralogisms, and their resistance to exposure is incredibly tenacious.

---

[14] New York, 1953.
[15] New York, 1963.

But non-psychotic behavior is also rich in the same way. Indeed, it is arguable that only mathematics and symbolic logic can possibly be free of them; certainly, all other behavior, no matter how logically structured, involves an infinite regress of paralogisms, each supported by a non-logical orientation.[16] Hence, there is little purpose in exposing a paralogism unless the supporting orientation is discovered. That is what I am looking for.

3. STYLE AND SYMBOL

As we have seen, the strong form of Daniells' assumption is that a particular orientation necessarily reveals itself in one, and only one, pattern of behavior. This proposition is so impossible to believe that it is only fair to assume that he intends the weaker form: It is a defining character of artistic behavior that an orientation reveals itself in one and only one behavioral pattern, or style. That is, scholasticism *must* produce a certain architectural style. But there are several errors here. The first is a confusion between emblem and symbol and symbol and style, a confusion found throughout his book. This is to anticipate my argument, and the distinction between the two will later be more fully explored. Here it is enough to say that Panofsky is talking about emblems, but Daniells is talking about symbols. An emblem is the equivalent in one sign system of a semantic function (or, loosely, "meaning") already existing in another. On a valentine a conventionalized representation of a heart is an emblem of "I love you." The language of the flowers consists of emblems. An emblem, therefore, is a *derived* semantic function. But a symbol, by contrast, is an *original* semantic function; its reference is not to a semantic function in another sign system but to an orientation. In Daniells' book, for example, the essence of Baroque style is a symbol of a ruling value, "the desire to assert the predominance of the will." This failure to distinguish between what Panofsky is talking about—emblematic iconography—and what he himself is talking about—style as symbol—rests upon a great pervasive and on the whole unexamined assumption in criticism and aesthetics, the simplest form of which is, "The style is the man." A more elaborate form is, "Style is an expression of personality," that is, a symbol of personality. From that it is but a

---

[16] Henry Margenau, *Open Vistas: Philosophical Perspectives of Modern Science*, New Haven, 1961.

step—a step made by hundreds of cultural historians—to the proposition that style is an expression—or symbol—of an age. And thence to Daniells' assumption, the assumption of his tradition of writing about the relationships of the arts, that the distinguishing features of a stylistic continuum in the history of art form a symbol of the "personality" (to use a metaphor often used for this purpose) of the culture of an historical period. Thus the style of each of the arts is an expression, or symbol, of the same orientation, the dominant orientation of an age, which pervades all behavior, at least at the higher cultural levels. This is a very large claim.

Now it is true that to-day the term "style" is used in a good many fields other than the field of art, but in fact it originated in literature, was then extended to the other arts, and in traditional critical and analytic discourse about the arts is felt to refer to a unique quality of art. The cultural anthropologists have been responsible for its extension to fields other than the arts, but in the humanistic tradition it is believed to be something within the particular province of critics and historians of literature and of art. Even to-day to say of a work of art that it lacks style is to assert either that it should not be regarded as a work of art at all or that it is seriously flawed; artists consider that they have not arrived artistically until they have evolved their own style, and critics agree with them.

But cultural anthropologists have been able to extend the use of the term outside of the field of art criticism and analysis precisely because all behavior is styled, just as all behavior is patterned. There is, however, a difference. The individual patterns his behavior as a response to his interaction with the environment; as a means, therefore, of controlling that interaction and thus controlling the environment. But within the limits of any pattern a good deal of variation is possible. After a pattern has been set up, put into operation, and has received cultural sanction and status, a residuum of behavior is left over which is not essential to carrying out the adaptational function of the behavioral pattern. Language, which has received more minute attention than any other kind of human behavior, provides an admirable example.

As far as sound is concerned, every language employs a limited set of sounds selected from the range of possible human sounds. The character of the sounds is a matter of indifference, as is the number, within a certain range. This arbitrary limitation is in itself a matter of the style of a particular language. Each such sound is called a *"phoneme,"* but in fact the term refers not to a particular sound but to a range of sounds acceptable by the speech community. These sounds are referred to by the term "*allophones*." Every *morpheme*, or meaningful sequence of sounds, that is, every sequence of sounds with a conventionally established semantic function, like "Chicago," can be uttered with great phonic variety. You can say "Chicago" or "Chicargo," "umbrella" or "umbrellar" and still be understood within your speech community. Each individual, therefore, makes his own selection of allophones, standardizes them in his speech behavior, and always uses them, except in moments of stress which alter his speech behavior. This is the individual's allophonic style. And there are also regional allophonic styles and allophonic styles of cultural level, geographical and social areas in which the allophonic range is smaller than that of the total speech community but larger than that of the individual. Thus regional and cultural allophonic styles may be distinguished. Any pattern of behavior, then, may be executed in an infinite variety of ways and still be socially functional. Every pattern of behavior, therefore, is actually a pattern of possibilities each of which lies within a socially functional range. We all put on our shoes in the morning, but there is an enormous range of ways of doing it, so long as we get them on our feet. Like the phoneme, then, a pattern of behavior is a construct; in identifying a pattern, we simply ignore the variations which do not seem to make any difference. In learning a pattern of behavior, an individual styles his pattern within the range of possible variations for each bit or segment of the pattern. The function is easy to see: such styling conserves energy by eliminating the necessity for choice when choice could not contribute to the adaptational effectiveness of the behavioral pattern.

Style, therefore, is not a defining characteristic of artistic behavior nor of the deposits of artistic behavior, works of art. Artistic behavior is styled because all human behavior is styled. Artists style their patterns of artistic behavior because they cannot help it. "The style is the man" only in the sense that we can identify an individual by the way he has styled his behavioral patterns.

"Style," then, means exactly what it has always meant: an identifying feature or set of features for each behavioral pattern an individual manifests. What happens when we are dealing with human individuals is this: If we are familiar with an individual we identify him by his stylistic features. But if we are sufficiently familiar with him we are also aware of his behavioral patterns. On perceiving a stylistic feature we then expect a particular kind of behavior. If we see that kind of behavior occur in a sufficient variety of situations we can abstract, as we have seen, an orientation. Thus when we perceive a stylistic feature we are led to expect that a particular orientation will govern the individual's behavior in a particular category of situations. In this sense a stylistic feature is a (predictive) sign of an orientation. What happens in art history is that our familiarity with the stylistic signs of a period and our familiarity with its values leads us to expect a set of values when we perceive a stylistic sign. And this in turn leads us to the conclusion that there is a necessary causal connection leading from the values to the stylistic features.

At one time, virtually all bookies wore jackets with heavily padded shoulders and long, wide lapels. Perhaps they still do. If you saw a costume like this in a situation in which it was likely that you would encounter bookies, you expected certain behavioral patterns and certain ruling orientations. But it is impossible to say that the professional orientation of a bookie necessarily *obliges* him to wear jackets with padded shoulders and big lapels. In art history stylistic features are excellent predictive signs. By relying on them it is possible to predict when and where the work was made and often enough by whom. We can often predict the attitudes which can be discovered by further examination, *if* we are already familiar with the kind of attitude likely to be encountered during that particular stylistic period. But as with the bookie, to assert that the stylistic feature is a symbol of the attitude—that the attitude caused that particular stylistic feature—is absurd; yet that is precisely the kind of assertion made by the tradition of which Daniells' book is so illuminating an example. On the one hand he has identified certain stylistic features: on the other, he has identified certain attitudes. He has then asserted a causal relation working from attitude to feature. Such connections must necessarily be spurious. It is not in the least surprising, therefore, that the various writers in this tradition so frequently disagree about what attitude goes with what stylistic feature; nor is it all astonishing that they link attitudes always present in human behavior with stylistic features found only within a particular stylistic continuum. The claim, therefore, that the arts are related because the style of each is a symbol (or expression) of a dominant orientation of an age cannot be substantiated. This is not to assert that the dominant orientations are not "symbolized" in works of art. Since orientations affect behavior, and since artistic behavior produces works of art, there is every reason to believe that works of art can somehow reflect those orientations: but the orientations cannot be deduced from the stylistic features. Nor is it to assert that the orientations do not affect style. Indeed it is one of the purposes of this book to show how they do; but they do not affect style as Daniells and Sypher and their fellows believe.

4. ORDER AND DISORDER

Daniells' assertion is that a defining character of artistic behavior appears in the fact that an orientation reveals itself in one and only one behavioral pattern or style. His first error lay in his confusion of emblem with symbol and of symbol with style, and in the spurious connections he made between them. The second error can be uncovered by considering his failure to account for stylistic change within the stylistic continuum of the Baroque period. That change did occur he asserts in distinguishing between High Baroque and Late Baroque, but he offers no explanation other than the implication that since the style changed there must have been an orientative change: in the Late Baroque style the drive to assert the predominance of the will was content to marshal forces without energizing them: the new style symbolized the new orientation. But this cannot be the case.

From what I have said about style it is obvious that human behavioral patterns must exhibit stylistic drift, a consequence of the innumerable combinations possible within any pattern. Actually my statement that each individual always uses the same allophones after he has standardized them in his own behavior, is not strictly accurate. Even in the individual's speech behavior there is allophonic drift, and with all his behavioral patterns there is the same kind of stylistic drift. Up to a certain point the range—the equivalent in non-verbal behavior—of the phoneme limits the variations; but at times the accumulation of variations may result in a general shifting of the range. Thus in England in the fifteenth century occurred the great vowel-shift, in which, roughly speaking, the phoneme for each of the vowels was placed higher in the mouth, and the highest became a diphthong and was pronounced lower in the mouth: "pearce" (as in "pear") became "pierce" and "shoores" (as in "booth") became "showers." Why this happened we have only the vaguest notion. To attempt to find out is to demand a knowledge of minutiae of human behavior which no historical records can possibly give us. Generally speaking, then, stylistic drift goes quite unnoticed because variation within the currently accepted range makes no difference to anyone, and because extreme variations are eliminated by the cultural domination of the range. Further, when stylistic drift is noticed, it usually meets with social disapproval.

But at this point something odd about artistic behavior becomes conspicuous. In this area of human behavior stylistic drift is noticed, is approved (except when powerful non-artistic cultural forces, such as religion or politics, resist it) and it is rewarded. And because of these factors, stylistic drift is so rapid in artistic behavior that we can no longer speak of "drift"; we must speak of dynamism and even, at times, of stylistic revolution. It is obvious that this is the reason why "style" has been felt to be a defining character of art; in art, style changes far more rapidly than in other categories of human behavior. Consequently it is far more likely to move outside of the previously existent range, as when Van Gogh started making his brush strokes part of his design. Stylistic dynamism in and of itself, then, is not symbolic. Within a stylistic continuum there is a stylistic dynamism, but it is obvious that it is quite independent of any symbolic functions, at least as Daniells and his tradition define them. To be sure, the stylistic dynamism of art may very well be governed by an orientation rather than being merely an energy-saving function, for stylistic dynamism obviously expends energy; Picasso had to expend far more energy in creating "Les Demoiselles d'Avignon" than he would have needed to paint still another blue harlequin. Further, the rate of stylistic change in art may be traceable to an orientation. But both of these statements are quite different from saying that change within a particular stylistic continuum is the expression or symbol of a change in values or orientation. Certainly, however, this odd dynamism of artistic behavior and the equally odd fact that it is looked for, noticed, approved, and rewarded requires explanation, and it is one of the purposes of this book to offer such an explanation.

Daniells' failure to grapple seriously with the dynamics of stylistic change is typical of the tradition in which he writes. The ordinary procedure is to consider the entire range of a stylistic continuum as existing simultaneously, or, as further speculation accumulates, to break it up into large segments, usually the uninstructive Early, Middle, and Late, and to regard works within these sub-continua as existing simultaneously. This kind of analysis can be handled at all only if the choice of stylistic feature is highly selective. Again, the use of Panofsky as a paradigm and justification has betrayed him. Panofsky was concerned only with geometrical emblems and ignored everything else. He was not talking about style at all. He was talking about something common to a great many structures distributed widely over space and time. Every object differs from every other object. When two objects are grouped together because they share certain features, those features are the stylistic signs of that category. But this categorization is possible only by neglecting features which are not in common. Each new level of categorization produces the same effect. The result over a long stylistic continuum is the selection of a very limited number of stylistic features. These are then said to be the defining features of all objects within that continuum, which of course is not the case. Thus the unique features of each work of art are ignored and only those are observed which one has spuriously linked with an orientation; if you select features common to all Baroque works and then identify them as symbols of a desire to assert the predominance of the will, it is no great trick to find that desire symbolized in every Baroque work. That so distressingly obvious a point should be missed requires explanation. Clearly some ruling orientation is at work in any writer who fails to perceive so glaring a problem. *That interfering orientation is the identification of art and order, the almost universal assumption of aesthetics and criticism and the historical analysis of styles.* I believe it to be entirely in error.

To repeat, certain stylistic recurrences within a given stylistic continuum are selected by a process of abstraction increasingly remote from the discrete objects exhibiting those features, that is, from the individual works of art themselves. By repeated behavioral reinforcement the investigator comes to regard this selection as a structure held together by certain forces inherent within it; and he usually identifies those forces with the orientation regnant within the continuum but which actually he has arrived at by quite a different process of investigation and from quite different data. This structure is then *hypostatized;* that is, the investigator thinks he is talking about something that "really" exists; or, more precisely, he ascribes to it "phenomenal existence." He commits, in Whitehead's phrase, *the fallacy of misplaced concreteness.* He fancies that he verifies that existence by observing in the discrete works of art the particular features he has selected and by ignoring the rest. Expecting to see those particular features, he sees them and suppresses his awareness of other features; he neglects the gap between orientation and perceptual data. But, in fact, the stylistic structure which he has thus hypostatized, and which he imagines he has verified, is only a construct. Or, rather, it is two constructs, one of them mental and one of them verbal, which do not have the same structure. That is, they are not completely *isomorphic* with one another, nor, as we shall see later, can they be. As he or his fellows become more attentive in the application of their construct, it is usually broken down, as we have seen, into segments of the continuum examined. But even that breaking down still leaves him with a series of interlocking hypostatized constructs. Consequently, he neglects the dynamic character of stylistic continua, and he also ignores the fact that the only entity which is really there, which really has phenomenal existence, is the individual and discrete work of art itself. Thus, though the Baroque is a dynamic stylistic continuum with chronological boundaries marked by so rapid an increase in the rate of stylistic dynamism that we can refer to stylistic revolutions at each end, there is no such thing as "Baroque style," in the sense that it is a phenomenally existing structure of stylistic features.

Several characteristics of the Sypher-Daniells tradition of writing show some of the consequences of this kind of thinking, as does much of the stylistic speculation in more conservative areas of art and literary history. One is the extreme instability of the various proposals about the stylistic structure of Baroque, and indeed any other historically identified style. It is, of course, particularly obvious at the boundaries of a stylistic field, but there is also only a very moderate agreement on what stylistic features are identifying signs of a particular style. For example, numerous authors, notably Frenchmen, have denied that late French seventeenth-century architecture, the Classicism of Louis XIV as it is manifested in the garden front of Versailles, should be properly called Baroque. Victor L. Tapié has found it necessary to write a large book,[17] in order to prove that seventeenth-century French and English architecture are as Baroque as the Roman work of the same time, English critics having tended to deny that the work of Wren is Baroque. Somewhat more naive than Daniells, Tapié identifies the informing principle of Baroque style, that is, the orientation which the style symbolizes, as simply the desire for magnificence. Since he concerned himself almost exclusively with large works, mostly buildings created for the government and the established church, he was bound to uncover magnificence. Such buildings are always as

---

[17] *The Age of Grandeur*, New York, 1960.

magnificent as the culture and its economy can make them, whether the city is Rome, Peking, Timbuktu, or Washington, D.C. The instability of the stylistic construct and its abstraction from the actual discrete works of art are also manifest in the attempts to identify a Gothic Baroque, a Hellenistic Baroque, or to call the High Renaissance a Proto-Baroque style. I have seen both Veronese and Tintoretto called Renaissance, Mannerist, and Baroque.

Another damaging characteristic of this kind of writing is the way any author in this tradition jumps from work to work, both within the field of an art and across boundaries between the arts. The principal source for virtually all twentieth-century writers on the Baroque style is Heinrich Wölfflin, whose *Renaissance und Baroque*, published in 1888, was the starting point for most stylistic inquiry in subsequent art history. To differentiate the two periods he set up five stylistic qualities, of which one is the contrast between the Renaissance harmonization of formal elements as opposed to the Baroque unification of such elements. In the visual arts, to which he confined himself, these terms generally have some continuity in their semantic functions, but it is obvious that once you get into literature very grave difficulties arise. Still, something can be done with them. You can contrast the rhymed stanza of Spenser and his series of more or less self-contained narrative units, with the blank verse paragraph and single narrative of *Paradise Lost*. But then you get into difficulties with the stanzaic poetry both of the Cavalier poets like Lovelace and the later metaphysical poets like Crashaw, as well as with such an Elizabethan poem as Marlowe's and Chapman's *Hero and Leander* with its single narrative. The fact is, of course, that when you are using such extremely abstract terms as harmony and unity, separated from the actual artistic situations from which Wölfflin derived them, it is almost impossible to keep the semantic functions of the two words separate. Having decided that "unity" is a Baroque characteristic and having decided that a particular work is Baroque, it is exceedingly easy to find unity in any work of art of the seventeenth-century and almost impossible to discriminate it either from Renaissance harmony or a non-Baroque kind of unity. If one is reasonably familiar with Baroque works in all the arts, it is no trick at all to think of one when one is looking for an example of Baroque unity. The term rapidly becomes so loose as to be almost without semantic continuity, and this is one of the reasons why reading this kind of writing eventually gives one such an extremely uneasy feeling. What semantic precision appears to be present at the beginning of the book is virtually dissipated by the time one gets to the end of it.

This mention of "Baroque unity" is particularly helpful when we try to understand the reason for the hypostatization of a stylistic construct. Unity of any kind is something the human being always tries to perceive if he possibly can. Indeed there is no set of perceptual data so disparate that human perception cannot create order and unity out of it. To orient oneself to a situation is precisely to perceive it as a unified field, though at the cost of suppressing and perceptually altering data and configurations which you cannot so unify. From this point of view it is easy to see why human mental behavior tends to hypostatize categorial constructs, such as "Baroque Style." The hypostatization serves as a defense against the problems and confusion and disorientation which are elicited in the individual when he notices disparate data, when he becomes aware of the gap between the behavioral pattern and the demands made by the interaction with the environment. To construct by categorizing abstraction a "style," to itemize its features, and to find those features and only those features in a work of art is precisely what I mean by a "behavioral pattern." Such behavior has its ultimate source in a basic drive which the human animal shares with at least the other higher animals. When a chimpanzee trained to use chalk is confronted with an incomplete cross inscribed within an incomplete circle, both done in chalk, he will complete both cross and circle, thus making a unified configuration.[18] The drive to hypostatization is a defense against the tension elicited when you hear one shoe dropped upstairs. However, in anything to do with art, there is an intervening factor, a concept which reinforces the general tendency to hypostatize categories, and that factor is the critical and aesthetic principle that a defining character of art is its unique power to create an ordered field. Thus in criticism, if a critic can demonstrate that a work of art is unified, he has, he believes, proved that it is good.

The most common form in which this notion occurs runs like this. Experience comes to us in a chaotic blizzard of phenomena; from this chaos art creates order. In transcendental form, the proposition goes on to add that this order is a constitutive order; art alone reveals the

---

[18] I regret to say that I can no longer locate the source for this statement, but I can assure the reader that it was highly respectable.

order which lies at the heart of reality beneath the chaos in which the world comes to us. In somewhat more sophisticated form an alternate continuation is that art must be "rich" or "complex" as well as unified, richness or complexity being a symbolic equivalent of the blizzard of chaos which is what we know, though it must be derived from the work's principle of unity. In situations in which the aesthetician is setting up art as superior to science, the order which art reveals is a discovered order: that is, art discovers not an order which transcends the blizzard but which is hidden within it, an order of which science can discover only fragments. In psychological forms of this notion, art reveals the order of the mind, sometimes conscious, sometimes unconscious, sometimes both. In the Romantic tradition one often finds the idea that by revealing the order of the unconscious mind art reveals the transcendent order of reality, which is immanent only in the unconscious mind. And so on, for thousands of years now, in innumerable documents and in an infinity of verbal statements happily lost.

A randomly discovered example will serve as well as any.

> The art of poetry is an art which, of its very nature, strips away inessentials to reveal only what is important, only what will suffice. What the poem discovers—and this is its chief function—is order amid chaos, meaning in the middle of confusion, and affirmation at the heart of despair.[19]

What heartening words these are! What a cozy glow they offer! It is a pity they are quite false. At least they are false if what is meant is what all such statements mean: order is a defining character of art.

Once a critic or an historian of the styles of art accepts this assumption, his tendency to hypostatize categorial constructs becomes irresistible. Such a ruling orientation leads unavoidably to the following reasoning:

> Style is a defining character of art; this is proved by the fact that stylistic continua can be discovered when an art is examined historically. Since order is *the* basic defining character of art, style must be a form of order. Consequently, the stylistic features of each work of art within an historical continuum of style form a paradigm of that style. That is, the order of each work is identifiable with the order of the style in which it exists. Hence, it follows that a style is the historical manifestation of the universal defining character of art, order. Consequently, every individual work of art manifests three levels of reality: (1) the

---

[19] Elizabeth Jennings, *Poetry Today* (British Council pamphlet); quoted by the reviewer of her volume of poems, *Recoveries*, in the London *Times Literary Supplement*, June 11, 1964, p. 512.

order of art; (2) the order of an historical style; (3) the stylistic features of each work of art. An historical style, therefore, really exists; it is a phenomenal existent. There really is such an actually existing entity as "Baroque style." Since it exists, its defining characters can be determined and defined; and, further, it can be decided whether a work is really Baroque or not.

As we have seen, in this line of reasoning three important facts are ignored: (1) that art has order is an assumption; (2) a continuum of an historical style is a construct; (3) stylistically every work has stylistic features which are inconsistent with the historical stylistic continuum in which it is placed. But the first element is the most important. So long as it is uncritically accepted that art has order as its defining character, all the rest irresistibly follows. As always happens, a paralogism causes one to suppress perceptual data.

The hypostatization of a stylistic construct, therefore, is an instance of special and unusual reinforcement of the basic drive to orient oneself to an environmental situation, and to do so by perceiving what lies within the boundaries of a perceptual frame as a unified field, structured, if possible, according to one principle. Now that science and philosophy have abandoned their claims to discover the order of the universe and of reality, the whole weight of this drive towards orientation has come to rest upon art. Probably this is the cultural situation which leads Miss Jennings to talk about "meaning in the middle of confusion and affirmation in the middle of despair." Any orientative construct is a guide to conduct, a behavioral control. If men at the higher cultural levels are used to guiding themselves by philosophy and science, the refusal of those disciplines to claim any longer the power to constitute the world leaves such individuals at a loss in a world they never made. The redemptionist tradition in aesthetics has thus currently received an extraordinary reinforcement.

But is there any real basis for these splendid claims for art in the name of order, and for order in the name of art? The claim is (1) that experience comes to us in a chaotic blizzard of phenomena, and (2) that only art offers us order. As for the first part of the claim, is it true? Does experience really come to us in a chaotic blizzard? No, it does not. All behavior is patterned and all behavior is styled, including perceptual behavior; and by "perception" I mean in this book all data reaching the brain through the various senses.

The individual is continuously, and largely unconsciously, casting his environment in the mold of his past experiences through a dynamic interaction between its components and his self-conception. He must perforce classify and interpret himself as well as other things; and since no two things (including himself) are ever identical from one moment to the next, he is constantly grouping together sensory and ideological data that are different. Perceptual organization is not a photographic process. It is fundamentally an innovative act; it is an interactive, adjustive relationship between the perceiver and the thing perceived. The two together make up a dynamic creative whole.[20]

This kind of analysis of perception, more fully developed, has been variously called transactionalism, set theory, expectancy theory, directive state theory, and the New Look in perception theory. I shall have much more to say about it later, but here it is enough to establish the point that any perceptual experience is organized by a pre-existent pattern in the mind. ("Mind" is an unfortunate term, but it will have to do for the time being.) Art, then, does not organize the chaos of experience. As far as human beings are concerned, experience is not chaotic and cannot be, at least for long; and while it remains chaotic the individual cannot act. To a newly sighted man who has been blind all his life, the visible world he now first sees is a blooming buzzing confusion. Outlines, for example, do not correspond with irregular and poorly boundaried patches of color. In one area of the visual field he sees the outline of a tree, in another a vague patch of green. To find his way around he has to close his eyes. Only when he has established visual categories does he begin to perceive rather than merely see. Thus the observer of the work of art already has an order which he uses to perceive it with; not art but perception is ordered.

So much for the first part of the claim for art in the name of order. Experience does *not* come to us in the form of a chaotic phenomenal blizzard. As for the second part, that *only* art offers us order, this is likewise patently untrue. A work of art is the deposit of artistic behavior. All behavior is patterned and styled, or ordered. So long as we follow the rules of our speech community, to create a sentence is to constitute reality; to put two sentences together is to create the world. It is not merely that Everyman is Innovator, as Barnett has put it; Everyman experiences order every second of his life. If he did not, he could not cross the room, let alone the street. That order is a defining character of art is so utterly untrue that it is downright absurd. As Miss Jennings revealed so clearly in her parallelism of order, meaning, and affirmation, the experience of order is the experience of value.

[20] *Innovation: The Basis of Cultural Change*, by H. G. Barnett, New York, 1953, p. 114. Copyright McGraw-Hill Book Company. Used by permission of McGraw-Hill Book Company.

In a poem quoted in the same review she asserts, "We want more order than we meet." The sense of value arises from the satisfaction of need, and our basic need is for order. Order, consequently, is our ultimate test for value. Why we value art nobody has adequately explained, but it is easy to see why aestheticians and critics conclude that we do so because it offers us order. The reasoning is this: *I value art; therefore art must offer me order.* The unconscious orientation controlling this paralogism is that the ultimate criterion of value is order. Man is inflamed by a rage for order, and the more he fails in controlling his transactions with his environment, the more the flames of that rage consume him. It is the damaged personality, it is the neurotic, it is above all the psychotic whose behavior exhibits an uncontrollable and passionate rage for order. Those who fail totally reach for the ultimate of order, psychogenic death.

If art is the satisfaction of this mad human rage for order, think of Hitler's rage for order, of his "final solution for the Jewish problem," and shudder. The death-wish is not a desire for death: it is a symbol of the desire for order on the part of men and women whose perception of the disparity between humanly created perceptual order and the demands of their transactions with environment has resulted in an unbearable tension. The desire for death is merely the desire for the most perfect order we can imagine, for total insulation from all perceptual disparities. If art is the satisfaction of the rage for order, then there is no reason why a healthy mind should pay any attention to it and every reason it should not. But does art indeed offer us order? Does the behavior of the artist leave as a deposit the opportunity to experience greater order than any other mode of experience?

We have already had a hint that it does not. As we have seen, the easiest way to comprehend behavioral patterning and styling as a means of biological adaptation is to interpret it as an energy-conserving function. By comparison with other behavior, however, because of its unusual dynamism, styling in artistic behavior involves energy expenditure. This is not true, of course, in any individual sequence of artistic behavior, as in painting a picture or designing a building. There the energy-conservation function of style is quite apparent. It is only in historical studies, whether over a stylistic continuum or a series of continua, or in the more limited chronological study of a single artist's body of work, that stylistic dynamism appears as something identifiably different from the normal stylistic drift which characterizes other behavior. Likewise, the shift of a possible range within which stylistic variation operates is in normal behavior only the consequence, it would appear, of the accumulation of stylistic variants involving large numbers of people over a long period of time. The great vowel shift, which took place over at least a hundred years, is typical. In fact, it never involved all words and was never completed. In the early eighteenth century Pope still rhymed "tea" and "obey" and many Irish still do. In ordinary behavior a striking change in the range of ordinary behavioral patterns normally occurs only as the consequence of a technological innovation. In artistic behavior, however, a shift in the possible range is rapid and is accomplished by one man. The shift in range in a great many patterns of artistic behavior which resulted in Picasso's "Les Demoiselles d'Avignon" was accomplished by only one man and occurred in the course of a few months. Actually, the ordinary language of criticism reflects this in its condemnation of an artist who becomes "mannered" as he matures. The authenticity of such artists—Swinburne and Debussy are instances—may even be seriously doubted. Contrarily, the highest praise is reserved for artists, like Michelangelo and Beethoven, who continued to grow until they died, that is, continued to exhibit a steady and sometimes an increasing rate of stylistic dynamism throughout their entire careers. This is an instance of the reward given to artists who are particularly impressive in presenting the world with examples of stylistic dynamism. Contrarily, a school of art which exhibits a minimum of stylistic dynamism is commonly dismissed with the pejorative, "academicism."

On these grounds alone we can distinguish between art and other kinds of behavior with which it is sometimes confused. I have encountered inverted snobs, liberals a little ashamed of being cultured, who attempted to get the best of both worlds by claiming baseball as an art. The test is that baseball has changed very little in the past forty years while all of the arts, particularly painting, have gone through a number of stylistic revolutions. In sport "style" is a laudatory word used when the player comes close to the ruling constructed norm for some sporting activity. It is particularly noticeable that in amateur sports, shifts in the ranges of a behavioral pattern nowadays occur only when approved by a conference, an organization set up to control and stabilize stylistic drift, or to permit it only under very special and pressing circumstances and after the whole problem has been presented to the public by sportswriters.

On the other hand, it is certainly true that professional sports change more rapidly, and for different reasons, than do amateur sports. When professional baseball experienced the public excitement over Babe Ruth's sensational batting, the rules were changed so that such batting became much more common. The same tendency is shown even more strikingly by the almost total divergence between amateur, college wrestling and professional wrestling, especially television wrestling. There is no excitement in the former except for someone exquisitely conscious of wrestling "style"; while the latter has clearly become a primitive kind of drama, a struggle in which the "goodie" *almost* always defeats the "baddie." The loss of amateur standing by someone who enters professional sports is a clear recognition that he has submitted himself to a different set of rules. The tests for excellence in amateur sports are no longer applicable, for the converted amateur has become an artist, or an actor in a drama. Professional sports show a greater stylistic dynamism than do amateur sports, but not nearly so much as the publicly recognized arts of painting, music, poetry, and architecture.

The same generalizations are true of scientific behavior, which also has often been claimed, sometimes by artists and sometimes by scientists, and particularly by mathematicians, to be aesthetic activity. So long as art is identified with order, there will be a tendency to collapse mathematics and art together, for mathematics is the creation of pure order and structure which does not degenerate into madness because it has no reference to the empirical world; it is not about anything at all. The behavior of scientists, however, is much more like the behavior of amateur sportsmen than it is like that of artists. We tend to think of science as an orderly and steady accumulation of knowledge, though the rate of accumulation has of course increased within recent centuries. But in a brilliant book Thomas S. Kuhn has shown that ordinary day-to-day scientific activity takes place within the limits of what he calls a "paradigm."[21] He has extended this term from its current reference to logical and verbal models. The important idea behind "paradigm" is that, in the absence of a completed theory, it can be used to control verbal behavior. Professor Kuhn now uses the term to refer to the total behavioral pattern of a scientist when he is engaged in some particular kind of research, not merely to the words the scientist uses. A scientific theory, Kuhn maintains, is only part of the whole paradigm each scientist uses to control his behavior. With this

---

[21] *The Structure of Scientific Revolutions*, Chicago, 1962.

extension of the term, he demonstrates that, as in all patterned behavior, the normal tendency of a scientist is to ignore problems which cannot be solved by the theory the scientist uses during the reign of a particular paradigm. Only when a rare genius comes along who sees these problems and, for whatever reason, can afford not to suppress them, does a scientific revolution occur.

In terms of its stylistic dynamism, then, artistic behavior is profoundly different from two human activities which in one case involve more expenditure of energy than art and in the other at least as much, but that energy is not expended in stylistic dynamism and much of it goes to resisting dynamism. Artistic behavior, as far as stylistic drift goes, seems unique.

But my question was not primarily aimed at artistic behavior, but rather at the work of art itself. As a deposit of artistic behavior, as an artifact, as a perceptual configuration, does it in truth exhibit an extraordinary degree of ordered structure, or even an ordinary degree, such as we find in a well-arranged supermarket? Or is it more like a fun-house in an amusement park? For my purposes here, one example will suffice, for I wish merely to put the identification of art and order in a dubious light. Let us take the matter of rhythm in poetry.

If "rhythm" means anything it means the regular recurrence of identical or similar features within a spatial or temporal field. For the purposes of writing and analyzing English poetry syllables are categorized as either stressed or unstressed: further, in English there are only two poetic rhythms, the alteration of a stressed with an unstressed syllable or the alteration of a stressed with two unstressed syllables. In the following (/) equals a stressed syllable (x) an unstressed syllable. Here is the stress pattern of the first ten lines of Milton's *Paradise Lost*.

$$x///x/xxxx/$$
$$x/x/x/x/x/$$
$$///xx/x///$$
$$x/x/x//x/$$
$$x/xxx/x/x/$$
$$//xx/x/x/x/$$
$$x/xxx/x/x/$$
$$x/x///x/x/$$
$$xxx/x/x/x/$$
$$/xx/xxx/x/$$

Although there are patches of regular recurrence, or rhythm, here, there are at least as many patches which exhibit in this scheme no regularity whatever. Certainly no one would deny that rhythm is a kind of order and of unity as well, yet one of the most highly praised of English poems begins, and continues for thousands of lines, in what can only be regarded as a mixture of order and disorder. If art is order and unity and if its value comes from that order and unity, greeting card verse is far better than the strangely messy work of John Milton.

Nor is this all. The traditional way of categorizing syllables as stressed or unstressed is in itself a considerable abstraction at a respectable distance from the empirical facts. According to current linguistic theory, known as the Trager-Smith hypothesis, any speaker of English uses not two but four levels of stress. Consequently rhythm as regular recurrence happens very rarely indeed in English poetry. The childish way of pronouncing "Hickory, Dickory, Dock" does have rhythm in the exact sense, but even greeting card poetry exhibits less order than this nursery rhyme. On the rare occasions when a poet writing for adults does manage, in the face of considerable difficulties or by accident, to hammer out a line of ten syllables with a regular recurrence, of, for example, second degree and fourth degree stress, he is condemned for writing sing-song and for a failure in technique.

There is nothing either novel or subtle about this. The phenomenon has been noticed and written about hundreds of times, though the complication of the presence of four stress levels rather than two is a discovery of only the last fifteen years. Before that, prosodists were aware of only two stress levels, and to this day few have attempted to deal with the Trager-Smith hypothesis. Rather, all prosodists, equating art with order, have attempted to reduce the obvious stress disorder of English poetry to an order. But the facts have resisted them and no such theory has been successful and accepted. In a later chapter I shall demonstrate precisely the same sort of phenomenon in all the arts I propose to deal with, poetry, painting, architecture, and music. Here it is enough to express my astonishment at the refusal of critics and aestheticians and stylistic historians to connect their theoretical statements about art and order with the perfectly obvious and always noticed phenomenon of rhythmical disorder in English and all other poetry with which I am familiar. But I really should not be astonished; I used to be a prater of order myself.

A prater of order:—that, I fear, is what aestheticians, critics, and stylistic historians are, at least those I have encountered, in books or in the flesh. The rest merely assume it as unquestionable truth. I once heard a professional philosopher whose field of specialization is aesthetics, widely known and highly regarded, prate (the word is not too strong) about how the task of the critic is to determine whether or not the work is characterized by unity and complexity (by which he meant features reducible to order and unity), and if it were, to pronounce it good. After the lecture I asked him if it would be legitimate to ask why he valued unity so highly. Gazing at me with astonishment and wonder, he admitted that it would be legitimate. I replied that I had no intention of asking it, but wished merely to assert that no form of human experience offered so much disorder as artistic experience. He replied that he found that statement so strange it almost frightened him. As well it might. But the point is that it was obvious that he had never asked himself why he valued unity so highly. Yet that is the kind of question philosophers are paid to ask of themselves. The task of philosophy is to bring to light the assumptions responsible for our paralogisms, our unconscious violations of logic, and if they are found wanting, to wring their necks.

One further quotation is to the point. Albert William Levi concludes a discussion of tragedy thus: "Peace is the understanding of tragedy." There follows a quotation from Whitehead to the same effect, and then Levi continues.

> Whitehead has caught it exactly: the intuition of an order, the disclosure of an ideal, the vividness of feeling, the sense of meaning amid the loss . . . . *Catharsis* is the natural conclusion of humanistic thought.[22]

Why is order so wonderful? Why must we praise it so? Why is it identifiable with all human value? Why do we see it when it is not even there? We have seen why: we praise order because it is an adaptational necessity for us that we experience order. And our praise merely reinforces the greatest of all human mottoes: *Millions for the orientation but not one cent for reality.* In his indelicate metaphor Aristotle, and after him Levi, has caught it exactly. We value order for precisely the same reason we value a good movement of the bowels. Both are human necessities. The reasons for praising order are comprehensible, but they are not impressive, at least not to me. They are not even exclusively human.

---

[22] *Literature, Philosophy, & the Imagination*, Bloomington, Ind., 1962, p. 316.

Earlier in this chapter I suggested the possibility that the failure of so many investigators successfully to relate the arts indicates something seriously wrong with the current and dominant conception of art. I believe that that serious wrongness lies exactly in the ancient effort to find order in a situation which offers us the opportunity to experience disorder. After so many centuries of praising order, I think it is time to praise disorder a little, and to give the proper recognition to the men whose task it is to offer disorder, the artists. To their social role and to the social role of the perceiver of art I shall now turn.

TWO:
ART AND BEHAVIOR

I do not yet expect the reader to take too seriously my assertion that art is characterized not by order but by disorder, though I hope by the time my exposition is completed he will take it very seriously indeed. Here it is enough to offer two reminders: first, that since we value—and often madly overvalue—whatever is ordered, we tend to impute order to whatever we value, even to the point of distorting perceptual data so that we see something as ordered which in fact is not; second, that perception is not mere passive response to stimulus but a creative, dynamic act, an act of interpretation. For this reason, to refer to the two ways of being related to a work of art, to create it and to respond to it, I shall use the terms "artist" and "perceiver."

1. A DISJUNCTIVE CATEGORY

If we proceed on the possibility that art offers not order but the opportunity to experience more disorder than does any other human artifact, and that artistic experience, therefore, is characterized, at least from one point of view and in one of its aspects, by disorientation, the question, What is a work of art? becomes very pressing. The reason is that all theories of art have been developed from the notion that art is uniquely characterized by order and that therefore works of art are characterized by structure. Now it is obvious that even if art is ordered, it is not the only ordered and structured artifact, though a good many aestheticians and critics appear to think so. The usual way out of this dilemma is to say that a work of art offers a unique kind of order, or as it is commonly put, unity and complexity. Further extended to the history of art, the notion of the uniqueness of aesthetic structure leads to the conclusion that stylistic continua are identifiable by a unique kind of stylistic structure; the weaknesses of this notion we have already explored. The ultimate conclusion of this thinking is that all works of art have in common a unique kind of structure, and that an artifact may be classified as a work of art if it has "aesthetic structure."

It is clear that to abandon the identification of art and order is to abandon the traditional distinctions developed in aesthetics and criticism for deciding whether an artifact is a work of art or not. On the basis of what I have offered so far, it is impossible to make any distinction between a saw and Michelangelo's "David." The only distinction possible is to be made on the grounds of stylistic dynamism. The saw has been stabilized for quite some time. Since the neolithic period, at the latest, its range of stylistic variation has been very narrow and at the present time is narrower than ever. If we arrange works of art in their historical order of appearance, the stylistic dynamism emerges at once. Works of art do not come to us, however, in neat historical sequence. On the contrary, the first job of art history is to establish that sequence, at the expenditure of great time and effort. But on what grounds do we put an artifact into the category of art so that we can include it in such an historical arrangement?

Few writers have attempted to face this question directly, for most of them simply accept without hesitation what their immediate cultural environment accepts as a work of art. In my Doctor's Orals I claimed that movies are works of art. Such a position aroused astonishment and admiration for my daring in some of my examiners; the shocked and repelled forgave me when I confessed that I had stolen the idea from Orwell; others said, "Of course." I have known a widely admired and honored critic and scholar, by no means an old fogey, to be horrified at the notion that the work of Edgar Guest should be considered as poetry. His immediate cultural environment does not accept such verse as "poetry." One writer to have faced this problem head on is George Kubler.

Let us suppose that the idea of art can be expanded to embrace the whole range of man-made things, including all tools and writing in addition to the useless, beautiful, and poetic things of the world.[1]

This is a promising beginning, but he continues by making an unsatisfactory distinction:

In short, a work of art is as useless as a tool is useful. Works of art are as unique and irreplaceable as tools are common and expendable.[2]

This is unacceptable; a unique primitive mask and a Raphael Madonna may be works of art but they are also tools in religious ritual. A unique cup by a great ceramicist may be a work of art but it is also a tool for drinking coffee. Further, the idea that to have an artistic experience before a picture is not to use it, involves difficulties and requires the making of distinctions which Kubler does not make. Ultimately, he is reduced, not surprisingly, to making a value distinction between "prime objects," works of art which are original, and artifacts which have ordinarily been classed as works of art but which are not very innovative. These he calls "replications." But the objection to this distinction is that value distinctions are never enough: they always rest on the authority of the writer or of a cultural tradition, and authority may always be questioned. Indeed, in the history of any culture the *canon* of good works of art is utterly unstable. Further, the distinction between "prime objects" and "replications" has two grave difficulties: it assumes the completeness of the historical record, but incompleteness may easily make a replication appear to be a prime object; and the distinction emerges only if the difference between the two categories is kept at a very gross level. Kubler offers no minute analysis of the finer stylistic grain of any single work.

Kubler's effort to establish a special and identifiable sub-class "works of art" within the general category of things is not successful. Indeed, every such attempt has failed and apparently must fail. In our culture "art" refers to a category of artifacts, though the attributes of this category may be ill-established and the range of objects may be ill-defined. Moreover, if we think of that range as a field it is not easy to decide what should properly occupy the center of the field and what lies towards the boundaries, so vague are the boundaries,

---

[1] In his instructive and valuable *The Shape of Time*, New Haven, 1962, p. 1. Kubler is a professor of art and archaeology at Yale.

[2] Kubler, p. 16.

especially if value is eliminated from the attributes of the category. Nevertheless, in most ordinary discourse if a person uses the word "art," his listener has at least a rough idea of what he is talking about. In discourse that attempts logical control, the existence of the category and what properly belongs in it are in fact rarely questioned. Certain assumptions have to be made if there is to be any discourse at all. This is true in our culture; but what are we to say of a culture in which the category "art" does not exist? Can it be properly said that the members of such a culture do in fact engage in artistic behavior? Actually, not long ago our culture presumed art to be a characteristic of only high cultures; primitive cultures did not have art, and that is all there was to it. To-day, such a notion seems absurd; yet not until the modern stylistic revolution did certain works of primitive cultures, such as African masks and fetish sculptures, begin to be perceived as works of art.

There is a close parallel to this in the artistic behavior towards works from our own culture. Most critics and aestheticians write as if a work of art automatically elicited a particular kind of response, and this by virtue of "aesthetic structure." But a work of art that moves me to-day may bore me to-morrow and often does. It is this phenomenon that makes the magisterial utterances of critics about how a work of art affects the perceiver so astonishing, not to speak of their statements about how it affected the perceivers of three hundred years ago. The customary way of dealing with this problem is to fall back on the authority of the qualified observer or on the consensus of tradition. But this is no solution. If to-day I respond to a work the way aestheticians prescribe, I am a qualified observer; but if to-morrow I do not, why have I ceased to be qualified? In the nineteenth century qualified observers rejected the poetry of Donne from the canon of English poetry; should you make such a judgment to-day practically all qualified observers would insist that you are not qualified. Indeed, to make the problem utterly unmanageable, what has the improvised fluting of an African cowherd in common with Leonardo da Vinci's "Last Supper?" All we can really say is that, upon questioning, some people would call them both art, some would classify only one of them as art, some people would find neither of them art, and some people, who had not learned the category "art," would not know what the question meant.

It is evident that two quite different systems of categorization are at work, excluding value categorization, which is so notoriously unreliable as to be useless, even if we settle for a theory of immanent value instead of one of ascribed value, or valuing (value behavior); for no one has found a way on empirical grounds to determine unquestionably the presence or absence of that value. On the one hand a quality named "aesthetic structure" is postulated and is said to be the defining character of works of art. On the other, a quality named "aesthetic experience" is postulated and said to be the defining character of the response to works of art. The problem is to decide how these two categorial ranges are to be related. If aesthetic structure is separated from experience, it collapses into all structure. The attributes of aesthetic structure have never been derived from works of art and cannot be. The perception of structure is a transaction. Initially the order is contributed by the perceiver, not by the perceptual field of the work of art. This is one reason why the attributes of aesthetic structure have always been derived from metaphysics or from an *a priori* value system. On the other hand, if aesthetic experience is separated from structure it collapses into all experience. Scientists, lovers, machinists, farmers, baseball enthusiasts, religious devotees, contemplators of the infinite, metaphysicians, have all claimed their activity as a true source of aesthetic experience; there is scarcely a human activity, not excluding fornication, which has not been offered as something which provides it. In both categories, of course, the notion of order is at work, in the second no less than the first, for the kind of experience Aristotle and Whitehead and Levi are talking about is merely the sense of having become fully oriented to a situation constructed in the memory; any consummated behavioral pattern can offer it.

Kubler's proposal is an excellent example of the attempt to put aesthetic structure and aesthetic experience together. Art is separated from tools on the basis of usefulness; that is, in art one experiences the uselessness of the object. Subsequently, this uselessness is connected with structure. The novelty in his proposal is that the structure is conceived historically; prime objects are structurally different from their immediate predecessors in time, which are but replications of prime objects farther back in time. Structural novelty is thus selected as true "aesthetic structure" and is connected with the experience of the uselessness of the object.

But the problem of relating the two categories may actually be a pseudo-problem. In the first place, the assumption that they must be connected may be only the consequence of a verbal illusion: Both aesthetic structure and aesthetic experience have something to do with art; therefore they have something to do with each other. But this point does not necessarily follow. The paralogism becomes clear enough if we say "art structure" and "art experience" (or "the structure of art" and "the experience of art"). What these two phrases have in common is the term "art." One refers to a range of discrete experiences; the other to a range of discrete artifacts. What binds these two together is the term "art," which leads to the assumption that they must be connected. But this is only an assumption. Properly, it should be considered as something to be proved. Thus Kubler has connected a particular kind of experience with a particular kind of structure, but he can do so only because he has already used the term "art." At the beginning of his book he has informed us that he is going to talk about art. We assume that everything he says is connected directly or indirectly with art as such. But nowhere has he given any reason for thinking that his experience is necessarily connected with his structure. As he uses "useless," it could equally well categorize drinking a highball or going for a ride on a roller coaster. Again, if the two are separated, each melts into larger categories, one into general structure, the other into the sense of orientation consequent upon the elimination of tension-producing disparities. Finally, as we have seen, there is no guarantee that a man-made object characterized by "aesthetic structure" will automatically elicit in any individual, even a "qualified individual," an "aesthetic experience." Since "art-experience" and "art-structure" are not necessarily linked, the term "art" at this point appears to be an empty category, one with neither range nor attributes. The work of art appears to vanish, leaving but a smile.

It is evident from all this that neither the notion of ordered experience nor the notion of ordered artifact can separately provide a defining attribute of the category "art"; and it is equally evident that the notion that they are interdependent cannot provide a defining attribute. It may seem strange that since I deny the validity of the notion that art either as artifact or as experience is characterized by order, I should go to the trouble to point this out. From my point of view the problem is entirely unreal, but it will be remembered that my question is: On what grounds may we put an artifact into the category of art so that we can include it in a stylistically dynamic historical sequence? Such a sequence cannot emerge until we put things into it. How do we justify such decisions? I have endeavored, therefore, to show that no basis for such decisions emerges even if we grant that both the work of art and the experience it offers are characterized by order and structure.

But there is more than one kind of categorization at work in our behavior. The usual assumption is that art is a *conjunctive category*, that is, that all works of art have something in common. But this is not so; it is not so even within the various arts. A sculptor uses a material that can be shaped and will hold its shape indefinitely. Alexander Calder, however, wants his mobiles to continue to change shape after they have left his hands; but since such a quality is not a defining attribute of sculpture, when you see a mobile, you cannot say that you are looking at a piece of sculpture. One of the most notorious events in art history is what happens when an artist offers as "art" a work so utterly different from what is currently accepted as art that a good many people insist that it is not art at all. The furors in the past fifteen years over abstract expressionism, pop art, and now op art have swirled around the question as to whether these things are works of art at all. When an artist hangs from the ceiling ten rows of twisted aluminum strips, has he created a work of art? This problem would not have arisen had Christmas tree ornaments been conventionally categorized as works of art. To any individual, on the other hand, who has in the past thought of such ornaments as works of art, the new op art—the art of "pure visual stimulation"—presents no problem whatever; without hesitation, he sees the new op art as art. And so with all the arts. But there is another kind of category which has been well worked out by Jerome S. Bruner. In such a category

all members do not share the same defining attributes. In consequence, one cannot infer much about the defining attributes of a member simply by virtue of knowing its category membership. The possibility of using the "common features" of a collection of positive exemplars is ruled out.[3]

Consider the members of a club. If you know they are members, you cannot predict their personality traits. Because of the way new members are elected, all you know is that each member was proposed by one or more men already in the club and that no other member

[3] *A Study of Thinking* by Jerome S. Bruner, New York, 1956, p. 159. Copyright John Wiley & Sons, Inc. Used by permission of John Wiley & Sons, Inc. Bruner takes this category from Bertrand Russell's *Introduction to Mathematical Thinking*, 1919. Bruner is a professor of psychology at Harvard. He is best known for his revolutionary theories on childhood learning.

blackballed him. He was elected not because he was something but because he was not. On the other hand, if you know there is such a club and you want to find out who are the club members, there is no way to find out except by asking people at random. The defining attribute of a member of a club is that he is a member of that particular club. The members already in the club have agreed that the new member shall be a member. It is entirely a matter of social convention. The defining attribute of a club member is that he can say that he is if you ask him. If you are a member of the club and know all the members by sight, a member's defining attribute is that he can elicit from you the statement that he is a member of your club. A man is a club member only because other men have agreed to call him a club member. There is little point in any one in the club or outside of it refusing to recognize an elected member as indeed a member. Since membership in the club is a social convention, the category "club member" is likewise a social convention. It is a behavioral pattern of the community in which the club exists, that community consisting of all the people who know it exists, a community which anyone can enter.

The notion of a disjunctive category is extremely helpful when it is applied to the problem of the category "art." To categorize an object as a work of art is to assign it to a category all the members of which have the power to elicit the statement, "That is a work of art," from those who know that such a category exists and know that that particular object has been placed in that category. But if the observer has not been directly informed by someone else that the artifact has been classified as a work of art, can he know that it has been so classified? Yes, he can. He knows by the situation in which he finds it, which is itself a social convention. In the same way there is a basic pattern of behavior by which the club servants conduct themselves towards the club members, a pattern adopted also towards guests, for a guest is a temporary member. Thus the doorman does not treat a guest as a member until he knows that he is a guest. His behavior alters as soon as he is sure. His job is to guard the door and refuse admittance to anyone who is neither guest nor member. In the same way, as soon as we learn or decide that an artifact is a work of art we change our behavior towards it. But just as with the doorman, our decision is a matter of convention. That is, just as the doorman shifts his social role when he has determined that a stranger is a guest, so when we learn or decide that an artifact is a work of art, we shift our social role.

At this point Kubler's distinction between useful and useless becomes genuinely helpful. As we have seen, to attempt to distinguish among artifacts on the ground of their utility is hopeless; but his proposal makes sense if we interpret it as meaning that when we decide an object is a work of art we forget about its possibilities as a tool for manipulating the environment. We can decide that a cup by a great ceramicist is a work of art and dismiss from our attention the fact that we can drink coffee out of it. And the fascinating thing is that we can do this while we are drinking. There is nothing about the cup which makes it a work of art except our attitude towards it. We apply to it a different orientation, an orientation involving socially standardized behavior. We are playing a role. The membership of a disjunctive category is fixed solely by social convention. Behavior, therefore, is determined not by common features but by convention.

A work of art, then, is any artifact in the presence of which we play a particular social role, a culturally transmitted combination of patterns of behavior. Yet to this proposition must be added others without which it is incomplete and perhaps even incomprehensible.

2. THE DRAMATIC METAPHOR

Let us begin with an anthropological definition of culture:

> All those historically created designs for living, explicit and implicit, rational, irrational and non-rational, which exist at any time as potential guides for the behavior of men.[4]

Such a design or pattern comes into existence at a point in history; it is an emergent It is a behavioral guide, or paradigm, as Thomas S. Kuhn uses the term, or model.[5] Above all, it is learned. Since the learning process involves communication, no pattern can be perfectly transmitted. However, this last statement is open to question, because it is questionable whether what is learned is actually a pattern.

The terms "pattern" and "design" when applied to human behavior are metaphors. Human behavior does not really come in patterns—sequences and combinations of always identical bits. A be-

---

[4] Clyde Kluckhohn and W. H. Kelley, "The Concept of Culture," in *The Science of Man in the World Crisis*, ed. R. Linton, 1945, p. 97.
[5] See notes 5 and 22 in Chapter I.

havioral pattern is not like a dress pattern or a piece of plastic imitation lace, all examples of which are indistinguishable. Pattern and behavior are not analogous. However, the use of the metaphor "pattern" permits us to say that if we ignore differences up to a certain level of observation, human behavior can be seen as made up of temporal configurations which are in turn parts of larger configurations. Each individual human organism learns to govern his potentialities, his limitations, his unique characteristics—his behavior—in a particular way for each category of situation in which he acts. When a situation is totally novel, either he improvises, or he adjusts his unique behavior as closely as possible to the behavioral pattern of someone who knows how to behave in that situation, or he does nothing at all. He may even die, as in the psychogenic death of a psychotic, whose disorientation is so great that all situations, no matter how often he has acted in them, seem novel and whose power to pattern behavior is quite lost. Primitives have been known to die after encountering the utterly different patterning of advanced civilizations. This is what happened to the Tasmanians. A more subtle but equally devastating effect is a decline in fertility, so that the tribe dies out. Excessive interaction among animals and humans can have similar effects. Somewhat less disturbed persons lose some patterning capacity; they may find themselves at a familiar street corner with no way of deciding which way to go.

But though "pattern" when applied to human behavior is only a metaphor, it is a very good one: it permits us to make successful predictions. When we see a bit of behavior in a certain situation, and if that bit falls within an accustomed range, we can successfully predict what range the next bit of behavior will fall into. A pattern is a predictable sequence of ranges of bits of behavior. Let us quite arbitrarily say that each range of a particular sequence of behavior consists of twenty-six possible bits and assign to each bit a letter of the alphabet. Let us further say that a sequence of behavior consists of ten such ranges. An individual, then, may learn the sequence *bdiwlcuent,* or *xmeoelsmxr,* or *sycielwhdp.* After we become familiar with a series of such sequences of letters, we can successfully predict in this situation that, if we are offered a letter, the next bit to be presented to us will also be a letter. We have created an orientation which controls our behavior by controlling our expectancies. This is why unpredicted behavior can disturb us so by disorienting us. So true is this that we are generally doubtful about the sanity of individuals whose behavior lies outside of the predicted range. But it must be very far out if we are to notice it, especially if the orientation for that expectancy has been reinforced on a large number of occasions. For example, after continuously encountering a thousand instances of a sequence of ten letters, and then encountering *cleocne3ros*, we may very well miss the intrusive number. This is why proofreading is so difficult, and doubly difficult for the author, who, knowing what comes next, tends to miss typographical errors.

When we learn a pattern, we actually learn a sequence of bits, each of which lies within a particular range. Here an example from learning to sing is instructive. Freshly trained singers always sing on pitch, but full professionals almost always sing a little off pitch. The singing teacher, by continuous reinforcement, requires the student to sing, as it were, *mmmmmmmmmmm*. When the singer is on his own, however, he indulges in a bit of latitude and may sing, for example, *lmkonmoln*. The reason for this is that in our interaction with others not a sequence of bits is reinforced but a sequence of ranges of bits. Furthermore, the actual state of the organism, its degree of tension, for instance, can shift the bit from one place in the range to another. Some singers are more than usually off pitch at the beginning of a performance because they are too tense; others because they are too relaxed. The behavior of some singers is highly patterned in such matters; they are always off pitch when they begin. The behavior of others is scarcely patterned at all; sometimes they are not, sometimes they are. In the first instance the appearance of such a singer on the stage is a sign to the concert-goer that for a few moments he is going to hear noticeably off-pitch singing: in the second it is not, the situation offering no statistical probabilities. Thus in any pattern of behavior the individual is continuously shifting within a range smaller than the socially permitted range. So true is this, that just as we are disturbed by a person who moves far outside the socially standardized range, so we are troubled by one who has a very narrow range or no range at all. Both are labeled odd, eccentric, neurotic, or psychotic. Thus we learn not merely a series of bits within a sequence of ranges, but we also learn the range. In this sense, it can be said not only that we learn patterns of behavior, but also that for each individual each pattern is unique. That is, each individual has his own style of behavior within any pattern: each bit of his behavior lies within a range narrower than the socially acceptable range.

In novel situations, we improvise patterns of behavior by combining bits from ranges and patterns of ranges we have already learned. If we do not know how to make our behavior predictable to others, at least we can experiment with what we predict may be appropriate, and at least we can make it predictable to ourselves, a matter even more important. Finally, as for our behavior in familiar situations, no two situations, no matter how similar, are ever exactly alike, nor is the individual organism exactly the same from moment to moment. The result is that not only is no sequence of behavior ever exactly repeated, but that the individual's style of patterning his behavior constantly shows anything from very slight to quite gross changes. We must not think of style and pattern as fixed or static but fluid and dynamic. Analysis at a higher level shows that all accepted members of a behavioral community operate within the permitted range of a behavioral society. Thus "style" is applicable to both the unique individual and the unique community within the society. (At all levels of stylistic analysis of behavior, of course, we are dealing with constructs.)

When we turn from style and pattern to role, we move to a higher, or grosser, or more inclusive category of behavior. Again, like pattern, this category has been established by the application of a metaphor. Actually, two metaphors are current for this purpose, the drama metaphor and the game metaphor, each of which brings out interesting aspects of human behavior. The drama metaphor, which ascribes to all human behavior certain attributes from the actor's behavior in the theater—acting a role—is much the older. At least it was introduced into the behavioral sciences long before the other, although how long both have been current in literature and speech there is no telling. A number of important aspects of human behavior are revealed when we think of it as if it were acting in a theater: Behavior is seen as conforming to an already existent set of specifications prepared by the author of the script. It is learned from the script and it is controlled by the script. But only in part. The scripts of Greek tragedy provide, first, the names of the characters—but since they come from mythology and legend, that is a good deal—and, second, what they say. The scripts of Shaw are far more detailed; he gives introductions to inform the members of the production what attitudes should control their decisions, provides biographical sketches for each of the characters, and often prescribes facial expressions, bodily carriage and movement, direction, speed, and so on. But not even the most elaborate script provides nearly enough prescriptions to control all the behavior necessary to act a play. The author, then, corresponds to the real human being's cultural tradition and the script to the specifications for action transmitted to each individual as he emerges from earliest infancy. But again, as with author and script, there is still a gap to be filled.

This is in part taken up by the director, who provides further specifications, both by precept and example. He is the cultural transmitter or, in the largest sense, teacher. All patterned behavior is learned, but no such behavior is learned without a teacher, whether he is fully conscious of it—his social role is to be a teacher—or whether he is an unconscious role model for the learner, who may or may not be conscious that he is using another as a role model. The task of the teacher is to take up some of the slack between the necessarily insufficiently precise specifications of the cultural tradition and its patterns; necessarily imprecise, because of the fact that a pattern consists of a sequence of ranges. For the individual to learn the ranges and then operate within his own restrictions of those ranges would be extremely tedious and laborious, and could be only partially successful. The director indicates a precise sequence of bits and then permits the actor a certain latitude. So with the cultural teacher.

But there is still something of a gap between specifications and acting. This is filled up by the actor, and what he provides depends upon his organic peculiarities, his training, his modes of perception, and his innovative powers. And the exploitation of these depends upon his awareness that he is acting a role. An experienced and successful actor can think of more things to fill the gap than can an untrained amateur. His excellence depends upon their pertinence to the orientations which dominate the play. If the only ruling orientation is that the performance should be funny, anything amusing will do. Consider the social success of the "natural comedian" at a party the tone of which dictates gay buffoonery.

But several other attributes of this useful metaphor remain to be considered: the stage and the audience. An actor is either on-stage or off-stage. A great deal both amusing and instructive has been done with this attribute of the metaphor by Erving Goffman.[6] He investigated hotel life, particularly the behavior of proprietor and servants, in the Shetland Islands, as well as the everyday life of the people; and he found that roles could be discovered by making a separation between stage and back-stage. Although he fails to consider the fact

<hr>

[6] In *The Presentation of Self in Everyday Life*, New York, 1959.

that back-stage life is also role-playing, at least he establishes the connection between situation and role, or in theater, setting and role. There the setting may be simply an area defined as the actors' space, as in the primitive theater or theater in the round; it may be generalized and used for all plays, as in the Greek theater; or it may be richly particularized, as in naturalistic theater settings. This corresponds to our various perceptions of situations in which we find ourselves. At times it may be enough simply to recognize that we are in some kind of situation and behave accordingly: we know that a social role is demanded and we pick up our cues from others. Or we govern our behavior by a minute examination of as much information in the situation as we can perceive and absorb. "Cue" also is a theatrical metaphor, and it is not necessarily limited to responding to another's speech or gesture according to the script. When we respond to a cue we interpret the situation as one which calls for behavior on our part, whether overt or concealed. Nor need cue behavior be only prescribed. During a performance an actor may get a cue for innovative behavior from a prop he has not observed in earlier performances or rehearsals. The total situation, objects and people alike, is a source for cues, and the richness of a theatrical production corresponds to the complexity of our perception of a situation as occasion for prescribed and innovative cue behavior.

Next, there is the audience. But the whereabouts of the audience in non-dramatic situations is by no means obvious. If we are alone, what has happened to the audience? Actually, playing to the analogical equivalent of the theatrical audience is rare. Usually we are embarrassed if our behavior is being observed by people who are not part of the situation, while an individual who glories in such observation is ordinarily condemned. Strangely, the non-theatrical audience is where we would be least likely to look for it; it is in ourselves. Acting on the stage is an art, the deposit of behavior, even though that behavior is transitory; but role-playing is behavior itself. Each of us is at once author, script, director, stage-designer, and styling and innovating actor. Behavioral bits, cultural behavioral specifications, teacher or role model, situation perception, styling, innovation—all these are but categorial abstractions from the only reality, the flow of human behavior. But categorization is inescapable; we cannot get away from it; only through categories can we predict; the dynamic structure of categories is the structure by which we relate ourselves to the world and ourselves to ourselves. Thus we structure the behavior of others and we structure our own behavior, and the character of that structure controls the character of our behavior. Everyman is ultimately his own playwright, and Everyman is his own audience.

Our mode of perceiving the behavior of others is identical with our mode of perceiving our own behavior. And our means of predicting and controlling the behavior of others is identical with our means of predicting and controlling our own. Failure of predictions and control over our own behavior is as disturbing and disorienting as failure to predict and control that of others. All interaction with others is an effort to control the behavior of others; all interaction with ourselves is an effort to control our own behavior. The self is an other.[7] We are, in fact, constantly engaged in testing and judging and planning ways to improve our playing of roles. We are our own audience.

This is why the audience is so hard to locate when we apply the dramatic metaphor to human behavior. The audience is not outside of us but inside of us. The behavior of the actor is not to be identified with the totality of an individual's behavior. The whole stage metaphor is to be applied to that totality; just as in the theater one sees a variety of roles, so in each individual there is a variety of roles. Indeed, the theater was probably invented in order to separate the self that plays the role from the self that observes, controls, directs, judges— or responds with delight or despair. This last is the role of the audience member who is involved with the actor to the degree that his own perceiving self is forgotten; precisely the same thing happens in life when we are so involved with the role we are playing that we lose corrective control over it. We get out of hand; we are carried away; we lose ourselves in what we are seeing in theater and what we are acting out in real life. As in the theater, the audience is lost in the actor.

The dramatic metaphor applied to behavior also permits us to see clearly into the difference between pattern and role. A further important possibility of the dramatic metaphor—the rehearsal—remains to be applied to human behavior. One aspect of the rehearsal is immediately apparent, the learning and the reinforcement of behavioral patterns by repetition, and it is obvious that in life much of our effort is devoted to rehearsal. But this is by no means the only or the most important kind of activity going on in rehearsals. The

---

[7] This point was established by George Herbert Mead, the great American pragmatist, in *Mind, Self, and Society*, Chicago, 1934.

primary job is to select from the repertory of behavioral patterns available to director and actor those patterns which fit the demands of the script as actor and director perceive them, mainly by trial and error, depending upon the difficulty and novelty of the play. A production of a play is always, therefore, an interpretation, even when the author is director and leading actor. He too has to decide what patterns of non-verbal behavior are called for by his script. When we look at the theatrical situation not as a metaphor for human behavior, but rather as human behavior itself, it is apparent that author, director, and actor, as well as scene designer and audience, are all social roles. Hence the difficulty of being all three at once. But when we turn back to this situation as metaphor, we see again that the individual human being *is* all of these at once, and is therefore constantly engaged in rehearsing, selecting and rejecting patterns of behavior, to be acted out either simultaneously—as words and gesture—or in sequence.

Much of this again is established by cultural convention. In some cultures, verbal behavior is always accompanied by elaborate gesture of the hand and arms; in others, one is expected to be physically quiet while talking. Further, the patterns available to the ingenue of a typical Broadway musical comedy are well established, as on the whole they are for the hero of a Shakespearean tragedy. The role has already been established. We may speak, then, of the structure of a role, but only so long as we remember that what patterns are available to a role, as well as the combinations and sequences in which they occur, have been established by cultural convention, not by any necessity immanent within that role. A role is really not so much a structure as a *package* of patterns. That is why in different cultures the same role is made up of such a wide variety of patterns. The role of college professor in Germany and in the United States is much the same, so far as social function goes, but the patterns culturally permitted in each do not correspond. Certain patterns are common to both; others are found in only one. A role is a package of patterns, but again, it is an incomplete package. The actual individual organism must style and improvise and innovate and at times be at a loss as to what to do next. That is why all our lives we are involved in role rehearsal.

Finally, in any theatrical situation—I have found no exception in primitive societies—there is the critic. We must conceive the audience as totally involved in the dramatic situation; during or after the performance, the critic places the performance in a tradition, decides what kind of role was being attempted, judges its adequacy, and passes out praise or blame, and often suggests interpretations. When we are growing up and learning roles, the first critics we encounter are our parents, then our siblings, playmates, teachers, lovers and spouses, friends, employers, and finally speakers of our obituaries. When we have learned the role of critic, we become critics of others and of ourselves; just as we spend our lives in an atmosphere of rehearsal, so we spend our lives bathed in criticism. How weary we get of it! It is even possible to be weary of criticising others. But it is one of the conditions of human existence; it is the brake against random and valueless innovation.

What happens when we gain what we call "psychological insight" is simply a shift from the audience role towards ourselves to the critic role. When we are totally involved in the audience role, we cannot control what we are doing; we are swept along by a compulsive pattern of behavior. We can neither correct it, adjust it, nor criticize its adequacy nor our adequacy in playing it. Psychological insight develops in various stages. First comes the realization that we are sunk in the audience role, that our behavior in certain situations indeed is compulsive, uncriticized, uncorrected, not adapted to the unique features of each unique situation. At this point we often seek help from a psychiatrist, a friend, a minister or priest. Eventually, often painfully, we learn the critic's role when we are not performing our compulsive behavior, and then when we are. But at this point a great difficulty arises; true choice emerges. One kind of criticism asserts the behavioral norms of a culture. But another kind recognizes the inadequacy of those norms; it may even select from the compulsive behavior genuinely functional possibilities, even though the cultural norms do not recognize them. For this reason, though criticism is the brake against random and valueless innovation, it also can be the barrier to adaptive innovation.

Above the level of human behavior which is illuminated by the dramatic metaphor lies another, and this at last is truly the level of the individual human being. Roles he shares with others. Human beings cannot be distinguished one from another on the basis of roles. Even style does not constitute the human being; it only marks him. What constitutes the human being depends upon the intermittency of role-playing; on the continuous shifting from one role to another; on the ironic playing of one role against another by displaying the signs of one role in words, for instance, and another in the tone of one's voice; on hypocrisy, or displaying all the signs of one role to one's fellow-player, but actually governing one's behavior by the patterns of another. The package of roles a human being plays is ever looser and less stabilized than the package of patterns that make up roles. This is the human individual's freest area of choice. At this level of analysis, the topmost level, the unique individual emerges.

To sum up, the drama metaphor for human behavior enables us to perceive in the seamless flow of action the following elements: the behavioral bit, the irreducible atom of behavior; the range, the collection of bits which are socially acceptable in a given situation; the pattern, the sequence in time of ranges; the role, the package of patterns; and the constituted human being, the unique package of roles. And in particular, the drama metaphor reveals the various aspects of each role: it is a cultural tradition; it is transmitted by a teacher to a learner; it always involves innovation; it is inseparable from a situation; it requires continuous rehearsal; we can be either unaware that we are playing a role, or we can be aware, and criticize both our playing of it and the role itself.

The game metaphor is fairly novel in the behavioral sciences, although it has a long history in literature. Kipling used it, and Pirandello wrote a play on the subject, *The Rules of the Game.*[8] Though it appears to be less fruitful than the drama metaphor, its attributes are capable of bringing out two very interesting aspects: rules and orientative reinforcement. A pattern prescribes what we shall do under certain circumstances; not so a rule. The role of the game player is to present his opponent, who may be himself, as in solitaire or fishing, with an unpredicted situation which will force him to behave in a particular way; while the player faced with such a situation has as his role the task of rearranging the situation so that the tables are turned. Playing a game involves continuous risk-running. The rules place limits on what may be done, but more importantly, they provide guides to improvisation and innovation. Behavior is aimed at following rules in predictable situations and interpreting rules in unpredicted ones. Hence, an important ingredient of game playing consists of arguments about how the rules should be interpreted.

When we apply this to individual behavior we see that it is helpful

---

[8] So far as I know, the first important attempt to apply it to human behavior is to be found in Thomas S. Szasz, *The Myth of Mental Illness*, New York, 1961.

in understanding what the dramatic metaphor left somewhat unclear, improvisation and innovation, how to handle the gap between the various levels of prescription—cultural tradition, teacher, and behaving individual—and actual situations, of which no two are ever the same. Faced with an unpredicted situation, the individual may either categorize it in such a way that he can select a rule to govern his behavior, or, if appropriate rules are unavailable, he can interpret an existent rule to cover the situation. He can, of course, fail. How often we hear people say, and say ourselves, "I didn't know what to do," or, defensively, "How was I to know what I was supposed to do?"

The essence of a game, then, lies in the reinforcement of the ability to face risks, to behave according to rules in unpredicted but familiar situations and to handle unpredicted, unfamiliar, and novel situations by deducing new rules from existing rules. Hence when people are weary of a game because they are encountering no truly novel situations, they develop old ones, as in three-dimensional chess, or invent new ones on the models of old ones, as Monopoly was probably developed from Parcheesi.

Role-playing takes care of most of our behavior. Game-playing fills the gap. The gap between the role and actual situations accounts for the dynamic character of human behavior; rule deduction accounts for the fact that the gap is neither filled with random action nor is a mere empty area of inaction. However, it is to be noticed that individuals insufficiently reinforced in risk-taking and rule-deduction frequently engage in random action or are frozen into inaction when confronted with an unpredicted situation. Finally, role-playing and game-playing are further alike in that each involves the separation of the self from the self as other. In the game of life, your real opponent is yourself, your awareness that a gap between role and environmental demand has appeared. Finally, both role-playing and game-playing have to be learned.

3. ART DEFINED

The possibilities of applying the dramatic metaphor to human behavior have made it possible to discriminate nine functions: author, script, director, actor, setting, cue, rehearsal, audience, and critic. When we apply this to artistic behavior, it is first necessary to repeat a distinction between the two kinds of behavior—we may now call them roles—referred to by the more inclusive category of "artistic behavior": artist and perceiver. The role of the artist can be easily disposed of. It demands only that he construct perceptual fields which occasion the role of the perceiver. (The term "perceptual fields" is preferable to "artifacts," for though it is possible, it is awkward to think of the dance, or acting, or music-making as artifacts, even though they are the consequences of the artistic behavior of the creator.) To know how to make his construction, the creator must learn his cultural tradition for that role; this necessarily involves learning the role of the perceiver. Using the drama metaphor for human behavior, it is easy to identify cultural tradition, prescriptions, teacher, making the work of art, picking up cues or ideas for innovation from his total situation, displaying the work in the appropriate setting, rehearsing all these activities, and being his own audience and critic, as well as submitting his work to other audiences and critics. The only thing unaccounted for is the development of a new kind of art, a perceptual field of which the media or the mode of handling traditional media is wholly novel. Here, as we shall see in the next chapter, the game metaphor fits in the next piece, but this must wait until the behavior of the perceiver has been fully understood as role-playing. Put brutally, the task of the artist is merely to manufacture objects and events for the perceiver to perceive. This is why the economics of art is such an enormous and fascinating field of study, although little has been done in it, principally because everyone concerned with the problem of art has been so bemused by the divine and magic myth of Artistic Creation.

Turning to the perceiver as role player, the first thing that leaps to one's attention is that artistic perception is learned. Nowadays this is easy enough to understand. "How to" books on art appreciation are all over the place, and the Metropolitan Museum of Art in conjunction with the Book-of-the-Month Club runs something it quaintly calls "Art Seminars in the Home." Art appreciation, of at least some of the arts, is taught in the schools; the more chic and modern the school the sooner it is begun. That on the whole it is taught badly is beside the point. Much of this has been a recent development. Nevertheless it can be traced far back in the history of formal education; the teaching of the rules of prosody, that is, the prescriptions or "script" of how to write verse, goes back in an unbroken tradition through the Middle Ages to classical times. The purpose of this was not so much to teach students how to write poetry as it was to teach them the rules by which poets write so that they could respond adequately to poetry. It was the ancient tradition of learning by doing. Singing was taught in the schools in the same way and for the same purpose. Generally speaking, however, perceivers learn from other perceivers, both consciously by precept and unconsciously by role model; indeed, this is still the principal way of learning how to respond to a work of art, which is the essence of the perceiver's role. Anyone interested in art has only to remember his youth to realize that mostly he learned from his friends and from books. Another old tradition, frankly appreciative criticism, serves as a written role model for the perceiver as learner; in literate societies the ordinary kind of criticism consists largely of prescriptions about the approved patterns of perceiving, for to judge the work, the critic must decide whether the traditional patterns may be applied to it, and to do so he must say what they are.

But even when all this is said, the fact remains that the perceiver's role is learned exactly as most roles are learned, by informal non-institutionalized interaction with other people who know the role or who are also engaged in learning it. The perceiver's role has been partly institutionalized in some societies and for a few of the arts. Mostly it is an informal matter. And the same conditions are at work in the critical aspect of the perceiver's role. Mostly it is in discussions with his friends that the perceiver quite unconsciously learns to be a critic of his own performance as perceiver. But it is amazing what one can pick up, both in learning one's performance and in criticizing it, from ten minute conversations with total strangers in museums, book-stores, and the promenades of opera houses and concert halls. It is one of the delights of the traveler in search of art. As with all roles, learn-ing, rehearsal, and criticism are life-long enterprises.

The question at once arises, of course, as to whether a culture which does not have the term "art" recognizes this category of behavior and has rules (to use the game metaphor for a moment) about what kinds of artifacts are the proper occasions for it. It is perhaps worth noting that our own culture does not so recognize it. If any of my fellow humanists run across this book, most of them will be repelled and revolted by the notion of applying the term "behavior" to art at all, and many of my most sophisticated students have been initially enraged at the notion that when they are engaged in aesthetic experi-ence they are playing a quite well defined and socially established role. I dare say many of them still are. But our culture has at least come to understand that somehow aesthetic experience is different from other experiences, though there is no agreement on how it is different. And it does at least recognize the existence of the category, "work of art," though there is little agreement on what its range is. To this extent the labors of aestheticians have not been entirely fruitless.

Oddly enough, the question is less real than one might suppose. To be sure, the more inclusive category of art as now used is only a few hundred years old in our society. The distinction between "art" to refer to anything well made or to any discipline formally taught and what is now meant by the term is of surprisingly recent origin. Nevertheless, all but the most primitive societies recognize the poet and his product, the sculptor and his product, the dancer, the actor, and so on. Such societies are small and the actual community surrounding the artist much smaller. Every child used to learn about poetry from a poet, just as he learned about forging from watching a smith. The social distance between artist and audience which now obtains is of fairly recent origin. Even the most primitive society we know—the Melville Islanders, Australian bushmen—has artists. They are painters of abstract art who do very little else, at least when they are old. The same society has a highly developed, very old, and quite magnificent art of abstract sculpture, used in funerals. Until quite recently in human history, then, the teacher, the transmitter, the role model, the "director" of art perceiving as a social role was the artist himself, and his behavior in a studio, or place of work, was easily accessible to the entire population. The ancient Welsh improvisatory bards are a good example, for they composed in public and were criticised and rewarded on the spot.

So long as we think of all works of art as having some mysterious character in common—structure, order, beauty—which necessarily elicits some equally mysterious mental state—mysterious because it is inaccessible to public examination—it is impossible to decide whether people who do not talk about art actually have it. But as soon as we consider art as a social role, its presence in a society is quite easy to identify. This way of looking at the problem offers a solution to another quite vexing one: Why have aestheticians assumed without question, except very rarely, that there is a necessary connection between artistic structure and artistic experience? It is now quite easy to see why: they have learned from their cultural tradition that the artistic role is properly played in front of only certain perceptual fields. And this instruction took place so early in their lives, so subtly, and so unconsciously, and has been reinforced so often that they have

quite forgotten that the connection was not natural. This kind of behavior is the most common thing in the world. Only a very small
proportion of the population of our own society has learned from
cultural anthropology that almost all behavior is learned, that only
a tiny fraction of human behavior is instinctual, that even monkey
mothers brought up from birth by humans do not know how to take
care of their own offspring. Teddy Brunius, a Swedish aesthetician, has
scolded his fellow aestheticians for being so completely ethnocentric.[9]

The fact remains, however, that the richest place to study the perceiver's role is our own culture. There is no question that it is more
highly developed, more thoroughly structured, more carefully taught,
and has developed a richer vocabulary in Europe and America than
in any other culture area. Above all, we have fully developed the
setting of the work of art: the art museum and the commercial art
gallery. In the past, as it is in other cultures, art collection was virtually a private matter. The Imperial Chinese art collections were not
collected to be shown to the public, or apparently, from any desire
to create a permanent archive of the finest of China's artistic genius.
They were the private collections of the Imperial household, belonging
to the Emperor as part of his personal property, and inherited by
successive dynasties with surprisingly little loss or disturbance. In any
society whoever is the richest and most powerful has the best and
finest of art, just as he has the best and finest of everything else. Poorer
people, however, could also collect art; and up to the time of the
French Revolution, in Europe any accredited gentlemen had access to
royal and noble collections. During the Revolutionary period, the
royal and many of the noble collections, as well as many ecclesiastical
works of art, were nationalized and the palaces were turned into
museums. This happened in almost every area of Europe the Na-
poleonic armies conquered and administered. Until recently the only
recognized model for an art museum was a royal palace, whether in
Europe or America.

This development had a peculiar effect. Since money and space
were involved, the question arose as to what belonged in such museums. This is still an acute question. As I pointed out in Chapter I,
quite recently, in both Philadelphia and New York, it has been con-
tended that symphonic music and opera should not be supported by

---

[9] In "The Uses of Works of Art," *The Journal of Aesthetics and Art Criticism*,
XXII, 1963, pp. 123–133.

public funds nor by tax exemption, because these things are entertainment. The basis for this argument was apparently that since they are not found in art museums, they cannot be called art. Such a contention would be impossible in Germany. There, the nationalization of the art collections of the numerous small German states involved the nationalization of the court theater, ballet, opera, and orchestra. To this day, as a matter of course, the various German states and towns support these institutions out of tax money, partly to keep admission prices down so that the young and the poor can afford to go; the rationale for supporting art museums and opera houses is exactly the same as the rationale for supporting public schools through the university level.

We have seen that, in human behavior, the setting can be anything from the simple perception of a defined space to an elaborate setting. The museum and the concert hall, the theater and the opera houses, are stages, or settings, not for art, but for the perceiver's role. In all human behavior we take our cues not only from other performers but also from the situation. It is the situation that tells us how we are supposed to behave. For example, any group of young men and women unhesitatingly assume the student's role the moment they enter a college classroom. They think it is the most natural thing in the world, forgetting that they have been carefully trained in that role from the moment they first entered nursery school, trained and rehearsed, and tested, and criticized, and praised and rewarded for the role of sitting still and listening to an older person, who has been as carefully trained in the teacher's role, though mostly by learning from the role models his own teachers offered him. But other societies are not deficient in defining artistic situations or settings. In all but the poorest Japanese houses a niche is reserved for the changing display of a painting or a print and a flower-arrangement, a highly developed art in Japan, as everyone knows. The very ancient arts of poetic recitation and story-telling require as their setting only a space with a group of people sitting around or arranged before the artist. The story-telling group for illiterate adults can be seen in the squares of Palermo to this day. The art of dancing, perhaps even more ancient, provides another illuminating example.

Everything points to the probability, then, that the connection between situation and perceiver's role is extremely ancient. Archaeologists, for example, have found in numerous sites concentrations of superior pottery. The cache of works of art is common enough and suggests collection. But a collection irresistibly suggests a setting. The museum appears to be only a very highly developed instance of something very, very old indeed: the space devoted to the perceiver's role. Those correspondents to the newspapers, therefore, who objected to public money being spent on what was not in museums were making an acute observation, though they were thoroughly wrong-headed about it. *A work of art is what the perceiver observes in what has been culturally established as a perceiver's space.* This can be anything: a dancing ground, a group gathered around a storyteller, the open place in front of a church or an important building, a niche, a mantelpiece, a cleared space around a centerpiece on the dining-room table, the frame around a picture. And it can be an entire landscape, which was the space for the pyramid and tombs in ancient Egypt and for temples in Greece and palaces in Crete.[10] The only requirement is that the distractions of other perceptual fields be eliminated or subdued, that orientation of the awareness upon the artistic perceptual field be made easy, that a certain psychic insulation be established. This is why works of art tend to be placed symmetrically on an axis, or in the center of a circle or at the apex of some segment of a circle, as in a corner. It is why very few attempts have ever been made to make a completely disorganized frame for a picture. It is also why nowadays many pictures are exhibited without frames or with minimal frames. Because of the high commercialization of the art world in our society, and because of our extreme elaboration and precision of the settings for the role, most pictures are first seen by the purchaser not in the artist's studio, as was the case until less than a hundred years ago, but in commercial art galleries or exhibitions of important institutions. It is also why art has so often been identified with order. The affect of ordered situation, the psychic insulation, has been confused with the affect emanating from the work itself.

But from this a surprising conclusion emerges. The role of art perceiver is learned, and this learning, when it does not take place through interaction with the artist or with a socially institutionalized preceptor, or with friends, occurs in the artistic setting or situation. Or more precisely, the perceiver learns the prescriptions for his role from artist, teacher, and friend, but he learns to be an actor in the artistic setting, on the artistic stage. And this is of course often very

---

[10] See Siegfried Giedion, *The Eternal Present: A Contribution on Constancy and Change; Vol. II: The Beginnings of Architecture*, New York, 1964; and Vincent Scully, *The Earth, the Temples, and the Gods*, New Haven, 1962.

difficult, as with all role-learning. The translation of the generalized precepts into behavior limited by an individual organism, by the patterns he has already learned, and by the peculiar style of those patterns, is by no means easy. This is why rehearsal is so important. The teacher or director may, and often does, give the pattern in terms of his own style, but the learner may not be physiologically able to reproduce that style. He must painfully create his own style without falling outside of the range of the pattern, when he does not yet know what that pattern is, that is, what ranges are permitted. Contrarily, a highly adept learner may learn his preceptor's style so well that he barely develops his own. This can be as noticeable in the young perceiver as it is in the young creator, who so exactly reproduces his master's style. However, once the role has been learned and mastered on the art perceiver's stage, once the perceiving role-player has become adept in his performance, he tends to forget, as in all role-behavior, that he has learned it.

At this point the work of art may be preliminarily defined as *an occasion for a human being to perform the art-perceiving role in the artistic situation, that is, on the artistic stage.* This definition helps us to understand the reasons for two of the confusions in aesthetics, one of them often discussed, and one but fairly recent in institutionalized aesthetic discussion, though, it seems probable, very ancient in actual artistic behavior, as well as very common, particularly in the criticism of the perceiver's role by himself and by others. It is one of the most common of human phenomena that we are often in situations in which we recognize the appropriate role for us to play but find ourselves unable to do so, even though we are highly adept in it. How often, for example, do parents criticize themselves for not playing the mother's or father's role as they recognize it should be played. How often are children unable to play a protective role for an aging parent, even though they have played it successfully for years and with at least no self-admitted hypocrisy. But irony and hypocrisy in role-playing arise from the same mysterious sources as inability to play the appropriate role at all, not even hypocritically. How many men, for example, have lost their jobs because they found themselves unable to play towards their employers the role of dutiful and grateful employee. The same phenomenon is true of the role of art perceiver, just as it is true of the role of art creator. As surprisingly few people appear to know, the role of art perceiver is very demanding, requires long training, involves an unusual degree of self-criticism, and is very inadequate in its preceptorial tradition, not to speak of the grave difficulty in connecting a precept with a particular internal or covert kind of behavior, rather than overt verbal or gestural behavior. The art perceiver's role is also extraordinarily fragile. Darwin experienced a total loss of the power to play this role in the presence of music and literature, except for light novels with pretty girls and happy endings. Illness, bad temper, bad weather, weariness, some dominant orientation such as a quarrel with one's wife or a business anxiety, can interfere with the effective performance of any role. Such matters can be devastating for the performance of the perception of art. And yet art also can break up a dominating mood as well as love or alcohol can.

Any social role is an ill-defined and socially fluid and dynamic assemblage or package of behavioral patterns. Now, orientations are linked to patterns and therefore roles. But the very existence of irony, hypocrisy, and performance failure indicate that orientation and pattern are two different matters. This is further indicated by the fact that the ironic or hypocritical performance of a role can lead to its sincere performance. This is the point of Max Beerbohm's brilliant story, *The Happy Hypocrite*. Sometimes, when one is in a dull and stupid frame of mind, or orientation, the mere stepping into a theater —the entering onto the artistic stage—is enough to break it up. But there is nothing unique to this. It is true of all role-playing. It is something we learn at the knees of our mothers, if they have any brains. "Try," they tell us when we balk at doing something we do not feel like doing, "try, and then you'll feel like doing it." At least half the time they are right.

The problem of the unpredictability of success in playing the perceiver's role has only recently emerged in institutionalized aesthetics; another problem that this way of defining a work of art helps us to understand is a very old one, the problem of art and nature.

The point is often made in definitions of art that a work of art is man-made. But we know that the Chinese connoisseurs constructed rules for the use of natural stones just as if they were works of art. These natural stones were taken from their original places, sometimes to be transported far away and put into a garden. They were not changed at all, but nevertheless they were works of art.

Thus the definition of art must be widened. Not all works of art are man-made. It is sophistry to say—as is often said—that man makes a natural work of art when he takes the stone from nature and puts it in a garden. From my point of view the chief fact is that natural objects are sometimes used according to the rules of works of art.[11]

---

[11] "The Uses of Works of Art" by Teddy Brunius, *The Journal of Aesthetics and Art Criticism*, XXII, 1963, p. 127. Copyright *Journal of Aesthetics and Art Criticism*. Used by permission of The American Society for Aesthetics.

Here the question is raised very well. In his talk of rules Brunius is on the right track, but he has not seen the answer fully. We have already observed that a role is not linked to a situation in the sense that the situation forces one to play it. Contrariwise, once one has learned to perform a role well, or at all, one can apply it with more or less success to any situation. We may be amused at the office buffoon or we may eliminate him from a situation in which he is playing the wrong role; but that the wrong role may be played is obvious. Roles are learned in terms of situations. Even if the learning takes place elsewhere than in its situation, the learner is informed about what kind of situation is appropriate for the role. Thus a cultural tradition transmits not information about the setting for the role, although it often appears in that form, but information about the setting in which the role *ought* to be played. But that very introduction of "ought" implies the possibility of "ought not." "Johnny," the kindergarten teacher is always saying, "we don't act like that in school." Because of this verbally stated distinction about the propriety of role to situation, it is possible to play deliberately the wrong role in any situation. This phenomenon is obviously one of the great sources for cultural innovation, and the recognition of it permits us to arrive at a further and more refined definition of a work of art, a definition which solves Brunius' problem.

A work of art is any perceptual field which an individual uses as an occasion for performing the role of art perceiver. (This assumes, naturally, that any individual who does this has already learned the role of art perceiver from his culture.) He can limit the occasion to a stone and take it home and incorporate it in another work of art, his garden. Or he can extend the field to include the entire landscape. Opposite me, as I write, is a wall of books. I have but to raise my head, assume the perceiver's role, and at once I see that expanse of book shelves as a work of art.

It will, I think, be instructive to apply this definition to certain novelties of contemporary art. One of the odd things going on to-day is that certain modern artists seem to have developed an inarticulate insight into exactly this way of defining art. John Cage, the composer, appears to be fully aware of at least one aspect, the situational cue. He has created a musical composition titled "3½." To perform it, he sits down at the piano with a stop-watch in his hand, and at the end of exactly three and one-half minutes rises, bows to the audience, and leaves the stage. Is it a work of art? By the last definition but one it unquestionably is: a perceptual field is a work of art if it is presented in a situation culturally defined as an artistic space. The hall, the audience, the printed program, the framing action of the performance —all are present. "3½" may be a singularly uninteresting piece of music, at least after the first performance, when, to judge from the comments at the time, it was wildly exciting; but a work of art it is.

Another example is less subtle and somewhat more confusing, the art of *objets trouvés* (found objects). In a 1964 show of Pop Art there was exhibited a long specially carved box, within which was a thin steel rod, highly polished. Was this a work of art? Since it was exhibited in an art gallery and listed in the catalogue and accompanied by the artist's name, title, and date, it was a work of art for the same reason "3½" was. Further, it was a work of art for the final and complete definition just given. Its exhibition amounted to an assertion on the part of the artist, "I saw this as a work of art; now, by exhibiting it in an art gallery, I invite you to see it as a work of art." Perhaps John Cage, having found himself listening to silence while performing the per- ceiver's role, invited his audience to share that experience with him, helping them along by placing it in a situation where they could recognize it as music. The discovery that anything becomes a work of art if you perceive it as a work of art, and that it can be given public status if you place it in an artistic situation, is, according to some critics and a concerned public, fraught with danger for art. For reasons I shall bring out in Chapter V I think this danger is non-existent. Certainly the same attitude directed towards stones seems to have done no great damage to Chinese art. And for reasons Brunius pointed out, the selection, exhibition, and sale of *objets trouvés* by imaginative and sensitive individuals may very well have henceforward a minor but important and refreshing place in the art business. Once you know that it can be done, anybody can do it. It is the first art truly for Everyman. And it settles the problem of art and nature.

4. STYLISTIC DYNAMISM

I have attempted to show that the notion that all works of art and all aesthetic experiences have something in common is in error, that art is a disjunctive category, established by convention, and that art is not a category of perceptual fields, but of role-playing. Brunius quotes from William E. Kennick, "the characteristics common to all works of art are the object of a fool's errand" and from Morris Weitz, "aesthetic theory is a logically vain attempt to define what cannot be defined, to state the necessary and sufficient properties, to conceive the concept of art as closed when its very use reveals and demands its openness."[12] Neither of these propositions could be truer or said better. I have endeavored to show that the paralogisms of aesthetics can be traced to attitudes which are cultural conventions. This leaves as yet unanswered, however, the question with which this chapter began: If we can arrange works of art in their historical order, stylistic dynamism emerges at once: but on what grounds do we put an artifact into the category of art so that we may include it in such an historical arrangement? Since the category of art as referring to a range of perceptual fields has turned out to be a logically empty category, there is no point in looking for artifacts with something in common. As Kennick says, that would be a fool's errand.

However, it would seem that artistic behavior is not an empty category, and for this reason: The fact is that though art is a logically empty category, in our culture it is not a conventionally empty category. Since aesthetics emerged historically at the highest cultural level, it is not at all surprising that aestheticians should have talked about the kind of art collected at that level, produced for that level, and valued by it. It is not at all surprising that a critic ethnocentrically bound to that level and taking pride in belonging to it should repel with horror the notion that Edgar Guest's verse is poetry and therefore art. Had there been no contact between Western culture and other cultures, if art historians had not set to work, if archaeologists had not started digging, if anthropologists had not started studying primitive cultures, if the Enlightenment had not started a tradition of paying attention to what lower cultural levels use for art, the probability is that none of the difficulties of aesthetics would have arisen and that it would not now be, as Brunius says, in ruins. Facts are always so embarrassing. Yet if aesthetics has given us little knowledge about art, it has given us a great deal of information about the conservative performance of the perceiver's role in nineteenth-century European culture. In fact, it is the only rich body of such information available anywhere, and it deserves to be thoroughly restudied as a collection of documents of great anthropological interest.

---

[12] Brunius, p. 133. His references are to William E. Kennick, "Does Traditional Aesthetic Rest on a Mistake?" *Mind*, LXVII, 1958, pp. 317–334, and Morris Weitz, "The Role of Theory in Aesthetics," *Problems in Aesthetics*, New York, 1959.

Further, the tradition of stylistic history was developed in the same cultural milieu and based on the same principles. Turning to the high level artistic culture of the European past, which to members of that culture could be readily identified, since it was being collected more assiduously than ever, and to ancient Greece and Rome and Byzantium, where the same cultural level could be identified with equal ease, stylistic historians readily established stylistic continua. They knew without thinking about it what kind of object was the culturally conventional occasion for the performance of the perceiver's role in their own culture and in the richly documented cultures which were the ancestors of their own. This was fortunate, because I do not know how otherwise the phenomenon of the stylistic dynamism of art could have been discovered. That stylistic continuum became the model for archaeologists and anthropologists.

When we examine stylistic history, of course, we are engaged with the other role of artistic behavior, the artist's. However, as we have seen, since he is engaged in an economic relation with the perceiver, he must know the perceiver's role in that particular culture. He knows what kind of object the culture requires as the occasion for artistic perception; it follows that the members of any sequence of functionally similar objects which show stylistic dynamism were occasions for the perceiver's role. It may, as in China, be the Imperial collection of paintings. It may, as in India, be numerous temples. Or it may, in prehistoric cultures, be simple household pots. Ceramic products have survived from prehistory better than anything else. In some instances it is almost all that has survived. Yet careful excavation and record-keeping about how deep in the earth the pot, or usually the potsherd, was found, can establish the historical sequence in which they were made. Nothing is more striking than the stylistic dynamism of such a series and the reliability with which that constructed series may be used in excavating other sites. There is no reason to change a perfectly efficient wine storage jar. As, too, with a house, there is nothing people do that they cannot do in a perfectly rectangular room. In ancient Greece, indeed, amphorae used for shipping and storing wine show virtually no stylistic change over long periods of time. In classical Greece they were standardized and the sequence was almost completely static.

Any object (or perceptual field) from any culture may, then, be properly categorized as having been the occasion for artistic perception if a chronologically arranged sequence of such objects shows both functional identity and non-functional stylistic dynamism.

I have chosen my major example from cultures about which we know almost nothing to show how artistic behavior can be traced throughout mankind's history. Even in the great Magdalenian and Aurignacian cave paintings of southern France of thousands of years ago stylistic dynamism can be easily detected, though, as might be expected, by the measure of modern stylistic change it was glacially slow in its movement. At the same time, the contemporary flint tools show only a range of refinement of shaping, which, once established, was maintained for tens of thousands of years, according to the efficiency of the workman and the difficulty of the job the tool was to do.

It appears to be clear, then, that we may categorize as a work of art any artifact (which is all we have from vanished cultures), or any perceptual field, if it can be placed in a sequence of similar objects or fields which shows a greater rate of dynamism than other such sequences from the same culture. If, moreover, we find a series of sequences ranging from a low rate of dynamism to a high dynamic rate, we may say that in that culture the last sequence was the occasion for the most intense and devoted artistic perception. Further, as cultures become more elaborate in history, sequences emerge which have little function except to be such occasions. As we have seen, however, even among the Melville Islanders something very close to this function has emerged, though recently and in sequence of objects still remembered as having been derived from baskets and still so recognizable. (We must not make the old-fashioned error of asserting that modern primitives are equivalent to the men of the paleolithic or neolithic ages, or lead the same kind of lives or have the same institutions, roles, and interests. Like ourselves, they are descendants of early man.)

One final point may be derived from this. The higher the rate of stylistic dynamism and the more frequent the stylistic revolutions, the higher the cultural level for which the art is being produced. To comprehend this, one has only to compare the stylistic history of comic strips for the past forty years with the stylistic history of paintings exhibited in galleries and bought by collectors and museums. Properly applied, this principle is a way of determining the cultural level which a particular sequence was made for.

From all this one obvious problem emerges. *Why* is art—a term we can now safely use—characterized by stylistic dynamism? Why does the performance of the social role of perceiving art demand it? Why does the poor artist have to sweat and toil to provide it? Why is the perceiver of art so greedy? This is almost the absolutely central problem of artistic behavior. But there is a problem at dead center which emerges from another consideration. It can be argued that even this conception of art as the occasion for a certain kind of role-playing is ethnocentric, that is, is culture bound. Art may be a logically empty category, but in our culture it is certainly not a conventionally empty category. But is there not a possibility that in other cultures it *is* a conventionally empty category, that the role-playing for which such perceptual fields provide the occasion is entirely alien to that played in ours? This possibility seems very remote indeed. There are too many similarities. Still, the question, logic-chopping though it may be, reveals the central question of all: If artistic behavior is a universal human phenomenon, what is its adaptational function? What is the biological basis for artistic behavior?

An analysis of the perceiver's role will eventually bring us to an understanding of stylistic dynamism and a theory about the crucial problem of this book, the relationship of the arts. Then it will be possible to make a proposal about art's biological function.

THREE:
SIGNS

Nothing about role-playing in the preceding chapter can be regarded as unique to artistic behavior, either to the artist's role or to the perceiver's. Hence, the stylistic dynamism of art is still unaccounted for. Between what behavioral patterns and roles can do and the emergent demands of transactions with a continuously changing environment is a necessary gap, which explains the existence of innovation, not as merely a common, but as a universal characteristic of human behavior. The awareness of the gap, or problem perception, accounts for the general dynamism of human behavior as simple stimulus-response theory cannot; an adaptational mechanism may be sufficiently successful to stabilize behavior within the ranges of a pattern, but it can never be perfectly successful. But the problem of the peculiarly dynamic character of artistic innovation remains unresolved. The application of game theory proves helpful at this point.

1. THE GAME METAPHOR

The game metaphor, it may be remembered, reveals two aspects of behavior which helped us to understand the gap left between role playing and individual human behavior. "A role is a package of patterns, but it is an incomplete package." In an actual emergent situation the individual may be at a loss, or he may improvise by trying out patterns or roles not conventionally used in the situation, or he may innovate. That innovation may involve novelty in role, in pattern, in style, or in bit (the irreducible atom of behavior), or in any combination of these. Obviously, simultaneous novelty at more than one level becomes increasingly difficult as more levels are involved. Indeed, I cannot think of nor even imagine behavior involving all four. What the game metaphor does is to show two ways of dealing with emergent situations, by the application of rules and by the deduction of new rules from existent rules.

In a passage quoted in the preceding chapter Brunius spoke of the Chinese having constructed rules for the use of natural stones as works of art. Though elsewhere he uses "rules" to describe an aspect of artistic behavior better accounted for by the drama metaphor, here "rule" is used in the proper sense: a rule is explicit, and from old rules new rules may be constructed by logical manipulation. There is no question that the artist's role is governed by rules and that new rules are developed by logical manipulation. Thus "A natural rock may be regarded as a work of art and consequently be incorporated into man-made works of art, a garden, for example, according to certain rules of design." This is extended by asserting, "Since a natural rock is a 'beautiful' product of nature, any 'beautiful' product of nature may be incorporated into an artifactual work of art." Therefore, "A flower may be regarded as a work of art and consequently incorporated into a work of art, may be placed in a pot according to certain rules of design." For all I know, this may be exactly the way the Japanese art of flower arrangement emerged; or it may have been the other way around. It makes no difference; the principle of extending artistic rules by logical manipulation is clear enough. The individual perceiver, however, who first saw flowers arranged according to familiar rules of design in a household pot placed in an artistic space, was confronted with an emergent, or unpredicted, situation. He could either cry, "No fair," insisting that the rules had been violated; or he could grasp the deduction and deny the validity of the categorization of "artistic rock" into the class of "artistic natural objects"; or he could grasp the deduction and accept it. In the first case, he would deny that the flower in the pot was a work of art; in the second, deny that it was a good work of art; in the third, assert it to be a good work of art. The game metaphor reveals the factor of the unpredicted in the role of artistic perceiving.

This brings out also the roles in games, which have already been hinted at, the role of challenger and the role of respondent. The artist is the challenger: his role requires him to create unpredicted situations. The respondent is the perceiver. His task is to meet the unpredicted situations. But here a striking difference between games and art emerges, and the game metaphor reveals its inability to account for all the data, as all metaphors eventually must.

A game is extended by logical manipulation of the rules. Three-dimensional chess was developed in this manner. It was first seen that chess does not involve the moving of men through space. The chessmen are, rather, emblems for variable rule-controlled patterns on a plane surface. Pieces are merely signs for communicating those patterns. Once this had been understood it was possible to write out chess games, that is, to substitute a new communication system for the traditional one. The next step was a long time in coming, and came only as the result of developments in mathematics. A plane surface was redefined in terms of three-dimensional space. This made possible the re-categorization of the plane surface of chess as one of an infinite possibility of planes. It was then possible to think of and to deduce the rules for three-dimensional chess. Until this occurred, chess had been stabilized in its traditional form for untold centuries, and for most chess players still is. When, however, three-dimensional chess was created, it too was stabilized, after a period of uncertainty during which the correct deduction of the rules was worked out and conventionalized.

Now it is quite possible to refer to three-dimensional chess as a new "style" of playing chess. Such a usage is quite permissible under the current rules for using the term. It is also quite possible to say that, though the movement may be glacially slow, even chess shows stylistic dynamism, and this remark becomes even more appropriate when we see how other games appear, flourish, and die within a short space of time. This is particularly true of word games, like the Swifties, which flourished in 1963 and will have been forgotten by most people when this book is published. The difference between stylistic dynamism in games, therefore, and stylistic dynamism in art must be determined, or art will collapse into games, as, in the thinking of some investigators, it already has. Unless Brunius realizes that he is using the game metaphor, he will find himself in serious difficulties.

As we have seen, the human function of the game is to reinforce the orientation which makes it possible to look for and experience unpredicted situations and to meet them by obeying rules or deducing new patterns of behavior from existent rules. If an individual creates new rules, he is excluded from the game or he has created a new game. A game proceeds by a system of rewards. If the respondent successfully meets a challenge he is rewarded by becoming the challenger. The game is cut off by weariness or boredom, as in many children's games, by completing a prescribed course, as in golf or croquet, by achieving an arbitrarily set goal, usually expressed in numbers, as in tennis or bridge, by the respondent's encountering a logical impasse, as when he is checkmated. (To meet the challenge he must move, but if he moves he violates the rules.) When an individual becomes too practiced in a game, and when he can predict that he can meet successfully all the unpredicted situations the game can offer, he abandons it, or he adds gambling, or he extends it by logical deduction, or he turns to a new game, or he invents a new one.

A game functions by producing an unpredicted situation which the respondent can meet only by solving a problem. If no problem emerges, or if all the problems are solved without offering the experience of solving a problem—if the solution is consistently immediate—there is no game for that particular player: that is, the respondent assumes the role of challenger with no awareness of problem-solving behavior. A game shows stylistic dynamism only when its function fails. The opposite is true of toolmaking. A tool changes style only when it is possible to improve its function by redesigning it. As tools become perfected, the style becomes stabilized. The proliferation of inexpensive power tools in the last few decades is to the point. A tool becomes perfected as the energy expended in using it decreases. Ways of inexpensively applying non-human power to hand tools has resulted in considerable stylistic change in a great variety of tools used in homes and in small businesses and by workmen without capital or who need portable tools. But just as the game metaphor is inapplicable at this point to tool behavior, so it is inapplicable to artistic behavior.

Originally all behavior which served to produce occasions for both the artist's and perceiver's role served also some other function. But certainly modern Western culture produces artifacts—wallpaper, for example—of which the primary function is to provide such occasions, even though, as we shall see, another function is always served. But any sequence of such artifacts is precisely one that shows the highest rate of stylistic dynamism. *When we apply the term "style" to artifacts, therefore, or to any pattern of behavior, like games, we may distinguish between functional style, as in games or tools, and the non-functional style or "free" style of art.* Yet if the non-functional stylistic behavior of artists were absolutely free, stylistic dynamism would be accounted for but not stylistic continua. If the artist were absolutely free, there would be no stylistic continua, not even within an artist's total work. Any theory of artistic behavior, therefore, must account for both.

Another difference between art and games also emerges from this analysis. The game metaphor reveals the presence in artistic behavior of the artist as challenger and the perceiver as respondent. But artistic perception does not involve a shift from one role to another when it has been successfully accomplished. It is true that the artist in the process of creation shifts into the perceiver's role and out of it again, but he does this as a means of deciding whether or not he has carried out successfully his artist's role, just as he has to learn the perceiver's role in order to be an artist at all. It is his technique of being his own critic. When a game player plays alone, however, he creates for himself, usually by rules that increase the frequency of certain kinds of chance, an unpredicted problem. If he solves it, he goes back to the challenger's role, or he loses to himself. In games, the individual must play both roles to carry out the function of the game. In art the roles are not interdependent for the perceiver, and it is possible for the practiced artist almost to neglect the perceiver's role. Even when the artist does play it, he employs the critical function, and then only a narrow range of its possibilities. The pattern for returning the respondent to the challenger's role, then, is absent in art. In games the winner is the player who blocked that return by creating an insoluble problem and forced his opponent out of the game. But the art perceiver may withdraw and re-enter his role at will. Winning and losing are likewise absent from art. Insofar, then, as art offers a problem, problem perception and solving are different from such behavior in games.

Certainly, as in the hypothetical instance of the development of the art of Japanese flower arrangement, rule extension is sometimes present in art. An actual historical example may be found in the rich information about the development of rules for perspective in Italy, especially in Florence, during the fifteenth century. But the artist also plays his role by violating rules. When the game player violates the rules, whether as challenger or respondent, he is thrown out of the game, or his partner withdraws from it; or, if he can get his partner to cooperate, he has invented a new game. Not so with the artist, though at times of stylistic revolution this may be the immediate effect. When Picasso showed Braque "Les Demoiselles d'Avignon," Braque's initial reaction was that Picasso had violated so many rules and so extensively that he had disqualified himself for the artist's role. Yet within not many months he was painting so like Picasso that their work became at times indistinguishable, even, in later years, to the artists themselves. How many times, since the days of the Impressionists, have we not heard, "This is not art"; then, "This is not good art"; then, "This is not only art and good art, it is great art, it is a masterpiece." But to this day, numerous students of literature deny the term "art" to Joyce's *Ulysses*, just as they deny it to John Cage's "3½," in which he violated *all* the rules, except that music may have silence. But in game playing, to say "This is not the game," is to stop the game in its tracks.

The artist, then, may present the perceiver with a problem to be solved, but it is not his primary function. The problem in a game emerges in the form of an unpredicted situation which has been created by following certain rules and which must be first perceived and then solved by the application of certain rules. But this is not true of art, since it may proceed by the violation of rules. Problem solution is impossible because there are no explicit rules to solve it with. Art may proceed by rule extension, but it does not have to. It can proceed by rule violation, of which rule extension, therefore, is a special class. Rule extension is but one way of presenting the unpredictable. It would appear that the artist's primary function is executed by offering a problem, but *not* a problem to be solved. He simply presents the unpredicted; he offers the *experience* of disorientation. Nevertheless, as we shall see later, if what the artist offers does not seem a problem to the perceiver, he will be unable to play his role. In games, however, it is not merely that the respondent can play even though he misses the problem; it is exactly the role of the challenger so to present the problem that the respondent does miss it. But in art there are no traps. The perceiver is supposed to experience the problem, the disorientation, as soon and as fully as possible. He often fails, but that is his failure, not the artist's success. The artist's role is to violate the rules, though he may fail to violate the rules enough to interest a particular perceiver. This is what Kubler is trying to get at in his rather crude distinction between prime objects and replications.

The indicators whereby the individual distinguishes another individual from everybody else are stylistic signs, for this reason: another individual is a class of perceptual fields, a conjunctive category. The style of that individual is made up of the signs by which that class of perceptual fields may be distinguished from similar perceptual fields, that is, other people. These signs are so reliable as predictive indicators that an individual offers more than a conjunctive category; he offers a category of identity—at least for all practical purposes of ordinary perception. (When we get down to the atomic level, of course, that category entirely vanishes.) Now when an individual wishes to be confused with other such perceptual fields by someone who has categorized him as an identity, he has only to change the attributes of that category. He grows a beard, puts on glasses, changes his style of dress, changes his walk, his posture, his gestures; he may even use a perfume to change his style of odor. This is no logical extension of rules. It is a flat violation of as many as he can think of. The familiar perceiver is now so disoriented—his orientation towards that individual is so useless—that he can no longer put this new perceptual field into the old category of identity.

This is an exact analogy to what the artist does, to a greater or lesser degree. Picasso so altered the stylistic features of that area of his behavior Braque cared about that Braque had to exclude those features from his category of Picasso's identity. Initially Braque did exactly what those other perceivers still do who cannot accept Picasso's subsequent work into the category of art. The traditional stylistic features of painting were so thoroughly violated that their orientation towards paintings was no longer applicable. Rather than permit themselves to be disoriented, they denied Picasso's work admission into their category of painting and consequently into their category of art. The artist, then, plays his role by building into his occasion for the perceiver's role a stylistic violation of the current stylistic orientation. This is the phenomenon Kubler was trying to locate. By a "prime object" he means a work which is heavily disguised, which for a wide range of familiar stylistic features has substituted unfamiliar ones, features unexpected in the culturally current stylistic category. This accounts for the dynamism of artistic style, though not for stylistic continua.

The probability that the primary role of the artist is to provide stylistic disorientation is increased when we examine more generally how human beings behave when they experience disorientation, of which we may distinguish three varieties: the awareness of the gap between the orientation appropriate to the situation and the actual demands of interaction with that situation; the absence from the individual's repertory of any orientation appropriate to the situation; the inability to make use of any orientation available in the repertory, the inability to interact with the situation at all.

The third can give us an initial hint. Under such conditions the individual's initial impulse on recovering the ability to act is to seek shelter, to insulate himself from the environment and its demands. In its most extreme forms the desire for insulation may lead to psychogenic death. Less damaging experiences of this sort, like that of a man at a familiar intersection who finds himself unable to decide which way to guide himself and unable to think of any reason to move at all, may impel the subject to seek psychiatric or religious aid. All kinds of spaces which offer help to the disturbed and disoriented, hospitals, clinics, asylums—the word itself shows the function—are characterized by psychic insulation from the environment. The psychiatrist's office is an intensification of this, and the orthodox analyst insulates the patient even from the sight of himself, reducing interpersonal stimulation merely to a voice, and often offering only silence. This additional insulation is a consequence of the analyst's desire that the patient should expose himself to the most disturbing forces within him, forces so powerful as to have a deep-seated physiological affect.

The game offers, in a milder form, the same pattern of behavior. All games, like all other roles, take place in a space temporarily or permanently defined for the performance of that particular role. The spaces or stages for disorienting activities such as the game, as we have seen, offer some psychic insulation. Even in the very noisy crap game, one often hears players shouting for silence. Games like chess, which requires immense concentration and the exposure to logical disorientation, intellectually the most difficult kind, require the greatent amount of insulation.

But more serious activities show the same pattern. As a role, game playing, along with its other role functions, which are all present, is particularly notable for its emphasis on rehearsal. As we have seen, it is a rehearsal for the confrontation with unpredicted experiences in other than game playing roles. Some roles, however, *require* the individual to disorient himself. The scientist, the philosopher, the scholar, the student—all require psychic insulation. This is why college campuses are modeled on monasteries, for the monastic role requires that one expose oneself to one's religious deficiencies and to the fragile and psychically dangerous disorientation of religious contemplation. This is again the reason for the tenure system in faculty life. The task of the scholar is to look for problems to solve, and these he can find only by exposing himself to intellectual disorientation.

Now, if we examine the settings for artistic behavior, we find the same phenomenon. The Japanese niche with its flower arrangement and its single painting, the picture frame which by bounding the perceptual field makes it easier to ignore what lies outside of it, the quiet museum of art, in which everyone talks in hushed tones, if at all, in which the guard upbraids the noisy, the darkened concert hall and theater, the defined space before or around a great building—all these stages for the perceiver's role are marked by psychic insulation.

Thus, creative activity, which can occur only after a disorienting experience, and art are quite different from normal day-to-day role-playing, such as one's job or the housewife's duties. In these the gap between behavioral patterns and the requirements of the transaction with the environment is of little importance. Exposure to disorientation is quite inessential, and in most paid activities a supervisor, a straw-boss or foreman, that is, a director-teacher, is present to observe the gap when it does occur and to correct the behavioral pattern by bringing it once again within an acceptable range. But even in business organizations, the higher the level of responsibility the greater is the insulation. Much of this is pure status seeking, but it is true that the men at the higher management and executive levels often engage in demanding problem-solving activities; and at the highest level their task is to look for problems or to wait for problems which have not been successfully solved at lower levels. A corporation president may not do much, but what he does is vital to the life of his company.

The function of psychic insulation is even clearer if we observe what happens in normal activities in which disorientation is not sought for or expected. Extreme disorientation precipitates flight; if people stand their ground, it is only because they can put up defenses, whether physical or psychic. Among the most useful are value defenses, the denial of the value of the disorienting transaction or stimulus. We have already seen something of this in the critical function of the artistic perceiver's role-playing. Particularly stubborn are the defenses of those whose disorientations are from within—to use very loose language—and are the consequence of the repression of an unsolved problem. Such people often require the repeated experience of psychic insulation before they can permit the psychotherapist to ask the overwhelming question.

The functions of psychic insulation are now clear: it permits the individual to let down his defenses and fully expose himself to disorientation; it permits him to avoid raising defenses when he encounters disorientation. It will become evident in what follows how both these functions are at work in the perceiver's and the artist's role.

From this examination of artistic behavior with the aid of the attributes of game playing, several problems have emerged. If the role of artist demands that he construct perceptual fields which offer a disorienting experience to the perceiver, how does this happen? What evidence can we find from actual discrete works of art that this possible explanation for stylistic dynamism is valid? Second, if this is the case, how can stylistic continua be explained and what is the evidence for that explanation? I shall now explore the first of these problems.

2. CATEGORIES

The first clue comes from the phrase "constructing perceptual fields." What the artist constructs are fields of signs: in producing stylistic dynamism, he changes the signs which the perceiver has been using as a means of categorizing the perceptual field as a work of art. Art is an open category, as Morris Weitz says. Generally, the new signs are so few, so similar to the old, and so controlled by rules, that the power of the situation continues to identify the field as an occasion for playing the perceiver's role. But at times, as in the ease of Picasso and Braque, the new signs are so different, and so many, and violate the rules so strongly, that the perceiver is unable to play his role, even with the best will in the world. In a perceptual field which is culturally conventionalized as the occasion for the perceiver's role, the artist presents unpredicted signs. This consideration of a work of art as a constructed field of signs permits us to place artistic behavior in a more inclusive category of human action: *semiotic behavior*, that is, *sign behavior in general*.

Semiosis is "the process by which something serves as a sign for an organism."[1] The most obvious class of signs consists of language signs; but, as we shall see, anything can serve as a sign. Indeed, I hope to show that every sensory stimulus becomes a sign as soon as it is estab-

---

[1] *Webster's New International Dictionary*, 3d ed.

lished in the individual's sensory perception as a configuration, that is, as a pattern, or figure, or *gestalt*. A *gestalt* is "a structure or configuration of physical, biological, or psychological phenomena so integrated as to constitute a functional unit with properties not derivable from its parts in summation."[2]

Roget's *Thesaurus* has several pages of words which may be used for various semantic functions in place of "sign." A few of these will suggest something of the range of sign behavior: indication, symbol, lineament, feature, trait, characteristic, means of recognition, marker, token, symptom, type, figure, emblem, gesture, signal, mark, badge, stamp, shibboleth, banner, insignia, flag, coat of arms, beacon, pointer, warning, trophy, stigma, call, trace, vestige, record, language, speech, hieroglyph, word, term, name. The great number of words for various sign functions indicates ("is a sign of") the importance of signs in human behavior, but only faintly. It is not too much to say that we live in an atmosphere of signs, and that the range of sign behavior—or semiosis—is identical with the range of human behavior. It is, therefore, all the stranger that so few efforts have been made to construct a general theory of signs. The American philosopher, Charles Pierce, most of whose work was still in manuscript at his death, was one of the very few philosophers who have been deeply engaged with the problem. Charles W. Morris has continued and developed Pierce's work.[3]

---

[2] *Webster's New International Dictionary*, 3d ed.

[3] Charles W. Morris, "Foundations of the Theory of Signs," *International Encyclopedia of Unified Science*, I, No. 2, pp. 77–137, Chicago, 1955 (this was first published in 1936); *Signs, Language, and Behavior*, New York, 1946. In 1957 the famous behaviorist B. F. Skinner issued *Verbal Behavior* (New York); the title is somewhat strange, since, as Skinner specifically says, his concern is with all behavior like verbal behavior, that is, with sign behavior, though he does not say so. Nothing on this subject has become standard or even, so far as I have been able to observe, has had a very wide or profound effect. Skinner, for example, does not mention Morris, although one criticism of Morris is that he is excessively behavioristic. It is my own opinion that a great deal of modern philosophy is weakened because it concentrates solely on language signs and neglects other signs. I also think that the difficulty linguistics is encountering in moving into the question of verbal "meaning" is a result of a similar failure. For my own part, I feel that Morris' weakness is his failure to consider modern perception theory, variously termed, to repeat, transactionalism, directive state theory, set theory, expectancy theory, the New Look in perception. He can hardly be blamed for this, since such theories were in infancy at the time he began to work. Nevertheless, the whole problem needs thorough reconsideration from this point of view. To make up for this deficiency in Morris, I have found particularly useful a book mentioned above (Chapter II, Note 3), Jerome S. Bruner, *A Study of Thinking*. It includes an important "Appendix on Language" by Roger W. Brown.

Anyone, therefore, is bound to get into trouble who attempts to use the accumulation of twentieth-century work in the philosophical analysis of language and in linguistics, and to integrate it with what little has been done in semiotic theory and research. This basic difficulty is particularly unavoidable in the effort to apply such ideas to a field of study so vexing and uncertain as artistic behavior. Nevertheless, I do not believe it is possible to approach art in any other way. although efforts to examine art from the semiotic position have not been very successful so far.

One who has made the attempt is Suzanne Langer, who has probably opened up the subject better than anyone else, for she has grasped the semiotic implications of modern philosophy; she has shown in that matter, at least, an insight that a good many other philosophers have missed.[4] Nevertheless, I find her work on art to be inadequate. She has failed to convince me that her conception of art as symbol is genuinely useful and informative, particularly since she admits that art "is not a symbol in full familiar sense, for it does not convey something beyond itself. Therefore it cannot strictly be said to have a meaning; what it does have is import." This is weasling. She goes on:

> The symbol in art is a metaphor, an image with overt or covert literal significa-
> tion; the art symbol is the absolute image—the image of what otherwise would
> be irrational, as it is literally ineffable: direct awareness, emotion, vitality,
> personal identity—life lived and felt, the matrix of mentality.[5]

Mrs. Langer assumes that art is a conjunctive category. To my mind, this is in itself enough to discredit her work. More importantly, if her explanation of "art symbol" is applied to any deposit of human behavior or to any perceptual configuration—a textbook or taking a bath—it collapses into all behavior. She has seen that art can be approached successfully only by categorizing it as semiotic behavior, but she has not, to my mind, arrived at an adequate solution. The reason appears to be that her analysis is still controlled by the paralogistic assumption that the defining attribute of the conjunctive category "art" is form, order, structure, organic unity.

Nevertheless, in spite of what I conceive to be Mrs. Langer's failure, she has demonstrated that the semiotic approach to art is not only valid but the only correct approach. Confusing and uncertain as

---

[4] She has published *Philosophy in a New Key,* 1943, 2nd ed., Cambridge, Mass., 1951; *Feeling and Form,* New York, 1953; and *Problems of Art: Ten Philosophical Lectures,* New York, 1957.

[5] *Problems of Art,* p. 139.

the science of semiosis may be, a few principles have emerged which appear to be reasonably reliable. In what follows, I shall use a few notions from semiotic, linguistics, and the analytic philosophy of language. Though relatively unrefined, they will be sufficient for my purpose. It is true that a general semiotic theory has not been completed, but it is consoling to remember that it is in the nature of scientific theories that they are never completed; one must use what one can, hoping that at least one has discovered real problems, the further exploration of which will supersede most of what one has managed to say.

The real trouble with Mrs. Langer's stimulating work is the confessed vagueness and subjectivity of her language. Charles Morris, on the other hand, presents a definition of "sign" which is carefully prepared for by a behavioristic analysis of the semiotic process in animals and in human beings. Though, at first reading, it may be difficult to grasp, rereading and meditation make it wonderfully sensible and satisfactory.

> SIGN: Roughly: something that directs behavior with respect to something that is not at the moment a stimulus. More accurately: If A is a preparatory-stimulus that, in the absence of stimulus objects initiating response-sequences of a certain behavior-family, causes in some organism a disposition to respond by response-sequences of this behavior-family, then A is a sign. Anything that meets these conditions is a sign: it is left undecided whether there are signs that do not meet these conditions.[6]

An example will help: If I see a heavy black cloud, and if I interpret it as a sign that it is going to rain, then I will have a disposition to avoid getting wet. The rain is here a "stimulus-object" of a certain behavior-family: the "keeping-dry" family of behavior sequences. But the rain stimulus-object is in fact absent. In spite of that, however, I respond with one of the various sequences of behavior from the "keeping-dry" family.

To take another example: If I see a library building, and if I feel a disposition to read, then a book is a sign that I can engage in reading behavior, even though printed language is absent from my field of vision.

However, supposing that I am a professional meteorologist, if I see a heavy black cloud, and if I interpret it as a sign that it is going to

---

[6] Morris, *Signs, Language, and Behavior*, p. 354.

rain, then I may very well have a disposition to engage in the various sequences of the behavior of professional meteorologists, even though I may in fact be preparing to cook a steak in the back yard.

Or, supposing that I am a slow and inefficient reader, when I see the library building I may very well have a disposition to lie down on the grass and take a nap.

On the other hand, when a dog hears the rustle made by a chipmunk, does he have a disposition to pursue the chipmunk or merely a disposition to continue hearing the rustle? If a stimulus-object from the "hearing-behavior" family rouses a disposition for the "pursuing-behavior" family, then the rustle is a sign. But if the rustle rouses the dog only to a course of action which will assure the continuance of hearing the rustle, if, that is, the rustle rouses a disposition only for the "rustle-hearing" family, then the rustle is, according to Morris, not a sign but a *signal*. Since this cannot be decided except by asking the dog, that is, by communicating with the dog through signs, "it is left undecided whether there are signs that do not meet these conditions." As far as we can tell, to the dog the rustle of the leaves is not a sign but a signal. We cannot know if the dog *interprets* the rustle or merely responds without performing an act of interpretation. This distinction brings out very sharply one of the great merits of Morris. He introduces the act of interpretation between stimulus and response. This act is responsible for the difference between the preparatory-stimulus family and the response-sequence family, that is, for the fact that a preparatory stimulus can initiate a response sequence from one of any number of behavior families. We cannot be sure if the dog performs this act of interpretation, which is essential to the definition of "sign." [7]

From Morris, then, I shall take certain factors for my discussion, partly redefining them for the purposes at hand.

Sign behavior involves four distinguishable factors.

(1) There is the *sign*, any perceptual configuration which leads to sign behavior.

(2) There is what the sign refers to, which Morris in 1938 called the designatum. [8] "The designatum is the kind of object which the sign applies to." A sign is a category, then, for "kind" equals "category."

---

[7] It is worth noting that recent work suggests very strongly that much behavior in the higher animals is learned from other animals of the same species; it is not, then, instinctual. This probability in turn suggests that such animals use signs and not mere signals.

[8] Morris, "Foundations of the Theory of Signs," p. 83.

In 1946 he abandoned this term and innovated two others. *Denotatum* is the categorial range which can rouse a particular disposition: that is, all the objects which can rouse that disposition. *Significatum* is what all members of that range have in common: that is, what character or quality an object has to have in order to be a member of that range. Other terms found in logical and quasi-logical discourse which are equivalent to *denotatum* are *categorial range, denotation,* and *extension.* The antitheses to these terms, and the equivalents, therefore, to *significatum,* are *categorial attributes, connotation,* and *intension.*

(3) There is the disposition to act in some particular way, to engage in some particular category of behavior. Morris calls this the *interpretant.* In this book I have called it "orientation," and in what follows shall use "orientative set," "expectancy," "set of expectancies," and "directive state."

(4) Morris also uses "interpreter," an organism that interprets a sign. Since a sign is not a sign unless it is interpreted by an interpreter, who "contains" an interpretant, the term seems to me to be uninformative. An interpreter is a mere bundle of interpretants. What I miss in Morris' work is a term equivalent to *interpretation,* a word which brings out the fact that the identical sign can be interpreted in a variety of ways, *by the same* interpreter. I may interpret a heavy black cloud near at hand as a sign of rain; or I may interpret it as a sign of beauty—it arouses in me a disposition to enjoy a natural phenomenon in some way apparently incapable of definition; or I may interpret it as a sign that the Gods are angry and respond with a disposition to offer up a sacrifice. This possible variety in interpretation brings out several important factors.

Let me first remind the reader that I have substituted "perceptual configuration" for "object," in Morris' "The designatum is the kind of object which the sign applies to." In later definitions he uses such terms as "whatever" or "anything," but his position is clear from his definition of "singular sign: A sign whose signification permits only one denotatum."[9] From such a definition it is impossible to develop the category of identity, which is not only common in logic but has been experimentally established by Bruner and further developed by Brown in his "Appendix on Language."[10] As a category of identity, an object is a category of perceptual configurations which always have the same

[9] From the book *Signs, Language and Behavior* by Charles W. Morris, p. 303. © 1946 by Prentice-Hall, Inc., Englewood Cliffs, New Jersey.
[10] Bruner, *A Study of Thinking.*

attributes. But in fact no "object" has ever precisely the same attributes. This is why such a maddening question arises as to whether or not a sound apple turned rotten is the same apple. For some purposes it is, and for some purposes it isn't. It may or may not rouse the same "interpretant" or orientation—it may or may not be perceived with the same orientation.

This brings out the fact that Morris has neglected "interpretation." It is not merely that a sign rouses an interpretant; it is equally true that no sign can function as a sign unless the interpreter perceives it in terms of an already existent disposition (or interpretant or orientation), that is, unless it answers to certain interests.[11] A configuration cannot be stabilized unless it is perceived as a sign. To stabilize it *is* to perceive it as a sign. The well-known duck–rabbit problem, in which a configuration can be seen as either but not as both at the same time, is an example. "When an individual is deprived of any objective means of stabilizing his perceptions, he will establish an internal point of reference for this purpose."[12] That is, applying to it an attribute or attributes of an already existing category, he stabilizes the configuration by perceiving it as a member of that category. Once that category has been established, it is difficult to place it in another. Recently, examining a photograph of a Greek relief, I perceived it as an intaglio or inverse relief, in which what in real life would be nearest to the observer is cut deepest into the stone or jewel. A friend saw it as a high relief, and in the very act of disagreeing with him I suddenly saw it the same way. I now find it increasingly difficult to see it as an intaglio.

From this, emerge several other factors in interpreting signs. Perception is categorization. Categorization tends to be stabilized in the interpreter. The tendency is always to see a particular configuration in terms of the same category when the configuration recurs.

> When groups of individuals are presented with a similarly unstructured field, they will, as a group, establish a hypothetical reference point and an organization of their perceptions based upon it that are peculiar to them and distinct from the norms evolved by other groups. If, then, an individual of such a group is presented with a comparable situation alone, he perceives it in terms of the group norm. . . . Both individuals and groups, then, unconsciously manufacture norms under the need to stabilize their sense impressions.[13]

---

[11] Paul Ziff, *Semantic Analysis*, Ithaca, 1960, p. 247.

[12] Barnett, *Innovation*, p. 116. He cites experiments and the bibliography in Jerome S. Bruner and Cecile C. Goodman, "Value and Need as Organizing Factors in Perception," *Journal of Abnormal and Social Psychology*, 1947, pp. 33–44.

[13] Barnett, *Innovation*, pp. 116–117.

Categorization is a matter of convention, of cultural tradition. Even in the individual, stabilization means that for that particular perceptual configuration the individual has conventionalized categorization, if only for himself. *To perceive is to categorize a configuration* by ascribing to it the attributes of a conventionalized perceptual category, whether or not the attributes have been made explicit by some form of overt and formalized semiotic behavior. Sign perception is not a passive response to a stimulus but a dynamic interaction involving both sign and interpretation, and it is conventionalized. This is why in using signs to talk about signs, as in this chapter, it is impossible to transcend sign behavior and to examine it from outside the sign field. In examining signs we are perforce within the sign field and cannot get out. Ultimately, to *perceive* is to *choose, will, intend*.

One further point, and we may turn to a categorization of signs useful for exploring the problem of art. It will not have escaped the observant reader that I have not used the word "mind." Do I not believe in the existence of such an entity? Yes and no. I do not believe that there is such an entity, but I do believe that the term "mind" is not an empty category. If a sign with its intension and extension, its attributes and categorial range, its connotation and denotation, is a sign of a category, and if a word is a sign, as it indubitably is, then no word can refer to an entity any more than it can refer to an object, for it can only refer to a category of perceptual configurations. The attempts to find in the world an entity which "mind" refers to have also been another fool's errand. If I say to you, "Find me a tree," there are millions of objects you could find; since we share the same culture, you are already familiar with the attributes and categorial range of "tree." Any tree will do, but the term refers to no particular tree. "Tree" does not refer to any unique object or perceptual configuration. But if I say, "On December 31, 1965, I shall meet you at the Christmas tree in the Plaza of Rockefeller Center," you will have no trouble in locating that particular tree. The reason is that each of the terms in the sentence has its attributes and perceptual range. When they are put together according to the rules of language, they create an intersecting network of categorial ranges which exclude everything but one unique perceptual configuration, or, more precisely, category of identity. If we share the conventional categories of a culture, I can tell you how to locate an object, but that is all. Turning back to the problem of "mind," if "mind" refers to anything, it must refer to something observable, some class of perceptual configurations. Since I cannot tell myself to find the mind of some particular individual, though I can tell myself to find his nose, and succeed in doing so, "mind" seems not to be a category of identity. Nor does there seem to be a class of perceptual configurations which can and does elicit from me the word, "mind." It appears not to be a disjunctive category; its categorial range derives from the fact that different people interpret the same sign in different ways, and that the same person interprets the same sign in different ways at different times. "Beat" may refer to a category of behavior involving one person striking another; to a category involving one person defeating another in a contest; to one involving a person hitting rugs in order to clean them; to a category of subjectively experienced states characterized by exhaustion; to a subclass of the class of people referred to by the term "Bohemian." The categorial range of "mind," then, is the variability of sign interpretation. It is a conjunctive category.

Nor is this all that is involved. A sign may be a sign of an unlimited number of categories. An individual's conventions and the conventions of a culture may and do continuously assign new categories to particular signs. Further, since we learn how to use signs only from situations in which we see others use them and from the incomplete and unsatisfactory information in dictionaries, it seems probable that no two people ever share precisely identical sets of categories and ranges for any sign. Moreover, try as one may, it appears to be impossible to stabilize the attributes and range of a term throughout any discourse, at least of any length. If the reader will look back through this section he will see that this instability is precisely the character of my usage of "sign." In the course of this book I have used the term "semantic function" a number of times. It should now be clear what I mean by it: each of the uses of "beat" in the preceding paragraph is a semantic function. The term is used to refer to the attributes and range of a term *in a given situation* (that is, environment interpreted by interests). It may even be that no two semantic functions are ever the same.[14] If so, one can account for the invention of symbolic logic, which involves the manipulation of terms with no semantic functions. Since the symbols of this kind of logic are empty categories without attributes or range, the boundaries of either can scarcely shift.

Our lives are bathed in a continuous flow of signs which we interpret

---

[14] See Richard von Mises, *Positivism: A Study in Human Understanding*, Cambridge, Mass., 1951.

to catch the world in an ever-shifting network of categories. The condition of human life is continuous categorial metamorphosis. We are forever engaged in constructing around us an architecture of categories as fluid and yielding to our interests as the air. There is nothing that man has not sacrificed, including millions of his fellow human beings, in the vain effort to fix that architecture, to stabilize his categories. But all knowledge, all science, all learning, all history, all thought are unstable, cannot be made stable, even by the majesty of the law armed with the power of brutal force. For "thought" is but the activity of "mind"; thought is but another term with which to refer to interpretative variability. No language, no sign system, therefore, is isomorphic with the world, or can be. No sign system has the same structure as the world.[15]

With these preliminaries out of the way, it is now possible to examine the kind of sign behavior involved in artistic behavior.

3. CATEGORIES OF SIGNS

Like anything else, like any other class of perceptual configurations, signs may be categorized in a multiplicity of ways. At the beginning of the previous section I gave a number of sign categories. For my purposes two categories and three sub-categories are good enough. The first distinction to be made is that between natural signs and artificial signs.

A cloud is a *natural sign*, but a drawing of a cloud and the word "cloud" are both *artificial signs*. An artificial sign is a perceptual configuration that, for all we know, would not exist were it not for man. A gesture is an artificial sign. If there were no men, there would be clouds, nevertheless, which are natural signs—to man. A natural sign becomes an artificial sign if man takes it out of its natural situation and places it in an artificial situation. So an artificial sign is not merely a man-made sign; it can also be a complex of natural signs which have been removed from their natural setting. It is the man-made relations established between the natural signs of a garden that make the garden an artificial sign. It must not be imagined that the sign status of natural signs is any less conventional than that of artificial signs. To

---

[15] That language is anamorphic with the world could not be put more beautifully or more impressively than has Nelson Goodman in "The Way the World Is," *The Review of Metaphysics*, XIV, 1960, pp. 48–56.

a man whose culture area does not have poisonous snakes, no snake can be a sign of danger. The semantic functions of natural signs have to be learned just as much as the functions of artificial signs, and both natural and artificial signs have the same semantic functions.

Arbitrary signs are first of all just what the name implies. There is no reason for them to be what they are. *Tree*, *baum*, and *l'arbre* work equally well. The most important kind of arbitrary signs consists, of course, of linguistic signs. The infinite complexity of linguistic signs has just begun to be explored in a scientifically controlled way, and so far linguists are reluctant to undertake the study of semantics, the categorial functions of a word, and pragmatics, the circumstances which govern the use of a word. At the lowest linguistic level is phonemics, the study of the word sounds; at the next is morphemics, the study of repeated sequences of sounds which have meaning, i.e., various kinds of semantic function. Next syntactics emerges, the study of the "way in which signs of various classes are combined to form compound signs. It abstracts from the signification of the signs it studies and from their uses and effects."[16] The peculiarity of language is that it contains a special class of signs the sole function of which is to indicate the relations between the signs which refer to something outside of the language system. In English, articles, some verbs, such as "is" used merely to identify something as a member of a category ("Man is an animal"), prepositions, noun and verb endings, and so on are *structural signs*.

Language, as opposed to other sign systems, is governed by an elaborate system of rules which must be followed if compound signs (sentences, for example) are to be meaningful. For instance, the meaning of the following sentence cannot be determined: "The dog is chased the cat." Faced with such a sentence as this, one must assume that a typographical error has occurred. The proper form of the sentence might be, "The dog *has* chased the cat," or "The dog is chas*ing* the cat." But from the original compound sign there is no way of telling. The rules for combining or compounding signs in other sign systems may be changed at will. Novel combinations may cause a little confusion at first, but they can soon be figured out by someone who has never encountered them before. Language, however, when it violates these rules dissolves the compound signs into separate categories. In language the phenomenon of interlacing categories depends

---

[16] Morris, *Signs, Language, and Behavior*, p. 355.

on the obedience to certain rules. The study of these rules is the special province of logic. I shall call these signs, which are found only in language, *structural signs*. Except for noting their presence as a distinguishing character of linguistic sign-systems, we may ignore them and the host of problems they give rise to.

Closely connected with these and probably historically emergent from them are *empty signs*. These are the signs used in mathematics and symbolic logic. "If you place two apples beside two more apples, you will have four apples." "2 + 2 = 4." "2" is an empty category, which acquires referential power only when it is linked to a categorial sign. This is why empty signs can be used in combination with structural signs. Neither has any reference outside of the sign system. This permits us to identify the kinds of arbitrary signs: empty, structural, and referential.

Visual arbitrary signs are another group of referential signs. The most obvious kind is the written word which is taken as the equivalent of the spoken. But of course it is not the equivalent. Like any sign it is a categorial sign which denotes a range of allophones (the sounds used by the speakers of a language). Looked at from the point of view of behavioral control, a written sign indicates that when you speak the word a certain sequence of allophonic signs is acceptable, depending on your speech community. What unites a written and a spoken word is that each has the same semantic function: i.e., the written sign may be substituted for the spoken without categorial shift. By cultural convention a particular visual configuration is arbitrarily selected to be the equivalent of an already established sound category in the spoken language. English has forty-six phonemes (acceptable allophonic ranges) for which twenty-six letters serve as signs. Some written languages use not the alphabet but other visual configurations to categorize not phonemes but morphemes or words. (A word is an independently recurrent sequence made up of one or more morphemes.) Once this principle has been established—a visual sign may have the semantic function of a recurrent phonemic sequence—the development of a written language is possible.

But the principle is applicable in another way. A visual equivalent may be conventionalized to serve as an equivalent for any established category. For the word "Stop" the much more readily identifiable red light may be substituted. This kind of sign and written words may be called a *derived sign*. There are also aural arbitrary signs, the ringing of bells, the sounds of buzzers, the blowing of bugles. These are all derived signs, substitutes for language signs, either simple or compound, in situations in which by reason of distance, for example, spoken language signs are unusable. In the Morse code the signs are derived from letters; in other codes, from words. Tactility can also be used for signs, as in Braille, and the various other senses can be so employed. Such derived signs I shall call *emblems* (for reasons to be presented under "configurational signs").

It may be argued that the kind of sign I call "derived" was actually the original human sign, the development of which can be more easily understood if arbitrary signs are conceived as developing out of signals, or if the evolutionary sequence was signal, natural sign, arbitrary sign other than words, and then words. This problem may yet be solved. Certainly wild animals signal each other with sounds and gestures. But at this stage in semiotic theory and knowledge, speculation seems to be unprofitable, at least here. For our purposes it is enough to identify non-linguistic arbitrary signs as derived signs.

The second major category of artificial signs is that of *configurational signs*. In art criticism and aesthetics this problem has been discussed for centuries in terms of "representation" and "imitation." It is not surprising that the argument should have been unfruitful, for the very terms imply an isomorphic relation between the phenomenal world and the "representation" itself. But since a sign is a sign of category, not of an object or entity, the structure of compound signs can scarcely be anything but anamorphic to the perceived world. To avoid the problem of representation—which appears to me to be a pseudo-problem—I shall use the term *icon* for a visual sign in which there is some resemblance between the sign and the perceptual configuration, and the term *iconicity* to refer to the degree of resemblance. The easiest example of an icon is a portrait. For the moment I shall deal exclusively with visual signs.

Two problems need some consideration at this point: the first is the ancient problem of perceptual identity: How do we know that when two people are looking at the same object, they have the same visual experience? For that matter, how do we know that they are even looking at the same object? The second is: What evidence is there for thinking that a visual sign is a categorial sign—an icon—and not a "representation"?

The first problem, for all its thorniness, is not very important to us. You may say to me, "How do I know that you see what I see when we both are looking at what we have agreed to call the Empire State

Building? How do I know that your perceptual configuration is identical with mine? How do I know that the two configurations have anything in common?" To these questions several answers are possible. One is that since brain activity is not continuous but intermittent, how do you know that your perceptual configurations of any two successive moments of brain activity are identical? But this is to place the problem precisely where it does not belong, in the phenomenal world. For it appears to be exclusively a logical problem and not a behavioral or scientific problem at all. The fact is that if I show you a photograph of the Empire State Building and add that it is in New York City, you can find it readily enough. A portrait is the most obvious example of an icon, and the fact that two people argue about the representational excellence of a portrait of someone they both know indicates that the portrait contains predictive information and varying amounts of that information, or *iconicity*. The interests of one observer lead him to select certain adequacies and inadequacies, certain sets of unsatisfactory information and certain sets of satisfactory information, while the interests of another lead him to select different sets. But both agree that the portrait does contain some satisfactory information: a stranger not knowing the subject of the portrait could find him. This is all we need. The ancient problem of perceptual identity may be a very important logical problem, but it is not a behavioral problem.

The second problem, whether or not a visual sign is a categorial sign, or "icon," as I have defined it, is also capable of solution. For one thing, to assume the validity of my proposal before providing any evidence, such a question could only have emerged in a society in which painting and sculpture had developed techniques of extremely high iconicity (or "realism") and in which a traditional criticism and aesthetics held a notion of art as imitation. It is, to use Brunius' term, an ethnocentric problem arising from peculiar cultural conditions. Actually the bulk of all painting, drawing, and sculpture through human history has not been "realistic," while such a late nineteenth-century notion as Herbert Spencer's that painting necessarily evolves towards "realism" has been thoroughly disproved by the subsequent events in the history of art. Indeed the first error of critics and aestheticians has been to consider the problem as one pertaining to art at all. Only peculiar cultural traditions and conventions and a professional concentration on art and inattention to anything else have made it appear to be a problem of artistic behavior. The problem should properly be studied in something like anatomical drawing from the early middle ages to the present. Such drawing increases in "realism" or iconicity until seventy-five or a hundred years ago; since then, it has shown little stylistic change. The famous anatomical drawings of Vesalius have charming landscape backgrounds, and their poses are modeled on classical statues; this characteristic suggests that they were executed with both functional and non-functional or artistic interests in mind. Such details have now entirely disappeared from anatomical drawing. Once it had attained what appeared to be the maximum amount of information drawing is capable of, its style was virtually stabilized. The same development can be illustrated from many other sciences and crafts which make use of drawings, paintings, sculpture, and three-dimensional models—as in ship-building—for the purposes of instruction and execution. Such examples show the predictive function of visual signs. "When you open up a body, this, or something very like it, is what you will find." Or, "If you build your ship according to this model, you will produce a seaworthy ship."

It is true that for a long time Western painting, drawing, and sculpture emphasized high iconicity, but this was not for artistic reasons but in response to non-artistic cultural demands which for a few hundred years controlled the artist's behavior and the perceiver's expectations. When, towards the end of the nineteenth century, a group of painters violated those conventions, the result was precisely what one might have expected. It was initially denied that they were artists, though their paintings are now collected assiduously, bring large sums, are exhibited in art museums, and are included in histories of painting.

My principal evidence that a visual sign is not a representation but a categorial sign comes from the investigations of Rudolf Arnheim.[17] His work is valuable in many ways, but little of it is about art. Arnheim has presented a large amount of theory and information about perception and has drawn his examples from works of art, logically quite a different affair. He has simply confused the two categories of "visual art" and "visual signs," selecting his material and studying the problem for the most part in terms of the conventional category of art as it functions in Western Europe and America in the twentieth century. Thus he has included children's art, which began to be perceived and categorized as art only some thirty or forty years ago, after the placing of primitive art in that category. This decision resulted from the

---

[17] *Art and Visual Perception: A Psychology of the Creative Eye.* Berkeley, 1957.

emergence of modern art, which was avowedly inspired in some degree by primitive sculpture.

In the chapter "Growth" he has studied the development of what he calls "children's art," what I would call the process by which the child first begins to learn the conventional configurational sign behavior of his culture. But let me quote him:

> Once the child has, during the early explorations of the new medium, hit upon the idea that the things he is making can be used as pictures of other things, the circle serves to represent almost any object at all, such as a human figure, a house, a car, a book—even the teeth of a saw, as may be seen in a drawing by a five-year-old. It would be mistaken to say that the child neglects or misrepresents the shape of these objects, because only to the eyes of adults is he picturing them as round. Actually, intended roundness does not exist before other shapes, such as straightness or angularity, are available. At the stage of the circle, shape is not yet differentiated at all. The circle does not stand for roundness, but only for the more general quality of "thingness"—that is, for the compactness of a solid object, which is distinguished from the nondescript ground.[18]

From the point of view developed in this book, what is going on could not be more obvious. To the child, the circle functions as a categorial sign for all perceptual configurations—or figures—visually separated from what surrounds them. The attribute of the category is the detachment of figure from ground, and the range is all such figures. The child begins with patches, probably the patches left on the floor or on the wall by dirty hands and feet. These are traces, signs of himself, and the excitement of the child which Arnheim explains as the "exciting experience of bringing about something visible that was not there before" is perhaps more probably a consequence of the child's interpretation of the patch as a sign of himself. Though it is not particularly to our purpose, if this is what the sign does mean to the child, it is a factor in its emerging sense of identity, and suggests that categorization by signs and the sense of identity are closely related. If so, this would be a clue to the tremendous human drive to stabilize categorization: one's categories are the instruments by which one identifies oneself; to lose one's personal categorial structure, to doubt it, to have it attacked, is to experience a threat to identity, a threat which by all but the most secure is hardly to be endured.

---

[18] From *Art and Visual Perception* by Rudolf Arnheim, Berkeley, 1957, p. 140. Copyright University of California Press. Used by permission of University of California Press. He uses the term "ground" because he is developing his analysis in part from Gestalt psychology, which makes the distinction between figure and ground.

Another investigator, Mrs. Rhoda Kellogg, has studied children's art all over the world in all kinds of cultures, from the primitive to the most highly developed, and has found the same shapes in the "art" or visual sign behavior in children: the cross, the x, the square, the circle, the triangle, and finally the free or biomorphic closed form, which is the stage at which an attempt is made to match the contour of the visual sign to the contour of the perceived figure or perceptual figuration.[19] At this point, normally, and certainly in our society, cultural tradition takes over in the form of teacher or parent, and the child is rapidly trained to draw according to the conventions of his culture. If that convention is high iconicity, then the child is rigidly trained in such conventions. This was the situation in American schools until the awareness of modern and primitive art penetrated from higher cultural levels down to the levels which control the schools. Thereafter, the rigidity of the training was abandoned in favor of fostering the child's "creativity." Perhaps this was not a bad idea; perhaps it was; but it happened only because of the confusion between visual signs and art.

The child, then, initially develops a basic set of visual signs which can be combined and varied in infinite ways to construct compound signs. This enables him, under the control of cultural convention, to include in the compound sign more and more visually verifiable information. With a basic vocabulary (to apply a metaphor from language signs) a trained adult can create as informationally reliable a compound sign as the situation calls for. If he needs a compound sign so reliable that it can preserve the appearance of someone after he has died, he will create a "realistic" portrait. If he needs to present only information about how to get to his house, he can merely draw a series of lines intersecting according to the actual distance and angle as seen from the air, add sketches of important landmarks, and be reasonably sure that a friend can find him. To these he can add referential linguistic signs: "Green Street," "Esso Station," "large white house." Or one can separate configurational signs from their normal environment or grounds and combine them into novel compound signs. The result is unicorns, chimeras, giants, and non-existing landscapes.

A great deal has been written about this last kind of visual sign behavior as if it were the manifestation of some mysterious entity called the "creative imagination." It certainly deserves investigation, but

---

[19] *Time,* "Education," March 9, 1962, pp. 62, 65.

there is nothing mysterious about it. Anyone can do it, and children do it all the time. All it means is that configurational sign systems do not include structural signs, and are consequently much easier to handle than verbal signs. There are no rules about how configurational signs may be combined; there are very stringent rules, however, about how referential signs may be combined in verbal behavior. For everyone who can successfully obey all the rules required for acceptable written verbal behavior at the highest cultural level, there are hundreds, thousands, who can handle configurational visual signs according to the conventions of a particular situation. Improvisation and innovation are comparatively easy in visual sign behavior, but are extremely difficult in high level verbal behavior. At this level it takes years of rehearsal and correction to be able to follow all the rules acceptably. Perhaps it is impossible; certainly all publishers employ editors to look for failures to observe the rules, and few scholars or scientists have the temerity to print an extensive discourse without having someone equally or better qualified examine it at least once.

In addition to visual signs the category of configurational signs also includes aural signs. Of these, onomatopoeia is the best known example. It was originally identified in poetry, which makes particular use of it, but it is, of course, quite common elsewhere in human affairs. Children like to frighten each other with aural configurational signs of dangerous animals. But generally speaking such signs are not very important. As we shall see, they play only a very small part in music. The primitive bull-roarer, which is conventionalized as an arbitrary sign of a god, was quite possibly in the beginning an aural sign of thunder. For the history of configurational aural signs there is almost no information, for obvious reasons. There is some reason to believe they were more important in primitive societies than in our own. Outside of music, the theater, and the cinema, in which they are used to meet the demands of high theatrical or cinematic iconicity, they are generally confined to children's culture, and to use them at all is regarded as childish.

A particularly important function for configurational signs in art is the emblematic function. Emblems are signs derived from verbal signs: by convention a configurational sign is assigned the semantic function of a single or compound verbal sign. The term "emblem" seems originally to have been derived from heraldry. A knight's shield may display a lion rampant, standing on its hind legs and pawing the air. Another knight may show a lion couchant, lying down, but watchful. Lions are in fact neither more nor less cowardly than other animals. "Cowardice" is a human term, the perception of which is the result of the human interpretation of signs. Nevertheless, for reasons on which it would perhaps be profitless to speculate, the lion is here used as a derived sign or emblem for courage. The lion rampant says, "This knight is always ready to attack on the slightest provocation. He is very brave and he is also very strong." The lion couchant says, "This knight is also very brave and strong, but he is not spoiling for a fight all the time. On the other hand, if you rouse him, watch out."

It is also worth noting for our purposes that the emblem as a visual sign can be referred to, like any visual sign, by language signs. Indeed, in using the terms "lion rampant" and "lion couchant" I did precisely that in the last paragraph. In *The Faerie Queene* Spenser refers to the veil of his beautiful heroine, Una. Further examination of the poem yields the interpretation that Una stands for—is an emblem of —"truth." The notion that truth is hard to perceive is expressed by the metaphor, "Truth is veiled." The term "Una's veil" is a substitute for the visual image of a beautiful young woman wearing a veil, which in turn is a substitute for the proposition, "Truth is both highly desirable and hard to perceive." From the proposition has been derived the visual image, and from the visual image has been derived the compound term in the poem. Obviously an important factor here is the human ability to imagine, to see a perceptual configuration which no one else can see unless he is instructed. The two images, naturally, will not be identical. What has escaped the visual image, of course, are the structural signs. Only the words that refer to something outside of the language system—only referential signs—can be used as the basis for derived signs, or emblems. This is the only sense in which I shall use the word "imagination." It is worth pointing out that some people do not visualize in this way, do not perceive visual images. They can, however, understand references to visual configurations and they can understand the allegorical use of emblems. Everyone can read and understand "veil" without actually having an image of one. Likewise after you have encountered Una's veil often enough it performs the semantic function of "Truth is hard to perceive" without your having to imagine the veiled young woman. The individual who does not image reads and hears everything this way.

The third group of signs, *primary signs*, is much harder to talk about. Little study has been devoted to them, and their existence, particularly in music, has often been denied. Yet there is a great deal of evidence for this category. They are quite different from configurational signs and it would be arguable that they ought to be included under arbitrary signs; but in one important essential they differ so strikingly from the other two categories that they seem properly classified in a group by themselves. They are particularly important in art, though they are not unique to artistic behavior. On the contrary, they are found throughout sign production and behavior and are present in media which are also the media of arbitrary and configurational signs. There is another reason for placing them in a special category. Let me give a few examples to suggest the general range of this category: verticality, horizontality, depth, color, pitch, volume, speed, rhythm, tactile smoothness and roughness, possibly sweetness and bitterness, and perhaps coolness and warmth, and the charm and offensiveness of odors. They may perhaps be found in each kind of sense behavior, but I shall restrict myself to visual and aural primary signs, because my application of primary sign behavior will be limited to Western poetry, painting, music, and architecture. They are what critics and aestheticians are often really talking about when they imagine themselves to be talking about the formal properties of works of art, particularly when they use terms like "significant form" or "expressive form."

The first thing to note about such signs, distingishing them from arbitrary and configurational signs, is that they are non-situational. The interpretation of the first two sign classes depends upon picking up clues from the situation in which the sign appears. Consider such a simple and widely used sign as "x." As a configurational sign it is used to warn motorists that an intersection is immediately before them, either an intersection of two roads or of a road and a railroad. In the former case it appears on a panel mounted on a post placed on the driver's side of the road; in the latter it is two pieces of wood joined to make a cross and mounted, usually on a taller post, ordinarily on the driver's side of the road, but occasionally on both sides. It is, of course, a configurational sign, but its meaning is determined by the total situation in which it is is found, place, post, and all. Such an "x" painted on a bounded plane and exhibited in an art-gallery becomes a work of art; the stage or setting or situation determines its interpretation. But "x" also has innumerable uses as an arbitrary sign: in a photograph or diagram to mark the spot where the murder was committed or the accident occurred; on students' compositions to mark a mistake; on manuscripts to indicate that a passage is to be eliminated;

in times of plague on a house door to indicate that a dead body is to be picked up. Like the child's circle, it can mean anything. The semantic function of "x" is that of an emblem meaning, "This is the area for attention in this particular situation," but why it is there and why one should pay attention and what one should do depends not on the "x" itself but on one's knowledge of the situation and the culturally conventionalized behavior patterns and, if appropriate, roles one should select from one's repertory and bring to bear on the situation. This arbitrary semantic function plays a part even in the situations in which "x" is also a configurational sign. At crossroads and railroad crossings it means not only "Intersection" but also "Pay attention! Watch out! Danger!"

It is not difficult to understand the reason for this principle of interpreting signs by picking up conventionalized clues from the situation and applying conventionalized behavior, if the notion of the fluidity of categories is applied to the matter. One of the problems in current linguistics and anthropology is the Whorf hypothesis. Benjamin Whorf, an amateur linguist, proposed several decades ago that the way one perceived the world was determined by the language one used. It was an extremely important statement and has caused everybody concerned with such problems to think hard and long.[20]

From the point of view presented here, the Whorf hypothesis is readily understandable and acceptable, with certain important qualifications. In the first place *language* determines nothing. Rather, any sign is interpreted by cultural conventions and elicits culturally conventionalized behavior. He has pointed out what Skinner insists on: language functions by controlling behavior, both for oneself and for others; but it does so only because every individual learns to behave in a particular way when he is presented with a word or series of words structured into discourse. But this is not enough.

As we have seen, and as any dictionary demonstrates, most referential words have a number of semantic functions; and the more common the word, the greater the number of functions. Which semantic function is appropriate on the presentation of a particular

---

[20] In 1953 a symposium on the Whorf hypothesis was held at the University of Chicago under the sponsorship of its Department of Anthropology and with the financial aid of the Ford Foundation. The twenty participants were anthropologists, linguists, a couple of philosophers and psychologists, and an historian of China. The papers and the ensuing discussion were edited by Harry Hoijer in *Language in Culture*, Chicago, 1954. In spite of the inconclusiveness of the results of the symposium, the book is well worth reading.

sign or compound sign is determined by the interpreter from situational clues. Moreover the semantic function of any term is unstable. The reason for this is that since any discourse, from a single word to a ten-volume history of philosophy, appears in a context of situational clues, which are themselves signs, there is and must be a considerable variation in the clues a particular interpreter picks up from the non-verbal sign environment of the language signs. As we have seen, the interpreter is not passive in any situation, but active. His orientation or interests or disposition determines what he sees and plays a part in how he interprets it, as does his capacity to perceive the clues. It is only after extremely rigorous training in common that a group of individuals will respond to the same signs in the same situation with the same patterns of behavior, though even then there will be stylistic variation. Indeed, this kind of behavioral conditioning seems to be possible only when fairly simple and repetitive and overt behavior is called for, as in military training or teaching children to respond simultaneously and by rote with the same verbal pattern. In elaborate situations where covert verbal behavior is demanded, common response among the members of a group is probably impossible. No two trained individuals have ever come up with the same overt verbal response to a reading of Kant's *Critique of Pure Reason*. No two people will have the same interpretation of either the whole or parts of such a simple sequence of verbal discourse as this book.

A further reason for interpretational variability lies in the fact, already explored in Chapter II, that no behavioral pattern is adequate to the environmental demands it is selected and improvised to meet. Consequently, to the degree the interpreter-actor observes the clues and is aware of the behavioral gap, to that degree he shifts the borders of both the attributes and the range of a particular category. When we say, "Now I understand that term better," we mean that henceforth on encountering the term we will employ different attributes and a different range than we used before this intellectually expansive experience. And this is as true of non-verbal as of verbal signs. An automobile mechanic learning his trade acquires a new conception of the meaning of carburetor-sign every time he rehearses repairing a carburetor. Trained specialists in carburetors are men who have in their repertory both an interpretational range and a behavioral range which makes it possible to find out what is wrong when the ordinary mechanic has failed. With the specialist the gap is very much narrower, though he too is always learning, only partly because manufacturers are continuously, for the same reasons, changing carburetor design. Every trade and profession has its specialists.

Another problem raised by the Whorf hypothesis is also pertinent to the interpretation-sign-situation complex. Do verbal categories correspond to "mental" categories? To reply, "Of course not, for there are configurational signs which are not emblems of verbal signs," would be trivial; this is one of many instances in which a writer is talking about verbal signs as members of the larger category of all signs, whether he knows it or not. Actually, the question really means, "Does the full range of sign categories correspond to the full range of perceptual categories and possibilities of interpretational variability?" There are three answers to this, all negative. First, since no language or sign system is isomorphic with what it refers to outside of itself, no sign category can correspond to a perceptual category: both the attributes and range of a category are structured, with center and boundaries. If an attempt is made, however, to make explicit the attributes and range of a category, its connotation and denotation, it can be done only by using terms which also are categories. One is involved at once in an infinite regress. Arguments about terms are arguments about what should properly belong to the set of attributes and to the range of perceptual configurations. They can never be settled, however, except by agreement, which is only partially successful at best; for an attributional set and a categorial range are held together in a structure not by any internal law or structural immanence or logical necessity but only by convention, only by behavioral pattern, within which there is always stylistic variation.

The second answer lies in the fact that there are obviously endless perceptual categories for which no words exist. If Freudian psychoanalysis did nothing else, it discovered and named a great many such categories. For instance, during the nineteenth century, even more than in previous centuries, teachers were supposed to beat children regularly, whether they wanted to or not. Some teachers found this task disagreeable but necessary; others excessively pleasing. Once sadism had been identified as an interpretational category and further categorized as a perversion, the tables were turned. Teachers who had found child-beating unpleasant now could use other training methods; while those who had found it such fun, now had to go to a great deal of trouble to establish both excuse and occasion for beating children. Some were reduced to whipping themselves and each other, on the whole a considerable improvement, at least for most children. In the phrase "unconscious mind," then, "mind" is equivalent to "interpretational variability," and "unconscious" is equivalent to "controlled by perceptual categories for which no verbal terms exist." Undoubtedly there have always been people whose behavior would now be referred to by the term "sadistic"; but such behavior was given social and cultural existence only when it had been categorized, and was regarded as something to be condemned only because one of the explicit attributes of the behavioral category "sadism" was "negative value" or "moral evil."

Third, if for every perceptual category there were a sign exactly corresponding in both attributes and range, there would be no way of explaining metaphor, or rather, there would be no metaphors. Whenever a new category was established, a cultural convention would explicitly establish the sign, whether configurational or arbitrary, and both its attributes and range. Indeed, something very close to this happens in the creation of neologisms, which are most common in science, an area of behavior in which new categories are constantly emerging. But even scientific neologisms are metaphorical, except for new terms in the area of empty-sign behavior, mathematics and symbolic logic. An understanding of metaphor not only shows the necessity for qualifying the Whorf hypothesis, but also returns us to the sign-situation complex.[21]

Consider the metaphor "laminated government," which Monroe Beardsley once improvised in class to demonstrate that metaphors can be nonsensical.[22] "A student later pointed out to me a very similar expression in a book on government that gives it, in context, a definite meaning." In a footnote Beardsley quotes from George A. Graham— "In contrast to the monolithic state, the strength of American political, economic, and social organization is its laminated structure . . . . In this *laminated society* of pluralistic loyalties, etc."[23] Since Graham was talking about social organization, I shall call "society" the "local term"; it is the expected term in the situation in which this discourse occurs. And I shall call "laminated" the "imported term"; it is the

---

[21] The best study of metaphor I have ever encountered, indeed, the only one that makes sense to me, is Murray Turbayne's brilliant and philosophically original *The Myth of Metaphor*, New Haven, 1962. Professor Turbayne is at the University of Rochester.

[22] *Aesthetics*, New York, 1958, p. 143. Professor Beardsley teaches philosophy and aesthetics at Swarthmore.

[23] *Morality in American Politics*, New York, 1952.

unexpected and initially inappropriate term in this situation. Though the oldest recorded English use of "lamina," to mean a thin plate or scale, occurs in the sixteenth century in the situation of metalworking, "laminated" is most commonly encountered today in a situation in which it refers to a category of sheets of wood made up of thin slices of tree trunks bound together with glue. This seems unquestionably what Graham was talking about.

"Laminated society" ascribes to the range of American social structures some of the attributes of plywood. It says that society consists of layers, that each layer is structured independently, but that each layer is also inseparable from the layer above it, by a category of social behavior different from the category which structures it as a layer. Society already has the attribute "levels," which involves up-and-down organization. For levels can be substituted "layer," which brings in the attribute of the lateral binding together of levels, a structure which makes each level able to operate independently from other levels. "Laminated" ascribes the attribute of "inseparably bound together." What has happened is that from the attributes of society Graham has selected "level," and from the attributes of plywood he has selected "internally structured layer" and "inseparably bound together." Such a society he contrasts with monolithic society, government in which there is only one organizing force, from the top, as opposed to the American type of society in which there are two organizing forces, vertical and lateral. Monolithic and laminated, then, select from the general range of society less inclusive and mutually exclusive ranges. Monolithic had already been applied to society when Graham wrote. Laminated was his way of distinguishing American society from monolithic societies and other kinds not yet distinguished. "Laminated society" is an emergent (or innovated) category. Graham used it because there was not in existence a term ascribing to the American type of society any structural attributes of the kind which he wanted to talk about; or else he did not know of such a term, even though it might have existed.

But observe, "laminated" could be successfully used in this situation only because the situation was already there and its character established. To Beardsley "laminated government" was nonsensical because he simply put two terms together in the absence of a situation, and then neglected to construct a situation in which one of his terms would have a local function. What Graham did was to apply to the situation a conventionalized category, conventionalized in a situation, the employment of wood. As we have already seen, in the definition of the perceiver's role, anyone can apply a category which he has learned to a situation or perceptual configuration for which it has never been used. But Graham did not apply all the attributes of laminated to society; he omitted "wooden." But someone else could apply to American society the attributes "artifactual" and "lifeless." His interest would be, perhaps, to defend what Graham calls "monolithic society," on the grounds that monolithic society is not heavy and rigid as stone but "organic," unified by a single force, to be sure, but filled with life, vitality, flexibility, and capacity to grow. And this is precisely what defenders of Fascist social organization, which its enemies call monolithic, have actually done.

The usefulness of metaphors is obvious, but their dangers and inadequacies are easily overlooked. If a metaphor is particularly successful, for whatever reason, it becomes conventionalized as a category, its metaphorical origins are forgotten, and it becomes a dead metaphor. Sometimes a dead metaphor can come to life: "A virgin forest is one where the hand of man has never set foot." The more one thinks about this, the funnier it is. Another disadvantage of metaphors is that they can be, and usually are, applied unconsciously. This is shown superbly by Turbayne's analysis of how the seventeenth-century philosophers applied a logical attribute to physical events, without realizing it; logical nexus became, unconsciously, cause-and-effect nexus. This unconscious metaphorical activity is responsible for the fact that by selecting only some of the attributes of the local term, others are omitted. The same effect is true of the imported term. When this takes place the unused attributes and the unaccounted for categorial range are ignored. It is as if Graham were to claim that "laminated society" applies to American society all the attributes which can be applied; the two categories are not seen as overlapping but identical, and the new category is not seen as an emergent category but as the whole truth. This is what happened in seventeenth-century philosophy. Those men ignored the omitted attributes and range of logic and also those of physical events. This process becomes more comprehensible when one notes that often in metaphorical usage the local term is omitted; only the imported term appears. The illusion of identity occurs; hypostatization and misplaced concreteness normally follow. This is what could easily have happened had Graham written, "This lamination of pluralistic loyalties," instead of, "This laminated society of pluralistic loyalties."

The first phrase, however, would have been more vivid to the reader simply because he would have had to work harder to understand it, vividness probably being the consequence of the expenditure of unusual amounts of energy on the categorial process.

To bring out even more sharply the importance of situation in metaphorical usage and in all sign interpretation, let us consider an instance in which "laminated" is the local term and "society" the imported. An animal trainer has to transport a number of powerful wild animals which if allowed to interact would tear each other apart. Plywood is better than ordinary lumber for such a purpose: two quite separate structural forces are involved and it comes in large sheets. When he has finished his cages, one side of iron bars and the remaining five sides of one-inch plywood, and has piled them together, he can say, "There is what I call a laminated society." He has applied the attribute of a "society," people who can live together, to a socially unstructured assortment of wild animals which cannot.

This may be a far-fetched example, and it is—for a purpose. It shows not merely that the situation determines which element in a metaphor is local, which imported: it not only suggests how much more obscure this metaphorical usage would have been had he said, "Now I have a real society": it also suggests the kind of situation in which metaphors are likely to arise. They hardly seem necessary in woodworking and cage making and animal taming. These are long-established roles, and their vocabularies are reasonably stabilized in what terms are appropriate and in what attributes and ranges are involved. But when one talks about "society," none of these conditions is true. Novel metaphors, then, are most likely to occur in situations in which the current terminology is extremely inadequate or non-existent. Freud's terminology is full of novel metaphors, apparently unconscious. By importing the terms of sexual perversities into a local situation of personality disorders, he identified the two, thus turning the perversities into the "cause" of the disorder. If this is so, the causal aspect of his theory rests on a simple, though extremely common, logical error. Original, as well as novel, metaphors crop up when the speaker is ignorant, lazy, or slow in recalling the terms conventional to the situation. There are also situations in which the cultural convention calls upon the speaker to use novel metaphors. This condition obtains in poetry from time to time. Well established metaphors, however, though once honored in poetry, are now most likely to be found in ritual situations, political orations, sermons, graduation speeches.

This last consideration brings to the fore two kinds of relation between the sign and the situation. On the one hand the situation is a necessary and inescapable part of both sign interpretation and sign innovation. On the other, the situation can determine the role, which in turn determines the sign. Primary signs are non-situational in the sense that they operate independently of the environmental situation. But they may be under situational control, for the function of some roles is to display primary signs.

What, then, is the significance of primary signs? What are they signs of? And what makes them non-situational? As a first example, consider the strange groups of young American males who apparently live to dress in black leather, ride on motorcycles to no place in particular, and if the spirit moves them, inflict a considerable amount of destruction and terror on the local citizenry when they get there. This was a fairly limited phenomenon until Marlon Brando appeared in a movie about these young men, *The Wild One*. Subsequently, a large group of youths perceived this kind of behavior as good. The movement has now spread to England, where it is causing considerable perturbation. Several elements in the considerably varying patterns and styles of these individuals may be distinguished: the penetration into space, the speed, the destructiveness.

The speed is the easiest to identify: it is a sign of energy release. Of course, all human behavior is a sign of energy release to an interpreter disposed so to interpret it. But other human behavior, to the producer of that sign, is simply energy release. That among the Wild Ones speed is a *sign* is suggested by the expressive slang expression that these young men are making a "thing" out of energy release. The purpose of their action is to signify energy release, not to accomplish anything functional, any adaptational interaction with the environment through which they plunge so rapidly. Further, they are releasing very little energy from their own organisms. Most of it is coming from the motorcycle, which must be capable of much greater speed than necessary. The Wild One must not merely release the motorcycle's energy: it must have vast reserves of energy.

The penetration into space is somewhat more difficult to comprehend. A clue may be found in the neuroses known as agoraphobia and claustrophobia, the fear, respectively, of open and closed spaces. When most people come up over a mountain pass, get to the top of a hill with a view or of a high building, or look out from the rim of the Grand Canyon, they experience a sense of release, a sense of tension reduction, a sense that there are no barriers between themselves and their environment, a sense, therefore, that there would be no frustration to any energy releasing action, to any behavior. I propose to call this "agoraphilia." Again, most people feel wonderfully cozy in a small fire-lit room, safely protected from the snow and wind outside through which no one surely will penetrate to make demands, to require interaction and manipulation of the environment. The satisfaction here comes from the sense of energy conservation. I propose to call it "claustrophilia," the love of the security of the cloister, as opposed to the love of the market place (agora), which is so full of novel possibilities. Functionless penetration into space, therefore, is likewise a sign of energy release. Our Wild Ones permit themselves a redundancy: they offer to themselves two signs of the sense of energy release.

The destructiveness is something quite different, except that it too is functionless. Its very pointlessness is precisely the quality which makes it so infuriating to anyone who so much as reads about it— anyone who is not himself a Wild One. It is the functionless imposition of the will upon the environment. "Will" is a word like "mind." It tempts us to think of a category of identity, of an "entity." But it seems rather to be, like "mind," a conjunctive category, referring to a range of behavior or of various patterns which, if successful, would meet certain demands of environmental interaction. But it is repetition which continues in spite of obstacles, of frustrations, of failure. The "man of strong will" appears determined to impose his demands upon the environment. Now, whereas, in ordinary behavior, that sense of making demands upon the environment has a function, with the Wild Ones it does not. They ignore the situation, though they can predict with some success that they may get into trouble with the police, just as they can and do predict with some success that their high speed on public highways can cause accidents to others and to themselves. They appear to be indifferent to the possible damage caused to others and the property of others and to themselves and to their own property. They are interested only in producing signs of making demands on the environment, not in actually making functional demands which if successfully fulfilled would enhance their environmental adaptation. The looting which accompanied the Negro rioting of the summer of 1964 shows the same interest.

There are two primary social patterns, masculinity and femininity; they are continuously being played no matter what the situation, and they are only partly controlled by the actor's interpretation of the situation. It is now a platitude that masculinity and femininity are not biologically based, that they are categories of behavior, not sexual categories, but it has become a platitude only recently. Masculinity is characterized precisely by making demands upon the environment, hunting, fishing, exploring, making a living, tilling the earth, fighting, protecting the home—by innovation; femininity by precisely the opposite. Femininity requires not that one should impose demands upon the environment but should rather respond to the demands of the environment with culturally conventionalized patterns of behavior, by staying at home, by conforming to the Hitlerian demand upon women that they should confine themselves to children, kitchen, and church, an institution devoted to the reinforcement of conventionalized orientations. Now it is obvious that both men and women exhibit masculinity and femininity. But just as women are expected to conceal their masculinity, at one time to execute their political demands behind the scenes—hence the violent male opposition to female suffrage—so men are expected to conceal their femininity behind a show of bluff maleness. Hence, men who perforce exhibit patterns of femininity or acceptance in their work commonly display masculine bluster at home, or at play. One function of the neighborhood bar is to provide a setting for this kind of masculine display and bluster.

If we examine our interesting Wild Ones further, we find that their costumes and behavior generally are made up of redundant masculinity signs: leather, chains, gleaming chromium, animal tails tied to the handle bars (man, the hunter), the swaggering walk, the loud voices, the aggressiveness, the drunkenness. The costumes are particularly interesting because they bring out a factor which is often highly visible when we apply the drama metaphor to human behavior. It was omitted earlier because it is not always present. It is, however, extremely common, and in this instance conspicuous. Just as the speed and penetration into depth are redundant with each other so the destructiveness and costuming and behavior are redundant. One of the more amusing aspects of the whole phenomenon, which by now has long since been packaged into a very precise role, is its imitation by certain groups of homosexuals. This gives us a clue to the function of this role. It is generally played by young men from the lower middle class, and it has emerged at a time when, particularly for white-collar workers, jobs require more and more acceptance and offer less and less opportunity for demand, for imposing one's "will" on the environment. It is also played by young men who have no particularly striking record of socially approved achievement in any role. They live lives of frustration in a society which demands achievement as the price for status. Unable to furnish the masculine achievement, they display its signs.

Such signs are non-situational signs, then, because they are not produced by interaction with the environment. On the contrary, the environment is chosen to be a setting or stage for the display of the signs. This is why the Wild Ones like to be destructive in small towns: they have enough interest in prediction to choose the proper stage, one where the police force is small and tends to be middle-aged and slightly decrepit. But it must not be imagined that they are unique in displaying these signs. Such signs are pervasive. Or more precisely, what I have called the sense of energy release, the sense of energy conservation, the sense of demand, the sense of acceptance, are the attributes of vast ranges of behavioral patterns.

What these men are doing is precisely identical with the explicit statement of the attributes of a verbal category, which, as we have seen, become signs once they are made explicit. And this is equally true of the members of a categorial range when they are explicitly stated. Any sign may lead its interpreter to engage in one of two kinds of categorial behavior. First, and by far the most common, is assumptive behavior. On questioning, such an interpreter will readily state attributes and members of that category. We have seen this at work in traditional aestheticians: "Everybody knows that the verse of Edgar Guest does not belong in the category of 'art'; it lacks certain attributes." This kind of categorial behavior is, obviously, the source of paralogisms. The second, by far the less common, is search behavior. The interpreter asks, "What is the membership of the category of which this sign is an attribute?" Or, "What is the common attribute of all the members of this range?" This last is what the proposed interpretation of the behavior of the Wild Ones is doing. It is interpreting the factors common to their behavior as attributes not only of their behavior but also of a wide range of all behavior.

When we define some particular attribute or membership as implicit we have, of course, make it explicit. And innumerable arguments are the result of the effort to decide whether what is not explicit really was implicit. Such arguments are difficult to settle because the implicit is inaccessible. That is why it has that name: the word is a dead metaphor imported from weaving. What connects two propositions is implicit, just as invisible threads hold together the design that you actually see. When Morris uses the term "disposition," when others use the terms "set," "expectancy," "directive state," or when I use the term "orientation," we are all talking about the same problem, what is implicit not in the environment—the environment as such has no implications—but what is implicit in the semantic interaction with the environment, the environment perceived as a situation compounded of signs, and the attributes and membership conventionally appropriate to those signs. Most pertinent here is Barnett's point that if the sign is ambiguous, the interpreter will resolve it one way or the other, or if the sign has no conventionalized implication of range and attributes the perceiver will supply them, by ascribing an attribute and then placing it in a category.

The only way it has been possible to discover these dispositions or orientations or directive states is by such experiments as Barnett cites and by observing certain similarities among widely different behavioral patterns in widely different situations. Freud discovered many of them simply because he was dealing with neurotics, individuals characterized by orientative inflexibility: sadism, he found, could manifest itself in innumerable patterns in innumerable situations, and the sadist is always looking compulsively for the situation in which the sadistic orientation can be applied. Or rather, Freud discovered a pervasive orientation and, applying a metaphor, called it "sadism." Freud's bio-sexual explanation may now be in ruins, but what he discovered is of the highest importance. After all, every explanation ends up in ruins sooner or later.

I call non-situational signs *primary signs*, therefore, because they are the attributes of all human behavior. This does not mean that all sequences of behavior have all the attributes, but that one or more of these attributes is always present. The making explicit these attributes, though not verbally explicit, is one of the most interesting developments of human history. We should really be grateful to the Wild Ones for having made their implicit attributes so exceedingly explicit. As with their behavior, the common redundancy of these signs is one of the few ways we have to identify them. I do not pretend to have identified all of them, or even to have identified finally those I have identified. The problem of translating them into language is bound to be somewhat unsatisfactory, and is analogous to the derivation of non-verbal emblems from verbal signs. To make it clear what I am attempting to talk about, I shall at this point merely list those I am reasonably certain of, with a note or two about the kind of sign used to identify them: adequacy to situational demands, inadequacy; demand (or organization), acceptance; energy release, energy conservation; smoothness of behavioral process, roughness; openness to the demands of others (white), rejection of such demands (black); inhibition, expression (soft as opposed to loud; dark purples as opposed to light yellows); transition.

It will become apparent that when we look at art from the point of view of the classical division of the arts into spatial and temporal, that the spatial arts tend to present these signs as contrasting, while the temporal arts are particularly useful for presenting primary signs as continua. The investigation of the arts as conventionalized sign behavior, then, is the next problem to be explored.

FOUR:
ART: THE SEMANTIC ASPECT

1. THE PYRAMID OF INNOVATION

With occasional exceptions the material I shall use for this and the next two chapters will be taken from what our culture conventionally recognizes as the "high art" of architecture, painting, poetry, and music from about 1600 to about 1830. I do this for several reasons. The center of the problem has two faces: stylistic dynamism and stylistic continuity. Non-functional style in art changes more rapidly than functional style, but it does not change in a random fashion but in such a way that stylistic continua may be perceived together with stylistic revolutions on the borders of continua. Until it is comprehended how this Janus-headed monster has his way in each of the arts, it will be impossible to make any even faintly valid statements about their relations.

Although detailed analysis will be for the most part confined to works executed after 1700, it is generally, though not universally, agreed that for the first twenty or thirty years of the eighteenth century the Baroque style was still in the ascendancy. In the third decade of the century the Rococo style began to be identifiably emergent and was gradually succeeded more or less simultaneously by Neo-Classicism and what is widely called Romanticism, though to my mind in error. What I believe is meaningfully called Romantic style began to emerge in the 1790's and became the starting point for a series of nineteenth-century styles which have various names, but all of which form a sufficient continuity with Romanticism to be called Romantic styles. This continuum reached its most recent climax in the first decade of the twentieth century when what we still call Modern style begins. To avoid confusion, and for other reasons which will emerge later, I shall refer to the Rococo–Neo-Classic–"Romantic" sequence as Enlightenment Styles and to the nineteenth-century sequence as Romantic Styles.

The advantages of this scheme are obvious. It deals with the termination of one major stylistic continuum, the revolution into a subsequent continuum, the full course of that, and the revolution into a third. Furthermore, the Baroque style, at the end of which we shall begin, was one of the styles, together with Renaissance style, with which modern stylistic study began in Wölfflin's *Renaissance und Barock*.[1] The very excellence of Wölfflin's studies made it subsequently necessary to insert Mannerism between Renaissance and Baroque, for any construct is excellent if it raises such important problems that it can be developed and in part—or wholly—transcended. To include the termination of Baroque, therefore, makes it possible to make some use of studies in the very period—1450–1725—for which the notions of stylistic dynamism and stylistic continua were stabilized. This insures at least some measure of relationship to the most important existent work in the field of stylistic history. It is, of course, for this very reason that most attempts to relate the arts, by Sypher and Daniells as well as innumerable others, particularly by German and German-influenced historians of literature, have drawn their material from the sixteenth and seventeenth centuries. This is the only period for which it has been possible to make any statements that look like generalizations about the attributes of stylistic continua.

Further, I confine myself to the "high arts" because they are the arts with the greatest artistic prestige. Almost no one argues that architecture, painting, music, and poetry are not arts. Moreover,

---

[1] This famous book, the foundation of modern stylistic analysis, was published in 1888.

aesthetic speculation has mainly revolved around these arts. They are the ones most valued at the highest cultural level. "Highest cultural level" is of course not synonymous with "highest social level" or "highest economic level." These are three independently varying factors in social structure, though there is a tendency for them to operate together. A man who has achieved a high economic level does not automatically belong to the highest social level, which tends to repel *les nouveaux riches;* further, he is usually expected to evince some interest, if only by giving away money, in the highest cultural level before he is accepted into "society," the highest social level. Where these three groups overlap, however, may be regarded, at least for the purposes of insight into the sociological place of non-functional stylistic dynamism, as the center of society. It is here that innovation of any kind tends to be most hotly pursued and most highly rewarded, whether it is in the techniques of business administration, of manufacturing, of fashion in clothes, or of stylistic dynamism in the arts. Wealthy "society" tends to take up, though not to admit to its ranks, not only artists but also philosophers, scientists, and at least in some societies, even scholars of the humanities, though this last phenomenon seems strange to Americans and is much more common in Europe. That is why American scholars love Europe so. Since people of wealth and status, people with economic and social power, tend to reward men at the highest cultural level who have a record of significant achievement, it follows that to be so rewarded is a sign that one has accomplished such achievement. Human judgment, however, is prone to err and the sign may be an illusion. Some people at the highest cultural level are better at achieving the sign than they are at achieving significant innovation. The Rockefeller, Carnegie, Guggenheim, and Ford Foundations, and the academic jockeying for recognition by them, illustrate this entire phenomenon.

The "highest cultural level," then, is the cultural level to which one can rise only after the longest and the most demanding learning period. It is what one normally learns only after achieving a functional mastery of the conventions and the roles necessary for survival in one's culture. It is much easier to become a millionaire or to win one's way into society than it is to become successfully operant at the highest cultural level. The four great categories of roles currently occupying this stratum are the scientist, the philosopher, the artist (both creative and performing), and the valuator, a role played in all fields of the sciences, the arts, and the various kinds of philosophy.[2] Within these classifications particular roles have their ups and downs. Astrologers, who once were in this group, no longer are, though astrology is more widely practiced and believed in at the present time than at any time in history. In the nineteenth century the great virtuoso performing artists, the Paganinis and the Rachels, enjoyed a somewhat higher status than they do now. This is probably one reason why such artists are now less common. Composers, on the other hand, enjoy a much higher status than they did at any time before the nineteenth century. The insults Mozart had to endure would scarcely be offered to-day; now it is the composers who can insult their audiences and be admired for it.

These four are creator's roles. But at this highest cultural level are also the roles of the perceivers, not merely the perceivers of art but also the perceivers of philosophy, valuation, and science as well. This role is that of the amateurs, the dilettantes. None of these creative roles would be possible were it not for the perceiver's capacity to respond to the occasion each presents. It is as true of the other three as it is of the artist that each can learn his role only by first learning the perceiver's role. One of the illusions of present-day American life—an illusion a teacher encounters with terrible frequency—is that if a work of art is great art it should be immediately communicable to everybody, no matter what his cultural level. Nothing could be more fallacious. The emergence of such a notion seems to be the result of combining ideas of aesthetic universality with the socio-political value orientations of the democratic tradition. It is said, for example, that Homer is universal. All this means is that the *Iliad* and the *Odyssey* are read by a tiny fraction of each generation and that a good many individuals of that fraction agree that Homer is very fine stuff indeed. The number of people who have been bored by Homer is, of course, enormous. Again, the only meaningful application of democratic

---

[2] Should anyone wonder what has happened to the humanities in this scheme, the answer is that to me they properly belong under the sciences. The humanities are concerned with investigating certain kinds of human behavior, particularly artistic behavior and culturally transmitted value behavior. All aspects of literary criticism, for example, purport to talk about a particular kind of verbal behavior. To my mind, literary criticism, except for evaluation, properly belongs to the behavioral sciences. The first effort to establish this claim was I. A. Richards, *Principles of Literary Criticism*, first published in 1924. See also Chapter I, note 1, above.

values to the problem is to insist that every man has the right to rise to the highest cultural level he can achieve, and that it is both the duty of the state and to its interest to facilitate those efforts. Vast numbers of highly talented people have no interest in becoming members of the artistic audience at the highest cultural level. Perhaps they should, but they do not. To be a member of that audience demands work, a huge expenditure of time and energy. There are plenty of other things to do with one's life; I see no reason why this role should be chosen simply because it has a high cultural status. Nevertheless, I shall attempt to show ultimately that there are certain advantages to be reaped from it which no other role can offer.[3]

I feel apologetic for spending so much time discussing obvious and well-known matters, but I should feel more apologetic had I not encountered so many students and adults for whom these terms are virtually empty categories, or to whom they are entirely unfamiliar. Further, the problems they entail are closely connected with the problem at hand, which emerges more sharply if one dwells a moment on the difficulty of maintaining one's place, whether as creator or perceiver, at the highest cultural level. One is required not only to achieve significant innovation to get there; one is required to continue such innovation in order to stay there. By "significant" I mean the kind of innovation valued by the members of the center of society, the overlap of high cultural, economic, and social levels. This is manifest in the publish-or-perish policy of the administrations of many colleges and universities in this country. A university, as an institution, can be rewarded the highest cultural status, including financial grants from the foundations and the federal government, only if its faculty is highly and conspicuously innovative. The current complaint about this amounts to the assertion that the perceiver's role at such a level must also be taught, that the teacher's role is very difficult and if performed well necessarily includes as much innovation as that of the creators, perhaps more, because the creator can specialize while the teacher must comprehend the specialists on a number of innovative fronts. Indeed, the university or college teacher is not only, to apply the dramatic metaphor, a director; he is also that peculiar kind of creator mentioned before, the virtuoso of interpretation as well as a valuator.

All these considerations serve to explain something about stylistic

---

[3] The finest and most penetrating analysis of the role of the dilettante is put in Goethe's mouth by Thomas Mann in *The Beloved Returns*.

innovation at the highest cultural levels, and to indicate the value, in this kind of study, of turning for one's evidence to the art produced for such levels. It shows the highest rate of stylistic dynamism. It is also the best preserved and the easiest to find. What I have called the center of society has the interests, the social power, and the wealth to preserve what it values. An instance is the Quartos, the first publications, of Shakespeare's plays. They were very common, but since the public drama was not recognized by the center of society, they were not preserved. Not all of his plays were so published, and these and many of those which had appeared in quarto would have been forever lost had it not been for Ben Jonson. A writer for the public theater, he collected his plays, gave them the trappings and the publishing format of the literary art of the highest cultural level and thus claimed that that was where they belonged. His claim was sufficiently recognized to turn his *Workes* into the model for the First Folio of Shakespeare, which preserves the only text of a number of the greatest plays. Subsequently the Quartos were hunted and preserved and now command staggering prices.

To apply a metaphor to this dual concept of innovative dynamism and social center, let us imagine we are looking directly down on the apex of a four-faced pyramid. The height is a metaphor for rate of innovative dynamism, the edges for the distance from the cultural center. Each face stands for one of the four innovative social roles, scientist, philosopher, artist, valuator. Any sequence in each of these fields can be located on the face by calculating its innovative dynamism. The greater the dynamism the nearer to the apex. Folk wisdom changes much more slowly than philosophy; the historiography of primitive cultures is mostly mythological and is rarely affected by historical events, but at the apex the history of the United States is re-written constantly. This country has had half-a-dozen major new pasts in my own lifetime, and minor historical events are in continuous flux. This is true of the individual as well. The man at the innovative fringe makes do with one past all his life, and he does not pay much attention to that. But the man at the center of society is continuously getting himself a new past, and modern psychotherapy has become an institutionalized Aladdin which peddles new pasts for old. Moreover, the pyramid metaphor brings out another characteristic of culture: the more rapid the rate of innovation, the smaller the number of people able to respond to innovation, the fewer immediately affected.

As for the arts, in the Middle East, domestic rural and urban building has scarcely changed for five thousand years or more; archaeologists have yet to discover the traces of a building of which they may say, "This was the beginning," though several times they have thought they have. During this immense period, however, a number of major architectural styles have come and gone in this area, not to speak of greater numbers of stylistic continua within those styles. Stylistic innovation affected almost nothing but temples, palaces, and tombs. It is evident that in this culture area, domestic buildings were not occasions for the art perceiver's role until very recently, and then only through Western influence. In our century, to take a mere recent example, neither were teakettles, until a short time ago. The old-fashioned gooseneck teakettle with the loose wire and wood handle is an object many of my readers will never have seen. It can be traced back at least to the sixteenth century. The stylistic changes were entirely functional, and the teakettle was stabilized in the late nineteenth century. The last important change was to make it of aluminum. But in the 1930's the "art of design" was applied to it. It became an occasion for artistic perception, like fine china. The various teakettles now on the market are very handsome, but none is nearly so functional as the now almost unobtainable gooseneck kettle. The teakettle has been moved much nearer the innovative center.

This pyramid metaphor was not imported from architecture but from solid geometry. It may be that when innovation is better understood it will be possible to mathematize the study of it, to calculate the rate of innovative change. Thus each behavioral sequence can be located on a face of the pyramid, and it will be possible to create a profile of a culture as a whole. The degree of the angle of inclination of each face—there can be as many as one pleases; for my purposes four are enough—will give the general rate of innovation, and cultures may be compared on the ratio of height to width of base. This possibility brings to the fore once again the question of the function of non-functional stylistic dynamism in the arts. It is easy to see the adaptational function of innovation on the other three pyramidal faces. Science strives to improve man's predictive powers; philosophy strives to improve man's control over his semiotic behavior, although so far its efforts have been concentrated mostly on verbal behavior; valuation strives to improve man's control over his value behavior, the orientations or directive states which are the interests which determine what he is going to select to make predictions about. It is obvious that all three of these efforts are interlocking. This phenomenon, I think, is further justification for calling the overlap of high culture, wealth, and status the center of society. But what is the adaptive function of the arts? This remains to be determined, but from this point of view no theory of art can be regarded as complete unless it answers this question.

2. SEMANTIC DYNAMISM

It will perhaps be remembered that the question at the end of Section I of Chapter III which I proposed to answer was this. "If the role of the artist demands that he construct perceptual fields which offer a disorienting experience to the perceiver, how does this happen?" The first step in answering this question was to place artistic behavior in the more general category of semiotic behavior. This was justified on the grounds that all human behavior which is not instinctual behavior —and most authorities agree that there is very little instinctual behavior left in humans—is semiotic behavior. The relation of man to his environment was seen as mediated by semiosis. A situation was defined as the environment perceived and interpreted in terms of conventionally established semiotic categories. This is true even for primary signs, in which the individual interprets the situation as one in which the display of primary signs is possible. For the purposes of analyzing semiotic behavior in art, the following classification of signs was proposed.

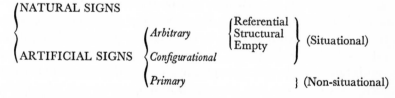

$$
\begin{cases}
\text{NATURAL SIGNS} \\
\\
\text{ARTIFICIAL SIGNS}
\end{cases}
\begin{cases}
\textit{Arbitrary} \\
\\
\textit{Configurational} \\
\\
\textit{Primary}
\end{cases}
\begin{cases}
\text{Referential} \\
\text{Structural} \\
\text{Empty}
\end{cases} \text{(Situational)}
$$

The immediate problem is this: If the artistic occasion offers to the perceiver a disorienting experience, we have a possible explanation for stylistic dynamism in art. Is that disorientation to be located in conventionalized sign behavior? We have seen that categorization, though conventional, is fluid and dynamic. We have seen also that there is reason to believe that in art, some stylistic dynamism is non-functional. In art is it to be identified with categorial dynamism? It is to be noted that though the phrase "non-functional stylistic dynamism in art" has been used with considerable frequency, nothing whatever has been said about it; it has been assigned no attributes; the direction of this discourse has been determined by the effort to locate it by elimination of possible candidates. Is categorial dynamism to be eliminated?

At first glance, it would seem not. Clearly, on the other three faces of our pyramid of the cultural center, innovation proceeds in terms of categorial innovation. Efforts in all three invariably boil down to definitional problems. The invariably emerging question is, "Have I accumulated enough data of sufficient quantity and significance to require a recategorization of my field of investigation? Have I had to change my mind about what I am talking about (range of categorial members) and how I am talking about it (bundle of categorial attributes)?" It has often been pointed out that in scientific discovery —and it is equally true of philosophic and humanistic innovation— the essential experience is the *Aha! Erlebnis!* experience, as psychologists call it. This phrase is never translated; the usual translation of *Erlebnis* is "experience," but in this situation the semantic function of *Erlebnis* is somewhat different.

Erleben means "to live through something." The phrase means something like, "I am startled: I have been taken by surprise. I suddenly realized that I have lived through something, and that which I have lived through is an entirely new way of experiencing. I have crossed the boundary into a new country. I have a new way of perceiving my field of investigation." In brief, "I have recategorized the situation." We discover nothing. We take care of a phenomenon which we cannot categorize by restructuring the system of categorization in the field of investigation. This is the experience accompanying scientific revolutions, as Kuhn defines them. It is equally true of humanistic revolutions and especially true in the study of philosophy, in which progress is not made by the accumulation of knowledge within existing categories but by leaps into new categorial systems; it is why philosophic study is so hard. Now it is perfectly obvious that the *Aha! Erlebnis!* can be experienced in any field of human activity. The agricultural worker who suddenly "sees" a new way of handling his hoe has it. It is equally obvious that the nearer one is to the center the more frequently it happens, at least on these three faces of the pyramid. But does it happen when one is playing the artistic role?

The first problem is to determine how four classes of signs are used in four kinds of art: poetry, painting, architecture, and music. The question may be approached from either side: the four sign classes may be applied in turn to each of the arts, or the four arts may be examined one by one in terms of each of the sign classes. Since the primary purpose here is to investigate art rather than signs, the latter method seems the more appropriate, though each has its advantages.

3. SIGNS IN POETRY

The first and one would think most obvious thing to note about poetry is that it is made up of words. But an enormous amount of discourse purportedly referring to poetry has neglected this simple fact. In recent years, however, there has been a considerable movement towards studying the language of poetry, almost without exception from an ethnocentric position. Edmund Wilson once churlishly remarked about the New Critics, as they are still called, that they were a lot of foolish young men who had made the discovery that poetry is made up of words. Wilson is an old-fashioned critic, and in many ways a superb one, but his notorious weakness is poetry. Actually, the discovery, or perhaps rediscovery, that poetry is made up of words was a momentous occasion.[4]

Two facts about it are of great interest. In the first place traditional critics and literary scholars could hardly understand it; they found both the aim and the execution quite mystifying. The second point of interest is that it issued from Cambridge University. Cambridge is not only the traditional English university for science, mathematics, and logic; in the 1920's it was the place where the work of Ludwig Wittgenstein and the logical positivists had the greatest influence in the English-speaking world. The revolution of this group was the proof that philosophy and science are also made up of words. Empson applied this orientation to poetry. American critics confused the positivist tradition and Empson's work with other issues, even though some of the greatest of the positivists had come here in flight from Hitler. *The International Encyclopaedia of Unified Science*, to which Morris contributed his first important study of signs, represented in this country the logical positivist tradition, to-day metamorphosed into the looser school of "philosophic analysis," and revitalized by the

---

[4] The ground was laid in the 1920's by I. A. Richards, but the first purely critical document was William Empson's *Seven Types of Ambiguity*, first published in 1930. Empson studied with Richards at Cambridge University.

later work of Wittgenstein, done after he returned to Cambridge in 1930, where he had not been since before the First World War.

Although there have been a few attempts to apply some of these newer ideas to poetry, the results on the whole have been meager. The traditional nineteenth-century way of going about talking about poetry was essentially to look for the poet's intention. This was to be located in his life and further located in his cultural situation. Valuable as much of this work has been—more valuable, potentially, to my mind, than the tradition of the New Critics—it is obvious that in this kind of discourse attention is focussed elsewhere than on the poem, and on something both historically and empirically inaccessible, the poet's mind, his personality, his imagination, his cultural background. The New Critics quite rightly pointed this out; that was their revolution. It was as if they had said, "What you are saying is very interesting, but you are not talking about the poem. You have stacks of fascinating information. Some of it, for all anyone can tell, may be highly pertinent. But your equipment for applying this information to the poem itself is crude and primitive almost beyond belief." This objection was irrefutable. That there has been a revolution both in published criticism and in the classroom is undeniable. On the whole, it has been salutary. But the innovative study of poetry for the past thirty years has suffered from two disabilities.

The first arose from its dependence on taking over from aesthetics certain unanalyzed notions, many of which we have already glanced at. The most important was that the New Critics thought that their task was to decide, once and for all, on what grounds the value of the poem could be determined. The peculiar drifting character of the canon of all art at the highest cultural level has already been suggested. Their efforts amounted to merely another instance of cultural ethnocentricity, and evinced exactly the same character as all such efforts: canonic drift. This confusion between a value problem and an analytic problem has vitiated most of their efforts to find out something about poetry, and still does.

But there was yet another matter that got in their way, which they saw as two interlocking problems, poetic structure and poetic truth. Their reasoning seems to have run along lines something like this:

Artistic value flows from artistic structure. Since poetry is art, its value must flow from poetic structure. Now, as we have recently discovered, poetry is made up of words. The most striking thing about words is that they have meaning. It must follow then that poetic structure is a matter of meaning structure.

Since poetic structure is a unique kind of structure (because poetry is art), poetic meaning must be a unique kind of meaning. Since to have structure is to have value, and since the only kind of meaning which can have value is truth, it follows the poetic meaning must have a unique kind of truth. Hence poetry has a unique kind of semantic structure which reveals a unique kind of truth. Poetry says things which cannot be said in any other language. And what's more, we shall now tell you in non-poetic language what that meaning is which cannot be said in non-poetic language, though, for this reason, you must not imagine that you will know what that meaning is. That meaning can only be experienced; it cannot be known.

I do not claim that the reasoning of any of the New Critics was as lucid as this conjectural reconstruction of their argument, but this is the line of thinking they developed. It is now triumphant in a new academic criticism, less readable and much less informative than the old.

For the present purposes, the only matter of significance is the claim that simple and/or compound verbal signs have semantic functions in poetry that the same verbal signs do not and cannot have outside of poetry. The argument that the truth of this position is to be found in poetic metaphor can be dismissed briefly. Metaphor as an emergent category has already been discussed, and it has been pointed out that at some periods poetic metaphor is very common in poetry, and in some periods it is not. Further, at some periods the poetry at the higher cultural level is conspicuous for its use of traditional metaphors; at other periods it is notable for its display of innovative metaphor. Since their claim is that unique poetic truth comes into poetry through metaphor, it is not surprising that these critics have been most interested in poetry of periods in which innovative metaphor, highly developed, is common. The unanalyzed equivalence of metaphor with poetry emerges nonchalantly in the following sentence, which comes from a more or less run-of-the-mill example of contemporary criticism: "Such a view . . . in denying metaphor . . . denies poetry itself."[5] In English poetry these periods are particularly to be found in one stream of early seventeenth-century poetry—what some have called Baroque poetry—and English and American poetry since 1910, modern poetry.

As has already been shown, metaphor is the only way to signify an emergent category, whether it is culturally emergent or emergent only for the speaker. When it is demanded at the cultural center that the

[5] Edward Engelberg, *The Vast Design: Patterns in W. B. Yeats's Aesthetic*, Toronto, 1964, p. xv.

task of the poet is to utter novel truths, the amount of innovative metaphor rises like a tide. Just such a condition obtained in the early Romantic period, in which the poet was to be prophet-priest, the utterer of new and redemptive truths. Cultural prescriptions kept him from discursive language, the kind of language found in metaphysics, though some poets, notably Wordsworth, occasionally used it. But another consideration kept him from discursive language. Poetic truth was supposed to be revelatory, and a carefully built up argument is rarely that. It is usually tedious; but poetry is supposed to be exciting. Innovative metaphor, above all linguistic devices, is notable for its capacity to offer the *Aha! Erlebnis!* experience. In actual historic fact, the claim of the New Criticism that poetry has a unique truth-value is by no means original with them but, amusingly enough, derives from the early Romantics, whom they despise so thoroughly.[6] Throughout the nineteenth century, the search for new metaphor was constant; and the New Critics are merely continuing, unconsciously, a cultural value already well established.

Metaphor, then, is found in poetry primarily because it is found in language, of which poetry consists. The amount of metaphor in poetry and its innovative character, however, is an historical variable. The question is, is it a non-functional stylistic variable, or does it vary with some extra-poetic cultural demand? The answer has already appeared. An increase in innovative metaphor for the past one hundred and seventy years of English poetry has obviously been in response to demands on the other faces of the cultural pyramid. These demands were made by philosophers and valuators; and when poets developed such ideas they were not acting in their role as poets but as philosophers and valuators. The increase in metaphor performed a non-poetic function. It arose neither from a realization of the true nature of poetry—every poetic and critical school has made that claim—nor from the efforts of poets to create a stylistic disorientation. In the time of Pope, for example, the task of the poet was not to utter new truths, but to utter old ones, platitudes, in a way that would make them appear fresh and vital. Not the discovery of truth but the renewal of truth was the poet's task. The poet felt himself quite consciously re-

---

[6] See Richard Foster, *The New Romantics: A Reappraisal of the New Criticism*, Bloomington, Ind., 1962. Foster presents an admirable demonstration of just this point. In fairness, I should add that of late some of the New Critics are beginning to see some merit in nineteenth-century poetry.

sponding to extra-poetic demands, and felt it was right that he should do so. In the early seventeenth century, among the "Baroque" Metaphysicals, metaphor responded to different demands. The task of the poet was not to be innovative in the sense of using metaphor to reveal new truths, but he was to be far-fetched in his metaphors, which were applied to very old ideas indeed: "My mistress is beautiful"; "God loves me." But the purpose of being far-fetched was not so much to astonish by importing wholly unexpected terms as it was to find opportunities to develop metaphors into "conceits." The poet executed this enterprise by using as many of the attributes of the imported category as he could. His object was to achieve the impossible: to identify the imported category with the local. The attempt was an effort to fulfill extra-poetic demands for problem perception, a matter to be returned to.

Much more serious than the attempt to identify metaphor and poetry is the claim that simple and compound verbal signs have semantic functions not found outside of poetry. The source of this notion can be traced to the failure of the New Critics to disengage themselves sufficiently from their predecessors, the intentionalists. It is instructive that the New Critics frequently talk about the poet, when on the basis of their own position, they should be talking only about poems, not even about poetry. The trouble is that they talk about poetry as if it were caused by a unique way of thinking, not as if it were a unique mode of verbal behavior, which it is. Thus both schools account for poetry by referring it back to the "mind," that pseudo-entity. Operating in the Romantic tradition, the New Critic gives the poet a unique kind of mind, with unique thoughts, and these emerge, of course, in unique semantic functions, though it is hard to see why they should. The proposition, then, amounts to a notion of semantic immanence. Meaning is "in" the sign, somehow or other. Since it is "there," it can be brought out. Yet semantic functions are entirely conventional, or are innovated from conventions, as with metaphor. And this, as we have seen, is particularly true of arbitrary signs, especially since interpretation depends upon knowing the conventions governing structural signs. The claim that poetry has unique immanent semantic functions is utterly untenable. But this denial permits us to make a further generalization. All of the semantic functions of poetry are under the control of extra-poetic convention. They are, therefore, all functional. Non-functional stylistic variability in poetry, consequently, lies elsewhere than in conventionally established semantic functions. But if this is true of poetry, it is true of all the arts, for which, at one time or another, precisely the same truth claims have been made. The semantic aspect of art, therefore, is always functional; in this aspect of his activity, the artist is controlled by extra-artistic, conventional factors. Henceforth, then, I shall refer to the semantic aspect of art when I wish to talk about its semantic functions.[7]

At this point the obvious objection is that it has been often asserted by very impressive writers that poetry *does* have a unique semantic function; the language of poetry and of all the arts is "symbolic." To this point, which is a strong one, I shall return at the end of Chapter VI. Here it is enough to state that in the sense in which "symbol" is ordinarily used in this situation, the Wild Ones must be playing the artist's role, because in this sense of "symbol" all their behavior, from speed to animal tails on their motorcycle handles, is symbolic, except for their clever predictions about the safest towns to be destructive in. If Wordsworth's "My heart leaps up when I behold a rainbow in the sky," is symbolic, then so is a Wild One's statement that *his* heart leaps up when he beholds a powerful motorcycle between his legs, his broad clutching him at his back, and a fast road before him. If art and poetry are symbolic, the artist is not making use of semantic functions unique to his role.[8]

Another claim for truth in poetry is the claim of "imaginative truth." By this is at times meant "symbolic truth," at times something different. One semantic phenomenon of "imaginative truth" is that of the meaning of a fiction, an invented narrative built by ascribing sequences of behavior to interacting characters. This deserves a word, for much poetry presents fictional narration. Actually, in exploring the role metaphor for human behavior, most of this has been discussed, except for the feature of "plot." Plot consists of sequences of action ascribed to proper names, that is, categories of identity. It may or may not correspond to normal notions of cause-and-effect in human behavior, but obviously such qualities are responsive to extrapoetic demands. The model for interpreting the significance of narrative is not found in poetry itself but in life, for, with one exception, we

---

[7] Actually, I should prefer "conventional aspect," but it would be hard to separate such a usage from the semantic functions of "commonplace" or "platitudinous" or "hide-bound." As with metaphor, for example, the semantic aspect of poetry can be radically innovative, but only by starting from a base line of semantic conventions.

[8] See also the discussion of Suzanne Langer in Chapter III, Section 2, above.

interpret human behavior in life just as we do in fiction, and we use exactly the same language in discussing fictional characters as we do our friends, relatives, enemies, and anybody else we know anything about. "What is the meaning of this?" is a question we ask constantly about observed behavior. With the coming of psychoanalysis we now ask the same questions of ourselves. Answers are given in the form of such statements as, "That means that he really loves her," or "That means he is trying to take my job away from me." These answers may or may not be right. These are essentially unconfirmed predictive statements, which may very well be subsequently confirmed, or disproved, or left open. The "meaning" of the action may forever remain a mystery. We proceed in interpreting personalities and events just as we proceed in interpreting any sign or compound sign, by applying categories to persons and situations. The same thing happens in the novel. The only difference is that all the necessary information is supplied by the novelist, and for his major characters it is generally more than we ever encounter in life, except—and only for some people—for what we know about ourselves. There are neither signs nor situational clues which the novelist has not provided, putting aside the fact that the signs and clues are, of course, conventional outside the fiction. Again it may be said that the total body of information taken together is a symbol, like Wordsworth's remark, or the behavior of the Wild Ones, or, as we shall see, like anyone's behavior at all times.

A further meaning of "imaginative truth" appears in the poet's ability to create through signs completely unpredicted situations, matters that nobody would think for a moment could actually exist. As the Puritans of the sixteenth century insisted, poetry consists of lies. What the poet does is to assemble a package of categories which, so far as we know, would never be found juxtaposed in the human environment. This can, of course, be found more or less in narrative poetry as well as narrative prose, but I am referring rather to the poetry of pure vision, as "Kubla Khan" would be, if those critics were right who insist that it has no meaning. In this sense "imaginative truth" simply means "a lie which I value." It is worth a brief exploration, and to begin it is interesting to listen for a moment to Laura Riding, herself a poet of considerable achievement and distinction. A lifetime of thinking about poetry has led her to this:

Thus, with neither poets nor their words put to the proof (except with respect to the artificially created conditions of poetry itself), nothing is ever *in fact* spiritually defined, morally determined, linguistically resolved, in poems. In no other field of human activity is there so much intensity of expectation and so little possibility of anything's happening to meet it. . . . The ultimate effect of poetry is to clarify nothing, to change nothing.[9]

Philosophy has traditionally been busy with the problem of how it is possible to tell a true statement from a false one. This is no place for presenting all the answers that have been offered. I suspect the answer is a very simple, one though, admittedly, if it is the right answer, it has been found only recently. A statement may be judged a true statement if it can be recast in an operational form and successfully tested. For example, "Water running down a millrace and striking the paddles of a mill wheel causes the wheel to revolve." To test this statement, it may be recast thus, "If I divert that water, the mill wheel will stop." And if I do divert the water, and if the mill wheel does stop, than the original statement is true. Nor need I trouble myself, for this purpose, about the meaning of the word "cause." In this situation all it means is that the sentence may be operationally recast. "True statement," here, means simply a statement which controls behavior to produce an *anticipated* result, which may have anything from a very low to a very high probability.

From the biological point of view of this book, semiotic behavior is an adaptational function. It has obviously been successful, at least from the human point of view. Man has learned to interpret a cloud as a sign of rain, and to put such an interpretative act into arbitrary signs established by purely human conventions. It is an extraordinary, an astonishing achievement, the expansion of evolutionary adaptation into a new dimension. What is the basic function of such a development that makes it possible to understand it? I think that signs of any kind function primarily by making prediction possible. The creation of arbitrary signs was, then, in essence an extension of predictive behavior. It enabled man to talk about a possibility; it freed him from having to act out every possibility. Thus he was able to select a limited number of signs from any actual environment. This act of selection turned the environment of signals into the situation of alternative signs. He attained "mind," that is, interpretational variability. That man should make true statements is nothing to be wondered at; once he had made the initial step of categorization—seeing configurations as

---

[9] Laura Riding (Jackson), "Further on Poetry," *Chelsea*, No. 14, 1964, p. 42.

signs enacted instead of as signals—he could not help it. To be sure, the structure of his signs is not isomorphic with his environment, but that does not interfere with the predictive capacities of sign behavior. No, the interesting and perplexing thing about man is not that he can tell the truth, but that he can lie.

Consider the statement which I have invented, "God is the ground of the universe who causes the world process to maintain its ongoing-ness." The operational meaning of this is, "If I remove the ground of the universe which is God, the world process will stop." This appears to be impossible. Whatever else God may be, he is clearly not a being who will cooperate with us by springing our predictive traps. It would be easy to maintain that "God" in this or any other statement is an empty category, not to speak of "ground" and "world process." But it appears that the only empty categories are the arbitrary signs of mathematics and symbolic logic, and these were derived from the enumerational attributes of categories. "God" has a great many semantic functions. In Christianity the attributes of the category "God" are omniscience, omnipotence, and omnibenevolence. Any member of this category has complete knowledge of the future, total predictiveness, complete operational control over the environment, and complete goodness, that is, a total absence of value conflicts, a knowledge of moral right incapable of error. Such a sign I would regard as a derived sign of a primary sign of adequacy. Any human who is totally adequate is a god, and this is exactly what the Romans meant when they deified their emperors, especially at the beginning, when they exercised some discrimination. Augustus, the evident master of all the world the Romans cared to worry about, was the first deified emperor. On the other hand, any ordinary mortal who imagined himself to be fully adequate was setting himself up in rivalry to the Gods. This was the Greek concept of *hubris*, which is precisely the same as that to be found in the colloquial expressions, "He's riding to a fall," and "He thinks he has it made." Oedipus thought he had it made. To think yourself totally adequate to your situation is to disarm yourself of the power to be aware of the gap between behavioral patterns and environmental demands. Tragedy, in the Greek concep-tion, is what happens to people when they are foolish enough to think themselves totally adequate, to imagine themselves safe and protected when they are not, for no one can be entirely and permanently safe and protected.

Such an interpretation at least gives meaning to the verbal sign "God" and makes it referential. It refers to a primary, non-situational, attribute of human behavior. Thus the original sentence about "God" and "world process" could be taken to mean: "If I never felt the sense of adequacy to a situation, I would feel unable to go on living." And this would be a statement capable of being confirmed or disfirmed. The problem now is, if simple operational statements like "If you put some water on the fire, it will go out," are true statements, how is it that apparently false statements can be made which, if interpreted, turn out to be true statements? How is it that false statements can be made for which no operationally valid interpretation can be found? An example is "A unicorn munches the diamonds of cats and imbibes the melted gold of the Fearful Mountains."

The human capacity to lie is, I suspect, responsible for the tendency to shift from the question of how one tells whether or not a statement is true to the question of how can it be that human beings can make true statements; for this is the form the problem sometimes emerges in. More radically, it often, indeed traditionally, appears as a question about how the mind gets to the world, the form in which Kant perceived it. What, in human behavior, has been responsible for such puzzles?

If the problem is put in the form proposed here, however, using the two categories of verbal signs, referential and structural, it is possible to arrive at an answer which tells us much about the splendid lying of poets. "A unicorn munches the diamonds of cats and imbibes the melted gold of the Fearful Mountains." Let us remove all the referential signs: "A ——— ———s the ———s of ———s and ———s the ———ed —— of the ———ful —s." These blanks can be filled in with referential verbal signs which turn it into a statement which may be tested for its predictive truth: "A *man eats* the *muscles* of *animals* and *drinks* the *fermented juice* of the *plentiful grapes*." It seems probable that linguistic behavior involves selecting for a bundle of signs a structural pattern as appropriate to the situation as one can manage. The pattern consists of a number of holes in a structure, and these holes may be filled at will with referential verbal signs. This is why foreign language teaching influenced by modern linguistics is devoted to drilling the students in the structural patterns. Thus the student learns simultaneously the pattern and the classes of referential signs which may be put into each kind of hole. Through drill he himself performs the categorial process, quite unconsciously. Subsequently he can learn explicit rules, but he begins by learning the implicit qualities of the language, just as children do.[10]

As we look back over the history of English poetry, it is apparent that one semantic variable is the ratio of fantastic propositions—valued lies—to predictive propositions. In the romances of the middle ages, purely fantastic propositions were highly valued. In the seventeenth century the poet was expected to apply his metaphors either to predictive statements or to the middle kind of statement which can be reduced to predictive statements. In the Enlightenment, the age of "nature poetry," the poet was required to include a large proportion of predictive statements about the natural world. This requirement first shows up strongly in James Thomson's *The Seasons*.[11] In the nineteenth century, predictive statements about social interaction and personal psychology were concentrated on, particularly the middle kind of statement which is transparently a psychological statement—or "symbolic" or "symptomatic" statement. A particular problem was the development of a semantic technique which would make it possible

---

[10] It is interesting that quite recently computers have been constructed programmed to generate syntactically correct sentences, that is, sentences which obey all the rules governing the use of structural signs. Such sentences, however, are nonsensical. The invented sentence offered above about the unicorn could be imagined as having a place in, let us say, a fairy story; but so far, the computer generated sentences have no place even in that very open situation. Obviously, the computer is not being fed any information about situational rules, either about verbal situations, such as fairy stories, or environmental situations. Nor can it make up such situations, since, so far, it cannot use referential signs without structural signs. Nor is there any way out of this logical impasse. Obviously, a way must be found to computerize configurational and primary signs. This conclusion brings out the necessary link between perceptual categories and sign categories: there must be a perceptual category before it can be signified. The reason is that rules governing the assembling of all primary, configurational, and referential signs, are entirely cultural, that is, conventional. Conventions cannot be controlled by logic, which is derived from structural signs. The computer has no interpretational variability, no mind. As the examination of metaphor showed, interpretational variability is controlled by convention. These conventions are probably beyond systematization and mathematization. A computer can be made to "think" only by supplying it with the codified data about a situation (an interpreted environment). But even this will have severe limitations. To "think," to have true interpretational variability, a computer, it appears, must be linked to a situation by means of perceptual categories. It must be able to deal with natural signs, directly, without mediation by programming, as well as with a full set of rules about the conventions which govern the assembling of primary, categorial, and referential signs. Right now, they can manipulate only empty signs. They can make sentences with holes, but the filling of the holes is random.

[11] "Spring," the first part of *The Seasons*, was published in 1726.

to reveal such metaphysical middle statements as the one about God as the ground of the universe as in fact predictive psychological statements, capable of being confirmed or disproved. In prose fiction, the demand for predictive statements was overwhelming. The problem was to make every statement about character, interaction, and situation capable of easy testing on a non-statistical probability ground. Pure fantasy statements sank to a much lower cultural level, in which poetic and prose fiction showed little non-functional stylistic dynamism. But these were all demands and problems derived from non-poetic, nonfictional sources, from the other faces of the pyramid of high-level culture.

In poetry predictive statements about the natural world are generally referred to as "imagery," but they are more easily understood as references to natural signs. In this sense they are derived signs. To anticipate, the original semantic function of a snow-covered mountain peak may have been to be a primary sign of adequacy; from it was derived the verbal sign "God." Or the already existent sign "God" was adjusted to the natural sign of a snow-covered mountain. Such adjustment is also achieved by sign derivation. In this sense poetry, then, can adjust itself to or derive its semantic function from any semantic function of natural signs. And the same capacity is true of configurational signs. In addition, however, it can derive configurational signs from the semantic functions of language. These are emblems. This is another sense of the term "imagery," but we have already seen it at work in the discussion of allegory in the preceding section. Again, however, these are not exclusively poetic functions. Non-poetic language can and does do the same thing. Sixteenth-century discursive language, for example, theological, political, even scientific, was full of allegorical emblems. Again, natural signs, configurational signs, and emblematic signs are put in poetry in response to non-poetic cultural demands. To repeat, this is a matter of style, to be sure, but of functional style, as with saws and teakettles before the 1930's, not non-functional style.

One question remains about poetry: Does the poet have any way of presenting primary signs, other than through sign derivation? In this matter the poet is faced with a peculiar difficulty which does not trouble the architect, the composer, or the painter. His raw material is sounds, but these sounds have already been selected by the language behavior of his culture. An infant is originally capable of all sounds selected by any language. Gradually, the adults around him serving him as role-models, he restricts the sounds he makes to the range selected by his language. The next step, oddly enough, is assembling these sounds into the sound packages of sentences. The next thing he learns to do is to say these sounds within the pitch or stress intonation of his culture. He does this by assembling the sounds into the pitch and intonation patterns of the sentences he hears spoken around him. This accounts for the peculiar ability of a child who has not yet learned semantic functions to produce sequences of sounds which have the phonic character of sentences, but such sentences seem to be spoken through a barrier which makes it impossible to ascertain what morphemes are at work. That is, as yet no morphemes are at work. Then, with this phonic basis to work from, the child can learn morphemes, which it does more or less in isolation from sentences. The final step is to put them into sentences, the phonic structure of which he has already mastered. It is true that the child learns morphemes and words before he learns to say meaningful sentences, but he can make this last step only because he already has rehearsed extensively the stress, pitch, and intonational patterns of sentences. With most children one further step may be identified—word-games which play with sounds. Almost any traditional nursery rhyme provides an example of this kind of phonic play, which is the raw material for the poet.

When the poet wishes to manipulate sounds, therefore, he can only manipulate the sounds selected by his culture, for if he uses other sounds, or sound combinations not so selected, he loses morphemic character, or semantic function. This is not true of the painter, who uses color signs and configurational signs, for these are not held together by structural signs which limit their juxtapositional possibilities. He can disintegrate the conventions of his culture, and as modern abstract cubism and expressionism have demonstrated, separate configurations entirely from any situational semantic function. This is novel in twentieth-century painting, but it is something the decorator and furniture designer have always done. The architect has the same potential, and has always used it. Music, likewise, is not held together by structural signs, as language is, but only by conventions of assembly, by packaging conventions. It can be completely disintegrated, and still be music, as certain composers of the 1950's and 1960's have shown by composing aleatoric music, which is made up of random selections of pitch, volume, timbre, rhythm, and so on. If music has primary semantic function, it is still at work in aleatoric music.

Not so with the poet; if he moves towards the random selection of allophones or phonemes, he disintegrates semantic structure. Gertrude Stein attempted to move in this direction, but she succeeded only in creating poetry of categorial disintegration. She left only referential and structural signs in situations which did not provide enough information to enable the reader to decide what semantic function was at work, if any. It is true that some poems contain nonsense sequences, like "Hickory-dickory-dock," but such lines are surprisingly rare, and are most common in nursery rhymes or poems written to be set to music. But even with "Hickory-dickory-dock" the poet has not moved in the direction of phonic randomness nor has he even moved outside of the accepted range of sounds and sound sequences possible in his language. He has moved in the opposite direction, virtually the only direction in which he can move, towards phonic overdetermination. It is possible, to be sure, to write such a poem as this:

> Slrsz bjam eiocn elpciwl?
> Thioe ekconelcighslei difonw,
> Ipncil tionalgpencklj dkendkthsi—
> Hyrsiel chtiowls cheiogls enciotns!

The fact that the lines are of unequal length and begin with capital letters is, in our culture, a sign that the poet offers it as an occasion for the perceiver's role. Anyone who wishes to do so may use these four lines as an occasion for poetic perception. Having spent my life in the study of poetry, I find myself irresistibly triggered into the perceiver's role, even though I composed the passage by randomly striking the keys of a typewriter. Actually the poem is not purely random, at least for anyone whose written language employs such letters of the English alphabet as appear here. A poet could also utter a phonic sequence making random use of all the sounds and sound combinations available in all the languages of the world about which it is possible to get information. If he presented it in a poetic situation, it would be a poem, even if he alone used it as an occasion for playing the role of poetic perceiver. So long as a poet uses the semantic function of verbal signs, he is limited by his language to a phonic range and a phonic formula, or rules governing sound combinations, which all languages have. Since there are barriers to phonic disintegration, to manipulate sounds he must move in the opposite direction. If he cannot be less selective than the language permits, he can only be more selective than the language requires. This narrowed selection is phonic overdetermination.

In English poetry the technique of overdetermination is fairly limited. It boils down to a more frequent repetition of phonemes or category of phonemes (such as vowels) than is to be found in ordinary utterance. To a speaker of a language who knows no other—the case when all poetry was originated, how long ago there is no telling—the normal phonemic flow is perceived as *random*. Any overdetermination, consequently, is perceived, by contrast, as *ordered*. In English the techniques of overdetermination are few but inexhaustible: rhyme, the repetition of the same sound combination at regular intervals or sets of regular intervals; alliteration, the selection of words to provide a more than normally frequent recurrence of the same consonant; assonance, the selection of words to provide a more than normally frequent recurrence of the same vowel or groups of vowels (such as front or back vowels); rhythm, the regular repetition of stress; and junctural regularity, or the regular repetition of juncture, a term I use here with non-technical fuzziness to indicate pauses in the stream of spoken sound. Such pauses are partly signified in written language by punctuation marks.

The first thing to observe about these devices is to note that not one of them is unique to poetry. All are to be found elsewhere in spoken and written English, though, admittedly, rhyme is the rarest. Still, in certain prose styles of the sixteenth century, rhyme was employed more or less plentifully. Nor are they confined to prose the conventions of which indicate that it is to be the occasion for artistic perception. They are to found in proverbs, advertising, sermons, and, though rarely after the middle third of the seventeenth century, in theological, philosophic, scientific, and general humanistic prose discourse. If such devices are to be regarded as signs, what are they signs of?

They are usually taken as indications of the poet's capacity to create order in language, and such an approach of course singles out the poet as the man gifted with a unique power to create order. The reasons for questioning this have already been suggested, though not yet the full reasons for denying it. But if this is the case, they may be regarded as signs of order. Order, however, as we have seen, is not something immanent in a perceptual field; it is something contributed by the perceiver. It is fully oriented perception, a condition in which disparities are ignored, in which one has the conviction that one's predictions will be confirmed. Such a conviction is independent of the situation; it is a non-situational, or primary, attribute of perception. If it is sustained, such a conviction may be marked by a sense of demand or of acceptance; by a sense of energy release or of energy conservation; by a sense of openness to the demands coming from the environment, by a sense of adequacy, or by a sense of smoothness of behavior. A situation in which one has, on the contrary, a conviction that one's predictions will be frustrated may be marked, if it is sustained, by a sense of rejection of situational demands, by a sense of inadequacy, or by a sense of behavioral roughness. Of this last, two kinds may be located: impulse smoothness and process smoothness. The first is a matter of initiating at regular or irregular intervals a series of behavioral sequences; the second is the smoothness or roughness of the execution of that sequence.

When we look for these in English poetry, the sense of adequacy may be located in rhyme. Comic verse is invariably rhymed, while double and triple rhymes, in which two or three syllables are rhymed, are so thoroughly identified with comic verse that they are entirely excluded from serious verse except when they are introduced for ironic purposes, like wry jokes about one's pain. Now, comedy as opposed to tragedy is the celebration of the sense of adequacy. Tragedy, it was suggested above, is a warning of the perils of feeling adequate. That is why it is about great men; the sense of adequacy can be a danger even to the greatest. But comedy is about ordinary men; anybody can experience the joys of adequacy, so long as he does not make too many and too heavy demands upon life. The great man, of course, is precisely the one whose role it is, for the sake of his people, to make such demands. Hence in English poetry, rhymed tragedy flourished only briefly, during the later seventeenth century. It was an experiment soon abandoned; but it is not difficult to see why it was undertaken. Such tragedy is about the conflict between private and public roles. It is about the difficulty the great man has in keeping up the front public role-playing requires. In this it takes up a quite different problem from either Greek or Elizabethan tragedy. Rhyme was used as a sign of the fact that public role playing requires the performer always to appear adequate. Such tragedy, so to speak, looks at the tragic hero through his mask of adequacy, while the Greeks and Shakespeare simply strip off the mask and show what is going on underneath. The same subtle ironic effect is to be found in Pope's "Elosia to Abelard," in which a nun presents the role mask of public adequacy—nothing is more exposed than the life of a nun—through which is revealed, by a kind of interior illumination, her struggles to keep erotic emotion and religious emotion in two separate categories—and her failure. Throughout the late sixteenth, seventeenth, eighteenth, and into the nineteenth and twentieth centuries poetic satire is almost invariably rhymed, for the role of satirist requires one to appear adequate to making morally correct judgments; the victim of the satire is shown as inadequate to this task. This comes out quite clearly in the early satirical lyrics of T. S. Eliot and in "The Love-Song of J. Alfred Prufrock," in which the object of the satire is the speaker himself.

These examples of unusual appropriateness of the sense of adequacy to the situation suggest the primary signification of rhyme in the usual run of lyric poetry. No-matter how great the suffering, in lyric poetry there is always present the sense that the speaker is adequate enough at least to talk about his feelings and, in that sense, face them. Like the man who says that he is feeling terrible, he is at least feeling well enough to say so. Thus lyric poetry is capable of the most varied and delicate ironies between the sense of inadequacy signified by the arbitrary verbal signs and the sense of adequacy signified by the primary phonic signs.

Alliteration and assonance are really identical; both are concerned with overdetermination of sound sequence. The judgment as to whether or not alliteration and assonance actually appear in a particular passage is frequently imprecise. Because the phonic character of any language is already preselected and limited, the mere use of the language is bound to produce what appears to be planned overdetermination, *if* one is looking for it. Unanticipated rhyme is always cropping up in ordinary speech behavior, and individuals at the cultural apex, accustomed to planning their sentences ahead, often go out of their way to avoid it. Because there are more consonants than vowels, alliteration is bound to be more conspicuous than assonance, and whether the latter is present in a poem or not is often questionable. For this reason it is not now judged so intrusive and offensive in prose as rhyme, alliteration, and junctural and stress regularity. Perhaps these last have become so exploited in poetry that their presence in prose seems to be a sign for the wrong role. But this explanation is probably not sound. Modern prose was established in the later seventeenth century by John Dryden, the Puritans, and the scientifically oriented Royal Society. The aim was to create a prose appropriate to science and business and other non-poetic kinds of discourse. Such prose, it was decided, should be purely "functional," purely predictive, prescriptive, and analytical, with no contributions from primary signs or verbal emblems. Swift's prose is still considered a model for humanistic discourse, though other models, based on the same principles, have dominated science and philosophy.

When alliteration and assonance are unquestionable, or when the values of the poetic perceiver lead him to be aware of them, even though such perception might be a surprise to the author, they appear to be primary signs of the sense of demand. Of the various kinds of phonic overdetermination they are unique in not being patterned. They come in patches, and their inherent capacity for ambiguity permits them to fade in and out. Poetic criticism is full of claims for "sound symbolism," claims that *s*'s are a sign of hatefulness, that *t*'s are a sign of contempt, that *r*'s indicate power, and so on. Such claims are so unstable from one critic to the next that they must be dismissed. But the making of such claims is interesting; it indicates that something has been observed, and it indicates that it is the conviction of most critics and readers of poetry that alliteration and euphony are signs. The interpretation of a particular sound as a sign of a particular attitude can invariably be traced to the semantic function of the compound verbal sign in which they are found. Alliteration and euphony serve, if nothing else, to intensify any attitude being signified. But if we consider that a poem is a dramatic expression, that even if the poet is saying what he really thinks is true, is speaking as it were, in his own voice, rather than in an invented voice, he is still playing a role. Pope satirized what he genuinely hated, but he was playing the role of satirist.[12] To intensify one's attitudes is to make a demand upon a situation, it is to be insistent. The same techniques are constantly to be found in advertising, which is nothing if not insistent, which exists only as means for the advertiser to make a demand upon the public. The hard-sell school of advertising, therefore, is marked by a conspicuous use of phonic overdetermination, particularly in slogans, which often use alliteration and euphony. For this reason I believe that if alliteration and euphony are to be considered as primary signs they are signs of the sense of demand.

One might easily think that the sense of demand could as easily be associated with phrasal length, the length of the phonic sequence between junctures. Long uninterrupted phonic sequences, however, are better conceived of as primary signs of energy release. In English poetry the long line of nine to twelve syllables is standard for serious

---

[12] To be insincere is not simply "to play a role." Like hypocrisy, it involves playing two roles, though with a different relation and intention.

poetry, while shorter lines tend to be used for poetry of a lighter vein. The consideration of what any culture regards as serious requires some preparatory girding up of the loins, some assumption of a stance designed to release large amounts of energy as the situation demands it, or even when it does not. A poem which uses long uninterrupted phonic sequences is ordinarily referred to as highly controlled, and defensive control against distraction is precisely what is needed for sustained release of energy. To cite a few instances, the lines of the stanza of Spenser's *The Faerie Queene* are ten syllables long, except for the last, which is twelve. The effect has often been compared to the wash up a beach of a broken wave. The metaphor points to energy released to depletion. Within the stanza, however, something else happens. The line is the normal ten-syllable English line; there is ordinarily a caesura in the middle, or thereabouts. The ordinary phrasal structure of Spenser's stanza usually is interrupted about two-thirds of the way through by a phonic sequence of anywhere from one to one-and-a-half or even two-and-one-half lines. This is an extremely long phonic sequence in poetry and appears to function as a sign of energy release. This is why the last line is felt as release to depletion. Were it not for the central gathering of power, it would be felt as energy release, but not to depletion.

In *Paradise Lost* Milton, having observed, apparently, Spenser's mid-stanza device, exploited it to the fullest degree it has ever received in English poetry. Tennyson's famous metaphor for the style of *Paradise Lost*, "organ voiced," appears to select this attribute of its verse, for the organ is the instrument with the greatest capacity for sustaining sound. Above all poems, *Paradise Lost* is characterized by long phonic sequences, and to it, more than to any other English poem, critics have attributed the quality of terrific force and energy. Some readers, in fact, find themselves so dazed and overcome by these primary signs of energy that they are almost incapable of understanding the verbal semantic functions. For this, however, there are other reasons to be discussed later.

Likewise, energy conservation, coziness, claustrophilia (a liking for closed spaces) are signified by short phonic sequences, as in the poetry of Milton's contemporary, Robert Herrick. Like Milton, Herrick specialized in the possibilities of phonic sequence as primary signs but, unlike Milton, devoted himself to exploiting the possibilities of the short line, with which he has done more than any other English poet. The ironic effect of using short lines in a serious situation appears in

A. E. Housman's *The Shropshire Lad*. The combination gives the effect of one who is engaged in serious considerations but refuses to commit himself to them or to any final position about them. To use an expressive colloquialism, he is playing his cards very close to this chest. Here the short line reinforces the skepticism which is the tone of the volume, while the rhyme, a primary sign of adequacy, supports its stoicism.

In poetry, as in music, two rhythmic devices are at work: the rhythm of juncture and the rhythm of stress, which I have identified as signs of impulse smoothness and of process smoothness.[13] Both, like phonic sequence, are easily identified: the same phenomena in human behavior are interpreted as predictive signs. When we see an individual executing smoothly a behavioral pattern we tend to predict that he will show a similar smoothness in patterns appropriate to other situations. Indeed, since a certain ability to sustain patterns on demand, to initiate patterns at regular intervals, as in mowing by hand, and to carry through the execution of the pattern without interruption stemming from the actor himself, is "normal," we tend to believe that something organically or psychically is wrong with an individual whose behavior evinces only short sequences, irregularity of impulse, and roughness or jaggedness of execution. On the other hand, training for sports is primarily training in these qualities. The same qualities are found in all behavior, including language behavior. Stammering, for example, is usually judged as a sign of organic disorder or psychic disturbance, though not always correctly. It may merely be a matter of style, like the adopted stammer of the old-fashioned British aristocrat. In poetry, such primary signs may properly be regarded as derived signs or emblems.

Rhythm offers one further primary sign, though it does not play an important part in English poetry. Two common kinds of expression about rhythm are "rising" and "falling" rhythm, and "masculine" and "feminine" endings. The difference between the first pair is whether or not the first syllable in the line is stressed. If it is, and the last syllable is unstressed, the rhythm is referred to as falling; and vice versa. But one frequently encounters "balanced" lines; these are often not random but are a part of the stanza structure. In a balanced line the first and last syllables are either both stressed or both unstressed. But when the last syllable in any line is unstressed, the line-ending is referred to as "feminine." The metaphors of verticality and sexual

---

[13] See above, p. 140.

role hint at the primary significance of the perceptual category referred to by these verbal signs. At one time, probably in the thirteenth or perhaps as late as the fourteenth century, a rising rhythm was felt as *masculine*, as a primary sign of demand. It has, however, become so standardized that it is no longer a primary sign of masculinity, unless it appears in a context which is mainly one of falling rhythm. Falling rhythm is rare in English poetry and has been for some centuries. However, in a context of which the basic rhythmic pattern is rising, a *feminine* or *weak* ending has primary significance. The metaphors used indicate that in such situations the feminine, or weak line ending, is a sign of acceptance. Byron, in *Don Juan*, constantly uses it in a context where it can be interpreted as an "Oh-well!-That's-the-way-it-is" kind of acceptance.

The poet, then, has at his command a number of primary signs, but it is worth repeating that they are there for him to use not because they are uniquely poetical but because they are a normal and perfectly ordinary aspect of the semantic functions of language. As my remarks about late seventeenth-century functional prose style suggest, it takes a settled and highly sophisticated set of principles to remove them. It is almost impossible to sustain discourse without using novel metaphor, and it is almost impossible to do so without recourse to the primary signs of language. Even scientific writing, especially if the writer hopes to make an appeal to an audience beyond his immediate co-workers, makes use of some primary signs, particularly phonic sequences and assonance, which, because they are so hard to perceive unless one is looking for them, can be smuggled in subliminally.

Yet there are certain functions of primary signs almost inaccessible to the poet. If rhyme is a sign of adequacy, lack of rhyme is not; if alliteration and assonance are signs of demand, their absence is not; acceptance can be signified only by feminine line endings; long phonic sequences lose some of their primary sign power if all sequences are equally long. Thus Milton is continuously throwing single short sequences or patches of them into an environment of long sequences; and when Herrick writes a long poem he tends to lengthen his line and to use occasional long sequences to keep the short sequences semantically functional. The reason for this we have already seen: there is a barrier to phonic disintegration. The background of ordinary speech only seems random; when the poet tests it, it turns out to be already selective. Further, there seem to be no signs of openness and rejection. Attempts have been made to call back vowels dark and front vowels light or bright; it may be, but such judgments can usually be traced to the verbal semantic functions of the passage concerned. They seem to be merely examples of assonance, or demand. As for expression and inhibition, these can be incorporated into poetry only by using verbal signs adjusted to natural signs or configurational signs which function as primary signs for these behavioral attributes. This device is the only way, therefore, that the poet can introduce into poetry openness and rejection, inadequacy, and expression, and he also makes use of the primary sign functions of configurational signs for demand, adequacy, and all the rest. For the prose artist, such derived signs are nowadays almost the only way to get primary signs into language, except for long and short phonic sequences, which tend, however, to become pallid over any long discourse. This is particularly true of modern prose fiction. Almost the last major English prose artist to make use of some variety of phonic overdetermination for primary sign functions was Walter Pater. Again, it is obvious that for the artist who uses language, the employment of primary signs is under extra-artistic control. Primary signs belong to the semantic aspect of poetry. It must, however, always be remembered that primary signs are not unique to poetry. The spoken language uses them, prose uses them; and, above all, advertising makes a constant use of them. Primary signs form a characteristic of language, which poetry exploits, in response to extra-poetic cultural demands.

Before turning to painting, a word of explanation may be advisable. The reader may very well be put off by this discussion of primary signs in poetry and by the attempt to find in ordinary terms categorial equivalents for the various kinds of phonic overdetermination. If he feels annoyed and disgusted I shall not blame him in the least. I have adopted this position only with extreme reluctance. Of the existence of primary signs in the other arts, I have almost no doubt whatever, but poetry, which is so rich, which has all the resources of language, hardly needs them. But it will be observed that the *kind* of statement I have made in locating primary signs in poetry is, other than the reference to primary signs, of the kind constantly and traditionally made. Sound symbolism, for example, can be so easily explained as a means of intensification, and the identification of particular sounds with particular emotions or attitudes is so patently absurd and so easily disproved that it was easy for me to reject the whole notion. Nevertheless, it is so easy for man to tell the truth and so hard to lie, it is so obviously true that even in the sentence about the behavior of unicorns each term retained its conventional semantic functions, that I was forced to the conclusion that there are no empty categories, except those of mathematics and symbolic logic. In short, we always talk about something; we always refer to some set of perceptual categories. Though the term used may mislead both the user and the listener to ascribe the wrong attributes to a category, it does not follow that no category has been located and established. Though, to take a personal example, I have been an atheist since the age of seven, I do not believe that the term "God" is an empty category; it is, to me, a derived verbal sign of the sense of adequacy. It is all too easy to dismiss such words as metaphysical and meaningless. This has been the failure and indeed the vice of the great philosophical schools of positivism and philosophical analysis. Indeed, many advanced thinkers trained in those schools are currently engaged in trying to find a way to use metaphysics. It may not be about a transcendental realm of being, but it is about something. Language is always about something, some category or set of categories held together by structural signs.[14]

Thus the constant claims through centuries of criticism that the various kinds of phonic overdetermination are meaningful, are signs, have semantic functions, even though the significance of those signs was mistakenly located, forced me to the conclusion I have offered here. I have not really offered a new language for talking about phonic overdetermination; I have rather attempted to provide a correction for the current language, to make sense out of it, to find an empirical and intra-subjective set of references for it. We cannot, it appears, create brand-new languages which will do exactly what we want them to do: we can only correct, we can only sharpen, we can only make more precise the existing language and develop it through metaphor, which is so dangerously hard to interpret, even for its originator. To improve a verbal situation of any complexity requires a fairly solid underpinning, a fairly thorough-going theoretical structure to hold the corrected language up and to justify its claims. This I have attempted to provide. I can only hope that the reader will apply this proposed language of primary signs to some thousands of instances of phonic overdetermination, as I have, before he makes up his mind.

---

[14] For an example of the same sort of analysis, especially of what I have called "middle statements," which can be translated into operationally verifiable sentences about attitudes or orientations, see the report on the application of linguistic analysis to theology in *Time*, July 10, 1964, p. 64.

With this pseudo-apologia disposed of, it is now time to turn to the next art, painting.

4. SIGNS IN PAINTING

With two exceptions, of all cultures which present something we could call painting—Roman, Greek, Egyptian, Babylonian, Indian, Persian, Chinese, Japanese are the principal ones besides our own—I know of only two which have made use of configurational signs so thoroughly deprived of iconicity that they make use of the basic signs of children, the patch, the line, the circle, the square, and so on. These are the abstracts of the Australian bushmen of Melville Island and the abstracts of our own culture, beginning with the innovations of the early 1910's of Kandinsky and Malevich. The abstractions of the Cubists and their followers were characterized by lowered iconicity and the use of different configurational categories, simultaneous presentation of two or more aspects of an object of which, by the previous conventions of perspective, only one side could be presented, or at the most two. With the exception of "decorative" borders and panels, which are also based on children's non-iconic configurational signs, all other schools of painting have devoted themselves to various degrees and possibilities of iconicity. Since everything about the visual aspect of a perceptual field cannot be signified on a two-dimensional sign package, selection is necessary, and this, as we have seen, is done by categorial signs. "Configuration," then, refers not to the fact that the sign corresponds to a perceptual configuration but to the fact that it is developed out of children's non-iconic configurations by the addition of categorial information. Thus it may or may not have color, line, perspective, or any other depth convention, chiaroscuro, shading, or anything else of the sort. These are all conventions and may be used or dispensed with at will. The question is, is their presence or absence a matter of non-functional style? Do they belong to the conventional, that is, the semantic, aspect of painting, or to that aspect of which non-functional dynamism is the character? Or do some belong to one and some to the other?

We may begin with two comparatively simple examples. Portraits of the Madonna, which function as religious tools, began to appear very early in the Middle Ages. Making them for churches and eventually for homes was one of the primary social functions of painters for some centuries. Even after the cultural center began to be interested in secular matters, such work was the bread and butter not only of the ordinary painter but of those who were operating at the highest cultural levels. Madonna paintings were a prime means for non-functional stylistic innovation for a long time. Gradually, however, they moved away from the cultural center; the style became increasingly stabilized; and they began to be not the first paintings to show the emergence of a new non-functional style, but among the last. To-day, portraits as well as sculptures of the Madonna, as they are found in twentieth-century churches and most homes, show either Baroque stylistic features or nineteenth-century traits. Recent efforts to return Madonna paintings to the cultural center have been highly self-conscious and not very successful in meeting the demands of the relatively low cultural levels of which the mass of the faithful consists. Even the Madonnas of Rouault are collected by art lovers, not by ordinary Catholic laymen.

The reason for anything so obvious is not far to seek. It would be a mistake to say that the Catholic countries of Europe drifted away from the cultural center, but it would not be an error to assert that from the seventeenth century on, the cultural center moved away from the Catholic church, taking with it not only the philosophical, scientific, and humanistic innovators, but also the innovating artists, who certainly could have continued to use Madonna paintings for stylistic innovation if they had felt like it. A few of them, here and there, did, but even Maulpertsch, a Catholic in eighteenth-century Catholic Austria, innovated in the Rococo style of his contemporaries and innovated unconcernedly in both religious and secular subjects.

In painting Madonnas at all, then, the painters were responding to non-artistic cultural demands. On the other hand, non-functional styles came and went. For a time the newer styles appeared in such paintings, but after a while this kind of picture was left to artists willing to execute them in fossilized styles, or, to be more precise, styles in which the innovative rate was low. The same thing is true of landscapes. Having been established as a genre in the sixteenth century, landscape painting remained at the center until the revolution into modern style, at which time it too, like Madonna painting, was left stranded in styles showing a progressively lower rate of stylistic innovation as the twentieth century unfolded. Currently some artists are applying some of the devices of Abstract Expressionism to landscape, but this new mode has yet to be firmly accepted by the social center.

Another example seems at first to follow a different pattern. Up until the end of the sixteenth century, landscape depth was conventionally signified by planes. In the plane signified as nearest the perceiver, there was high iconicity, including color. In the second plane, colors were subdued to tones of brown, and in the third to tones of blue. This recession was further signified by reduction in scale according to the rules of perspective. Early in the seventeenth century a new convention emerged. The same conventions of color iconicity were now to be found to the point signified by perspectival convention as the most distant from the perceiver, nor was there a planar regression; frequently a road led from the foreground straight back to the horizon line. The effect was of a plunge into space. It would be easy to say that such a plunge was a mark of Baroque style and was part of the revolution in non-functional style which occurred in the years straddling 1600. And such statements of course have been made. But in that event, why did it not disappear as the Baroque style disappeared? On the contrary, it remained a standard device in landscape painting through the work of Gauguin and Van Gogh and Cézanne, although they used iconic conventions strikingly different from those of their predecessors. I shall offer later an explanation as to why this new device should have appeared when the Baroque style did, but it is obvious that, like Madonnas and landscapes, it appeared in response to other demands than those for non-functional stylistic innovation. If it was a sign, it was serving a function other than an artistic function.

One other example of this sort will be enough, the problem of iconicity itself. Iconicity is to configurational signs as predictiveness is to arbitrary signs. A portrait gives certain information about the sitter. The portrait painter implies that, in the absence of the sitter, the painting gives information about him which the observer can verify by examining the sitter after he examines the painting. The sitter may also be described in words, though the kind and reliability of the information will differ. (The painter can specify more exactly the color of the eyes than words can.) In either case, however, predictive information has been offered which can be verified. Iconicity, then, is the equivalent in configurational signs to predictiveness in verbal signs. It is, then, obvious that a painting is iconic, or has iconicity, to the degree that it gives such verifiable information. Iconicity is a quantitative aspect of painting, or of any kind of configurational signs.

To understand this problem better, it may be granted without further argument that to a Chinese, the conventions for presenting atmospheric perspective are as iconic as the different conventions of the West, which are geometric. But it is not necessary, however, to grant that the short-legged, big-headed African statues are as iconic as classic Greek statues. The African works are obviously less predictive than the Greek; the Chinese classic landscape paintings, however, give as much information about landscape depth as an etching by Rembrandt or a landscape by Rubens. This is the difference between iconic convention and iconic degree. That "illusion" is a matter of convention has been demonstrated with finality by E. H. Gombrich.[15] Within a continuum of convention, however, there may be degrees of iconicity. In China, landscape painting in the sixteenth century showed the same degree of iconicity as it did in the twelfth. Between the landscape painting of the Netherlands in the sixteenth century (Paul Brill) and that of the seventeenth (Hobbema) there is a profound difference. The convention of planar depth shifted to the convention of plunging depth, but both were controlled by the rules of perspective. On the other hand, the newer painting offered a higher degree of iconicity, because the highly iconic colors of the sixteenth-century foreground were now extended to the farthest point. This change in iconicity is exactly the change in the purely functional iconicity of anatomical drawings from the Middle Ages to the late nineteenth century, when it became stabilized.

In this connection, it is instructive to remember the first volume of John Ruskin's *Modern Painters*, published in 1845. After a general introduction on the scheme of the book, the rest of the first volume was devoted to what Ruskin called "truth," which is called here iconicity. Since iconicity is the configurational equivalent of predictiveness, I do not feel that Ruskin's term "truth" was badly chosen. Almost the entire volume was devoted to demonstrating that Turner's paintings and drawings showed greater iconicity than did the work of any of his predecessors. It is enough to compare any Turner landscape before 1830 with any Gainsborough landscape to see that Ruskin was quite right. He was insisting that Turner, using the conventions of his predecessors, had nevertheless put into his paintings more information about the real appearance of the world than anyone before him, that the eighteenth and seventeenth century painters were using conventions of iconicity without concern over their predictive powers, without checking on the iconicity, the attributional refinement of their

---

[15] In *Art and Illusion*, New York, 1960.

configurational categories. Actually, Ruskin's demand, though not so extensively, had been made by various predecessors in the nineteenth century. It is unquestionable that nineteenth-century Romantic painting, as we shall see later, was marked by a considerable and easily noticeable increase in iconicity. But then, as we have seen, so was Romantic poetry and prose fiction, with its "realistic" and "naturalistic" schools and their incorporation of vast amounts of easily confirmable predictive statements. Sociologists can use them, just as geographers and topographers can use nineteenth-century paintings. Everything leads us to believe that the novelist's information about the nineteenth-century individual psychology, culture, social life, and the Romantic painter's information about the appearance of the world and about, for example, the battles of the Italian Risorgimento are highly reliable. Further, this was the century of the invention of the daguerreotype, as well as the century of the invention of sociology and the separation of the physical and natural sciences from philosophy.

From these representative examples, which may be multiplied by a thousand by anyone, it is possible to make certain conclusions: Subject matter, or, more precisely, the configurational categories used by the painter, varies independently from nonfunctional style; so do primary signs, of which depth is one; so do the conventions of iconicity; so does the degree of iconicity. All of them may be and have been used in configurational sign fields which the culture has not used as occasions for performing the art perceiver's role. Not one of them, therefore, is a matter of non-functional stylistic dynamism. They are all under the control of the cultural forces on the other faces of the pyramid, to which the artist responds, which are prescriptions which he obeys and demands which he meets. This is true even when he himself originates the demands, for when he does so he is playing not an artist's role but a scientist's, a philosopher's, or a valuator's. In this kind of analysis it is an error to think of an individual as a "person," a unified entity; he is a package of roles, each played with varying patterns and a unique style.

Paintings which present fields of configurational signs of some degree of iconicity, therefore, present no particular problems as far as the conventional aspect of painting is concerned. But paintings which present fields of non-iconic configurational signs are a different matter and offer peculiar difficulties—or at least have offered peculiar difficulties as such painting has emerged in this century, to the public and to aestheticians alike. An aesthetics ethnocentrically built on the assumption that painting of high iconicity is the product of high culture, of the cultural apex, was, initially, at any rate, comparatively helpless towards Cubism and non-objective paintings, such as Kandinsky's and Mondrian's. Frequently it was antagonistic. I have heard with my own ears a famous aesthetician, one with important academic status, the author of a very large, though not very instructive, book about the arts, publicly sneer at all stylistic innovations in painting beginning with "Les Demoiselles d'Avignon." His reaction was like Braque's, but unlike Braque, he remained stuck in his cultural ethnocentricity. Even the matter of a slight shift in the conventions of iconicity has caused untold trouble. Manet caused considerable shock by adopting the conventions of photography in the 1850's, but the problem was hardly seen clearly and fully resolved before Gombrich's work. Even that had to wait until the development of modern perception theory, and even Gombrich, like Arnheim, is really directing his attention towards signs and not, as he imagines, towards art.

It is only decent and just to admit that I too was utterly bewildered when I saw my first exhibition of abstract painting, though little of it was of the non-objective variety. I mention this only because after I had begun to grasp it and had begun to play the perceiver's role before it with some success, I noticed a peculiar phenomenon which a good many others who had also taken the plunge into modern painting had likewise become aware of. Traditional painting began to look very different. It began to look, in an odd way, like abstract painting. Gradually it became apparent that modern painting had added nothing new to the old, that it had merely stripped away, totally or partially, the conventions and the degree of iconicity to reveal what was there all along. Comments of two of the originators of totally non-iconic painting are of some use here.

Under Suprematism I understand the supremacy of pure feeling in creative art.

To the Suprematist the visual phenomena of the objective world are, in themselves, meaningless; the significant thing is feeling, as such, quite apart from the environment in which it is called forth.

The so-called "materialization of a feeling in the conscious mind" really means a materialization of the *reflection* of that feeling through the medium of some realistic conception. . . .

Feeling is the determining factor . . . and thus art arrives at non-objective representation—at Suprematism.[16]

---

[16] *The Non-Objective World* by Kasimir Malevich, Chicago, 1959, p. 67. Copyright Paul Theobald and Company. Used by permission of Paul Theobald and Company.

The following is Kandinsky's own analysis of the famous "Improvisation, No. 30," at the Chicago Art Institute, the one with the cannons.

> The contents . . . are indeed what the spectator *lives* or *feels* while under the effect of the *form and color combinations* of the picture. . . . This entire description is chiefly an analysis of the picture which I have painted rather subconsciously in a state of strong inner tension.[17]

Both artists are in agreement on two matters: first, such painting is concerned with feeling, second, it is a representation of feeling. Translated into the language used here, a painting is a sign of a feeling state. Malevich further insists that such feeling states are independent of the environment: therefore the artist should not present the environment in the painting. Kandinsky, in his title, "Improvisation," clearly suggests that he believes that what he is doing has some relation to music. And indeed, non-objective painting, as well as abstract painting, has been called "visual music" by the English author-painter Wyndham Lewis, among others.

It is reasonably plain, I think, that what Malevich and Kandinsky are talking about is what I have called primary signs, or non-situational signs, non-environmental, as Malevich would call them. (It will be remembered that "situation" has been defined above as "interpreted environment.") Malevich is asserting that he does not wish to interpret the environment to get at the feeling. In a passage on the same page he makes it clear that he thinks that, although only feeling signs give value to a painting, academic naturalism can also have value, since, in spite of themselves, such painters (he includes Cézanne among them) present, submerged by their environmental information, feeling signs.

His insistence that only such signs have value is of course merely another instance of any innovating artist's insistence that he, and he alone, has discovered what true painting really is. It need not be taken seriously. The importance of both passages lies in the testimony they offer that non-objective art was a matter of making explicit those "feeling states" which are separable from a particular situation because they are found in all situations. This, obviously, is virtually the definition offered above of primary signs. However, in his book Malevich offers also evidence that he would not have made his great

---

[17] As quoted in David M. Robb, *The Harper History of Painting: The Occidental Tradition*, New York, 1951, p. 819.

discovery had it not been for the cultural situation in which he found himself. As he says, Suprematism could also be called aeronautical painting, because he was stimulated by aerial photographs of cities and by photographs of flying planes. Both of these, particularly the latter, bear striking resemblance to some of his paintings. It was, he tells us, new ways of looking at the world, new sky patterns, and new ground patterns, which made him realize that the traditional ways of looking were conventions, or, as he calls them, illusions. Thus, even the new ways were illusions. The only thing not an illusion was what was in common to both. This phenomenon we have met before. The pertinent passage may be quoted here once more.

> When an individual is deprived of any objective means of stabilizing his perceptions, he will establish an internal point of reference for this purpose.[18]

As an artist, accustomed to dealing with primary signs, though he had not known it, Malevich stabilized his perceptions by establishing an internal point of reference in his feeling states. But instead of merely saying he felt odd, as an ordinary man would do, Malevich categorized the experience and thus was able to make explicit in his paintings the signs of the attributes of all behavior, regardless of the situation.

Now if one looks at my behavior in this book as tied to a cultural situation which I cannot transcend, if I look at myself operating within a cultural field without attempting to get out of it, because I know that I cannot, it becomes apparent that my development of the notion of "primary sign" arose exactly as Malevich's did. I felt that there was something in common to both the old painting and the new. This is all the more probably because I was haunted by Malevich's "White on White"[19] from the day I first saw it, just as I was haunted by Lewis's and others' references to abstract painting as visual music. I did not know what the phrase meant, nor I believe did they, but I was convinced that like the term "God" it meant something, that it was the product of seeing something common to conventionally quite different categories of perception. The famous statement, which I shall return to, that "Architecture is frozen music," has much the same quality. It is a metaphor; but is the imported term "frozen music" or merely "frozen"? Does the sentence "Architecture is music" mean anything, if "is" is interpreted here not as a statement

---

[18] Barnett, *Innovation*, p. 116.
[19] Painted in 1918, it now hangs in the Museum of Modern Art, New York.

of identity but a statement that both referential terms belong to the same category? It is as if Kandinsky were asserting with his title "Improvisation" that "Painting can be frozen music."

Finally, the title of Kandinsky's volume of 1912, *Über das Geistige in der Kunst*, or *On the Spiritual in Art*, is of some help. This was written in 1910, before he had created his first non-objective pictures, but after he had freed color from iconicity and had begun, under the influence of the Fauves, to reduce the iconicity of bounded forms.

> The leading idea of his book . . . is that a harmony of colours and forms "can only be based on a purposive contact with the human soul" and that "composition is a combination of colored and graphic forms which exist independently, which are summoned up by an inner necessity and, thus living together, come to form a whole that we call a picture." But this does not preclude the possibility that the inner vibration may be provoked by a represented object. . . .
>
> How Kandinsky moved slowly away from object-signs and at the same time fashioned a pictorial organism capable of sustaining the new communicative signs can be clearly discerned in the series of "Compositions," as his great works are entitled.[20]

Haftmann has translated "Geist" as "Soul" rather than "Spirit." Either one will do. "Spirit" and "Spiritual" are terms like "mind," "mental," "thought," "soul," and, to my mind, "God." They hypostatize pseudo-entities. Nevertheless, "spirit," like those terms, is not an empty category. As Kandinsky uses the term, it seems to have the same semantic function as it has when we talk about the "spirit of a place," "the spirit of a poem," or the "spirit of Bach's organ fugues." We are talking about something pervasive, something that abides from moment to moment or spot to spot in spite of phenomenal differentia. We appear to be referring to an attribute of a category of identity or a conjunctive category which is always present, no matter how widely distributed in time or space are the perceptual configurations which, for us, make up that category. Again, Kandinsky, like Malevich, seems to be separating some attribute of behavior from the situations in response to which behavior takes place. I cannot forbear emphasizing that Haftmann, as I do, regards Kandinsky's non-iconic configurations as "signs."

I have inserted this discussion of Malevich and Kandinsky, together

---

[20] *Painting in the 20th Century*, by Werner Haftmann, New York, 1960, p. 140. Copyright Frederick A. Praeger, Inc. Used by permission of Frederick A. Praeger, Inc.

with something of my own experiences with modern painting, to gain, frankly, the sympathy of the reader. As I have already suggested, it seems to me that he must find the status of primary signs highly questionable. I am trying here to discourage cooperative readers from accepting that status too readily, to encourage the doubtful, and to persuade the stubborn by flourishing something that looks like evidence and may very well be evidence.

It appears, then, that the basic configurational signs of children can be developed into primary signs as well as into iconic signs, but that in the history of painting they were developed simultaneously, as in poetry. We cannot know, of course, the perceptual mode of thousands of years ago. The earliest configurational signs we have found are already so highly developed that it seems necessary to postulate a long previous development of configurational signs executed, perhaps, first on sand and soft earth and clay, then on skins and easily worked materials like wood, and then only on materials which it takes some previous skill to manage at all, bone, ivory, and stone, and which are not affected by organic decay. "Man's oldest paintings," a phrase so often applied to the great Aurignacian and Magdalenian cave-paintings of southern France and northern Spain, should not be interpreted to mean, as it so often is, "the first human art." It is merely the oldest we moderns have discovered. These ancient works of at least ten thousand years ago and not more than fifty show clearly, though at a very slow rate, non-functional stylistic change, but I think that it would be correct to say that the first use of configurational signs was purely functional. Only when non-functional stylistic dynamism begins to appear can we say that artistic behavior has begun in painting, and when that was we can never know. There is, however, every reason to guess that it first began in gesture and verbal behavior—dancing and oral literature.

Further, the first examples of configurational signs we have are both iconic and non-iconic. The chances are that the former were emblems, derived from verbal signs. Some of them may very well be empty signs, or signs of numbers. It is impossible to tell. But the first primary sign one can reasonably be sure of is rhythm, sequences of overlapping animals highly suggestive of an effort to create a sign of behavioral smoothness. If the dance was the first, or one of the first, successful attempts to make explicit pervasive attributes of human behavior, it was surely behavioral smoothness that it signified. It is not surprising, therefore, to see such primary signs appear in the paintings of animals, both in the caves and on bones. In discussing the great cave paintings, it is common to say, also, that man felt himself small and ugly and weak beside the beauty of the animals he pursued as sources of energy. Though I have seen this statement innumerable times,[21] I find it singularly unconvincing; it seems to ascribe to early man characteristically modern notions. Nevertheless the observation is just. What one feels above all in such a cave as Lascaux is the sense that these animals are perfect. They seem deities, so majestic, so powerful, are they, so capable of overcoming all obstacles. If they were not divine, we see in them to-day the attributes of divinity.

They are, I think, the first signs we have of adequacy and demand, explicit attributes of human behavior, but executed before such primary significance had been stabilized in configurational signs as light and verticality. Siegfried Giedion has shown how primitive man had not yet organized sign fields vertically and horizontally; verticality and horizontality emerged only in the first civilizations, in Egypt and lower Mesopotamia.[22] But it is worth noting the cave paintings could only be painted and seen by artificial light. Since there are no torch smudges, the light seems to have come from lamps made of shells and hollowed bits of stone filled with animal fat, with clumps of moss as wicks. Presumably only part of an animal could be seen at a time, and then he would be seen as emerging into the patch of light thrown by three or four of these lamps. If one were sufficiently moved and disturbed, the patch of light in the absolute blackness of the cave might appear motionless, and the glorious animal would float tranquilly into it. Light is the sign of the divine, of the sense of adequacy. Certainly by the seventeenth century it had long been so conventionalized.

One of the striking developments of the late sixteenth century, the invention, it is generally thought, of Caravaggio, was "cellar lighting." The entire signified volume beyond the surface of the painting is dark, except for a shaft of light from above. Rembrandt picked up this device and used it so much it became a kind of trademark. In religious pictures the light invariably strikes upon the principal religious figure present, God, Christ, an Apostle, a Saint. This is certainly consistent with the suggestion that "God" is an explicit verbal sign for the sense of adequacy. Yet "God" cannot be a primary sign, for the striking

---

[21] Notably in Gertrude Rachel Levy's *The Gate of Horn*, London, 1949, and in the first volume of Siegfried Giedion's *The Eternal Present, The Beginnings of Art*, New York, 1957.

[22] *The Eternal Present: II: The Beginnings of Architecture*, New York, 1964.

thing about primary signs is that they cannot be hypostatized into pseudo-entities. The reason is that they are non-situational and pervasive; hence they cannot be conventionally identified with a situational configuration. On the other hand, they can be the source for derived signs, or emblems. In Genesis God says, "Let there be light," which can easily be judged as what I have called a middle statement and translated into, "I want to experience the sense of adequacy in meeting the demands of the environment." But light can also be made into an emblem for divinity, probably by derivation through a verbal sign. In Christian iconography light is often an emblematic sign for God.

An indication, however, that light is more than a mere emblem for deity, that it is a primary sign, is to be found in Watteau's first version of "A Pilgrimage to Cythera" (see Plate I). This painting, mistakenly retitled "The Embarkation for Cythera" in the late eighteenth century, dates from 1717.[23] The scene is a low rounded hill beyond which opens out a deep arm of the sea, with a great range of snow-capped mountains on the horizon. In the foreground, on the right, placed against and among a clump of trees, are a herm of Venus and seen through the trees, the phallus of a herm, presumably of Priapus. To the left are three pairs of lovers in sequence, culminating at the center of the picture. The figures on the left of the picture consist of a crowd of lovers, partially organized into pairs, who are lining up to enter a boat, the prow of which is headed into the darkness at the left side. The extreme lower left is filled by a dead tree, dark brown in color. The most brilliant light falls on the first pair of lovers on the right, each successive pair reflects less light, and the final pair to the extreme left is half obscured by shadow. At the extreme right intense light falls upon the breasts of Venus, the roses twining about her herm, and the erect phallus of Priapus.

Cythera is the island sacred to Venus, whither she was wafted by the winds after she was born from the impregnation of the sea by the phallus of Uranos, severed from his body by his son, Kronos. Aphrodite and Priapus are the gods of sexual adequacy, or, more precisely, of erotic adequacy. Sexuality is environmental, but eroticism is the interpretation of that environmental feature. Eroticism is situational. Cythera, then, is the setting or stage for Aphrodite and Priapus, erotic

---

[23] Édouard Michel, *et al.*, *Watteau: "L'Embarquement pour l'Île de Cythère,"* Paris, (?1939).

adequacy. After worshipping at their shrines, the lovers are homeward bound, back to the world of ordinary eroticism, marked by the sense of inadequacy. The farther the lovers are from the herms and from their shrine, which is a sacred grove of lush trees, the more each pair interacts with other pairs, and the darker the lighting. At the extreme left are not only the dead tree, but also a great pile of rocks. These are emblems for death, just as the living trees are emblems for life. The situation in which these emblems are found requires they be interpreted as "erotic life," and "erotic death." In religious pictures they are emblems of religious life and death. The primary significance of light, then, is consonant with other signs and emblems.

The use of depth and shallowness is similarly consonant. In the foreground on the right, at the entrance to the shrine, is a pair of lovers closer to each other than any other pair, and the boundary of their configuration shows less overlap with the boundary of another pair than does that of any other pair. To their right, between them and the herms, sits a cupid. The cupids on the left are flying away. The first pair of lovers also sits within a kind of half cave or shelter made by the trunk and branches of a great tree. Their shelter is dark, is shadowed, though they are brilliantly lit, a touch that not only increases the brilliance but adds a touch of poignancy, a threat of inadequacy. The sun is setting, and the whole landscape is filling up with shadow; the sense of adequacy is slowly being drained away. The title should be "The Embarkation *from* Cythera." Nevertheless they are at least partially sheltered, they are on the threshold of the shrine. The energy expenditure required for the erotic attack and initial encounter is no longer necessary. But they are on the line of a diagonal across the painting from lower right to middle left, and along this diagonal is the great arm of the sea, lying between the rocks of a mountain on the left and the foothills of the great mountain range in the background. This vast lunge into space thrusts almost infinitely into the background. One would at first think that this lunge, the primary sign of energy release, should be to the right, toward the shrine and the most fulfilled, though not entirely consummated, pair of lovers. And this would have been just as possible. It would, however, have had a different meaning. Here the thrust is to the left, in the direction of the departure of the lovers. In this situation that tremendous depth signifies the enormous expenditure of energy it takes to tear oneself away from a consummate erotic situation. And this is consonant with the regretful backward glance of the woman of the central pair, who is being led away by her lover, whose pilgrim staff links them with the lovers who have left the isolation of eroticism and have returned to normal social interaction.

But, as so often with primary signs, there is another probable semantic function here for the penetration into space. Far in the distance toward the setting sun lies a vision of a paradise which human lovers can never attain. It lies far beyond the lovers preparing to sail into the darkness off the left of the picture, a darkness immediately beneath the termination of the plunge into clouds brilliantly illuminated by the setting sun, a glowing light into which the cupids are flying away. A complete release of erotic energy would take humans to the perfect and consummate erotic adequacy of the gods, but this human lovers can never achieve. This is what accounts for the tragic note in a painting in which the most obvious signs are highly iconic configurational signs of lovers.

Horizontality and verticality are also at work here. In painting as in architecture, verticality is the sign of demand, horizontality of acceptance. It has already been suggested that these attributes have also been conventionalized in the masculine and feminine roles; such attributes come out very strongly in this picture, for one of the sharpest and most conspicuous vertical accents is the brilliantly lit erection of Priapus. The oldest goddesses are of the earth, goddesses of the horizontal plane, while male gods emerge invariably in verticality. Perhaps the first primary sign of demand was the erect phallus of the most primitive man. At any rate, here verticality is predominant in the right third of the painting, in the dominating tree of the sacred grove, in the verticality of the pink robe of the first woman on the right, in the herm of Aphrodite. The sacred grove and shrine of Venus is where one should make demands. Each of the pairs of lovers on the right has strong verticality, but on the left the crowd of lovers is organized into a horizontally extended mass. Most significant of all, a fallen branch of the dead and mutilated vertical tree in the lower left corner is absolutely horizontal, and that horizontality is reinforced by its division into a group of horizontal twigs. Further, even the great vertical lush tree at the right extends a brown half-dead branch which curves into almost perfect horizontality and points to the left, the area in which the lovers, returning from Cythera to ordinary life, have no choice but to accept the inadequacy of ordinary eroticism. Similarly, in the background, the home of the Gods, a vast peak rears up a strong vertical cliff, brilliantly illuminated by the setting sun. Only the gods make their demands with impunity. Yet, in the left lower quarter of the picture, the horizontal group of lovers breaks up into strong vertical accents, extended by the two figures of the supernatural oarsmen and the prow of the boat, as well as by the vertical mass of the cliff rocks, and the mutilated tree-trunk. The mutilation is an emblem of half-destroyed masculinity, or demand; the emblematic function is emphasized by repeating in the silhouette of trunk and mutilated limb the herm and phallus of Priapus. Nevertheless, the verticality is part of the area of demand assembled with signs of inadequacy and energy conservation. This area offers, as it were, consolation, and prevents the picture from being entirely tragic. One need not surrender entirely to the limits of ordinary eroticism. There will always be the memory, a point emphasized by the fact that the last pair of lovers on the left is looking back towards the other lovers and in the direction of the shrine; perhaps the suggestion is also that though one must leave Cythera's isle as adequacy and demand fade, they will return, and one can come back to the shrine of Aphrodite and Priapus.

Blackness and whiteness also have significance in relation to this erotic situation. The largest area of white is the dress of the woman at the extreme right. One other woman wears an only partly visible underdress of white and a short white pilgrim's cape; another has a white sleeve and another what appears to be a white blouse or kerchief or possibly pilgrim's cape. The largest area of whiteness, then, is associated with the woman who is most open to the advances of her lover, and this openness is picked up by the white sleeve of the cupid sitting between her and the herms. Yet the cupid wears a short black pilgrim's cape, as does her lover, the lover in the center of the picture, and one other man and two women. The cupid dressed in black and white combines the two signs: in love it is necessary to be both absolutely open to the demands of the lover, and, on other occasions, absolutely closed, insistent on one's own way, like the Wild Ones.[24]

---

[24] The obvious question here, the kind of question invariably raised when any interpretation of a semiotic-structure is offered, is, "Did Watteau intend all this?" The first answer is, "I have no idea." The past is irrecoverable, and the covert and implicit intentions of any absent originator of a semiotic structure can never be recovered, or known. (For an extended discussion of the empirical status of historical sentences see the "Introduction" to my *Beyond the Tragic Vision*, New York, 1962.) Any interpretation of any sign depends upon a knowledge of the conventions governing the semantic functions of the sign and the situations in which they are used. But, as we have seen above, this knowledge need not be "conscious,"

The pilgrims' capes are worth a note on emblems. From at least the fourteenth century on, religion was used as a metaphor for eroticism, and eroticism for religion. Such a conventionalization of interchangeable local and imported terms is unusual. Which was which depended, of course, on the situation in which the metaphor appeared. What made the conventionalization so easy was that erotic and religious experiences both require and offer a total focussing of the entire interpretative powers. Such stabilized focusing can produce a state something like a trance; in both kinds of experience it was frequently labeled an "ecstasy," and Donne so uses the term in his poem of that title. By the time Watteau painted this picture, the erotic-religious metaphor was so much of a cliché that he needed to introduce only the short cape and the staff. Here they are emblems for the erotic-religious ecstasy and for the devotion required for a perilous journey to a distant shrine. That distance, of course, is a psychic distance from ordinary experience, of which the predominant character is not focussing but orientative scanning.

Black and white, and color in general, have been heatedly argued about; the arguments are reminiscent of the arguments over alliteration. Do colors signify specific attitudes, or do they not? Certainly,

---

that is, explicit in other signs. If signs function by controlling behavior, the individual whose behavior is thus controlled need not know the "meaning" of the signs that perform the governing. ("Meaning" refers to the explicit statement of a semantic function by using another sign.) When an individual originates signs, either to control someone else's behavior or to control his own, he does not simultaneously translate them into other signs or control his sign behavior by such translation. We often say, "I know what x means, but I can't put it into words." And such statements, which have been subjected to much ridicule, are, from this point of view, perfectly comprehensible and perfectly correct. We put a sign into a structure of verbal signs because it "feels" right to put it there. For example, in the sentence, "He milked the cow," we put "the" before "cow" not because we can give a linguistic analysis of the semantic function of "the" but simply because our cultural conventions demand that we put it there. It feels "wrong" to omit it. In the same way, it feels right to say either, "He milked cows" or "He milked the cows," depending upon the situation; either is English, but "He milked cow" is not. However, at some future time it very well may feel right, if it is conventionalized for a particular category of situations. Making explicit the semantic functions of signs is, in fact, a characteristic of the highest cultural level, from which, through public education, it has filtered down to the lower levels. But primitives, for example, use signs just as well as we do, though they have neither lexicon (explicit statements of semantic functions) nor syntax (explicit statements of the rules which govern the use of structural signs). Watteau used the various primary signs as he did because it *felt* right to use them that way in the particular situation of this painting.

they are effective in various kinds of therapy, both physical and psychiatric. Hospitals have discovered that a patient gets better sooner in a room with colored walls rather than white ones. If white is a primary sign for the absolute openness of a sacrificial victim, it is not surprising that this should be so. Even so, neither commercial color experts nor psychiatrists agree on what each color signifies, though all agree that color has significance. The following statement by a woman who has spent many years using "art" in psychotherapy is, however, illuminating.

> I have found that certain colors do tend to be associated with some universal human experience. Black, as you would expect, is chosen to express depression and mourning and hatred against self. When it is used in combination with red it is frequently an expression of hatred, hostility or rage against a parent. Red, alone, is often associated with blood, and has been used to express various degrees of intense feeling, ranging from passionate warmth to anger or rage. Green has frequently appeared as a positive feeling in relation to growth and self-development. The meaning of blue seems to vary, according to the tone and quality of its color: deeper dark tones may be interpreted as depressive; bright and brilliant blues as joyous; and delicate tones are often spoken of as related to pure and ethereal feelings. A combination of flame and orange color often expresses positive and hopeful emotions. The exception to this occurs, sometimes, if a fire image is employed to express destruction. However, I have found that patients have always used yellow as a positive color, to express such feelings as joy and reaffirmation of life.[25]

One patient "was an extremely repressed and insecure boy, who refused to express an opinion about anything." As he gradually emerged and became more capable of expression—of signifying his attitudes—the colors in his drawings moved from predominantly brown through magenta to red, green, and yellow. Other patients cited show progression in the same direction, from dark blacks, purples, and reds, to scarlets, greens, and yellows.

Miss Naumburg's investigations appear to make it impossible to associate a particular color with a particular emotional state. The significance of a color lies in its place on a continuum; a color appears to be a sign not of a particular emotion but of a certain balance between inhibition (repression) and semiotic freedom (expression). The continuum can perhaps also be seen as running from compulsion to

---

[25] "Expanding Non-Verbal Aspects of Art Education on the University Level," by Margaret Naumburg, *Journal of Aesthetics and Art Criticism*, XIX, 1961, pp. 444–445. Copyright, *Journal of Aesthetics and Art Criticism*. Used by permission of The American Society for Aesthetics.

freedom. At one end lies a narrow range of interpretational possibility, at the other a sense that one can interpret situations to one's own benefit. I once knew an artist who, when he painted oils, permitted himself only grays and very dark colors, mostly purples and reds; but when he made block prints, cutting the designs in slabs of seasoned oak, he was able to print them in bright colors with a heavy emphasis on greens and yellows. He was the son of a Pennsylvania Polish coal miner, and felt very guilty that he was spending his life in something so physically easy as art. Thus, apparently, he could permit himself expression only when he earned the right to it through the hardest work his metier permitted him, cutting delicate designs in oak slabs.

There would seem, actually, to be two dimensions at work. One is the color range from dark purple through blue, red, and green to yellow. The other is the saturation of the color, which depends on its admixture with black or with white. Thus in a given continuum, as Miss Naumburg suggests, signification is not only a matter of color but also of saturation. An admixture of white pushes the color toward the positive end of the spectrum, of black towards the negative end. These last colors are often called "brooding," a recognition of their significance of inhibition through withdrawal from open interpretational expression. In any assemblage of color signs, consequently, it is not merely a question of which end of the range is the predominant color but also what continua of color and of saturation are at work within the sign area.

Color reproduction, however, is so unreliable that one must always speak with extreme caution unless one has the picture before him, and even then, fading, dirt, and cleaning, which can remove glazes and often has, can change the original color signification. Ruskin insists that the most glowingly colored of Turner's late masterpieces were, less than a decade after his death, only wrecks of what they originally had been. This misfortune, if it really happened, was the result of Turner's constant experimentation with color media and his use of different media in the same work. I have been informed that the rather dull colors of Sargent's murals in the Boston Public Library and in the Art Museum are a consequence of his having used kerosene as a medium. I have never seen two reproductions of Watteau's "Pilgrimage" with the same color character, and the original makes a total color impression different from that of any reproduction I know.

Nevertheless, a few points may be made. The deepest reds may be found at the left, while the woman in the white dress wears a pink cloak close in color to the roses on Venus' herm. This seems to be a way of signifying the sense of relative inhibition in ordinary social interaction as compared with the ease of expression in a successful erotic situation. Again, reading from left to right, the blues, at first grayish, become increasingly saturated, and then become brighter with the admixture of white. Because I am not in Paris, I prefer to say little more on the subject, except that the picture as a whole has a golden tone, particularly in what I have called the area of the gods, the great sunset illumination in the distance. A further example may be found in the trees of the shrine area. In the foreground, the foliage is relatively brown, but there are holes in this green-brown area through which shine saturated and light greens. In the upper right-hand corner, diagonally opposite the brown mutilated tree trunk, is a patch of intense green, only a little brighter than saturation. This effect is consonant with the hint from the primary symbols throughout the right-hand third of the painting that perfect consummation of eroticism has not been achieved, or perhaps that the climax of it is over.

Finally there come the aspects of rhythm, impulse and process. In painting, the former is signified by the regularity of recurrence of identical or similar configurations, the latter by smoothness of line, which in iconic art appears as the boundary of a configuration. Again, as might be predicted from the analysis of primary signs so far, the three groups of lovers on the right are more regularly disposed than those on the left; in the latter, the identity of pairs is lost in one area and nearly lost in another. This is redundant with other signs, because the isolated pairs on the extreme left form not only a different kind of configuration—an implied rectangle rather than an implied triangle—but also have lost the intimacy of those on the right. The boundaries of the configurations are equally informative. At the extreme right the implied triangle is more explicit than in the next configured pair, and so on. Considerable confusion then ensues, and the relatively explicit rectangle emerges to contain the final pair on the left. One moves from relative smoothness of boundary line through extreme irregularity to relative smoothness, that is, from easy eroticism through a difficult period of transition to easy social interaction. What is thus signified is a transition from the erotic role to the social and courtly role. This is echoed at the extreme left of the picture. A cupid is arranging a red cloth canopy over the more or less regularly broken outline of the prow of the boat which is to take the lovers back to normal life. The edge of this canopy, which disappears off the edge of the canvas, is almost perfectly straight. It is the longest straight edge in the picture. It contrasts with the rhythmical undulations of the body of the statue of Aphrodite, with, on the right, the easy flow of erotic process from one stage to the next, and with, on the left, the straight line of conventionalized patterns of polite interaction. It makes one think of the wonderfully expressive modern configurational metaphor. "He's a square." That is, "He has little orientative and interpretative flexibility."

Obviously, this kind of analysis should be pushed only as far as the individual thinks appropriate. In all these matters there are compositional or formal interests which have no sign function at all. To these I shall turn in the next chapter. The principle of such analysis, however, is clear enough. It is based on the appearance of the same kind of sign in similar situations and on consonance in the same situation. From these it is possible to abstract the primary significance, as I proposed with "God" and "light," and then to see it at work in at first surprising situations. Applied to this painting, the analysis of primary signs provides what appears to be an explanation for what almost every commentator has remarked, its union of pathos and consolation, of tragedy and comedy, an explanation for its fascinatingly ambiguous and ambivalent character.

One final note about painting before architecture is considered. When Picasso introduced verbal signs into his Cubist paintings, he caused considerable surprise and shock. But the introduction of verbal signs is by no means a novelty. It was standard practice to introduce the names of saints into religious paintings and verbal signs into allegorical tapestries—Fortitudo, Patientia, and the like. Thus the sign field offered in juxtaposition both the configurational emblem and the verbal sign from which it was derived. This practice, of course, is standard in the emblematic sign fields of political cartoons. This is not an artistic problem at all. It is standard in sign packaging, as on maps. It was only an extra-artistic demand of the other faces of the pyramid, the requirements for high iconicity, that required the artist to give up the practice. This is not a very important question for painting, but it is more important for architecture, and of the highest importance for music. In art and out of it, primary signs are invariably present in configurational and verbal sign fields, and there is no reason why a configurational sign field should not include or be accompanied by spoken or written verbal signs. Most paintings have titles, usually affixed to the frame, and Rossetti inscribed his own poems on the frames of some of his pictures. I see no reason why a painting should not be accompanied by a poem, recorded on tape or on disks, which one could play, as one wished, when one wanted to enjoy the painting. Indeed, an exhibition of such paintings opened in New York in July, 1964. The problem seems most important when words are sung to music, but it is really no problem at all.

This is not a matter of the relationships of the arts. That a painter should illustrate a poem, or that a poet should write a poem for a picture, or that Debussy should write a piano piece on the painting we have just examined, has nothing to do with art. At least fifteen different sign systems are at work in any ordinary production of a play. This is entirely a matter of the semantic aspect of art, of adjusting the categories of one sign field to those of another, or creating an ironic relationship, like saying, "Why you *bastard!*" in a friendly tone. Whatever may be the identifying attribute of art, it is responsible for non-functional stylistic dynamism, and the semantic aspect is a functional aspect, under extra-artistic control. It is only a demand of the other faces of the pyramid that determines whether or not an artist combines configurational signs with verbal signs. It has nothing to do with the unique demands of his role as artist.

5. SIGNS IN ARCHITECTURE

Architecture offers configurational signs, both iconic and non-iconic, of the sort found in both painting and sculpture, but it has its own kind of configurational sign as well. Like music, however, its greatest power lies in its presentation of primary signs. As we shall see, this is one reason why architecture has so often been categorized with music.

I have been able to find no information on the source for the sign material of architecture such as Arnheim and Mrs. Kellogg provide for the emergence in child behavior of these configurational signs which can be developed into both the iconic and non-iconic signs of painting. Nevertheless it is perfectly obvious that children improvise three-dimensional signs as well as two-dimensional. This has, of course, been institutionalized in giving children blocks to play with, and the again famous Montessori method capitalizes on the child's desire to create signs of solids and of spaces. There is one modern instance, however, which shows a striking parallel to Kandinsky's and Malevich's recovery of children's non-iconic configurational signs. When he was seven, Frank Lloyd Wright was given the "gifts" of Friedrich Froebel (1782–1852), the great German inventor of the kindergarten.

> In 1876, Mr. and Mrs. Wright . . . traveled from Boston to Philadelphia to "take in" the great Centennial Exposition of that year. In the welter of Victorian things spread out to view in Fairmount Park, Mrs. Wright made, for her, a tremendous discovery; an exhibit setting forth the principles of the new Froebelian kindergarten concept. She was fascinated by the clean toys, the intelligent way in which the games were organized, and the conversation of the young woman in charge. . . . Here, indeed, was a radical departure in child education which, Mrs. Wright believed, she could put into practice back in the Weymouth parsonage. It seemed to her that her son particularly (whom she had predestined to be a builder) could not fail to derive a sense of structure and a feeling for simple materials from playing with the wonderful Froebelian toys. She made up her mind—and, in so doing, contributed one source of influence upon her son's career which seems certain and undeniable. Frank Lloyd Wright is fully aware of the enduring effect of his kindergarten experience, and he used to speak of it to George Elmslie. No doubt he also discussed it with Robert Spencer, who so wisely stressed it in his valuable early article on Wright (1900), pointing out that Wright was probably the only American architect of his generation to have received kindergarten training.[26]

Only an examination of Manson's juxtaposition of drawings of the Froebel games with photographs and drawings of Wright's subsequent work can give one a sense of the astounding resemblance between the two. It is no exaggeration to say that Wright became the first great modern architect because at the advanced age of seven—this is no irony—the continuity of childish space and solid manipulation with adult spaces and solids was institutionally established. Thus the recovery of the child's pre-iconic and pre-primary sign improvisation was common to both modern painting and modern architecture. Gertrude Stein and, to a lesser degree, James Joyce did the same thing; they discovered the link between adult high-level literature and the phonic over-determination games of the child.[27] Music, however, has such a rich set of rules that in spite of the new freedom in pitch and harmony Schönberg achieved; it was not until the aleatoric (random) music of the 1950's that the recovery of the childish base for music was accomplished.

---

[26] Extracted from *Frank Lloyd Wright: The First Golden Age*, 1958, by Grant Manson, p. 5, with permission of Reinhold Publishing Company.

[27] See above, Section 3 of this chapter.

Even a cursory examination of how a child plays with blocks, especially if it is enriched by what memory can summon of one's own play, shows that he is manipulating three-dimensional signs of his environment. Like the two-dimensional signs which are developed perhaps simultaneously into the culturally conventionalized primary and iconic semantic functions, a block or any solid is a sign of any solid shape, and a void of any hollow space. But, as modern architectural interpreters have insisted, it has been a mistake to think that architecture is an art only of solids and hollows. The examination of children's play shows two other configurational signs of equal importance to the architect and the architectural perceiver: light and movement. The experience of a work of architecture is not that of standing still and looking at a defined spacial field. Architecture is the least defined of all the arts. We move towards architecture, into it, through it. Its absolute scale constantly changes as we approach, and even changes relatively, because if we are far enough away from it, the other objects—trees, bushes, human beings, animals—by which its relative scale is judged, are too small to be identified. Perhaps this is one of the many reasons why the greatest Egyptian pyramids were placed so far from human habitation. Only when the perceiver is close enough to use himself as a scale can their size be comprehended. When, moreover, we consider that moving into a work of architecture is as important as approaching it or moving through its hollow interior, it is apparent that to empty space and solid form must be added the screen, which is interpreted as a screen rather than one face of a solid only when it is apparent that it can be penetrated. Approach, penetration, and dynamic or static containment are the elements of architectural experience. This is one source of the common categorization of architecture and music. Music flows, as it were, around us, as if we were standing in a river. In architectural experience, the reverse is the case: we flow through a building and its spaces.

One further element contributes to the dynamic character of architectural experience: light. This is, of course, most obvious in enclosed interiors, but it is equally important to the exterior of a building, and in two ways. At high noon the Grand Canyon seems absolutely flat, a painted backdrop, but as the sun is rising or descending the enormous distance from rim to rim becomes obvious. At noon, the southern face of a building can look as if it were cut out of paper and the north face can have an almost equal lack of definition. Further, if we approach a building on any line except one running between the sun and the center of the facade, the relative proportion of light and shadow changes as we near it. A building approached on a winding directional path, therefore, shows this dynamic element as well as continuously changing shape and a constant sliding back and forth against the background. A building is a fixed object, but nothing could be more fluid than our experience of it. Only in the twentieth century has this been fully realized. In his extraordinarily sensitive discussion of Greek religious architecture Vincent Scully offers remarkable insights into the dynamic nature of architectural experience.[28]

This emphasis on the function of light in the visual experience of approach, penetration, and containment sounds like a justification for the orthodox Freudian explanation of an interest in architecture as the sublimation of a voyeuristic fascination with the sexuality of the human body. But the Freudian explanation suffers from the same disadvantage as all Freudian interpretations: the interpretation of all experience is derived from instinctual sexuality. This is why infantile sexuality is logically essential to Freudianism. To be sure, there is no particular reason for doubting infantile sexuality, but interpretation is not instinctual; it is conventional, a consequence not of sexuality but of perception. Nevertheless, the Freudian interpretation may very well point in the right direction: perhaps a building is ultimately a sign of the body, and the child's play with the configurational signs of space, solid, screen, and light may be his initial categorization of his own body and its relation to the environment, as something confronting the environment, as something which is penetrable, as something which contains hollows, and as something which he can relate to the environment.

Among many primitive tribes certain unshaped stones are held as sacred, cherished, manipulated ritually, and carefully preserved and hidden in safe places. The Australian Bushmen call them *churingas*. They are spirit-stones, intimately involved with the being and continuity of the individual and groups of individuals. The sacred Stone of Scone of the Scots appears to be a sign of the same order, a sign of the Scots "nation" as a category of identity.[29] So it may be with the

---

[28] *The Earth, the Temples and the Gods*, New Haven, 1962.

[29] Only a few years ago a group of Scots Nationalists stole the Stone from the coronation throne in Westminster Abbey. They wished, they said, to draw public attention to what they considered to be the fact: The people of Scotland are a traditional "nation"; they all are members of the same entity. The Stone of Scone, to these Nationalists, was a sign of the category of Scots, a category which they are passionately convinced should be formalized and recognized by other "nations."

Australian aborigines, and with the three-dimensional signs with which children play. At a later stage in their development, children turn any three-dimensional small object into signs of themselves, their parents, and their siblings. Fingers can serve this purpose, as in the sign joke at the end of which the thumbs are spread apart to reveal the interior of the church with all the people. A sacred stone, or a finger, or any small object can be interpreted, then, as a sign of one's own being, one's own continuity through time, or, more precisely, a category of identity the range of which is an intermittent series of perceptions of one's own body as the stage for interpretational variability. In our culture, boys are given blocks, and girls, dolls. Boys tend to develop a capacity to deal with non-iconic three-dimensional configurational signs, with, therefore, primary signs; girls with iconic signs of the same sort, dolls. Sculptors, of course, are an exception; they play with dolls all their lives.

Perhaps this is why a building seems to emanate an aura of human presence. Perhaps this is why columned buildings are so satisfactory, why modern functionalist architects—who, to be sure, are responsible for the least functional buildings in history—have to go to enormous trouble to find a pseudo-functional excuse for using what, for other reasons, they cannot resist using, columns. A column somehow always seems to be a man, an interpretation sometimes signified by making columns of iconic three-dimensional configurational signs of men or women, atlantes and telamones or caryatids. The Vitruvian architects of the fifteenth century derived all architectural proportions from the human body.[30] The Dogon tribe of Africa are quite conscious that the "big house" of each lineage is laid out as a sign of "a man lying on his right side and procreating," or in his bed asleep, or in his grave. Each functional part of the house is identified with part of the human anatomy.[31] This suggests the first important step in the development of the rude shelter into the building.

If we apply the dramatic metaphor to buildings, it becomes at once apparent that to subdivide a house into rooms is to provide a stage for each role. As society develops and new roles emerge, buildings are split up into rooms, and some rooms are separated from the house and given buildings of their own. The space around the household altar

---

[30] James S. Ackerman, *The Architecture of Michelangelo*, New York, 1961, p. 97.
[31] Marcel Griaule and Germaine Dieterlin, "The Dogon," *African Worlds*, London, 1954.

was developed into the household chapel. It was then separated from the house and included in a temple, which was given its own surrounding space; sometimes, as in Egypt and Greece, the entire landscape was made into its stage or setting. This placing again emphasized its aura of human presence, here as a performer on a stage.[32] Similarly, the primitive tribal headman occupied, perhaps, a particular space in a circle of men sitting around a fire. The next step would be to orient that space toward some important sign. Next would be to place the headman in a space at the bright end of an axis, to signify his power to demand, to be adequate, and to release energy. From this, early civilizations evolved the throne room. And the Egyptians, combined all these spatial organizations and primary signs in tombs, into which light was carried to the eyes of the statue of the dead king.

Between the rooms of the house were walls, and in walls were doorways. Penetration through a doorway, then, meant moving from the stage for one role to the stage for another. Penetration of a screen became a primary sign for transition from one interpretational set, or orientation, to another. This may be an explanation for the peculiar porthole doors, radially symmetrical doors with their thresholds above ground level, found in Maltese temples and Spanish tombs, as well as elsewhere in the era of early European megalithic architecture.[33] Since such doors were not used for constant coming and going but only ritual purposes, some functional practicability could be sacrificed to the demands of a primary sign of orientative shifting.

The consideration of architecture as a fluid and dynamic experience to be interpreted rather than merely a solid or a void to be seen makes it much easier to identify primary significance in architecture. For the purposes of such an analysis the usual distinction between architecture and building can be ignored. As it is usually employed, "architecture" refers to buildings which show non-functional stylistic dynamism. Until very recently ordinary houses, whether rural or urban, showed almost no dynamism of this sort, except around important transitional areas, outside doors and, to a lesser degree, windows. In the peasant tradition, furniture was the occasion for artistic perception, not houses, which remained almost unchanged from the neolithic period. This is

---

[32] See Giedion, *The Beginnings of Architecture*, and Scully, *The Earth, the Temples and the Gods.*

[33] Sibylle von Cles-Reden, *The Realm of the Great Goddess: The Story of the Megalith Builders*, New York, 1962.

particularly true in the Mediterranean area and the Middle East, as well as the Far East, wherever the climate did not require a complicated functional adaptation to winter and summer conditions. For millennia, "architecture" was strictly an activity of the center of society; only in the last century and a half has architecture penetrated to the middle and lower cultural levels. The results have been, it must be confessed, most unfortunate from the perspective of the higher levels, for architecture is the unavoidable art. The too great respect for architecture has brought about the visual deterioration of the city and the countryside. The nineteenth and twentieth centuries have been only too successful in spreading the misled doctrine of the supreme importance of art, of the redemptive powers of art, and of the necessity to democratize art. And of course increased economic abundance has inspired the middle and lower levels to imitate their cultural betters, without bothering to become properly qualified. As far as primary signs are concerned, there is no difference between architecture and building. However, because of the economic resources of the center of society, which could build on a large scale and thus exaggerate the primary signs, such signs are more visible and easier to derive from ritual situations in architecture than in buildings of a simple subsistence function, homes, agricultural buildings, and workplaces for craftsmen.

Certainly the most conspicuous primary signs of architecture are verticality and horizontality, which work just as they do in painting, the one signifying the sense of making demands upon the environment, the other the sense of accepting the conditions the environment imposes and adapting oneself to its demands. Especially in architecture, demand can also be referred to as the sense of organization. Thus verticality asserts as a primary value in any situation the sense of organizing the possibilities of that situation to meet one's own interests; horizontality the sense of establishing an equilibrium between oneself and the environment. The vertical-masculine role is to make war; the horizontal-feminine role to keep the peace. Home should hug the ground.

The easiest way to see this in architecture is to examine the difference between European and Chinese architecture in these terms, and to compare the dominating values of the two societies. The European tradition has plenty of horizontal architecture, but in both of its two sources, Mesopotamian and Egyptian, there was a tremendous effort to create verticality. The Greek temple, taken by itself, appears to be horizontal, but seen in terms of its position as part of an entire archi-tecturally conceived landscape, the temple of an Olympian god is the crown of a conspicuous height with a strong vertical character. Further, from the Archaic period it was surrounded with columns, and as one approaches a Greek temple, its verticality becomes more marked as the bulk of the building disappears behind the narrow facade. Even when one looks down a side, the verticality of the columns is more impressive than the horizontality of the roof-line and the great beam which supports it and is supported by the columns. Eventually this beam, or architrave, was broken up by panels, or metopes, into vertical accents. The verticality of the great Roman buildings needs hardly be emphasized, and as the Empire developed, the buildings became higher. The Romanesque and Gothic towers and lofty naves need only be mentioned, not to speak of the sky-scrapers of America. In contrast, the horizontality of Chinese buildings of the last few centuries is striking. In Peking the Altar of Heaven is not a spire; it is a great flat disc, elevated above the ground level on three broad terraces. Verticality is there, but the effect is the piling up of platforms far wider than their height. To be sure, certain Chinese cities once held tall towers, but these are now gone, except for the pagodas, which are mostly in the countryside.

It is instructive that China has, or at least had, fewer heart failures than any country in the world. This is not, as has been sometimes suggested, the result of a rice diet. Tokio is the heart disease capital of the world, and in contrast to Chinese architecture, Japanese shows far greater verticality and spikiness, even in domestic architecture. Rather, the whole Chinese cultural tradition, especially as it is built around the cult and instructions of Confucius, emphasizes equilib-rium, tranquillity, behavior that will keep tension low, the tension necessary if one is to make demands upon the environment. The greatest Chinese paintings are scrolls unrolled from right to left, so that each section viewed implies an almost infinite extension in either direction from side to side. Their vertical paintings show human figures, especially sages, wise old men, sunk or buried in the land-scape. The role of the sage was to be a model for accepting the demands of the natural world and for adjusting to those demands.

By contrast, European culture is incredibly restless; to the cultivated Chinese of the last century it was the restlessness of uncivilized bar-barians. The degree to which Europe has valued imposing one's will upon the entire world comes out strongly in a recent book, *The Politics of Hysteria.*[34] But now, under the stress of modern conditions, China is returning to its old policy of conquest, of imposing demands. There is always a difference between cultural value and actual behavior. In the course of centuries of being left alone China gradually came under the control of Confucian values, and as it did, its architecture lost its verticality. Acceptance became the dominant value; in the West demand never lost its preeminence.

The cultural sources of European scientific mastery are to be seen in the towers of Gothic cathedrals. In China, even the tall pagodas do not soar upward but are divided into horizontal bands much broader than high. In the American skyscraper, as it developed, every attempt was made to emphasize its verticality, to make it seem higher than it actually is, and to sweep it upward into the most rarified heights. Perhaps even the traditional phrase "higher cultural level" and the identification of it with the innovative center is indicative of one of the most pervasive attributes of European behavior.

There are, however, two ways of perceiving horizontality and verticality in a building. The way just discussed looks at the building without reference to its site. But when the total fluid architectural experience is taken into consideration, any building is vertical compared with the ground it sits on, no matter how wide it may be in relation to its height, and the ground always is horizontal. Even when a building is built on a mountain peak, the earth is horizontal at the base of the mountain. It is easy to see that when a Babylonian temple is built on top of a ziggurat, the ziggurat is a work of architecture. But it is equally true, as Scully has demonstrated, that though the buildings of the Acropolis sit on a natural formation, the great rock itself is part of an architectural vision embracing the entire landscape.[35] It rises out of a shallow bowl. Scully's argument, recast into the terminology of this book, is that in Greek temple siting the natural signs of the landscape were incorporated into a sign system of which the temple was an artificial sign. As indicated earlier, natural signs are also conventions and can be used for any purpose which artificial signs are used for; though they cannot be verbal signs, they can be emblems derived from signs, which seems to be what happened in Greece.

His study of palace and temple siting from Cretan civilization down

---

[34] By Edmund Stillman and William Pfaff, New York, 1964.
[35] Scully, *The Earth, the Temples and the Gods.*

through the Hellenistic period shows how originally the palace or temple was sited to be within the protective hollow of the earth mother, how gradually the temple site (including the temples of the female Olympians) was raised to hilltops and then mountain tops, so that the vertical element became predominant. In the classic period, he concludes, the siting of the temples of Zeus created a perfect balance between the two, between the protection of the earth and the exposure to the dangers of reality, a perilous balance which has been recovered only in our time. After the classic period, the Greeks once again turned back to valuing protection over exposure.

This suggests that hollowness is the equivalent of horizontality and solidity of verticality, for the building itself always appears vertical compared with the total site. Certainly hollowness, horizontality, and femininity are as clearly associated in ancient and prehistoric periods as solidity, verticality, and masculinity. The former, then, are primary signs of acceptance, the latter of demand. A total architectural experience involves the penetration into a hollow, which is perceived as a hollow only because the solid building itself is visible. To perceive a building is to perceive a space around it. One enters that space at the precise moment the building is seen, whether one first glimpses it as it slides up over the horizon, or whether it is invisible until one passes through a concealing wall. In either case, one penetrates onto a stage in which the building is performing a part. One comes under the domination of the primary social role of the building, whether it is a hut on a plane or a vast temple or palace. During the approach to the building there may be other barriers; each is the sign of an orientative transition. Each becomes a solid as one nears it, and then, beyond it, one passes again into another hollow. The climactic transition is that into the building itself. One is now in the hollow of the very building, but the termination of the approach may well be once again the demanding vertical of an altar or a throne.

The masculine or demanding role of the building is increased if one approaches it on a straight axis but softened if the approach is sinuous. Scully thinks the winding approach descends from the sinuous entrance to the natural buildings of caverns in the earth. It may be. At any rate, kings and divine kings, like those of Egypt or the Roman Empire, are approached through a series of barriers in an absolutely straight line. The palace at Versailles is built across an axis which extends from the king's ceremonial bed several miles in either direction. But Bernini wished a sinuous approach to St. Peter's in Rome.

There is another reason, but one seems to be that any church, though the central church of Catholic Europe, should not be so demanding as to require the worshipper to experience the demanding sequence of the facade and piazza along an axis until he reaches the barrier of the unbuilt colonnade between the ends of the wings. Even so, the great arms of the colonnade, which were completed, create a vast hollow from which the bulk of the church itself is effectively reduced. Certainly, everyone feels that the Fascist creation of an immense axis for the church down to the Tiber was a great error. It makes the basilica more demanding than it should be. In medieval towns the cathedral was always at the center of a maze. The approach was sinuous, and the experience of the overwhelming verticality of the towers was fairly brief, for the worshipper soon entered the body of the church.

A building, then, is only part of a total field of primary signs in which the experience is alternately hollowness and solidity, of acceptance and demand. The social function of the building determines which is predominant, and which the ultimate interior emphasizes. Every building is a screen with a demanding outside and an accepting, fostering, protective interior. This is probably why the statues of the dead Egyptian kings were completely enclosed, except for a tiny window through which the statue could look out into the world, and why the Olympian gods were also contained with a relatively small hollow space surrounded by walls and columns. Thus the sign of demand was softened by compounding it with the sign of acceptance. If Scully is correct, the sacred places of the Olympian Zeus show the same fusion. And the Altar of Heaven in Peking, though exposed nakedly to the sky, protected the sacrificing Emperor with the circle of the platform on which he stood, a circle defined by a balustrade.

But there is another way of conceiving the axis, not as an approach to the building but as a radiation of force from its heart. It depends upon whether one is the audience to the building's role or the actor for whom the stage has been created. As the latter, the line of axis is experienced as a line of energy release which penetrates to the boundary at which the ultimate space of the building begins. So from the court front of Versailles, the force is released until far in the distance the road turns towards Paris; and on the garden front it is released for a full two miles until it terminates on a low hill on the horizon, on a sign of demand. Similarly, from the entrance colonnade of the English palace of Blenheim, the Duke of Marlborough, the English general who defeated Louis XIV and decorated his palace with his trophies, could look down a long axis to the horizon; and again the axis disappeared over a low hill. Depth, as in painting, is a sign of energy release. On the other hand, when, in the 1660's, Bernini designed St. Andrea al Quirinale as the novitiate church for the Jesuits, he laid out an oval and placed the entrance on one side and the high altar on the other. Bernini himself said, "Often when I need rest from my troubles I come here to gain consolation from my work."[36] As opposed to the customary straight nave, the ends of the ovals, opening out like the interiors of the megalithic Maltese temples and the arms of the colonnade of St. Peter's, are a sign of acceptance, while the shallowness from entrance to altar was a sign of the energy conservation which Bernini himself sought after the expenditure of great labors and the exhaustion of enduring great frustrations. That shallowness is also highly suitable for a novitiate church, in which the novices are sheltered from all random energy expenditure to concentrate on one task, that of becoming a priest, whose social role is to offer protection, psychological shelter, and a technique for reducing pointless energy expenditure.

Light and shadow are among the most powerful primary signs at the service of the builder. The lean-to was presumably the first building, nor is there any particular reason to doubt that very early man could make tents out of animal skins. But a house is a tool as well as a primary sign. The first large three-dimensional configurational but non-iconic sign-compounds for the purpose of assembling and displaying packages of primary signs were caves. These were in part, of course, natural signs functioning as primary signs, but to them was added, by artificial means, another important natural sign, light. In fact, since the caves could not be entirely illuminated, they must have been experienced as enveloping darkness with a small area of illumination inside. Nothing is so disorienting as absolute darkness, which appears in building, as in painting, to function as a sign of inadequacy; we need light to relate ourselves to our environment; light, then, is a sign of adequacy. But these caves are far below the surface of the earth. A long and difficult penetration is necessary. Even though the cave walls could not be seen, there must have been an awareness of the cave as a container or hollow. The total sign-compound meant, then, adequacy dominant over inadequacy in an atmosphere of acceptance, a pervasive attribute of human behavior which is so

---

[36] Douglas Haskell, *Patrons and Painters*, New York, 1963, p. 86.

easily experienced as dependence, passivity, or imprisonment. Acceptance as well as demand requires an ability to manipulate the environment and to make successful predictions, as the dependent and passive slave is extraordinarily successful at making predictions about the behavior, the reasonable demands and the unreasonable whims, of his master. If to the primary signs of hollowness, darkness, and light are now added the highly iconic two-dimensional signs of the animals, themselves possibly signs of adequacy and demand, as suggested above, early man could thus feel the otherness of the animals and oppose to them his own adequacy. It may be, as has so often been suggested, that the source of the Aurignacian and Magdalenian cave behavior was man's sense of inferiority to the animals, but the ritual of the cave was to make him feel equal to the animals and perhaps superior. One of the most constant phenomena of slave households is the slave who runs everything.

This same sign-compound of light in darkness in a hollow is found again in the Eleusinian mysteries of Greece, in which, so far as we can tell, the initiate ended up feeling adequate to death, and it survives right up to the present time in dark churches illuminated only by candles. In such Catholic churches, the illumination, as in the caves of southern France, is concentrated on the saint's highly iconic image. The worshipper wishes to feel adequate to the kind of inadequacy his particular saint has overcome, to the kind of victory of which that saint's picture is an emblem. The Baroque architects were particularly effective in using light and shadow. Frequently the space around the high altar, railed off by a barrier so that it became an interior space or hollow, was filled with darkness into which a shaft of light burst from above. The ingenuity they exercised in introducing light from concealed sources is astonishing.

Building appears to have at its disposal still another sign of adequacy, rectangularity in plan and in profile. The original form of the city plan in ancient Mesopotamia was curvilinear, and the oldest temple discovered was a rectangle in an approximately oval *temenos*, the sacred area. In Ur, however, the temple area was rectangular but the city wall was roughly oval. But in Khorsabad, nearly a millennium and a half later, temple, temple enclosure, palace, and city were all rectangular.[37] An oval or round shape is felt as embracing as a hollow,

---

[37] Plans and reconstructions are in Giedion, 1964, and in Henri Frankfort, *The Art and Architecture of the Ancient Orient*, Baltimore, 1955.

but here rectangularity, proceding from within, gradually conquered the curvilinear. Egypt is the classic land of rectangularity, of which among the earliest as well as the most striking examples are the pyramids. In Egypt geometry was a sacred science; its primary function was laying out sacred sites, and the Great Pyramid is almost exactly oriented to the points of the compass. Again emerges the theme of orientation. Even in the metaphor, "He has his feet square on the ground," squareness is an imported term which ascribes to such a man the attribute of knowing exactly how and where he is placed in the world, of being consciously aware of his relation to everything else. The four-square is the adequate, but to-day we mock a "square" because he thinks he is adequate, because as a middle-class type, with all its limitations, he is unaware of those forces in human experience which show up his adequacies as illusions.

A few words on the Great Pyramid will show how far man had come since the introduction of light into the dark hollow of the cave. Originally the tomb of Cheops was to have been below the foundation of the pyramid, deep in the earth. Later it was raised to a position slightly above ground level, but still directly below the apex. The third stage of planning raised it considerably higher, though slightly off center, perhaps so that the core of the pyramid should not be further weakened. Now the King's container was hung between earth and heaven. The pyramid was perfectly oriented, faced with polished granite which reflected an almost blinding light, and placed in a vast landscape, empty of human habitation, with low rock escarpments at a great distance and the hollow of the sky above. A more powerful development of a simple sacred stone, like the Stone of Scone or the Australian *churinga*, has never been built. Pharaoh was the sign of the organized community of the Egyptians, and in his tomb was signified the adequacy of that society to meet the conditions of life on a narrow band of green hemmed in by deserts and to impose its demands on that environment. The hollow in the cave had been extended to the hollow of the universe itself. Perhaps this is why it is so difficult for us to feel the sky as anything but a container. Verbal signs inform us that space extends from us indefinitely, but we find it extraordinarily difficult to perceive the sky as an emblem of that proposition. It remains to us a primary sign of hollowness, of acceptance and protection. Perceiving the sky, in day or at night, as an empty infinitude makes us feel exposed and inadequate.

The Great Pyramid is still terrifying, and it must have been even more frightening when it was sheathed in polished granite, for those smooth surfaces made it seem absolutely closed. The erection of such a gigantic monument seems almost insane to us, and even the Egyptians built pyramids for only a very short time. It has the rigidity of the psychotic, if we forget the importance of its light-reflecting function. Only the light and the colors it still takes on at various times of the day redeem it. Were it not for light and color, it would be totally inhibited and inexpressive. In unpolished buildings—and polished buildings are rare—the equivalent of the color of painting is the manipulation of the surface and solidity of a building; here light and shadow are not present as primary signs but to make the building expressive. The phrase that a building is "expressive" leads to another fool's errand, for the logical question is, "Expressive of what?" Like color, the breaking up of profile and surface of buildings is not expressive of any particular attitude, but is a primary sign of the continuum from inhibition to expressiveness. The Renaissance adoption of Classical forms tended to make building surfaces and outlines far more inhibited and closed than Europe was used to from its experience with the Gothic, although it is to be noticed that when Renaissance styles were adopted in Italy, in still Gothic Europe there was a striking reduction of Gothic irregularity at precisely the same time. One is tempted to think that the Classic forms were adopted in order to clarify the problem of creating less expressive buildings and to facilitate the solution. Clearly the same cultural forces were at work both in the Gothic and the revived Classic areas. This trend toward simplification of profile and wall manipulation, towards inhibition, continued through the sixteenth century, reaching its climax in the work of Palladio. One of the great tasks of Baroque architecture was to continue, for completely extra-artistic reasons, the Renaissance means of manipulating wall surface and profile and yet to get the extreme sense of expressiveness or orientative flexibility which was so striking a character of the Gothic, and the effort to attain which was perhaps the reason for the development of the relatively inhibited Romanesque forms into the sculpturesque openness of the Gothic, the architects of which so often planned and attempted to build beyond the capacities of their engineering, not to speak of their economic resources.

What happened to the dome of St. Peter's in the sixteenth century is instructive. Bramante designed the profile to be semicircular, Sangallo made it oval, Michelangelo in progressive designs once again reduced it to semicircularity, and Giacomo della Porta, whose design was executed, again made it oval.[38] The rigid signs of inhibition which marked Egypt and the Roman Empire were not appropriate to modern Europe. In Egypt the function of such primary signs was to lock the observer in a given orientation. The attitude of the worshipper at the shrine of a dead or a living king was to be fixed from the moment he saw the building: ancient Egypt was the most stable and long-lived society ever to have existed. It was not a slave society, but we are tempted to think of it as such, for it asserted that only the God-King is adequate and empowered to demand. But the European tradition offers the worshipper signs of orientative expressiveness and flexibility; the sense of adequacy is to flow upon him from God, or from the saints, the intercessors for particular roles and environmental difficulties. Even the king was not God, but only the representative of God. Hence the great political problem of Europe which still vexes us to-day, in one form or another. Is the king—or president—to be worshipped because he is an emblem of adequacy? Or should he be removed when he is in fact inadequate, a condition that obtains with depressing frequency?

The problem of the European architect of the period after the Classical revival is with us again to-day. The International School of "functional" architecture generally succeeded in stripping down its surfaces and its profiles to signs of inhibition. The public tends still to dislike these shoeboxes, factories, prisons. Yet, because a smooth wall and a regular profile are cheaper to build then complex surfaces and broken profiles, the International Style has been commercially successful. Currently, such architects as Edward Stone, Louis Kahn, Philip Johnson, and Paul Rudolph are trying desperately to create expressive buildings which at the same time shall be functional as a tool is functional, or a machine. If they realized, as indeed some of them seem to, that nothing is more functional to man than primary signs, whether he finds them in nature or in buildings, they could stop troubling their consciences.

Both impulse rhythm and process rhythm function in architecture in two ways: to pass through a screen is to initiate a new impulse, while regular or irregular features along the way of approach signify the smoothness or irregularity of behavioral process. Likewise, the manipulated screen has the same two primary semantic functions. Screens may present a series of identical three-dimensional configura-

---

[38] James S. Ackerman, *The Architecture of Michelangelo*, Chapter VIII.

tions, signifying only process rhythm, as a colonnade, or they may present a hierarchy of configurations. In this kind of screen design, panels subdivided into panels signify a series of impulses, while the subdivisions within the panels signify process. The screen actually may exhibit as many levels as the designer wishes; his media are recessions and projections and the light that makes them visible. The same kind of hierarchical organization may be used in profiles.

By this time it is hardly necessary to say that the primary signs of buildings vary quite independently from non-functional style. In European architectural history, for example, there have been only three short periods in which highly regular closed signs of inhibition were dominant: for a century or so in the late fifteenth and sixteenth centuries, for a couple of decades at the end of the eighteenth century, and in the twentieth century. It is not uninstructive that Fascism and big business have been most interested in the inhibited regularity so characteristic of Egypt and Imperial Rome. It is also hardly worth more than a mere mention that much of what has passed for stylistic analysis in the Wölfflin tradition, particularly as it has been applied to the other arts, has in fact been concerned very much with primary signs, scarcely with non-functional style at all. And again, as with poetry and painting, I have not made a kind of statement different from the kind normally made about architecture. The architecture of Imperial Rome, for example, has often been called brutal or powerful, as well as the architecture of Fascism, Communism, and American big business. I am attempting, rather, to find some reason why such statements are made and to translate them all into a common language which will serve both in artistic and non-artistic situations. This problem is particularly important when we come to music.

6. SIGNS IN MUSIC

The arguments about whether music does or does not have meaning are perennial. The demonstrations that it does not have been air-tight; the only trouble with them is that virtually all composers, except those under the influence of modern aesthetics, and almost the entire audience of music have insisted that music is meaningful, or at least expressive. Everyone will admit, of course, that music can have an emblematic function and that configurational signs are found in music. Both of these have already been discussed, but so far as instrumental music is concerned they are trivial and generally not even present. Mahler has made striking use of emblems, but it is striking partly because it is so very rare. In his cantatas, Bach, like other Baroque composers, also used emblems. Christ walking on the waters is accompanied by a wave-like melody. But this device again has been used too rarely to be of any fundamental importance.

Two of the best arguments against the meaningfulness of music are very simple. If music has meaning in the sense of necessarily referring to a given attitude, all musical settings of "I love you," or "*ich liebe dich,*" or "*Je t'aime,*" or the equivalent in any language should have something in common. They do not. Aside from the fact that all such musical settings are music, they have nothing in common. In instances in which the composer controls his compositional process by a definite set of verbal signs, the listener should be able to deduce the set of signs, in the original order, from the music. Here are a couple of sentences from Schönberg's own analysis of the meaning of "Verklaerte Nacht," the composition of which was controlled by a poem of Richard Dehmel's.

> She had married a man whom she did not love. She was unhappy and lonely in this marriage (Ex. 5), but forced herself to remain faithful (Ex. 6), and finally obeying the maternal instinct she is now with child from a man she does not love. She had even considered herself praiseworthy for fulfilling her duty towards the demands of nature (Ex. 7). A climactic ascension, elaborating the motif, expresses her self-accusation of her great sin (Ex. 8).[39]

Could anybody deduce this from the music alone? Speaking for myself, although I had known this music well for thirty years, the composer's explanation came to me as a great surprise. Even someone who knew the poem would find it impossible to decide exactly which phrase informs us that the woman is pregnant or which phrase "expresses her self-accusation of her great sin."

These examples are representative of two types of theory of musical meaning. One is that music is equivalent to verbal statements. This depends upon the notion that the "mind" has an "idea" and that both of these are independent of the signs that "express" them. Consequently the "idea" (for example, "she is pregnant") can be expressed either in words or in a musical sign. This must necessarily also involve a theory of immanent meaning, rather than conventional meaning.

---

[39] Arnold Schönberg, "Verklärte Nacht," *The Music of Arnold Schönberg*, Vol. II, Columbia Records, 1962.

But the hypostatization of "mind" and "idea" are enough to show the absurdity of this position, not to speak of the simple pragmatic test. The only way to get from a verbal sign to a musical sign is to conventionalize the latter as an emblem. If the audience knows the convention, it can then, and only then, arrive at the composer's verbal sign.

The other theory is the expressive theory: music is a sign of a particular attitude, rage, love, joy. These terms are also considered as names for emotions. However, if "emotion" means anything, it means the awareness of physiological change, a change of internal temperature, or a change in control over fine or gross movements, as when emotion prevents one from making delicate adjustments or forces one to tremble; or even violent bodily changes, such as a breakdown in learned behavioral patterns, retention of urine, for example. Now rage, love, and joy can cause any of these physiological changes or all of them. A man can feel hot from rage, love, or anxiety, or tremble from joy or hate, or feel cold from an encounter with a loved object or a feared one. The names we give, therefore, to an emotional state are not derived from anything physiological; they are derived from our interpretation of the situation. "I feel hot all over, and my interpretation of the situation tells me that I do so because I am terribly angry." "I cannot move from shock, and the situation tells me that the reason is that I have just heard that my wife has been murdered by a rapist," or "that I have inherited a million dollars." The situational interpretation of a physiologic change is why there is no consistency whatever in the way particular words are set to music. Both Handel's *Dettingen Te Deum* and his *Utrecht Te Deum* were written to celebrate political occasions; both use exactly the same words. But the Utrecht version is mostly in the minor, and the Dettingen is in the major; in the one there is a strong tendency for the melodic line to descend; in the other it mostly ascends.

A common statement is that the major and minor contrast, which was established in the early seventeenth century, is equivalent to the contrast between happy and sad. To be sure, the major-minor contrast works reasonably well in a good many instances; indeed, composers who have been so instructed will use the contrast emblematically. However, it inevitably collides with Gluck's setting of Orpheus' lament for Eurydice, which is partly in the major and partly in the minor. If minor means sad, the situation clearly calls for the minor. Any attempt to ascribe meaning to the major-minor contrast must take account of this famous instance.

Again, it is often said that chromatics are erotic. But this is only because of the enormous impact of Wagner's *Tristan und Isolde*, which was the most heavily chromatic work of any extent at the time it was composed. Scriabin's *Poem of Ecstasy* is likewise heavily chromatic and obviously derivative from *Tristan*. "Ecstasy" is usually taken to mean erotic ecstasy, and I have seen many references to the perfumed eroticism of the work, frequently in a context of lightly disdainful puritanism. Yet Scriabin himself said it was about the ecstasy of feeling one's identity in confrontation with the chaos of human experience. It is, so far as the composer was concerned, not erotic but epistemological. Certainly the Prelude to *Tristan* is filled with, for want of a better word, tension, but it would not be erotic tension unless we knew it was written for an erotic situation. It is just as applicable to the tension of waiting for a bus.

The kind of argument that attempts to link a specific attitude to a specific musical character has been encountered before, in the attempts to link phonic overdetermination of a particular sound, specific colors, and architectural expressiveness to specific attitudes or emotions. The structure of the argument suggests that here it is appropriate to work backward: the same thing may be going on here. Such talk is really mistaken talk about primary signs. The principle that no categories are empty prompts the conclusion that people who attempt to make an inadmissable link between a musical element and a particular emotion are nevertheless talking about something: they have recognized those elements as signs but have made an error in identifying what they are signs of. Much mockery has been made of "impressionistic" descriptions of musical significance, yet even some of those who most strongly deny it find themselves, in spite of every effort, falling into the habit.

Monroe Beardsley has made devastating critical analyses of the various kinds of theories of musical significance, and has decided, "It seems that we must tentatively conclude that music does not express or signify." "Music, then, is no symbol of time or process, mental or physical, Newtonian or Bergsonian; it *is* process."[40] To which I can only reply, "Of course. What is not? Music is experienced. What experience does not involve process? As you are using the term, is

---

[40] *Aesthetics*, New York, 1958, pp. 337–338.

process much more than another name for experience?" Yet he also says,

> Even after we have analyzed a piece of music . . . exposing the details of its structure and texture—there is . . . something . . . left out of our description. For we have not mentioned those pervasive regional qualities that are distinctive to it and relished in it. We list such qualities—it is dramatic, it is turbulent, it is restrained and lyrical, it is boisterous and bluff—we know our description can never be complete."[41]

And again,

> Considering her special predicament, it is true not only, as the composer has said, that "the tune should be feminine, young, nervous, and if possible, pretty like the girl," but also that her problem and her state of mind should be partly given by that tune itself—as they are.[42]

If I tell my gardener I want him to plant me a willow tree "feminine, young, nervous, and if possible, pretty like a girl" I have not the slightest doubt that he would be able to find me such a tree and plant it. But I do not think for a moment that he would judge these attributes anything but metaphorically transferred from a girl to a tree. If I said to Beardsley that I found a mountain majestic, I do not suppose that he would think I meant that majesty was immanent in the mountain. Yet he tells us that the tune is not a sign of femininity, but *is* feminine. If this is not a theory of immanent meaning I do not know what it is. It seems unwise of him to refer to the similar language of others as "affective free-associationism disguised as semiotical profundity." In short, here is a highly sophisticated and knowledgable aesthetician falling into the trap he spends pages warning us against.

His justification is the phrase "pervasive regional qualities." And his defense is "We know our description never can be complete." He is aware that terms like "feminine, young, nervous, pretty" tell us something about the music, but only something. Thus "affective free-associationism" selects some attribute of the work and links it to an association. When, therefore, someone says of an untitled piece of music that it is profoundly and disturbingly erotic, he means that in a semiotic situation identifiable as one in which a profoundly and disturbingly erotic interpretation would be appropriate, this music would

---

[41] *Aesthetics* by Monroe Beardsley, New York, 1958, p. 318. Copyright Harcourt, Brace & World, Inc. Used by permission of Harcourt, Brace & World, Inc.

[42] *Aesthetics*, p. 348.

be appropriate. Or if he says, "The conclusion to this symphony is triumphant," he means that it would be appropriate to a setting of that part of *Paradise Lost* in which the Son returns to Heaven and his Father after triumphing over Satan. Yet violent music is as appropriate to a fight in the street over a crap game as it is to a quarrel among the Gods. Schopenhauer pointed this out long ago in *The World as Will and Representation* (1819), although his explanation is not precisely satisfactory, consisting almost entirely of what I have called middle statements. Thus Beardsley's remark about the character of the tune and the character of the pretty girl is perfectly correct, so long as it is remembered that the same tune could be applied equally well to an ugly old man, and without irony. One of the most striking instances is Wagner's and Verdi's independent use of an almost identical melody, one as a leitmotif throughout *Parsifal*, the other when Othello stands by the sleeping Desdemona, determined to kill her. The fact that in *Parsifal* it is known as the "Redemption" motif is irrelevant; these names were not given to the Wagnerian motifs by Wagner, but by ill-advised commentators. Happy is the man who has never learned them.

The language people use in interpreting music, then, suggests another reason for identifying music as being made up of primary signs. They vary independently of the situation, just as they do in poetry, architecture, and painting. No particular sign is required by the situation. Only in poetry are signs structured, and then only verbal signs. Primary signs may or may not be absent, and there is no stable relationship between the primary sign and the verbal sign. This relationship is a packaged relationship, the relationship all signs have in non-verbal sign systems. But there is further evidence. One of the few efforts to make an extensive study of musical signs is Deryck Cooke's.[43] This book has been variously received, with both great praise and great scorn, the latter, as one might expect, emanating from a reviewer in the *Journal of Aesthetics and Art Criticism* who denies utterly the notion that music can have meaning. Cooke went about it the only way one can go about it. He attempted to find some stability between words and music in innumerable compositions of Western music from the middle ages to the present. His attempts to identify particular harmonic combinations and particular melodic sequences with particular emotions are open to the same objection that all such attempts

---

[43] In *The Language of Music*, London, 1959.

have been: one wonders if the same words have been set to different harmonies and sequences. However, when he turns from that and goes to the elements without which music cannot be music he seems on surer ground.

If his harmonic and melodic signs are signs at all, they are emblems, derived by subjecting the basic material of music to situational control. Indeed, he has so much evidence that it seems probable that there has been musical emblematism at work since the early seventeenth century. In fact Baroque theorists quite consciously created musical emblems ("affections"), and it seems probable that they became standardized.[44] It would have been very strange had Verdi accompanied the death of Traviata with a military march for a brass band. However, in examining so many situational instances, Cooke necessarily was concerned with basic musical devices common to all situations; pitch change, rhythm, volume, and the like. He has applied what I have called the principle of consonance.[45] Like all signs, primary signs are conventions, even though they may be, like the conventions or arbitrary referential signs, thousands of years old. Before any sign can be used ironically, it must be conventionalized.[46]

This is what Cooke says about pitch. He identifies "up-and-down," "out-and-in," and "away-and-back" as referring to a quality in human experience; he continues:

> The expressive quality of rising pitch is above all an "outgoing" of emotion: depending on the tonal, rhythmic, and dynamic context, its effect can be active, assertive, affirmative, aggressive, striving, protesting, or aspiring. The expressive quality of falling pitch is of an "incoming" of emotion: depending on context, it can be relaxed, yielding, passive, assenting, welcoming, accepting, or enduring. These qualities clearly absorb the "rising and falling vitality" of the "up-and-down" symbolism and the "continuation and finality" of the "out-and-in" symbolism. The passion of the *Tristan* Prelude is outgoing—active, assertive, striving; the fulfillment at the end of the *Liebestod* is "incoming" —it is received, welcomed, accepted.[47]

He is talking about a pervasive character, for pitch change is only less pervasive than rhythm. Rhythm alone creates music, that is, what our

---

[44] Manfred F. Bukofzer, *Music in the Baroque Era: From Monteverdi to Bach,* New York, 1947, pp. 388–390.

[45] See above, Section 4, this chapter.

[46] See note 24 of this chapter.

[47] *The Language of Music,* by Deryck Cooke, London, 1959, pp. 105–106. Copyright Oxford University Press, Inc. Used by permission of Oxford University Press, Inc.

culture recognizes as music; phrase, the forming of rhythmic sequences by pauses, seems the next essential; speed, or frequency of beat, and volume change seem to be next. Pitch change appears likely for the next emergent, followed by pitch relationships, or harmony. All of these can be derived by abstraction from the phonic character of language, though poetry does not use all of them, notably pitch and speed. Or if poetry uses speed, it appears only in performance, at the discretion of the performer, and in any case, its range is not wide.

These are the musical elements that vary independently of situation. Cooke calls them the vitalizing agents: volume, time, rhythm, pitch. About the others he has useful things to say, but is on the whole less satisfactory than on pitch change. Here is my own list of the primary significance of these basic elements.

Rhythm	Process smoothness
Phrase	Impulse smoothness
Speed: fast to slow	Energy release to energy conservation
Volume: loud to soft	Expression to inhibition
Upward pitch motion	Demand
Downward pitch motion	Acceptance
Fixed pitch	Rejection
Wave pitch	Openness or flexibility
Major	Adequacy
Minor	Inadequacy

A note on major-minor is necessary. Music of the Middle Ages was modal. Early in the seventeenth century two modes were selected and contrasted as major and minor. There is some reason to believe that the modes were emblematic situational signs. This would have taken care of adequacy and inadequacy. Nevertheless, what were ultimately recognized as major and minor harmonies were present in medieval music and may have had some function there for adequacy and inadequacy. Certainly, all the examples Cooke gives of his major and minor significances can be reduced to these two attributes. The disappearance with Schönberg of this semiotic distinction I believe to be consonant with the disappearance of the tragedy-comedy contrast, for to the modern mind, the adequacy-inadequacy contrast is no longer relevant, as I have proposed in my *Beyond the Tragic Vision.* Scully, it will be remembered, makes the same point. Perhaps Euripides, who has so modern a feeling and who has once again emerged from the shadows cast over him by worshippers of Aeschylus and Sophocles, is not truly tragic for the same reason. When the major-minor contrast was abandoned by Schönberg, chiaroscuro, or light and shadow contrast, disappeared from the most advanced painting. Architectural rectangularity is now in the process of disappearing, but to abandon it presents technical difficulties, since engineering technique has developed almost entirely from the need to create rectangular shapes. In architecture, light and shadow survive more as a means to manipulate surface, that is, for expressiveness, rather than as primary signs in their own right. Interiors tend to be increasingly uniformly and brightly lit. This is becoming true even of domestic interiors.

I have put off considering music to the last, because, if I had put it first, nobody could possibly have taken seriously the primary sign functions offered here. Several examples must suffice, and then the reader generous and curious enough to try it out in innumerable situations, as I have done for the past five years, motivated by the profoundest suspicion, may find it acceptable. Again, let me urge that I am more interested in trying to account for the almost universal assertion that music has significance than I am in forcing my significations down anyone's throat. Further, my ultimate concern, the non-functional stylistic dynamism of art and my proposal about the relations of the arts do not rest upon this. Rather, if the reader believes that music has significance, he will see that its signs do not vary with non-functional stylistic variation. If he does not believe that music has significance, the ensuing explanation of non-functional style will not be affected one way or another.

Let us begin with a famous example of musical significance, an explanation of which was offered by the composer. The four notes at the beginning of Beethoven's Fifth Symphony he explained as fate knocking on the door. "Fate" refers to our sense that there are environmental forces greater than ourselves over which we have no ultimate control: "knocking on the door" refers to our sense of awareness of such forces, a sense we do not always have. If we did, we could not act. Applying the scheme of interpretation proposed, we get process smoothness, impulse smoothness (the repetition of the four notes), energy release, expression, initial rejection followed by acceptance, and inadequacy. The phrase as a unit signifies the sense of a powerful, irresistible force, which one at first resists and then accepts with a sense of one's own inadequacy. This seems to be perfectly consonant with "fate knocking at the door." Beethoven's statement was a middle statement, and translated into predictive statements, means, "Sometimes I feel that I am inadequate to the demands the environment makes upon me, and my attempts to meet them and to control the environment merely make me feel the more helpless." That there are such forces, and that we do frequently feel this way is undeniable. Further, the phrase can readily serve quite a different function. Used in World War II as the victory sign, it meant, "The Hitlerian Reich will succumb to forces more powerful than itself, and when it succumbs it will be destroyed." The force of fate was redirected from the interpreter and the composer to the environment. In the conclusion to the Fifth Symphony, in the fourth movement, Beethoven himself reverses that direction, but it will be more interesting to turn to another fourth movement, one for which no such neat explanation can be obtained from the composer.

The fourth movement of Tschaikowsky's Sixth Symphony violates a number of rules, particularly the rule about the triumphant fourth movement, which, ever since Beethoven's Fifth, was expected to be loud, fast, in the major, and have as its principal theme an upward-moving melody. This movement is usually identified with Tschaikowsky's attempt at suicide, and its pervasive character is such that it always comes as a shock to realize that Tschaikowsky wrote it in particularly good spirits. He had rarely felt so cheerful in his life. It is, however, an instructive and salutary shock, for it shows how an artist, like anyone else, can manipulate primary signs of pervasive attributes of human behavior without himself experiencing those attributes. An artist, like anyone else, can be hypocritical, dishonest, insincere, and ironic. In fact, more than anything else, sincerity is conducive to an ineffective and confusing manipulation of both the semiotic material of art and its non-functional stylistic features. It leads to a confusion of actor's role and audience's.

I have seen this movement of Tschaikowsky's called tragic, sad, melancholy, lugubrious, despairing, sentimental, self-pitying, self-torturing, suicidal, and any number of similar terms. Applying the above interpretational verbal signs, we get: process and impulse smoothness, energy conservation, inhibition, acceptance, and inadequacy. In other terms, a fixed, settled, gnawing sense of inadequacy which nearly inhibits all energy release and all orientative expression. In situational terms, it is a fixed, settled grief which the individual can neither come to terms with nor throw off and which is present as the interpretational background of all situations in which he finds himself. These terms, I think, will be acceptable to anyone who admits that this music has any significance at all, or any "pervasive regional qualities."

The difficulty of talking about the significance of music, then, lies in the fact that most of its primary signs are at work at the same time and that, for non-situational music, there is no guide from consonance. However, once music is put into a situation its meaning is readily comprehensible. For this reason most talk about the suitability or non-suitability of music to words, which are situational signs, is nonsense. Music is always suitable to the words it is set to. Handel's *Utrecht* and *Dettingen Te Deums* use the same words; but in one, roughly, the music signifies a sense of inadequacy and acceptance, or submission, before the Deity; in the other it is a celebration for a victory in which God was clearly on the side of the English. The *Utrecht Te Deum* was written to celebrate the coming of peace after years of war; the *Dettingen* to celebrate a very minor victory. The music for each is appropriate, but the titles of the two works could be switched. Then the music for the *Utrecht* would signify rejoicing that God has rewarded the English for their perseverance in a righteous cause; and the *Dettingen* that, in spite of their victory, they must always remember that they are in the hands of a stern and just God and that vengeance is His, not theirs. And so on, as far as anyone wishes to carry it. Thus, again, the Prelude to *Tristan*, in its situation, means, roughly, a sense of making an erotic demand in the face of frightful frustrations and difficulties and with a strong sense of inadequacy. At first the demand is intensely inhibited, and there is both process and impulse roughness. Gradually, however, the initial tendency to accept failure and to conserve energy is overcome, smoothness of process and impulse is achieved, energy is released, orientations are expressed, the demand is imposed, and adequacy is experienced. But unfortunately, all these attractive attributes of behavior last but a moment, and the original character of the piece returns, except that demand is converted to acceptance. As I have suggested, this is perfectly applicable to waiting for a bus which, on arrival, turns out to be so full that though the driver lets off a passenger he refuses to let another one on. All one can do is to wait for the next bus, or the next Isolde.

Finally, though music cannot say much it can say it over and over with extraordinary flexibility. Men never weary of primary significance. These are, above all, the attributes which, because of their pervasiveness, are precisely for each man among the most important means of creating his own experiences of himself as a category of identity. Personality, roles, patterns, style can and do change, some from hour to hour. Indeed, we have rituals for shifting roles; alcohol, with its depressant effect, is an important ingredient in much role shifting. It relieves the individual of the anxieties attendant upon the gap between environmental demands and behavior in one role and relaxes him enough to take up the anxieties of another. It is not, therefore, surprising that certain kinds of highly repetitious music are often the accompaniment of such rituals in our society, and not only in bars. Popular music, and almost all dance music, is particularly characterized by wave pitch, up-and-down motion across some particular tone. This, like the regular irregularity of the Gothic, appears capable of signifying a sense of orientative openness and flexibility. In popular music, even when the wave-pitch character is absent, there is usually during the course of the entire tune a symmetrical disposition of the melodic elements on either side of a note. Cole Porter's "Night and Day" is an excellent example.

The semiotic flexibility of music becomes apparent if the reader will glance once again at the table of significances offered above. Only one element need be changed to alter the whole character of the work. Even the fourth movement of Tschaikowsky's Sixth Symphony has several moments of expression, but because nothing else is changed, they are entirely frustrated. A massive change of all of them in the middle of a movement can have a prodigious effect. Mahler was particularly adept at this kind of manipulation of primary signs. Further, music can signify intense conflict, by simultaneously presenting contrastive signs. Over a steady rhythmical pedal point, the violins can present signs of the most disturbed and irregular behavior. Towards the end of *Parsifal* two equally powerful melodic lines in the major move in opposite directions, one up, one down. Wagner is saying that true adequacy is to be limited neither to acceptance nor demand but should fuse both, or, situationally, that the individual should be both masculine and feminine. Perhaps to feel both demanding and accepting at once is impossible in life, but in sign manipulation it is not only possible, it happens all the time, in all the arts. For, since art is, in one of its aspects, semantic, and since it is therefore a construct of attributes, not life itself, it can present the impossible with no difficulty whatever. It is only signs. The signs have categorial reference to experience; but the sign packages are not isomorphic with experience. As sign packages, poetry, painting, architecture, and music present behavioral models, just as the model of a building gives no information about the stresses to be placed upon the posts and beams when the building is actually built. They must be calculated and predicted in other sign systems.

Art: The Semantic Aspect 195

7. THE SEMANTIC RELATIONSHIPS
OF THE ARTS

From all this emerges one conclusion about the crucial problem of this book: the relationships of the arts. Certainly the arts are related through their primary signs, but the fact is of no significance, because all the signs of art, natural and artificial, situational and non-situational, arbitrary and configurational, are to be found outside of the arts. They are in the arts because the arts are the deposits of human behavior, of which perhaps the central and certainly one of the most important elements is semiotic behavior. The semantic aspect of art varies not with the non-functional stylistic aspect but to meet non-artistic demands. Much of common discourse about art is concerned with a property known as form, but as this analysis has shown, much of that discourse is not about form but about configurations which serve as primary signs.

From this point of view, the classic pairings of poetry-painting and music-architecture are reasonably understandable. Poetry can make predictive statements and painting can present iconic configurations. The information poetry gives, whether about nymphs or skyscrapers, can be used as the basis for derived signs in painting; and the configurational signs of painting can equally be the guide to the poet. Keats's "Ode on a Grecian Urn" is a classic example of one; the innumerable examples of illustrations, from Greek bas-reliefs and painting to the *Saturday Evening Post*, are examples of the same process working in the opposite direction. Gombrich has demonstrated how extra-artistic demands were responsible for the highly iconic Greek sculptured illustrations of mythology and heroic legend. Currently, of course, high-level culture looks down on illustrations; they are, it is said, not true paintings but literary paintings. This is but another instance of a non-artistic demand being made upon the painter. Like all such demands, it will eventually pass, and indeed, with the emergence of Pop Art, it has already begun to lose its power. However, the primary signs available to the painter do not correspond with those the poet can use. The poet has fewer and is further limited by the phonic selectivity of his language and the necessity to meet the requirements of structural signs.

The music-architecture pairing is even more obvious. Though the architect can plaster his building with configurational signs in two and three dimensions and can inscribe as many verbal single or compound signs on its walls as he pleases, nevertheless these are only additions to primary signs, which can get along perfectly well without them. So it is with the composer, who can use verbal signs, whether as title or program, for guides to the situation he wishes the listener to apply the music to, and configurational signs, sounds like barking dogs or wind machines or recordings of bird songs. Nevertheless, these, too, are but additions which the musician adds to his basic package of primary signs. This is why abstract painting has so often been called visual music. It uses two-dimensional configurational signs which are non-iconic and primary. It could as well be called flat architecture.

But another pairing is common, music-poetry. This is understandable if we add painting and oppose the triad music-poetry-painting to the monad, architecture. Only architecture offers a primary sign of the sense of transition; only architecture offers the experience of penetrating through a screen. Just as such penetration requires leaving one spatial orientation and entering another, so music, poetry, and painting offer transitions from one orientational construct to another. This, of course, is not unique to the arts. This is characteristic of all experiences of sign constructs. The instability of human categorization is the basic reason for it. Certain behavioral patterns, however, are signs of transition. The opening through the architectural screen is one. Any ritual is another. The anthropologists Elliot Chapple and Carleton Coon point out that a ritual of initiation is a repetition in miniature of the transition from one social function, or role, to another.[48] The hazing in fraternity initiations is a repetition of the humiliation and dependency the pledges have to go through. In the initiation it is followed by the admission of the pledge as a fraternity brother. The hazing is a sign of the testing for the pledge's capacity to submit his interests to the group interests when there is a conflict. The hazing, then, is a sign of his ability to add fraternity loyalty to family loyalty. Should there be a conflict between the two, how the conflict should be settled is not prescribed. In the life of a nun, however, who goes through a novitiate and then a vigil—the functional equivalent of the initiatory hazing of the fraternity—the resolution of any conflict between family loyalty and loyalty to her religious group *is* prescribed. Hazing and vigil, then, are signs of the sense of transition. A musical composition, a poem, and a painting are also such signs. This primary significance of painting becomes apparent if one thinks of the ancient

---

[48] In *Principles of Anthropology*, New York, 1942.

use of configurational signs as attitude controllers around entrances through screens and, if the penetration is corridor-like, on the side walls of the penetration. An example may be found in the entrances of medieval cathedrals. The first line of decoration directly above the worshipper's head consists, ordinarily, of signs of occupations and roles, but the last is of angels, and directly above the door is the Virgin, or Christ, or God. Another instance is the Chinese scroll-painting, which the perceiver unrolls. It is a true visual music. This primary semantic function of music as a sign of the sense of transition is very possibly what lies behind Beardsley's assertion that music is process. It is probable that tragedy was derived from ritual poetry, and our knowledge of ancient transition rituals like the Greek mysteries suggests the use of music, poetry, dancing, sculpture, and painting as well. Architecture, as a sign system, thus can be thought of as the stage or setting for a ritual of transition. In this sense it truly is, as has so often been claimed, the mother of all the arts.

In the semantic aspect of the arts, then, the artist is meeting demands, prescriptions, rules of the other faces of the cultural pyramid. He includes signs in his work because he is a human being, and in meeting such demands he does exactly what everybody else does; he even innovates semantic functions, but the degree and nature of his innovation is determined extra-artistically. He innovates meanings because he is a member of the human community, not because he is an artist, just as the poet creates metaphors not because he is a poet but because his emergent categories can be signified only by metaphor. At the end of this chapter is offered a table of the primary signs in the various arts; but, to repeat, let it not be imagined that completeness is claimed, or that the terms I use could not be improved on. Indeed, almost any one who can accept the notion of primary signs will be at least partially dissatisfied with the verbal identificatory terms I use and will wish to improvise his own.

Though much discourse about "form," then, really refers to primary signs, yet much does refer to something else, to non-functional style, to what may properly be called "form." The task of the next chapter will be to clarify that problem.

Primary Signs in Four Arts

Sense of	POETRY	MUSIC	PAINTING	ARCHITECTURE
DEMAND	Alliteration and Assonance	Upward pitch motion	Verticality	Verticality and Solidity
ACCEPTANCE	Feminine ending	Downward pitch motion	Horizontality	Horizontality and Hollowness
ADEQUACY	Rhyme	Major	Light	Light and Rectangularity
INADEQUACY		Minor	Shadow	Shadow
FIXITY (REJECTION)		Fixed pitch	Black	Closed solids
FLEXIBILITY (OPENNESS)		Wave pitch	White	Open pavilions
EXPRESSION		Loud volume to	Yellow White saturation to	Deep plasticity to
INHIBITION		Soft volume	Purple Black saturation	Shallow plasticity
ENERGY RELEASE	Long phonic sequence	Fast speed to	Depth	Deep axis
ENERGY CONSERVATION	Short phonic sequence	Slow speed	Shallowness	Shallow axis
IMPULSE SMOOTHNESS OR ROUGHNESS	Junctural rhythm	Phrasal rhythm	Configurational sequence	Screen, panel, profile sequence
PROCESS SMOOTHNESS OR ROUGHNESS	Stress rhythm	Ictus rhythm	Line	Subdivisions within screen, panel, and profile
TRANSITION				Screen opening

FIVE:
ART: THE FORMAL ASPECT

At the end of Chapter I it was proposed that not order but disorder was the character of art and artistic experience. In Chapter III the application of the game metaphor to behavior made it possible to hypothesize that playing the perceiver's role involved exposure to disorientation. An analysis of semiotic behavior and the application of that analysis to various works of art, however, offered nothing to support that hypothesis. On the contrary, the interpretation of signs in art, as well as in all human behavior, involves the use by the interpreter of an interpretant (to use Morris' term), or already existing orientation, culturally conventionalized. The only conceivable exception is metaphor, but even when metaphors in poetry are highly innovative, and therefore disorienting at least to the slow-minded, that possible disorientation is the consequence of the poet's assenting to demands not specifically poetic in origin; and it is equally true that during some periods standardized metaphors are demanded. If disorientation is present in the perceiver's role, and therefore the artist's, which is dependent upon and derived from the perceiver's, its source must be found elsewhere than in the semantic aspect. The only other aspect is the formal.

1. THE PERCEPTION OF POETRY

Rather than an attempt at a definition of the "formal aspect," something which, in any event, cannot be done, for reasons to be forthcoming, it will be enough to give a few invented examples of the kind of statement which may be taken as referring to this aspect of art. "The Christ and the apostles in Leonardo's 'Last Supper' are organized into a series of interlocking triangles, of which the figure and head of Christ is the most independent and dominant." "The formal development of Shakespeare's style is characterized by a more or less steady reduction of the relative quantity of closed couplets and end-stop lines." "The form of the symphony consists of four movements, fast, slow, fast, fast. César Franck's symphony is an exception. But the form of this is cyclical, in that certain themes appear in more than one movement." "Formally speaking, nineteenth-century architecture has nothing of interest: the forms are merely repetitions of historical forms."

The question is, "What are the attributes and range of such terms as 'form' and 'formal?'"

A glance at an unabridged dictionary shows the nature of the problem. We are up against one of those words which by now have so many semantic functions that to use it at all guarantees communicative failure. Whenever I hear "form" used in connection with art, my mind goes blank. So many possibilities of interpretational variability open that I am incapable of using any of them. This is why it is essential to begin with specific statements, such as those in the previous paragraph. Consider the first one. A glance at Leonardo's painting, or a careful examination of it, reveals no triangles at all. It is true, however, that it would be easy to draw a triangle around the figure of Christ that would include all of his body visible above the table and would exclude almost all the rest of the painting. It is also true that if we connected the brightest spots in his figure, the two hands and the forehead, we would get something very close to an equilateral triangle and that the two upper sides would correspond almost exactly with the axes of the two arms. But the important consideration is that the painting offers no triangle, either in the figure of Christ or in any of the groups of the apostles.

Consider this statement: "The verse form of Milton's *Paradise Lost* is iambic pentameter. This means that it consists of five feet, each of two syllables, and that in each foot the second syllable is stressed."

This is the stress pattern of the first six lines of *Paradise Lost,* with the feet marked by a vertical line.

$$x/|//|x/|xx|xx|/$$
$$x/|x/|x/|x/|x/$$
$$//|/x|x/|x/|//$$
$$x/|x/|x/|//|x/$$
$$x/|xx|x/|x/|x/$$
$$//|xx|/x|/x|/x|/$$

Of these only the second line conforms to the rule. If the sentence referring to its form is a descriptive sentence, it is obviously false, like the sentence about the triangles in "The Last Supper." However, if it is prescriptive sentence, then we already have some notion of what it is doing in this situation. The application of the game metaphor to art broke down precisely in the application of rules. The role of the challenger requires him to create a disorienting situation by obeying the rules of the game: but the role of the artist permits him to create a disorienting situation by violating those rules. If that happens in a game, the game is over. If it happens in art, the "game" has just begun. As soon as it is recognized that many statements about the form of art are prescriptive statements, or rules which the artist is at liberty to follow or to break as he pleases, the situation begins to make some sense. But it is more than that: the role of the artist *requires* him to break prescriptive rules about form. There are no exceptions. But this still does not give us very much understanding of what the rules are talking about, about what is meant by form. For one thing, the rules for games are complete and explicit. But the explicit rules for art obviously cannot be complete. For example, they rarely say anything about breaking the rules. They are set up in such a way that their only possible meaning is that if the prescriptive statements are followed, the ensuing work of art will be of such a nature that the prescriptive statements will serve as descriptive statements. This is why so much of aesthetics and criticism is engaged in a desperate struggle to make prescriptive statements serve as descriptive statements.

If we apply this analysis to the opening of *Paradise Lost,* the difference between the two kinds of statements emerges at once. Here are the same opening lines, but this time with both words and stresses. But to these are added something else: The sign "#" means a juncture.

$$x \quad / \quad / \quad /x \ / \ xx \ \# \ x \quad x \quad /\#$$
Of Mans First Disobedience, and the Fruit

```
x   /  x  / x   / #  x   / x / #
```
Of that Forbidd'n Tree, whose mortal tast

```
/    /  / x x    / # x / /   / #
```
Brought Death into the World, and all our woe,

```
x   / x / x # / /    / x   /
```
With loss of *Eden*, till one greater Man

```
x /  x # x   x  / x   / x  / #
```
Restore us, and regain the blissful Seat,

```
/ # / x  x  / # x / x  / x /
```
Sing Heav'nly Muse, that on the secret top

```
x / x   #
```
Of Oreb . . .

The first obvious difference between this and the former scheme is that the feet are not marked off by vertical lines. The reason for this is simple: there are no feet. "Stress" and "juncture" are signs of perceptual configurations, but "foot" belongs to an entirely different category of semantic function. Feet and divisions between feet are no more observable in poetry than lines of longitude and latitude are observable on the surface of the earth. The foot is an importation from Latin and Greek prosody and applied by a pedantic classicism to English poetry. Stress and juncture can be experienced: feet cannot. They can, therefore, be entirely dispensed with. The effort to use them is a result of the confusion between prescriptive and descriptive statements, and the confusion of the rules of games with the rules of poetry.

The first prescriptive rule appropriate to the actual text of this poem is that a line should have ten syllables. In these six lines that rule is violated twice. The second rule is that the rhythm should be duple, consisting of alternating stressed and unstressed syllables. That rule is obeyed only in patches. The third is that a line should end with a juncture: that rule is violated twice. The fourth is that there should be a shorter juncture after the fourth, fifth, or sixth syllables. That rule is violated in lines 1, 5, and 6.

An application of what has been said about signs to the artistic situation will clarify this matter. The last definition of art but one in Chapter II was, "A work of art is an occasion for a human being to perform the art-perceiving role in the artistic situation, that is, on the artistic stage." The last definition led to the conclusion that an artifact or behavioral sequence can be regarded as having been or as being the occasion for the perceiver's role if a chronologically arranged sequence of such objects shows both functional identity and non-functional stylistic dynamism. That conclusion made it possible to decide what, in a given culture, should be categorized as art. The last definition but one, however, is useful in the present situation, one in which the cultural apex has already decided what is art. But this gives rise to the question, "How does an individual know whether an artifact or behavioral pattern is or is not a work of art according to the decisions of the cultural center?"

In Royall Tyler's *The Contrast*, the first comedy written by an American, and the second play, there is a famous scene in which a country bumpkin describes how he was taken to a large building with many seats and was astonished to see a group of people, obviously high in society, behaving in public as if nobody else were present. His explanation is that the wall of the house next door had been removed. The joke lies in his naïve failure to recognize the situation as a play. He did not have the perceptual categories "drama" and "theater." Nor did he have knowledge of those situational signs which were there to inform him that what he was about to see was not to be confused with reality. The obvious joke and this painfully obvious explanation are equally instructive. Consider the famous definition of poetry which has been so constantly offered as an indication of naïve stupidity. "It is poetry if the lines are not the same length and if they all begin with a capital letter." A better definition of poetry would be impossible to devise. These are precisely the signs by which, in our culture, one knows that it is poetry. They are not, of course, the only signs, since for the past forty years it has been increasingly common to print poetry without the capital letters at the beginning of each line, but for centuries it was an essential sign. Consider the following passage of poetry:

And Cupid being healéd of his wound,	1
Because he would endure no longer	2
The absence of her he loved, gliding through	3
The narrow window of the chamber wherein	4
He was holden, his pinions being now	5
Repaired by a little rest, fled forth swiftly	6
Upon them, and coming to the place	7
Where Psyche was, shook that sleep away from her,	8
And set him in his prison again, awaking	9
Her with the innocent point of his arrow.	10

The reader is invited to make a prosodic analysis of this passage, indicating the stressed and unstressed syllables and the junctures.

Consider now the following passage:

The first war of the Essenes was with the poetry of selfhood, those sagas and epic rhapsodies which had burst forth to flood all Europe in the time of the northern invasions, when the hideous Huns, extending the right wing of their havoc, swept down on the old land of the Goths.

The first passage is from Walter Pater's novel, *Marius the Epicurean*, Chapter V; the second is lines 498 to 503 of Book III of Robert Bridges' poem, *The Testament of Beauty*. Actually Bridges does not begin his lines with capital letters, and it was considered quite daring for him not to. The Pater passage, of course, was written as prose. Nevertheless, when printed as poetry, almost all trained readers would put junctures at the ends of lines 1, 2, 5, 6, and 7. Yet no trained reader, seeing it printed as prose, would pause or recognize in any way a break or juncture after lines 5, 6, and 7. Further, a trained reader would make the stresses conform as closely as he could to a duple rhythm if he saw it as poetry, but if he read the passage aloud in its original prose form he would pay attention only to supra-segmental stress, which focuses on semantically functional stress.[1]

The appearance on the page of poetry, therefore, is a sign that the passage has been written by both obeying and violating certain prescriptive statements. Conformity to those prescriptions may be predicted; failure to conform cannot: the poem may be, in its stress and

---

[1] An extraordinarily apt example of just this point appeared in the London *Times Literary Supplement* during January and February, 1965. A reviewer praised a particular passage in a poem by the Scots poet Hugh McDiarmid. The next week the editor published a letter pointing out that the passage was word for word from a prose essay, *not* by McDiarmid. The author of that essay wrote to confirm the discovery and to offer a generous explanation that McDiarmid had, as so often happens with authors, confused what he wrote with what he had previously read and remembered word for word. McDiarmid wrote to the TLS, admitting the claim and assuring the public that the passage would be expunged from subsequent editions of his poems. At the time of writing this note (March, 1965) a number of letters had been published, and I expect that more will be. The problems raised were fascinating. First, after the rearrangement by McDiarmid of prose into poetry, was it now poetry, that is, prose still in the original but poetry in McDiarmid's poem? On this there was considerable disagreement. Second, had McDiarmid committed plagiarism? According to the explanation offered in this book, to incorporate prose into a poem by employing the typographic conventions of poetry, makes it a piece of poetry. As for the legal problem, that, of course, would have to be decided by a court of law. Were I asked to give testimony as a literary scholar, I would testify that, in my opinion, there had been no plagiarism and no violation of copyright, because McDiarmid had changed the total semantic function of the passage by adding primary signs and by informing the reader that it was to be read with poetic expectancies, not prose expectancies. The expectation determines what it is. The situation now calls for the poetry-perceiving role.

junctural patterns, entirely regular, or it may be irregular, but the degree, the frequency, and the locus of the irregularities, if there are any, is entirely unpredictable. The appearance on the page, therefore, is a sign of probable success of certain predictions. It is a sign just as much as a heavy black cloud and thunder is a sign of rain, not entirely reliable but reliable enough to lead the careful person to take precautionary action. In each case the sign rouses and is interpreted by an interpretant or orientation which is not derived from the data at hand but has already been conventionally inculcated. Both sets of signs arouse in the interpreter a certain set or expectancy. The interpreter of the rain cloud sign can predict that it either will or will not rain; but although the interpreter of the printed signs of poetry can only predict that some degree of regularity of stress and juncture will be forthcoming, he can make no predictions about how much irregularity he is going to get, or even whether he will get any. The rain cloud interpreter is not going to be disoriented, whether it rains or not; but the interpreter of the printed signs of poetry will be. Furthermore, his predictions for both stress and juncture have none of the reliability of the interpretation of the natural sign. Even if he gets regularity of pattern of stress and juncture, he will not get configurational regularity, because of the four levels of stress and the four degrees of juncture, which have already been discussed. The prescriptive statements applied to an actual poem provide him with a model, but the actual poem violates that model. He has, therefore, a form in the simple sense of "mold," but what he gets never quite fits it, and frequently scarcely fits it at all. The actual experience of the poem is characterized by a discontinuity of experiential process.

It seems reasonable to say, then, that the categorial reference of artistic "form" is not to a range of configurations perceived in the artistic field, but to a range of expectations, or sets, or molds, or models in the perceptual set or orientation. If this can be seen at work in all the arts, justification for the hypothesis of disorientation as the defining character of artistic perception will be forthcoming, and the perceiver's role will have as its defining character a particular kind of perception.

Let us go back a moment, however, to prosody in order to clear up an explanation which has been offered for the contrast between the prescriptive regularity of stress and its actual irregularity. In recent years this phenomenon has often been noticed, but it is usually called "counterpoint," and the application of this term, taken from music, is considered to be a sufficient explanation. This is an excellent example of unhappy analogies made between the arts. For it is not an analogy, which points out similarity of structure, but a metaphor. Further, its application is a bad use of metaphor, because those who have used it have failed to observe in what area of the prosodic stress field it does not work. "Counterpoint" as an imported term in this metaphor is usually taken to mean the simultaneous presentation of two rhythms, the regular rhythm, and the irregular rhythm. But of course, an irregular rhythm is not a rhythm. Further, even if it were, the poem does not present two stress patterns but only one, and that is only occasionally a pattern, with varying frequency from poem to poem and within a poem. In music the meaning of "counterpoint" is simple: it refers to the simultaneous presentation of two or more melodic lines. Hence, the counterpoint metaphor applies an attribute of pitch change to stress. In music the contrast is between two melodic lines, each of which can be extracted from the composition and performed independently. This is obviously not true of verse. The use of "counterpoint" in this situation imports only the attribute of simultaneity, but it totally fails to locate one factor in the poem and the other in the mode of perception.

We are back, then, at the problem of perception and the generalization that perception is possible only because prior to the act of perception the perceiver already is trained to have certain expectations or behavioral sets for particular situations. It will be advantageous to begin with a series of quotations from psychologists of some authority. It is a complex matter, and it seems best to let the professionals speak.

2. A THEORY OF PERCEPTION

The first quotation comes from a massive survey of the problem of perception by F. H. Allport.

> Seldom does intellectual crisis in science attain such cosmic proportions [as that resolved by Einstein's theories]. Nevertheless in every field, and in every topic within a field, this well-known drama seems to repeat itself. In the theories of perception we observed how an early system of introspective analysis of mental phenomena was developed: and for a while it seemed that the notion of "conscious elements" as the units of which the "mind" is composed was the only answer to the question of why things appear as they do. Later, logical considerations began to show this view to be unsound. . . . There arose a conception of wholes, relationships, and supersummation. [Gestalt theory.] Patterning, rather than what is patterned, seemed to be the essence of mind. . . .

Yet this solution, in turn, gave rise to an issue. . . . It was . . . seen that configurationism had achieved its successes at the cost of practically ignoring the motor side of the organism. . . .

Of late we have witnessed one of the most dramatic episodes in the history of perceptual theory. Perceived dimensions were traditionally supposed to be firmly rooted in psychophysical theory and autochthonous principles. But recently this idea has been assailed. As we have seen, it has been claimed on the basis of experimental evidence that conditions internal to the organism, such as drive, value, or need, can affect the way in which the physical world appears, even in its supposedly stable quantitative properties. Phenomena appeared that seemed to suggest, at least to many, the presence of a functionalistic preperceiver who selected the sensory data that were to be permitted the right to organize as perceptions. Here was a crisis indeed. If this sort of thing was perception, then most of the knowledge gained from the earlier study of stimulus-percept relations must be an illusion, or at best insecure.[2]

There are two main traditions in this dramatic episode, which is by no means finished, but is already usable. The older is *transactionalism.* This resulted from a fusion of the pragmatism of John Dewey (who originated the term) with the experiments begun by Adalbert Ames, Jr., as far back as the 1920's, and continued by Hadley Cantril, W. H. Ittelson, and Franklin Kilpatrick, originally at Dartmouth, then at Princeton, and now at Brooklyn College. A recent statement of this position is worth quoting at length.

This belief in the possibility of reducing observation to absolute objectivity is basic to much of our current thinking. It leads to dichotomies, such as fact versus value, organism versus environment, subjective versus objective, etc. It underlies most theorizing concerning the nature of science. In psychology one is hard put to find an approach to human behavior which departs from this basic premise. Stimuli or stimulus patterns are treated as though they exist apart from the perceiving organism. Mechanical or interactional relationship between the organism and an "objectively defined" environment are sought, and purposes and values are often ruled out as not belonging in a strictly scientific psychology. A growing awareness of the false nature of such dichotomies, and the acute contrast between the theoretical possibility and the practical impossibility of leaving values and purposes out of scientific observation, has pointed up the necessity for re-examining the basic formulations from which these problems stem.

Historically, these formulations stem from experimentation which reasoned from *object* to *organism.* If one begins, thus, with an external object, an invariant correspondence between object and stimulus pattern is demonstrable. For example, it is simple geometry to show that, in standardized illumination, a specific object at a specific location relative to the eye will always yield the same stimulus pattern on the retina. Once this invariance is *in the organism*

---

[2] *Theories of Perception and the Concept of Structure,* by F. H. Allport, New York, 1955, pp. 438–439. Copyright John Wiley and Sons, Inc. Used by permission of John Wiley and Sons, Inc.

(on the retina), it is completely logical to propose that what is seen basically corresponds to what is there. This sort of analysis depends upon introducing the object at the beginning; having been introduced, it is always present.

But what happens when one turns matters around and attempts, instead, to reason from a given physiological stimulus pattern to a unique related external configuration? It becomes apparent that the treasured invariant relationship disappears. For example, in visual perception one is faced with the fact that any given visual stimulus-pattern can be produced by an infinity of different external conditions, and this holds true for both monocular and binocular vision. But we never see an infinity of configurations; we see just one. This means, of course, that perception cannot be "due to" the physiological stimulus pattern; some physiological stimulus probably is necessary, but it is not sufficient. There must be, in addition, some basis for the organism's "choosing" one from among the infinity of external conditions to which the pattern might be related. Thus, any notion concerning a unique correspondence between percept and object must be abandoned, and a discovery of the factors involved in the "choosing" activity of the organism becomes the key problem in perceptual theory.

Our work has been aimed at a systematic examination of such problems, and out of this examination there has been developed a basic formulation concerning the nature of knowing and of observation, which is neither solipsistic denial of reality nor a postulation of its independent existence. This basic theory is one which has elsewhere been called "transactional." According to this view, living is an enormously complex evolving process which includes space and time and environment, as well as the organism, in an indissoluble whole. A segment in time of this process may be labeled as a "transaction" (Dewey) or "occasion" (Whitehead) in which all aspects of the process are contained, including purposes, past experience in the form of assumptions, and the future in the form of expectancies. Cantril explains this position in the following way: "Each transaction of living involves numerous capacities and aspects of man's nature which operate together. Each occasion of life can occur only through an environment; is imbued with some purpose; requires action of some kind, and the registration of the consequences of action. Every action is based upon some awareness or perception, which in turn is determined by the assumptions brought to the occasion. All of these processes are interdependent. No one process could function without the others."[3]

Evidence for the necessity for such an approach is to be found in the demonstrations and experiments reported in this volume, which suggest strongly that the search for absolute objectivity is a vain one. Apparently, the correspondence between percept and object is never absolute. Instead, perception is of functional probabilities, of constructs which emerge from the consequences of past action and serve as directives for furthering the purposes of the organism through action. "Percept" and "object" are but two abstracted aspects of this total process and correspondence between the two is simply a function of their being part and parcel of the same thing.

At a somewhat higher conceptual level, it would appear that the perceptual process itself is but an abstraction from a total evolving process which includes space and time and environment, as well as the organism in an indissoluble whole. Perception is that phase of the total process which is an implicit awareness of the probable consequences of purposive action with respect to some

---

[3] A note ascribes this passage to Hadley Cantril, *The Why of Man's Experience*, New York, Macmillan, 1950, p. 59.

object. Man never can know more of the external world than those aspects which are directly relevant to the carrying out of his purposes. Each man's perceptions are therefore his own, unique and personal; common perceptions become possible in so far as common experiences and common strivings are shared among individuals. This approach places perceiving squarely within the context of human striving, the "thing perceived" being inseparably a part of the "process of perceiving" and both reflecting "reality" only by virtue of the active participation of the perceiver in the full-bodied ongoing process of living!

By perception, then, is meant that part of the transactional process which is an implicit awareness of the probable significance for action of present impingements from the environment, based on assumptions related to the same or similar impingements from the environment. By assumption is meant that generally unconscious aspect of the transactional process which may be described as a weighted average of past experience in dealing with those portions of the impingements from the environment to which it is related. Assumptions function as probabilities which are built up by action, checked by action, and modified by action as the consequences of these actions are registered in relation to purposes. Taken altogether, our assumptions form our "assumptive world" which we bring to every occasion and on which our perceptions are based; therefore, the only world we know is determined by our assumptions. The assumptive world is conceptualized as that complex set of internalized, interrelated generalizations or standards which are not dependent for their effectiveness on any given reference point in space or in time. It thus provides whatever constancy there is in our environment and whatever continuity there is in our experience.

From this description the perceptual process emerges as a dynamic fusion involving cues from the environment, assumptions, and action. The process is one in which cues from the environment are related to assumptions, giving rise to perceptions which are "prognostic directives" for action. Action based on perception not only results in different cues being received from the environment but its consequences in relation to purposes are reflected in the modification of assumptions and/or to the bringing into play of different assumptions. Of course, it should not be supposed that the perceptual process proceeds in the step-by-step fashion necessitated by verbal description; it is a process involving at any one moment a complex integration of at least those factors mentioned.[4]

The similarities of this position to the assumptions on which I am building up this investigation into artistic behavior are so great as to provide a theoretical explanation for my procedure. For example, in the third paragraph of this passage the statement that the organism "chooses" one from among an infinity of external conditions corresponds to what I have called interpretative behavior in the discussion of categories in Section 2 of Chapter III. Again, the reference to Dewey's "transaction" and Whitehead's "occasion" refer to what I have called "situation," and what is called "assumptions" I have called "orientations." The phrase, "implicit awareness of the

[4] *Explorations in Transactional Psychology* by Franklin P. Kilpatrick, New York, 1961, pp. 2–5. Copyright New York University Press. Used by permission of New York University Press.

probable significance for action of present impingements from the environment," describes what in the preceding section I called the poetry perceiver's awareness that some degree of regularity of stress and juncture will be forthcoming. Finally, the definition of perceptions as prognostic directives for action is precisely what I mean by locating artistic form in the mode of perception rather than in the work of art.

The other principal theory is what Allport called in his 1955 volume the "directive-state" theory, a term which Jerome Bruner, its principal proponent, has accepted. Bruner, coming to the problem through social psychology, had, apparently, become aware of the role personality plays in the organization of perception and interpretation.

> The past few years have witnessed a notable increase in interest in and investigation of the cognitive processes—the means whereby organisms achieve, retain, and transform information. . . .
> One need not look for the origins of the revival. Partly, it has resulted from a recognition of the complex processes that mediate between the classical "stimuli" and "responses" out of which stimulus-response learning theories hoped to fashion a psychology that would by-pass anything smacking of the "mental." The impeccable peripheralism of such theories could not last long. As "S-R" theories came to be modified to take into account the subtle events that may occur between the input of a physical stimulus and the emission of an observable response, the old image of the "stimulus-response bond" began to dissolve, its place being taken by a mediation model. As Edward Tolman so felicitously put it some years ago, in place of a telephone switchboard connecting stimuli and responses it might be more profitable to think of a map room where stimuli were sorted out and arranged before ever response occurred, and one might do well to have a closer look at these intervening "cognitive maps."[5]

This is what he does in his book, which was so useful for Chapter III, above. The earliest state of his theory, which by now of course has been considerably refined, was published in 1951 and was the basis for the experiments which resulted in *A Study of Thinking*. It is still worth quoting.

> My collaborator, Leo Postman, and I have been drawn increasingly closer over the last few years toward an expectancy or hypothesis theory of perception. . . .
> Basically, perceiving involves a three-step cycle. Analytically, we may say that perceiving begins with an expectancy or hypothesis. In the language of Woodworth [1947], we not only see, but we look for, not only hear but listen to. In short, perceiving takes place in a "tuned organism." The assumption is that we are never randomly set or *eingestellt* but that, rather, we are always to

---

[5] Jerome S. Bruner, *A Study of Thinking*, New York, 1956, p. vii.

some extent *prepared* for seeing, hearing, smelling, tasting some particular thing or class of things. What evokes an hypothesis? Any given hypothesis results from the arousal of central cognitive and motivational processes by preceding environmental states of affairs.

The second analytic step in the perceiving process is the input of information from the environment. . . .

The third step in the cycle is a checking or confirmation procedure. Input information is confirmatory to or congruent with the operative hypothesis. If confirmation does not occur, the hypothesis shifts in a direction partly determined by internal or personological or experimental factors and partly on the basis of feedback from the learning which occurred in the immediately preceding, partly unsuccessful information-checking cycle.[6]

The conclusions to which Allport comes, though they are now a decade old, are also of great interest and pertinence to the problem of artistic perception.

> It is clear . . . that the problem of perceptual theory has now been broadened. We can no longer view it as separate from that of learning. The aggregate that we have been calling perception is now becoming an aggregate of behavior. It must be considered as a physiological process or pattern developing and strengthening through time and performances, as well as one that underlies immediate experience. Instead of saying either that perceptual phenomena are strictly "perceptual" or that they are fundamentally the operations of "learning" we could say that perceptual theory and learning theory are two different ways of looking at the same facts.[7]

> . . . a perceptual act is really a dynamically operating *structure*, . . . it presents the very picture of a self delimited and self-contained structuring of ongoings and events. . . . It appears as a structure that is closely knit, yet not isolated from surrounding happenings, that is built up of the events of ongoing and interacting elements—events that have assembled, as it were, through space and time, a structure that can endure, that is flexible and yet ordered and resistant to disruption, that has both a nonquantitative and a quantitative aspect, that pools or averages its energies, that "gears in" with some adjacent structures and opposes or reduces others, and that operates as self closing or self renewing cycles.[8]

All this is consonant with what has been said earlier about the impossibility of creating a meta-position. If perception is the consequence of a "transaction" or a "directive-state," if an act of perception is an act of interpretation, then the transactionist's or the directive-statist's perception of perception is also an interpretation. But this is

---

[6] "Personality Dynamics and the Process of Perceiving," by Jerome S. Bruner in *Perception—An Approach to Personality*, edited by Robert R. Blake and Glenn V. Ramsey, pp. 123–124. Copyright 1951 The Ronald Press Company.

[7] Allport, p. 463.

[8] Allport, pp. 612–613.

the human condition. Our thinking is always ultimately circular; all we can hope to do is to include as much in the circle as possible. Perception theory and philosophy are beginning to converge.[9]

If the reader wishes to test for himself these theories about perception, there is a very easy way for him to do so. Not every one knows that if you look at a picture with one eye closed, it will have a stereoscopic effect; it will appear to have depth, the kind of depth we experience in two-eyed or stereoscopic vision. If you close one eye and look, not at a picture but at any ordinary field of vision, it will appear to be without depth, to be flat. According to pre-transactional, mechanical theories of perception, it must be impossible for a one-eyed man to have depth perception or the equivalent of stereoscopic vision. Yet I know of a one-eyed artist who has perfect depth perception. If the mechanical theory were true, it would be impossible for a one-eyed man to drive an automobile, or certainly very dangerous. But it would also be impossible for two-eyed people to experience depth perception when with only one eye they look at a photograph or any picture, even one with very low iconicity. Further, the Grand Canyon would appear to be just as far across at noon as it does when the sun is lower in the sky.

This odd phenomenon is easily explained if one observes that when one looks at a picture with only one eye, one looks at it against a background ordinarily perceived stereoscopically but now perceived without depth. The depth perception, or stereoscopic effect, is consequent upon our interpretation of certain clues, light and shade, relative size of objects, and so on. In stereoscopic vision among these clues are the non-identity of the two retinal images. This may be checked if you look at a tree or a telephone pole or a box so placed that you can see two sides, rapidly alternating your vision from one eye to the other.

---

[9] It is a quite extraordinary example of cultural convergence that the German philosophers Edmund Husserl (1859–1938) and Martin Heidegger (1889–   ), followed by the French philosopher Jean Paul Sartre (1905–   ), have arrived at conclusions strikingly similar to those of the American Transactionalists, though their path has been through philosophy rather than through scientific psychology. Currently, American psychology is being convulsed by the "phenomenological" movement, derived from Husserl and Heidegger. The reason is that these two philosophers have called into question the traditional sharp distinction between "subject" and "object," which, as Kilpatrick implies, are hypostatizations, or, according to the theory of signs presented here, are not entities but categorial terms. Behavioristic psychology has assumed (has used as its "directive state,") that the subject responds to a stimulus from an object. This position has become untenable for the current crop of rebels in academic psychology.

You will then perceive that with each eye you get a different image, different information. Like a one-eyed man, given enough practice you would be able to perceive depth without this kind of information but from other information. Stereoscopic vision is, then, a highly redundant information situation, from which any element can be eliminated without harming depth perception if the perceiver has enough practice, that is, learns to get along without it, as our one-eyed artist has.

When, therefore, a two-eyed individual closes one eye and looks at a picture of some iconicity, not being accustomed to doing without the two images of stereoscopic vision, which ordinarily make the picture look flat and without depth, he sees the background field as flat. This enables him to perceive the depth in the picture by picking up other clues, for with only one eye open there is no conflict between the clues in the picture and the clues in the background field against which the picture is perceived. Consequently, he can interpret the clues in the picture and perceive depth, as if he were looking at the two images of a stereoscopic photograph through a two-lensed stereoscopic viewer. Only, the latter is actually less satisfactory than one-eyed perception of a single picture.

The reader may further check this by comparing the depth "illusion" in a picture of, let us say, the nave of a cathedral, looking towards the altar, with a picture of hay-stacks or anything else presented as a series of receding planes, rather than as a powerful set of perspective lines. Our culture trains everyone in the conventions of perspective as they were first worked out in the fifteenth century and have been subsequently refined. However, even Chinese landscape paintings, or reproductions, will show depth if looked at with one eye and if the perceiver gives himself a chance to assimilate and interpret the information, which is mostly a matter of shading and size. The shift from seeing such pictures flat, when I look at them with one eye, and then suddenly re-interpreting the information and seeing them as deep has a very peculiar visceral effect; for a moment I feel slightly sick to the stomach.[10]

Perhaps the reader will forgive another bit of autobiography, for it has considerable pertinence here and for what will follow. My father, Dr. Ray Morse Peckham, lived in Connecticut in the 1920's and practiced optometry. He became friendly with Adalbert Ames, then

---

[10] See Robert L. Fantz, "The Origin of Form Perception," *Scientific American*, Vol. 204, May, 1961, pp. 66–72; Eckhard H. Hess, "Shadows and Depth Perception," the same, Vol. 204, March, 1961, pp. 138–148.

at Dartmouth, and worked with him on some of his experiments. He also devised some of his own. I well remember his experimentation with stereoscopic vision and photography. From these he developed an elaborate series of exercises to correct faulty vision, including a way of straightening crossed eyes without operation—the first time it was done. But far more interesting was his discovery, quite without any psychiatric training or indeed general reading in psychiatry, that the emotional condition of a patient could affect the vision. Particularly interested in the problems of children's vision, he discovered that whenever he found a child with myopic vision—short-sightedness—he almost invariably discovered that the child came from a broken or highly disturbed family situation. Better evidence for the general position of transactionalism—that our interests affect our perceptions— could scarcely be found.

In any event, it should now be clear that the last fifteen years have seen a revolution in the theory of perception so extensive that it is no longer really possible to tell perception theory, learning theory, and behavior theory apart. They are all different ways of talking about the same data. Obviously one major question remains open. Why is perception dynamic? Why do perceptual categories "develop?" What Bruner and Postman call the confirmation procedure, the third step of perception, clearly involves some kind of checking of the set or hypothesis against the informational input. This can only mean that disparities between the set or hypothesis and the information input are observable. Failure of confirmation means a frustration of cognitive activity. Why does the organism continue its search?

> Cognitive frustration, within tolerable limits, helps keep search-behavior going. The "insight" experience leads to new bursts of testing activity. We are completely without evidence for such assertions or even without proposals as to how one might gather evidence.[11]

But for our purposes all that is necessary is the notion of cognitive frustration, the recognition that the organism can respond to disparities, and the realization that this response leads to further problem-solving behavior. This was discussed in Chapter III, but is worth bringing out again.

Since artistic experience involves perception, one would think that this revolution in perception theory would by now have had a pro-

---

[11] Bruner, *A Study of Thinking*, p. 17.

found influence on aesthetics. It has had almost none. Gombrich has used some of it in *Art and Illusion* to settle that what was traditionally called representation is really a matter of conventions and that these conventions are under extra-artistic control. Monroe Beardsley's *Aesthetics* has no reference to any of the psychologists quoted here. Actually, there is no difficulty in understanding why modern perception theory has had so little impact. As Kilpatrick put it, aestheticians "have reasoned from object to organism." The object "having been introduced, it is always present." In fact, they rarely have reasoned beyond the object. But the point need not be labored.

The only exception of any significance I have been able to discover is the work of Leonard B. Meyer, who has applied the expectancy theory to music with singularly rich and rewarding results.[12] His book is all the more astonishing in that the only reference in the notes to set and expectation is to an article by O. H. Mowrer, published in 1941. Presumably Meyer was familiar with other literature, but it is quite possible that he developed his theory out of little more than this hint. In his introduction he mentions John Dewey and George Mead, the very philosophers from whose writings transactionalism emerged, as well as Charles Morris, who read his manuscript and advised him.[13]

It is a pleasure to say that I owe Meyer a great debt. My own original and odd form of expectancy theory emerged from my extreme discontent with explanations for prosody, in very much the form I have presented them in at the beginning of this chapter. Since, fortunately, I had not encountered the counterpoint explanation, I had not been trapped by that confusing metaphor. The only usable term I was then familiar with—this was in the late 1940's—was *gestalt*. It seemed to me that a prosodic pattern was a *gestalt* that was then violated by the actual stress configuration given, and that the same thing was true of phrases, or phonic continuities between junctures, as I now call them. My suspicion that Meyer's conclusions emerged from the

---

[12] *Emotion and Meaning in Music*, Chicago, 1956.

[13] The New Look in perception theory, as the various kinds of transactionalism and directive-state theory have been called, is very much in the tradition of pragmatism, instrumentalism, and operationalism. Indeed, given the position of Kant, its logical emergence was bound to occur sooner or later. (In fact, Samuel Taylor Coleridge worked out the essential pattern in the 1820's. See James D. Boulger, *Coleridge as Religious Thinker*, New Haven, 1961.) This is why Percy Bridgman, the great physicist and operationalist, was so profoundly influenced by the Ames-Cantril experiments at Princeton. His account is in *The Way Things Are*, Cambridge, Mass, 1959, p. 8.

pragmatic tradition derives from a recognition that my own thinking was certainly derived from it, perhaps from my father's discovery of the relation between myopia in children and disturbed family situations.[14] I also felt that the logical positivists' distinction between meaningful statements and emotive statements was unsound, and that predictive statements must be thought about in terms of predictive behavior. Familiarity with a central tradition of modern anthropological theory led me to ask what the function of "emotive" statements might be, as well as the function of "meaningful" statements, that is, predictive statements. It seemed clear to me that there could be no prediction without an orientation which selected what the prediction was to be about. This is of interest, of course, only because of the fine example of cultural convergence it offers. When I read Meyer's book, therefore, I felt for the first time that I was on a fruitful line of inquiry. Up to that point I had felt extremely lonely. The subsequent reading of Barnett's *Innovation* gave me further confidence. After that came the discovery that my general position, if not its application to art, had massive support in psychological theory and experimentation. The real moral of this story lies in its revelation of the problems posed by academic specialization. And it also seemed that it would interest the reader to know that the general approach offered here, at least as far as the formal aspect of art is concerned, has been applied with striking success to at least one of the arts. Finally, it would be both unfair and dishonest to present a position as if no one had successfully used it before. Certainly, however, whether the reader agrees with Meyer and myself or not, it is evident that aesthetics lies in ruins not only because of logical faults but also because modern perception theory has destroyed its entire psychological foundation.

3. DISCONTINUITY

With this background, it is now possible to return to the application of modern perception theory to poetry; and for the sake of simplicity I shall henceforward select the word "expectancy" from the terminology available. The rules for poetry do not describe poetry, but rather prescribe; the situation in which the poem appears induces in the perceiver—tunes the organism, in the Bruner-Postman phrase—

---

[14] *World Hypotheses* by the philosopher Stephen C. Pepper (Berkeley, Cal., 1942) also played an important part.

certain expectancies which would be totally congruent with the poem if the rules were descriptive; consequently it is apparent that the term "form" refers not to anything "in" the poem but is rather a sign for a category the range of which includes as members such expectancies. "Poetic form," then, is a category of expectancies which the poetic situation induces in the perceiver when he plays the perceiver's role. As we have seen, there are all kinds of reasons why the perceiver's role should not be played. But when the perceiver's role *is* being played, what the perceiver experiences when his expectancies are frustrated or violated is a *discontinuity* of experience.

A simple example will make this clear and also bring out another aspect of expectancy frustration, the emotional affect. Consider the case of a man who lives alone on the forty-fifth floor of an apartment building. He, and he alone, has a key. His habit, when he comes home at night, is not to use the light switch at the door but rather to walk diagonally across the living room and switch on a light standing on a low table at one end of the couch. A coffee table sits in front of the couch, but the couch is so placed that the line of approach from door to lamp is completely clear and perfectly straight. Very well: One night the man comes home, walks towards the lamp—and falls over the coffee table. No one could have entered the apartment, yet when he left the apartment in the morning, the coffee table was in its customary position. His expectancy is that his path will be clear, yet that expectancy has been frustrated: the "form" of his perception has been violated.

His first response is disorientation; his mode of prediction in this situation has failed. He experiences a profound emotional disturbance, as "emotion" has been defined above. The sympathetic nervous system, which equips us physiologically for the great energy release necessary to meet emergencies, has been violently activated. How that affect shows up in him is a matter of individual physiologic response, or personality style. But however it shows up, the man has experienced a "discontinuity" of experience. The next activity is to renew search-behavior, which is the norm of all oriented human perceptual activity, in other words, to reorient himself. He must interpret what has happened to him. Since it is impossible that the table should have moved itself—our man does not believe in poltergeists—someone may still be in the room. If he entered without permission he is there for no good, robbery or murder, very probably. How the man behaves now is a consequence of his previous experience and cultural conditioning. He may make a leap for the lamp, or run for the door, or collapse into hysteria or shock. Whatever happens to him, he has interpreted the situation as an emergency situation. This gives a new charge to the emotional affect, a further violent stimulus to the sympathetic nervous system.

This is the basic pattern of the poetic or any other artistic experience, as we shall see. It is not, as I shall attempt to show later, the function of art to provide us with powerful emotional experiences. Rather, emotional affect is the *test* of a successful performance of the perceiver's role. This is obvious when one listens to one's own or to anyone else's discussion of an artistic experience. It is judged a valuable artistic experience if it has occasioned a profound emotional response. "I was not—or I was—profoundly moved" is not, as it appears to be, a judgment on the work of art, but a judgment on the success of the perceiver's performance. In poetry, as in all art then, there are two emotional sources, discontinuity and conditioned response to the natural and artificial signs the artistic field presents. "Conditioned response," however, is perhaps too old-fashioned a term; it would be more consistent with the general position presented here as well as expectancy theory simply to refer to "learned affect." This usage would be consonant with Allport's conclusions.

It is now possible to use a different term for the hitherto not quite empty category of "non-functional stylistic dynamism." Henceforth, for that compound verbal sign, I shall use "formal discontinuity," or, ordinarily, merely "discontinuity," the violation or frustration of the expectancies set up in the individual by the situational signs that it is appropriate for him to play the perceiver's role. This formulation makes one aspect of the central problem of this book immediately apparent: the rules govern the artist's behavior in manipulating a particular medium. A rule governing what an artist does to language is obviously utterly different from a rule governing what he does with paint, or with solids, spaces, and screens, or with musical tones. *On purely non-functional or formal grounds, therefore, there is no relation to be found among the arts.* Different arts set up in the perceiver completely different expectancies. At the same time, however, it must be realized that just as one art can and does set up a package of numerous expectancies, so "mixed arts," like the plays or operas or recitations of poetry to a background of music, can set up expectancies of one or more arts. If any relation among the arts is to be found it is not to be discovered in their formal aspects, in the discontinuities themselves.

There is no more relation between the rules governing artists working in different media than there is between the rules governing a game of tag and those governing atomic investigation.

Two points are worth recalling here. One is that the term "rule" is derived from the application of the game metaphor to human behavior. Some rules are explicit, but some are only implicit. There must have been a time, for example, when human beings played games but had no explicit rules. "Rule," therefore, does not limit the investigation into discontinuities to explicit rules. Here is another area in which the application of game metaphor is inadequate. The artist and the researcher into atomic physics, or any human being playing a role in any situation, are alike in that only some of the rules are explicit. One of the things Kuhn is doing in his study of scientific revolution is making explicit many of the rules governing scientific behavior.[15] His point is that rules govern the scientist until the application of the rules can no longer take care of data which is recalcitrant to being structured according to the current body of rules or, as he calls them, the current "paradigm." Generally speaking, the ordinary scientist ignores such data. It takes the scientific genius, the scientific innovator, to force a rule change, which is resisted in science as much as it is in any other branch of human behavior—except art. It is clear that the artist is rewarded with praise, status, and money for breaking or violating rules, for offering discontinuous experience. But all other human activity is normally rewarded for offering a continuity of experience, for following rules. It follows that any explanation of either of the art roles, artist and perceiver, must account for the odd phenomenon of discontinuity, which is the distinguishing or differentiating attribute of artistic behavior.

Applying, now, the completed definition of a work of art from Chapter II, "any perceptual field which an individual uses as an occasion for performing the role of art perceiver," it is now possible to say that *the distinguishing character or attribute of the perceiver's role is search-behavior focussed on awareness of discontinuities.* This awareness of the disparity between expected and experienced configuration is remarkably analogous to the structure of problem solving. But again, as we have seen in applying the game metaphor, the perceiver, in this sense, is not interested in solving a problem, only in experiencing as

---

[15] Thomas S. Kuhn, *The Structure of Scientific Revolutions*, Chicago, 1962.

affect the perception of a disparity or discontinuity. Nevertheless, any attempt to account for the function of art as a biological adaptation must relate it to problem solving.

Discontinuity, then, is the defining attribute of the perceiver's role. As we have seen, however, in Chapter II, when an attribute of a category is made explicit by some single or compound sign, it becomes itself a categorial sign. "Discontinuity" refers to a category of experiences. Further, the range of the category "discontinuity" may be broken into sub-categories. It is possible to distinguish at least four of these: "implicit discontinuity," "internal discontinuity," "modal discontinuity," and "external discontinuity." Using the terminology already offered, it is possible and useful to present at this point definitions for each sub-category, though, of course, these definitions, for the moment, will not mean much to the reader.

Implicit discontinuity is the violation of any perceptual form implied by the perceiver's recognition of a perceptual field which, in his culture, is an art situation, or by his application of those rules to any perceptual field not hitherto, in his culture, so conventionalized. This is why the Chinese connoisseur can see a naturally formed rock as a work of art, and equally why a contemporary sculptor can see a mashed automobile as a work of art.

Internal discontinuity is the violation of a perceptual form established for that particular work of art. It, too, can be experienced in the perception of fields not hitherto defined as works of art.

Modal discontinuity is the violation of those perceptual forms which are the sources of implicit and internal discontinuity in a given work of art. It is also the violation of an expectancy that a particular mode of sign structure or package already established in a work of art, should be continued in that work of art. It is changing horses in midstream, and it too can be experienced before culturally novel perceptual fields.

External discontinuity refers to the discontinuous relation between a work of art and its predecessors in the same category. The explanation for external discontinuity lies in the fact that when particular devices for achieving implicit, internal, and modal discontinuity have been used for any period of time the perceiver can come to anticipate them, or predict them; the artist's role, therefore, requires him to innovate new devices. To a person at the cultural apex, works of art which employ devices of discontinuity to which he is pretty well adapted appear old-fashioned. Obviously they will not look out of date to someone who is just entering the artistic world of high-level culture. An external discontinuity, then, is the historical consequence of the stabilization of an innovative device for implicit, internal, and modal discontinuity. It explains why art has non-functional stylistic historical dynamism, why one dimension of artistic behavior must be historical.

External discontinuity suggests three conclusions. One is that when we use the term "non-functional stylistic dynamism" we are referring to the accumulation during a stylistic period of external discontinuities, which are, of course, dependent upon the presence of the discontinuities in individual works, implicit, internal, and modal. "Discontinuity," then, is not merely a substitute for "non-functional stylistic dynamism"; it implies and offers an explanation for it. The second suggested conclusion is that the kind of person who climbs from lower to higher levels on the artistic face of the cultural pyramid is one who is dissatisfied with the experience of discontinuity available at his cultural level. The final suggested conclusion is that the farther down one goes into the culture, the farther down the art face of the cultural pyramid one descends, the less discontinuity one will find for individual works of art and the slower the rate of external discontinuity. These suggested conclusions will be developed in the two concluding chapters; they are offered here only as devices to give the category "external discontinuity" and "discontinuity" a little more attributional richness. Finally, external discontinuity may also be experienced before a perceptual field not hitherto culturally defined as an occasion for art just as well as any of the other kinds.

4. POETRY

When this scheme is applied to poetry, the first thing to notice is that what is true of phonic overdetermination is also true of the devices for discontinuity which poetry has developed. They are limited by the rules of language. Compared with the other arts, poetry is comparatively poverty stricken, just as it is more limited in the primary signs at its disposal. But the fact that it does have discontinuities accounts, in part, for the extreme difficulty of translating poetry. To get the exact correlation in another language of verbal signs, primary signs, and discontinuities appears to be beyond human capacity. Theoretically, such a task could be programmed for an electronic computer and perhaps successfully achieved. But at the present time even the programming would be impossible.

However, if poetry does not have the quantity of discontinuities available to music, painting, and architecture, it has one advantage which they do not have. In those arts, to respond to the discontinuities the perceiver must first learn the rules. As we shall see, the only thing he already has is the perception of configurational regularity which he learned as a child and which has, of course, been reinforced on innumerable occasions by the time he becomes an adult. Poetry, on the other hand, can violate a habit of expectancy, a set of rules, reinforced thousands of times a day, the expectations of sentence structure, or syntax. The basic pattern of the English sentence is subject-verb-object (or other pattern completer, or complement). This is the SVO pattern. Other syntactical elements are connected with these basic elements by modification, the principle being that the modifier should be as close to the element on which it is dependent as possible. Thus the English sentence can be considered as a hierarchy of modifications: at the first level is SVO: individual words, phrases, and clauses which function as any of these; at the next level are the modifiers of each, articles, adverbs, adjectives, and phrases and clauses which function as adjectives and adverbs: at the next are the modifiers of the second level, and so on. The explicit rules governing the word order of the English sentence are designed to make this hierarchial structure as clear and lucid as possible. Anyone who has tried to handle a sentence with a number of levels and numerous elements in each level is aware of how difficult this can be, and how often the rules are in conflict with each other. The good writer of expository prose is the writer who, besides meeting other demands, can manage the linear presentation of two-dimensional structure. But even the best readers can have difficulties with the work of a writer who employs many levels and many elements in each level. The good writer of poetry, however, is not the one who makes the structure of the sentence clear and lucid. On the contrary; here is a set of rules all ready for him to violate, and he violates them constantly. He frequently creates a syntactical tangle which only a great deal of practice enables one to untangle readily as one reads. In this sense, all poetry is badly written, and the higher on the artistic face of the cultural pyramid it lies, the worse it is written. A couple of examples will suffice. The first comes from Part I of Alexander Pope's *Essay on Criticism* (1711).

Still green with Bays each *ancient* Altar stands
Above the reach of *Sacrilegious* hands,
Secure from *Flames*, from *Envy's* fiercer Rage,
Destructive *War*, and all involving *Age*.
See from *each Clime* the Learn'd their Incense bring;
Hear, in *all Tongues* consenting *Paeans* ring!
In Praise so just, let ev'ry Voice by join'd,
And fill the *Gen'ral Chorus* of *Mankind*.

In normal word order, this would read as follows:

Each ancient altar stands still green with bays [and] above the reach of sacri-
ligious hands; [it is] secure from flames, from the fiercer rage of envy, [from]
destructive war, [and] from all-involving age. See the learned from each clime
bring their incense! Hear consenting paeans ring in all tongues! Let every
voice by joined in praise so just [in order to] fill [out completely] the general
chorus of mankind.

A second example comes from "Casino" (1936) by W. H. Auden.

Only the hands are living; to the wheel attracted,
Are moved as deer trek desperately towards a creek
    Through the dust and scrub of the desert, or gently
    As sunflowers turn to the light.

In normal order:

Only the hands are living; [they are] attracted to the wheel [either desperately,
just] as deer trek towards a creek through the dust and scrub of the desert,
or gently, [just] as sunflowers turn to the light.

A third is the first nine and one-half lines of *Paradise Lost* (1667).

Of Mans First Disobedience, and the Fruit
Of that Forbidd'n Tree, whose mortal tast
Brought Death into the World, and all our woe,
With loss of Eden, till one greater man
Restore us, and regain the blissful Seat,
Sing Heavn'ly Muse, that on the secret top
Of Oreb, or of Sinai, didst inspire
That Shepherd, who first taught the chosen Seed,
In the Beginning how the Heav'ns and Earth
Rose out of Chaos:

[O] heavenly Muse, sing of man's first disobedience, and [of] that forbidden
tree whose mortal taste brought death into the world and [brought] all our woe,
[including the] loss of Eden, [a loss which we must endure until] one greater
man [shall] regain [for us] the blissful seat and restore [it to] us. [I am addressing

thee, heavenly Muse, who] on the secret top [either] of Oreb or of Sinai inspire[d] that shepherd who first taught the chosen seed how in the beginning the heavens and [the] earth rose out of chaos.

These translations from poetry into prose make it possible to explain why there is always a loss when poetry is paraphrased: the syntactical discontinuities disappear. The perceiver cannot experience the emotional affect consequent upon syntactical disorientation. One source of external discontinuity is a matter of increasing or decreasing the amount of syntactical discontinuity to be found in the recent poetry against which a particular poem is written. For example, James Thomson, who was a generation younger than Pope, simplified his syntactical violations considerably from Pope's practice; and Gerard Manley Hopkins made the level of his syntactical violation considerably higher than that of his mid-Victorian predecessors. To be sure, the poet does not calculate mathematically and with the aid of a computer that amount; he arrives at it by what Kilpatrick calls a "weighted average." The poet, as perceiver, has adapted himself to a certain degree of syntactical discontinuity; all he has to do is to violate in either direction his formal expectancy; he tests the presence and degree of that violation exactly as the perceiver does, by whether or not it makes him feel uncomfortable, disturbed, disoriented, excited, ecstatic, that is, by whether or not it produces an affect.

It is obvious that there was a considerable decline in syntactical discontinuity between *Paradise Lost* and *An Essay on Criticism*. However, there were compensations. Pope is famous for being "correct" and always showing "decorum." In any situation correct behavior is behavior which is governed by a scrupulous attention to the behavioral rules for that situation. But to show decorum means more; it involves slight adjustments of the rule to the particular situation, or, to be a little more precise, to the perception of that situation as belonging to a narrower, or sub-category, of the situation. "Decorum," then, invariably involves a certain amount of picking up clues from the situation, a certain amount, therefore, of innovation. By saying that Pope was unusually "correct," his contemporaries and subsequent critics are referring to the fact that his poetic behavior attempted to meet the demands of an unusual number of rules, and that in turn meant, of course, that he had unusual opportunities for violating those rules. This comes out particularly strongly if we consider the heroic or closed couplet, as it was used by Pope.

The ten-syllable couplet, which rhymes aa, bb, cc, dd, etc., had been in use since the early fourteenth century. Early in the seventeenth century, however, new requirements were imposed upon it. This change is generally asserted to have begun with George Sandys' translation of Ovid's *Metamorphoses* (1621–1626). The basic rule was simple: the couplet should coincide with a self-contained syntactic unit, that is, either a sentence or a modifying clause. The couplet should have, then, a complete SVO pattern, preferably independent. Occasionally a triplet instead of a couplet might be used in order to fulfill this second requirement. This gave, of course, a possibility of internal discontinuity: a pattern which the poetic situation did not imply, though it might be found in other poems, was violated. Pope quite consciously rejected the possibility of the triplet. Consequently, when he does use it, it is so rare that it is felt as a very considerable discontinuity. He further made the syntactical rules more stringent: each line should be syntactically self-contained; each pair of lines within the couplet should be syntactically parallel. Since juncture is a verbal means of indicating the two-dimensional structure of the English sentence, and appears at the ends of syntactical units, whether words, if the speaker wishes, or, almost invariably, clauses, and always at the ends of sentences, the closed couplet meant that there must be a juncture at the end of every couplet, while the Popean rules for the closed couplet meant that every line also ended with a juncture. This meant that junctural violations are, in Pope's verse, exceedingly rare; and that meant that when they do occur, they are felt as very powerful discontinuities.

Pope, like all Baroque theorists of the arts, was perfectly aware that art must include variety and surprise, that is, discontinuity. For a constant and more or less steady source of milder discontinuity, or "variety," he depended upon juncture within the line, that is, *caesura*. As we have seen, in some poetic styles the caesura can fall almost anywhere within the line and a line can have any number of them. Milton shows little obedience to any rule about the caesura except that there should be at least one per line. But Pope makes the caesura more fixed; his rule was that it should come between the fifth and sixth syllables of his ten-syllable line. Consequently, whenever it appears elsewhere, or does not appear at all, or is doubled or tripled, it is felt as a stronger discontinuity than Milton's caesura.

When these rules are all put together it is apparent that Pope, though he makes less use of syntactical discontinuity than Milton, has more than made up for it, and that his poetry is characterized by more rules, and therefore by greater discontinuity, than Milton's. It is for this reason that some have been tempted to call Pope the most perfect, the technically most satisfying of all English poets. It is not really that he was more gifted. Rather, it is that he submitted himself to a greater number of rules, and consequently his poetry shows a continuous flow of discontinuities and, in juncture, for example, a hierarchy of discontinuity from the caesura to the end of a couplet. Rarely does Pope violate the rule that a couplet should terminate with the completion of a self-contained syntactical unit. When he does, therefore, the resultant discontinuity is powerful indeed, for it functions at once as an implicit discontinuity and as an external one.

In the same way, Milton, in *Samson Agonistes*, for example, uses a kind of modal discontinuity which Pope eschews as not being demanding enough, just as he reduces sharply the frequency of the triplet from the practice of Dryden, who came between Milton and Pope. Consider the following from *Samson Agonistes:*

> Then had I not bin thus exil'd from light:
> As in the land of darkness yet in light,
> To live a life half dead, a living death,
> And buried; but O yet more miserable!
> My self, my Sepulcher, a moving Grave,
> Buried, yet not exempt
> By priviledge of death and burial
> From worst of other evils, pains and wrongs,
> But made hereby obnoxious more
> To all the miseries of life,
> Life in captivity
> Among inhuman foes.
> But who are these? for with joint pace I hear
> The tread of many feet stearing this way;

This passage from near the end of Samson's opening speech offers examples of two kinds of discontinuity. The prosodic rule Milton is following is that for blank verse, or common meter, duple rising rhythm, ten syllables to the line. The rhyme in the first two lines is an example of internal discontinuity, for the basic pattern of the poem does not call for rhyme. Beginning with the fifth line we suddenly enter a field in which the prediction based on the rule that calls for ten syllables becomes unreliable, and the length of the line varies for seven lines. Then it returns to blank verse. Stanzas and sections of stanzas of patterned inequality of line had been used in the sixteenth century, and earlier in "Lycidas" Milton had used unpatterned sequences of this sort. The rule, then, is that a poem may include passages of varying line length in poems predominantly governed by one rule. This passage, therefore, would not have been felt by Milton or his contemporaries as an internal discontinuity but as a modal discontinuity, a shift into a new, and here, less demanding set of rules. Pope, who governed his poetic behavior by more stringent rules, has no such examples.

The passage exhibits, moreover, a further characteristic use of discontinuity available to the artist, dramatic discontinuity. In this device an increase in discontinuity is correlated with a disturbance on the part of the speaker (or implied speaker in situations in which a speaker is not dramatically identified, as in this passage). Since discontinuity varies independently from the information presented by the other signs, there is no necessary link between the two. A rise in the level of discontinuity, therefore, may function as a sign that the speaker of the poem is to be thought of as experiencing powerful affect. But it need not so function. When the general style at the time calls for a high level of discontinuity, only a higher will function as a sign of disturbance. To function as a sign, then, discontinuity must be above the current level and also above the pervasive level of the poem. Jazz, for example, is filled with discontinuities, but the pervasive level is constant within a particular jazz style.

Pope is extremely adept at what may appear to be dramatic discontinuity (principally because he uses it so rarely that it is very noticeable) but is not. Generally speaking, about two-thirds of the way through each verse paragraph there is a rise in the level of discontinuity; the rise is almost always greater in the last verse paragraph of the poem. It is succeeded by a pair of couplets, or sometimes only one, particularly in interior paragraphs, which matches the configuration offered to the implicit and internal expectancies. This is responsible for the cadential effect at the end of Pope's internal verse paragraphs and especially in the last paragraph. It is exactly analogous to the cadence of music, in which the explicit configuration is very close, and, in the final chord, identical with the implicit configuration. Such a rise in the level of discontinuity is not, therefore, dramatic but is presented purely for the effect of tension reduction. It may be what Aristotle was talking about when he used the metaphor "catharsis" for the affect of tragedy. To say that a tragedy is cathartic is a mistake. It is the end of the tragedy which may, or may not, have the cathartic affect, as may the merest soap opera.

It would be tiresome to attempt to be exhaustive in discussing the discontinuities available to any of the arts. The important thing is the principle: the reader, if he is taken with this mode of analysis, can find considerable pleasure and profit in discovering them for himself. Yet there is one further kind, particularly noticeable in poetry, but found in the other arts as well, the double function of transition from a field within a poem characterized by one kind of primary sign into a field marked by another. An implicit rule in English poetry has been the creation of a higher level of alliteration and assonance than is to be found in the ordinary use of the language. This is one of the reasons the presence of assonance and sometimes of alliteration, particularly when the latter involves the single repetition of a consonant, is so frequently ambiguous. Since some phonic overdetermination of this sort is almost always present, one cannot be always sure when the primary signs are actually performing a semantic function. There is, then, almost always a subtle significance of demand. Milton, for example, is very concerned to have an unusually high degree of assonance. Hence it is rare that it clearly functions as a primary sign. But it is one of the reasons that Milton is always felt to be trying very hard. Some poetry perceivers like this and some do not. When, in any poem, there is a rise in this kind of phonic overdetermination which lasts long enough to establish a field, it serves not only as a primary sign but also as a modal discontinuity. It is a change of the rules, a shift into a different mode. The transition out of such a passage, then, is also felt as a modal discontinuity.

Now it is not true that for the native speaker any sound or sound sequence is easier to pronounce than any other sound. Nevertheless, there are conventions, generally considered to have been established very massively by Spenser in *The Faerie Queene*, for what are euphonious sound sequences. Most poets have tended to avoid as much as possible plosives, like p, or sibilants, like s or z. The rules remain implicit rather than explicit, but they have governed poets by a weighted average. A few poets, then, have exploited the possibilities of a heavy use of "ugly sounds," thus creating a striking implicit discontinuity. Donne and Browning, who learned from Donne how to do it, are particularly notable examples. Swinburne, on the other hand, presents a level of euphony so high that it is unique in English poetry. In a peculiar sense it has, therefore, a dramatic function; for it is not consonant with the emotional affect signified by the verbal signs. Only initially is it felt as an external discontinuity; thereafter it functions as primary significance, utterly divorced from and always ironic to the terrible things he usually writes about. The putative speaker, or "spokesman," inappropriately signifies adequacy, demand, energy release, and impulse and process smoothness. There is an extraordinary split between the primary significance and the verbal significance. And this split is found in all of the arts of the period Debussy's *Pelléas et Mélisande* is another example. This is the period I have called, in *Beyond the Tragic Vision*, "Stylism." Involving as it did the separation of primary semantic function from verbal and configurational semantic function and social function in architecture, it was the necessary preliminary to abstract art of low or no iconicity. Such art, as we have seen, consists of little or nothing but primary signs.

One last possibility for discontinuity in poetry is worth mentioning, particularly because it is so peculiarly appropriate to the comprehension of Pope and has had a great deal to do with the misunderstanding which, after the 1740's, his poetry so frequently has suffered. This is the matter of poetic diction. Most periods in English poetry, particularly since the Renaissance up to the emergence of modern poetry around 1910, have been marked by certain limits placed upon the vocabulary available to the poet. This is partly a matter of decorum. Pope, for example, rejected, in his edition of Shakespeare, the metaphor in *Macbeth* about sleep knitting up the raveled sleeve of care. It was a breach of decorum that a king should use such an extremely homely figure of speech. A king should use only royal language. Poetic diction, therefore, is very much situationally determined, both by dramatic situation, as in *Macbeth*, and non-dramatic; the kind of vocabulary available to satire was not identical with that available for epic. These non-artistic considerations also govern architecture, music, and painting. What is proper for a pavilion in the royal gardens is not proper for the facade of the palace. What is proper for *tafelmusik*, music written as background for dining, is not proper for a church service. One of the complaints against the first examples of modern poetry in the second decade of this century was that the poets were not using "poetic" language. Certain language was held to be inherently or immanently poetic. The modern situation is that any vocabulary is available for poetry. But this was not so in Pope's day. He was, as in other elements of the formal aspect, of his own choice under the control of rules of poetic diction. But since they were rules, they could be violated. One of the reasons he was so admired for his decorum was that he was able to extend the range of poetic diction to its very limits, and just a shade beyond, while justifying such an extension by the dramatic situation of the speaker or the role the poet was playing, that of satirist, for example. Thus he was able to reach the casual diction of the last satires, still playing the severe moralist adequate when the rest of the world is not.

> Shut, shut the door, good *John*; fatigu'd, I said,
> Tie up the knocker! say I'm sick, I'm dead,
>
> • • • • • • • • • • • • • • •
>
> Is there a Parson, much be-mus'd in Beer,
> A maudlin Poetess, a rhyming Peer,
> A Clerk, foredoom'd his Father's soul to cross,
> Who pens a Stanza when he should *engross*;
>
> • • • • • • • • • • • • • • •
>
> Who shames a Scribbler? break one cobweb through,
> He spins the slight, self pleasing thread anew;
> Destroy his Fib, or Sophistry; in vain,
> The Creature's at his dirty work again . . .
>
> ("Epistle to Dr. Arbuthnot")

5. MUSIC

In understanding the nature of discontinuity it is instructive to turn from poetry, which is relatively poverty-stricken, to music, which certainly has the richest formal aspect of any of the arts. The reason is easy to see. The basic rules of prosody can be learned in a few minutes, though it may take years to master the possibilities for discontinuity they offer. But this is not a matter of the difficulty of the rules. It is a matter of gaining experience, of practice in meeting two quite different sets of rules, those governing the language and those governing poetic language. Music, however, is an entirely different matter. It takes years to learn the rules themselves, and more years of practice to make the formal aspect serve the interests of the primary signs, and still more years of practice to catch up with the innovative frontier. Thus poets can, in a few years, reach that frontier of the formal aspect. Some highly gifted poets have reached it in a matter of months. It is in part a matter of how many rules are in force at the time the poet takes up his task. But most musicians are in the position of Brahms, who, when he left for Vienna from Hamburg, destroyed all his compositions. Consequently his Opus 1, a piano sonata, was the work of a man who had already mastered his medium.

Nevertheless, in spite of the complexity of music's rules, the situation obtaining when Johann Sebastian Bach emerged as a mature talent in the first decade of the eighteenth century can be described with relative ease and rapidity; and that formal situation obtained until about 1907, even on the innovative frontier. Bach was born in 1685, three years before Pope, and like Pope he governed himself with more rules than any musician before or since. This has led to a profound misunderstanding of his music from which the general public is only now beginning to recover. Because the writing of a fugue is governed by a great many rules, it is commonly believed that listening to one is very difficult, that it is highly organized or ordered music, and that the listener must know all the rules in order to appreciate it properly. The ordinary listener, with the best will in the world, often concludes that Bach's fugues are quasi-mathematical and beyond the grasp of any listener who does not have technical training in the art of composition. Nothing could be farther from the truth. Listening to a fugue is nearer to the experience a roller-coaster offers than any other kind or type of art. When a perceiver who is used to fugues hears a typical fugal theme, he braces himself for an exciting ride. Anything can happen, and with Bach all hell is about to break loose. The reason is that no musical type offers greater possibilities for discontinuity than the fugue. But to comprehend this statement, it is necessary to begin with the implicit elements of musical composition as they were assumed at Bach's time, and still are for most music played in public performance and for the enormously vast majority of recordings available and bought.

The seventeenth century saw the emergence of new principles of composition, based not on a number of modes, as Medieval and Renaissance music were, but on only two, which we now call the major and minor scales. Of the latter there are two forms, but this is of little importance. The first rule for Western music is that all pitch possibilities should be limited to half-tones. The technicalities of this may be ignored. For our purposes the successive black and white notes on the piano constitute the chromatic scale of half-tones. The major scale consists of the following pattern: two successive tetrachords, each consisting of three tones and a half-tone. Between the first and second tetrachords there is a step of one full tone. The C major scale is

C-D-E-F-G-A-B-C. To get the minor scale, E and A are flatted or moved down a half tone. These are the scales against which diatonic melodies are perceived. They are also the scales against which modal melodies came to be perceived; Bach and certain subsequent composers occasionally composed their melodies in the note sequences of the eight medieval modes, but they were perceived in terms of the diatonic scale. The major and minor diatonic scales, therefore, are the forms, or the expectancies, which are violated in order to produce melody. Thus when C is followed by D, the expectancy for E is very great. If E is forthcoming the expectancy for F is even greater. The presentation of F makes an enormously powerful expectancy for G, and so on. But the composer may not only skip up and down; he may also introduce accidentals, notes not part of the scale he is composing in, and he may shift or modulate (a metaphor, of course, from mode) to another key. But with "key" we come to harmony.

Here again the possibilities of rule manipulation are enormous, but the basic rule is simple enough. The first, third, fifth, and eighth notes of the scale, when sounded together, produce the harmony of that scale. A melody in C major is to be accompanied by one or more of these harmonic intervals: $1 + 5$, or $1 + 8$, or $1 + 3$, or $1 + 3 + 5$, and so on. In the key of C major these are $C + G$, $C + C$, $C + E$, $C + E + G$, and so on. Here, of course, the composer again can introduce accidentals to create a discord. The composer, then, had to obey two sets of rules both derived from the same scale pattern. This was profoundly different from the Medieval or Renaissance compositional problem. Before the seventeenth century the composer wrote only horizontally. Or, to be a little more descriptive, the rules for vertical organization were not derived from the modes. There were, to be sure, rules which indicate that some intervals were felt to be more satisfying than others, so that to use the unsatisfying intervals was to create discords, or something very like the discord in the diatonic system. But this distinction may have been more in the nature of primary significance than it was a matter of discontinuity. The augmented fourth, for example, $C + F$-sharp, was called the Devil's interval and was felt to be particularly disturbing, even dangerous, a kind of quasi-forbidden interval. Before the seventeenth century, therefore, a composer writing for four different voices selected the successive notes for each voice from the notes available in the mode he was writing in, with, of course, occasional accidentals to introduce implicit discontinuities. The intervals could be freely chosen by a system not integrated with the melodic system. Consequently, there was little opportunity for any harmonic expectancy to develop. For us, it takes a long time to get used to listening to such music, so powerful are our harmonic expectations. Seventeenth-century music, however, after it had successfully made the harmonic-melodic rule integration, was capable of far more powerful discontinuities than its predecessors. The reason for this was that particular melodic sequences and harmonic combinations were reinforced with infinitely greater frequency than in the preceding era. The absolutely untrained listener, therefore, could develop a weighted average of expectations which corresponded with the rules for harmony and scale.

In 1907 Schönberg made the first steps towards abandoning this system and substituting for it the twelve-tone system, which, though it sounds complicated, is really much simpler. Actually, any set of rules can be developed for composing music. First comes the selection of pitch tones to be available. Then comes the selection of tones for the scale or the modes and a selection of tones for the intervallic combinations of tones. What Schönberg's twelve-tone system amounts to is that each composition is written in its unique mode of twelve tones, which are, however, not presented in ascending sequence, but in expressive sequence, as a melody perceived against the background of the chromatic scale. This mode is also the basis for harmonic selection. Like diatonic music, twelve-tone music also permits the use of accidentals. But generally, it is only after the music has gone on some time that accidentals are introduced. Otherwise they would not be felt as accidentals. The basic mode for each composition must be reinforced in the perceiver or he will be unable to perceive a violation.

At the time of Bach a melody either followed the scale or it followed the triad, the first, third, and fifth notes. That is, an upward or downward melodic movement either moved to the next tone on the scale, or it moved to the nearest tone available from the triad. This can sometimes become rather tedious for our ears. In Vivaldi's *concerti grossi* the fast movement themes are almost always built on the triad, and the slow movements on the scale. This is less true of Bach, who was born ten years after Vivaldi. Another peculiar phenomenon is to be found in the contemporary judgments made on Wagner's *Tristan*. Though to our ears this music is always melodic, apparently most of the audience at the first performances heard almost no melodies at all. The reasons were two. In the first place, *Tristan* makes use of so many accidentals that ears accustomed to melodies made up of standardized and short patterns of triadic sequences of three or four notes following the scale could not perceive any melody. To them it sounded like a series of random notes. The other reason was that by the time he wrote *Tristan* Wagner was governing himself more and more by his own rule of endless melody, melody not made up by repeating well-known short sequences within a melodic sequence. Ears accustomed to the Verdian type of melody, which is either made up of standardized triadic and scale sequences or, if unusual sequences are used, by frequently repeating such sequences, could not retain their perceptual grip on Wagner's melody. The implicit discontinuity was so extreme that they experienced not discontinuity but total disorientation, one damned note after another. Most listeners are still bored by much of the Wagnerian melodic recitative, though perceivers who have adapted themselves to "endless melody" find that the most "boring" passages, such as the Wotan-Fricka duologue in *Die Walküre* or Mark's second act monologue in *Tristan*, are the most fascinating and moving of all. Schönberg's twelve-tone system was an implicit discontinuity from Wagner's diatonic endless melody. Having become conventionalized, the twelve-tone system is an external discontinuity from heavily chromaticized diatonic music, itself an external discontinuity from lightly chromaticized diatonic style. To listen to Schönberg, it is only necessary to listen with chromatic expectations, rather than diatonic. Enough experience with it will automatically bring this about. The perceiver can ignore the twelve-tone rules; they are there to govern the composer's behavior; he too actually writes against chromatic expectancies.

This brings out a very important fact about discontinuity that we have not encountered before: toleration for discontinuity varies from individual to individual. An enormous amount of argument about the value of art is concerned precisely with this problem: one individual can tolerate a discontinuity and experience it as a discontinuity which another experiences as pure randomness offering nothing but total disorientation. But this also suggests a further fact. Music and all the arts, for the individual, wear out. If one can predict with total success everything that is going to happen, the work of art can be a bore. Consequently, the performing arts show a steady measure of external discontinuity against the background of previous performances. One particularly amusing example comes from the 1930's. At about the same time, Toscanini and Stokowski changed the tempo of the second movement of Beethoven's Seventh Symphony from its traditional speed: Toscanini played it faster, and Stokowski played it slower. On the other hand, to restore a piece of worn-out music to life it is only necessary to limit oneself to an earlier period of music for some time. The amount of time, of course, is an individual matter. If you are weary of Beethoven's Fifth Symphony, for six months listen only to music composed before 1800.

The shift into diatonic music was one of the most striking examples of external discontinuity in the history of the arts, at least in Europe, and the shift out of it was equally striking, except that it was accompanied by external discontinuities in some ways even more discontinuous than music showed until some decades had passed. Further, once the perceiver has learned this basic diatonic form, these two integrated expectancies for melody and harmony, all music between the early seventeenth century and to-day, with the exception of twelve-tone and aleatoric music, is open to him. I limit this to two expectancies, excluding the minor, for in the first place the minor is derived from the major, and in the second place anything not major sounds minor. Thus, at first, Schönberg's music sounds merely as if it were written entirely in the minor, that is, after the listener can hear its melodic and harmonic character as something more than random.

At Bach's time, then, the diatonic system provided the basic implied expectancies for all music. But Bach introduced a most interesting external discontinuity. As we have seen in the discussion of rhythm in poetry, counterpoint consists of the simultaneous presentation of two or more differing melodies. The strict counterpoint of the diatonic system meant meeting the melodic and harmonic requirements, as well as violating them. The effect of the harmonic-melodic integration of the seventeenth century was that only the top and bottom voices were normally distinguished when all voices were given at equal volume. In the previous period of non-integrated harmony and melody all four, or more, or fewer, voices were heard independently. The reason for this was that the ear was as concerned with the harmonic progression as with the melodic as soon as the seventeenth-century integration had been established. Nevertheless, the harmonic progression continued to be subordinate to and dependent upon the melodic. In the 1710's Bach began writing fugal passages of pure harmonic progression, in which the distinguishable element was successive chords with at best one melodic line, the upper, and sometimes not even that. This external discontinuity introduced a new kind of modal discontinuity. A further external discontinuity was a little like

Pope's extension of the possibilities of poetic diction. At about the same time, or even earlier, Bach began using chords of a complexity, of a distance from the simple triad, hitherto unparalleled. In fact, early in his youth and for the rest of his life, his congregations were always complaining about the strange chords. Although these harmonies were justified by a development of the harmonic rules, they sounded to the uninitiated like discords. It was the phenomenon that greeted Wagner's *Tristan*. It is of considerable interest for our purpose that many of Bach's most extraordinary and ingenious harmonies did not appear again until Wagner. From then on, they became the common property of all innovative composers. There was no *musical* reason why Bach's example should not have been followed, just as there is no musical reason either for the introduction of diatonic integration or its abandonment by Schönberg. The reason must be sought elsewhere, like the abandonment of the closed couplet in the 1720's by innovative poets.

But although the diatonic system is the basic formal implicit expectancy for music in Bach's time, it was by no means the only one. The other sources lay in the individual forms, such as the fugue, the ricercare, the sonata, the concerto grosso, the fantasia, and so on. In order to avoid confusion I shall use here an alternate term for these: musical types. What is a symphony? Is Tschaikowsky's Sixth Symphony a symphony? After its first performance in 1893 a good many people insisted that it was not, and there are still a few diehard formalists who deny that it is truly a symphony. Such a denial is based upon some notion of platonically pure symphonic form. But this is absurd. A symphony is a musical composition written according to a set of rules. The title "symphony" informs you not that those rules governed the composer but rather that the composer wishes the perceiver to listen to it with the formal expectancies prescribed by the term "symphony." He may or may not violate them. At the time Tschaikowsky wrote his Sixth, "symphony" led one to expect a sequence of four movements: fast, slow, fast, fast. There were also other prescriptive statements about the way each movement was to be organized: that is, each movement was also a type. Among other violations in the Sixth, Tschaikowsky presented a first movement alternating between music derived from fast movement types and music derived from slow. This was followed by two fast movements, and then by a slow one, in the minor, instead of the customary major. It was an error to deny it the title "symphony" because it did not conform to prescriptions for the symphony; rather, the attempt to deny it membership in the symphonic type or category was a result of the confusion between descriptive statements and prescriptive statements about the formal aspect of art, an error we have met before.

A brief examination of the fugue and what Bach did to it will serve to explain what happens to all musical types (see Plate XVI). A fugue is, first, written in strict counterpoint. It may have anything from two voices, that is, independent melodic lines, on up, though the upward limit appears to be six. It should also be noted that Bach never gave the title "fugue" if he used only two voices; instead, he used the title "invention" or "sinfonia," titles he also on occasion used for three-part fugues. The rules for fugue writing are quite complex, but the basic principle is exceedingly simple. A fugue begins with one voice presenting a melody; usually it is a sharply contoured configuration so that it may be heard against the other melodies. Though this is often said to be the essential and necessary character of a fugue melody, it is not. Bach and other composers have written fugues on melodies which are barely distinguishable, which melt into the contrapuntal background. After the initial presentation of the melody by itself, it is never heard again in the same contrapuntal background. There may be counter-melodies, and second subjects, or second subjects that are in fact developed out of the principal subject. The melody may be presented in twice its normal time span, or half of it, or any multiple. The surrounding voices may have very little character, or they may have enough character, that is, be far enough away from scale and triad sequence, to be rivals to the melody. In short, anything can happen. Passages can be introduced which are totally unrelated to the melody. The fugue is a type which permits maximum discontinuity, but it is basically internal discontinuity. All musical types are basically means of setting up the necessary conditions for internal discontinuity.

Musical internal discontinuity, then, requires some further explanation. It is the principle usually known as musical variation. It consists simply of the presentation of a melodic pattern and then the violation of that pattern. The melody itself offers implicit discontinuity; the variation offers both implicit and internal discontinuity, since it is perceived simultaneously in terms of the diatonic scale and in terms of the original melody of which it is a variation. A somewhat richer type of external discontinuity appears when the melody is accompanied by a harmonic pattern. Thus the composer may offer a variation on the harmonic sequence without presenting a variation on the melody itself. He may even offer a completely new melody accompanied by the harmonic sequence of the initial melody. The fugue is virtually alone in presenting its melody without harmonic accompaniment. A still further way of enriching the possibilities for internal discontinuity in musical types is the presentation of two melodies, or more, each of which is then subjected to internal discontinuous manipulation. The sonata-allegro form, the traditional first movement form for symphonies from about the middle of the eighteenth century to the twentieth century, is an example. Two melodies are presented, usually contrasting in their primary significance; this presentation may or may not be repeated. In the eighteenth and early nineteenth centuries it usually was; the repetition is now usually ignored. There follows a section of free fantasia, in which the composer manipulates one or both melodies as he pleases, sometimes simultaneously. This in turn is followed by presenting the two melodies in much the same form as originally, except that now both are in the same key. Later, from Beethoven on, an originally implicit discontinuity was stabilized as an external discontinuity: the recapitulation of the two melodies was followed by another free fantasia. The pattern thus was changed from a-b-a to a-b-a-b. When composers got weary of this, they changed the movement types and sequence.

Modal discontinuity in music is, of course, a change of rules that have been in use for a long enough time span to raise the expectation that they will continue to govern the composer's behavior, or a little more accurately, to make it impossible to predict how long they will continue to be in use. The perception of modal discontinuity is, of course, very much an individual matter. For the highly practiced musical perceiver, a bar or two in the minor in fast tempo will be perceived as a modal discontinuity from the preceding major. Less practiced perceivers may not even notice that for a moment the music shifted into the minor and then out again. One of the most important devices for obtaining modal discontinuity is the division of a musical type into separate movements, each of which is capable of being played by itself. There has been much pedantry on this subject. Sometimes there are rules governing the key relationships. When these are standardized, the composer may create implicit discontinuity by ignoring them. At other times in the history of music or for certain musical types, they are not standardized; the type title does not raise in the perceiver at the same cultural level as the composer expectancies for certain key sequences. And as usual, there has been much talk about how a composition in movements is "unified" by key relationships. This is again to confuse prescriptive statements with descriptive statements. The modal shift, therefore, from the rules governing one movement type to those governing the next movement type, is extremely important in music. Again, pedantry has destroyed some of the discontinuity inherent in the sequence of movement types. The practice of printing in programs and on record sleeves and labels information about the tempo and key of each movement ruins the modal discontinuity from one movement to another, or at least ruins so much of it as is a matter of tempo and major-minor discontinuity. The best way to listen to a musical composition in movements is to remain utterly ignorant of the number of movements and their individual character. Among music-lovers the feeling that they ought to have this information in order to listen to the music properly is deeply ingrained; it can be overcome, however, with a little effort and self-discipline.

Finally, modal discontinuity is much easier in music than it is in poetry. In its formal aspect as well as in its semantic aspect, music is packaged, not structured. In spite of its rich complexity of rules, many of which have been developed in prescriptive statements of a quasi-mathematical order and thus made capable of extremely complex manipulation and development, the decision as to what rules to use in a given composition is entirely at the discretion of the composer But he never exercises that discretion. His external discontinuities are, as in the other arts, innovated on the basis of what has preceded him, as Bach established an external discontinuity by extending the implied length of the fugue to four or five times what it had been. This of course enormously increased the fugal possibilities for internal, modal, and implicit discontinuity. We are left again with the problem of what keeps external discontinuity from being random.

6. PAINTING

In poetry the fundamental and most important implicit form—the subject-verb-object pattern and the more or less standardized patterns for indicating the two-dimensional structure inherent in modification —is given by the language; in music the implicit forms have to be learned from music itself, either by acquiring weighted averages through experience or by learning them through prescriptive teaching.

The implicit forms of painting and architecture have a different source, the non-iconic two- and three-dimensional signs which the child spontaneously works out for himself. The regularity of these signs is another instance of the consequence of forming assumptions by the process of the developing of weighted averages. In the widest sense, the notion of the weighted average is identical with any orientation, no matter how elaborate and rich a package that orientation may be. These weighted averages, as we have seen, become instruments or hypotheses of perception. In perceiving two or three dimensional configurations, the ordinary tendency is to ignore the disparities between the regularity of expectation and the configuration the situation actually offers. Only when our interests so direct us do we search for and respond to those disparities. The art situation requires of the individual playing the art perceiver's role that kind of interest and that kind of search behavior. The implicit forms for painting are the square, the rectangle, the circle, the oval, the triangle, the straight line, the cross, the x. The implicit forms for architecture whether for solids, hollows, or screens, are three-dimensional projections of the square into the cube, the rectangle into the extended cube, of the circle into the sphere, and of the oval into the ovoid. I shall first take up painting.

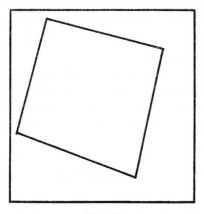

Fig. 1

The above figure is derived from Malevich's "White on White." An exact reproduction is unnecessary, but this is reasonably close to the original. I have purposely exaggerated the interior configuration to make it obvious that, unlike the exterior one, it is not a perfect square. In the original the difference is so slight that it is extremely easy to overlook it. In the original, also, there is a difference in shade of white between the area outside the interior configuration and the area inside of it. In the original, it is so easy to overlook the difference between the two configurations that, in my own case, I was familiar with the picture for some years before I realized that the interior "square" was not a square at all; others I have talked to about the painting have had the same experience, and one individual refused to believe the difference between the two configurations until he had checked the assertion against the original. I have had students who refused to recognize the difference when they were looking at a slide projection of the picture. This is the most minimal painting I know, and hence the most instructive. It is completely non-iconic and there is but one primary sign present, the square, a perfect balance between horizontality and verticality, between demand and acceptance. It can be regarded, then, as a sign of the sense of being oriented: no more than that, certainly. Consequently, the semantic aspect is capable of only almost the lowest possible affect. For that reason, what affect it has comes almost entirely from its discontinuities. The external discontinuity can be briefly disposed of. No sign field so simple had ever been offered before as the occasion for performing the painting perceiver's role. For this reason alone "White on White" is of the highest interest in the history of modern art. But it is the implicit and external discontinuities that make it even more interesting as a superb means of showing how these operate.

The square shape of the painting itself is not merely a boundary to the perceptual field; it is part of the design itself. This outside square, then, is an explicit presentation of the implicit form of "square perception." Its presentation reinforces that implicit formal expectancy. This is why it is so easy to ignore the fact that the internal configuration is a variation on a square, a departure from it, a violation of squareness expectancy. It is, therefore, an implicit discontinuity. Another implicit discontinuity is to be found in the almost complete triangle at the upper left and in the somewhat less complete triangles implied by each outside line of the inner configuration, each inside line of the bounding configuration, and the right angle at each inside corner of the boundary.

Each of these implied forms also serves as a basis for the presentation of internal discontinuities. The outside square establishes the pattern from which the inside configuration is a departure. A square has four interior right angles: here, the interior "square" has only one, that at the upper left. This obviously is the same principle as internal or variational discontinuity in music. Now consider Figure 2.

One first perceives "a" as an implied triangle. This having been established, the next most obvious triangle, "b," emerges. The next most obvious triangle is "d," but behavior, having started the clockwise pattern, continues it, and perceives the implied triangle "c"; then comes the perception of "d." This is exactly analogous to the

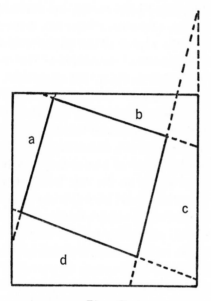

Fig. 2

variation principle in music and even analogous to the cadential principle discussed above, the gradual rise in level of discontinuity and its abrupt fall to something very close to the implicit form.

Modal discontinuity is also present, though not in these figures. In the original it emerges in the difference between the two shades of white. A further very delicate implied and internal discontinuity in the original is to be found in the fact that though the edge of the painting, the boundary of the square, is perfectly straight, the lines forming the interior configuration are slightly irregular, not ruled.

A further word about the perceptual transaction offered by painting is, however, necessary. In one respect poetry and music are contrastive to painting, with architecture falling in between, partly like the first two and partly like the third. This is the matter of time. A common way of categorizing the arts is to divide them into arts of space and arts of time. But since every artistic transaction involves time, such a division is absurd. In fact, the Chinese scroll paintings clearly offer a time experience. Though the difference is in its ordinary form meaningless, it does, nevertheless, point to something of significance. The poet and the composer predetermine the order in which the perceiver experiences the formal aspect, as well as the semantic aspect. The painter of paintings to be seen all at once does not. He may, as Malevich does and as many painters do, use various devices to make some implied form more prominent than any other, and the general tendency is to look at the center of the painting first, then along the axes in the order of hierarchical prominence. The next tendency is to read the painting from left to right. All these were exhibited in my analysis of "White on White." First the external shape, then the center, since there are no axes, the left, and thence to the right and so around the painting in clockwise order, picking up the implied triangles as a series of internal discontinuities. This, according to Arnheim, is the average way of examining a painting—at least in our culture.[16] The architect, on the one hand, dictates the order in which his spaces, his screens, and his solids are to be encountered; but on the other hand, a facade is experienced as a painting is.

However, there is no particular reason why an individual should not have a unique style of examining a painting. Thus, he might very well become aware of the implication of triangle "c" before any of the others. Statements about the order in which we see the configurations of paintings, especially statements that include words like "must" or "is required" or "does" or "necessarily," are to be regarded with the highest suspicion. They are value statements; they may be based on the weighted averages of the particular critic; most of them are prescriptive statements masked as descriptive statements. They are statements like, "The figures of the Madonna and the two saints form a triangle." There is no triangle; a triangle is implied. Such statements really mean that the artist had to be controlled by a triangular mode of perception before he could violate it.

The most important element, however, in the transaction with a painting that makes it a temporal experience is internal discontinuity.

---

[16] See Rudolf Arnheim, *Art and Visual Perception*, Berkeley, 1957.

Generally, one may say that when a painting offers a series of implied shapes as occasion for experiencing internal discontinuity, the tendency is first to see a configuration as an implicit discontinuity which is closest to its explicit configuration. But in a painting of considerable complexity, this very well may not happen. In Baroque painting, for example, which made considerable use of dramatic discontinuity, the main figure of the painting, the principal configurational sign, frequently is more discontinuous from its implied form than anything else in the painting, including similar implied forms which offer internal discontinuities. In other words, the hierarchy of discontinuities may be congruent with the semantic hierarchy, or may be exactly the opposite, or it may be completely unrelated.

That is really all there is to say in general terms about discontinuity in painting. Like music and poetry, painting can be and has been extraordinarily complicated, but the basis for that complication is actually quite simple and derived not from artistic experience but from ordinary experience, experience so ordinary it is necessary to survival. This is less true for music, but even in that art the basic principle of pitch selection and scale is first established in the phonic aspect of language, at least if the Trager-Smith hypothesis is true that a speaker of any language, though he may use a unique range and though his pitch tones are not constant, nevertheless uses the same number of pitches that every speaker of that language uses. The Chinese, for example, are said to have been unaware that they used pitch change to establish semantic functions for words using the same phonemes until the Indian Buddhist missionaries pointed it out.

Although nothing can be added to the scheme of formal analysis presented here, it may be of some value and interest to analyze some of the discontinuities in Watteau's "Pilgrimage to Cythera." Indeed, it is necessary in order to establish some basis for tackling the next problem, the continuity of external discontinuities (see Plate I).[17]

Discontinuities may be established by line, by boundaries, by color areas, and by contrasts of tone, as light and shadow. Watteau uses all of these in this painting. A practical hint may be of some use. The simplest way to rehearse perception of discontinuities in paintings is to squint the eyes so that the painting is out of focus. This reduces the

---

[17] I use Watteau's painting again for two reasons: the reader will thus have before him a detailed semantic and formal analysis of the same picture; and both aspects will be useful in the next chapter, which proposes both an explanation for stylistic continua and for the relations of the arts.

insistence of iconicity and permits focussing on the formal aspect. This reduction of iconicity also permits the emergence of the configurations and boundaries and patches that imply forms. Another and in some ways more satisfactory way of doing the same thing is to project slides of paintings out of focus. As the focus gradually blurs, various configurations emerge from their implications and often achieve, as the defocussing proceeds, surprising regularity.

In Watteau's painting the most obvious implied form is made by the parallel implied lines which bound on the left the pile of rocks and the boatmen and on the right the foliage of the shrine. On the left the implication is made stronger by the staff of a pilgrim; on the right by the spot of black and white clothing of the sitting cupid. This strengthens the implication just before it disappears. These two slanting approximately parallel implied lines are joined at the base by an implied line slanting up to the right to the cupid, who occupies an implied 90° angle. Thus these three lines imply a vast slanting rectangle, the upper left area of which lies outside the painting, just like the apices of two of Malevich's triangles.

But almost as obvious, and to some observers no doubt more obvious, than this implied rectangle is the implied triangle of the low hill in the foreground. This is repeated by the implied triangle of the central three figures, an implication picked up and extended both left and right. This creates an external discontinuity sustained by the presentation of a number of other similarly implied triangles. In addition, each of the pairs of lovers in the foreground implies a triangle, as well as the boatmen and the two pairs of lovers standing in front of them. Here the same staff that established the implied left-hand line of the great implied rectangle serves again to establish this triangle. This gives across the painting a sequence of internal discontinuities. Another large-scaled formal implication is established by a curved line of lighter green seen through the foliage of the shrine. This is picked up to the left by a similar curve and below by the slightly curving herm of Priapus, by a curve at the bottom of the painting near the center, and by a darker patch of clouds and the cupid floating away at the upper left. These elements imply a vast circle overlaying the great implied rectangle and cut across by the large implied triangle of the hill and the outline of the figures.

Modal discontinuity appears in the difference between the way the figures and their costumes are painted and the technique used for the landscape and foliage. One is sharp, crisp, and highly reflective of

I. Jean Antoine Watteau (1684–1721), "A Pilgrimage to Cythera" (1717). [Musée du Louvre. Photograph: Alinari-Art Reference Bureau.]

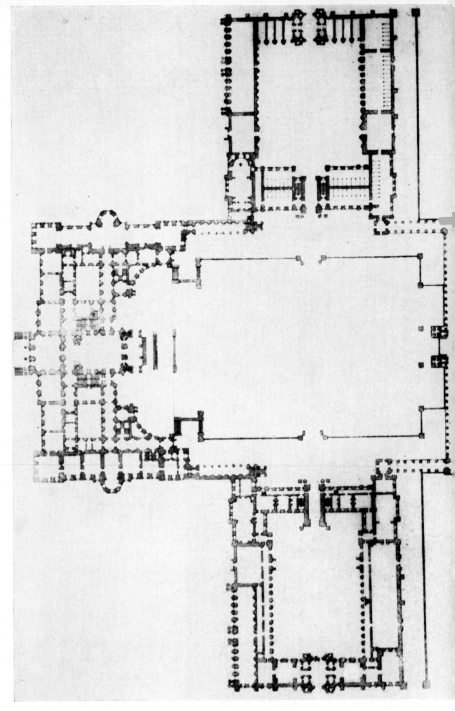

II. Sir John Vanbrugh (1664–1726), Blenheim Palace, Woodstock,
England (commissioned 1705). General plan. The screen, the terrace
stretching in front of the complex, and the three outer sides of the
right wing were not built. [From *Vitruvius Britannicus*, Vol. I, 1717.]

III. Blenheim Palace. The East Wing and the façade of the Central Block, from a distance. [Photograph by Dr. Robert Smith; courtesy of the University of Pennsylvania Libraries.]

IV. Blenheim Palace. The inner half of the East Wing and the facade of the Central Block, from within the courtyard. [Photograph by Dr. Robert Smith; courtesy of the University of Pennsylvania Libraries.]

V. BLENHEIM PALACE. THE FACADE OF THE CENTRAL BLOCK, FROM THE NORTHWEST. [PHOTOGRAPH BY DR. ROBERT SMITH; COURTESY OF THE UNIVERSITY OF PENNSYLVANIA LIBRARIES.]

VI. Filippo Iuvara (?1676–1736). The Hunting Lodge of Stupinigi, near Torino, Italy (1729–1733). The Main Block. [Photograph by Dr. Robert Smith; courtesy of the University of Pennsylvania Libraries.]

VII. Balthasar Neumann (1687–1753). The Pilgrimage Church of Vierzehnheiligen, Bavaria (1742–1744). Facade. [Photograph by Dr. William Murtagh; courtesy of the University of Pennsylvania Libraries.]

VIII.   Neumann and others. Vierzehnheiligen. Interior (completed in
the 1770's and 1780's). [Photograph by Dr. William Murtagh; courtesy
of the University of Pennsylvania Libraries.]

IX. Jacques Ange Gabriel (1698–1782). Petit Trianon, Versailles (1768). The garden facade. [Photograph by Dr. Robert Smith; courtesy of the University of Pennsylvania Libraries.]

X. Étienne-Louis Boulée (1728–1799). Design for a Cenotaph for Newton (1784). Facade and cross section. [Drawings in the Bibliothèque Nationale, Paris.]

XI. GIOVANNI BATTISTA TIEPOLO (1696–1770). CEILING OF THE STAIRCASE,
RESIDENZ, WÜRZBURG, BAVARIA (1753). APOLLO, THE OLYMPIANS, AND THE
FOUR CONTINENTS. THE PHOTOGRAPH SHOWS AFRICA, EUROPE, AND ASIA.
[PHOTOGRAPH: MARBURG–ART REFERENCE BUREAU.]

XII. RICHARD WILSON (1714–1782). "SNOWDON FROM LLYN NANTLLE"

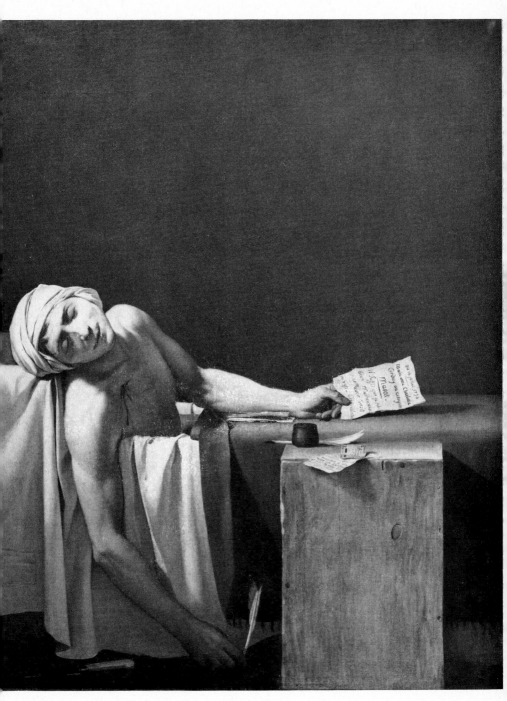

XIII.   Jacques Louis David (1774–1825). "The Death of Marat" (1793).
[The Chateau of Versailles. Photograph: Alinari–Art Reference
Bureau.]

XV. Pablo Picasso (1881–   ) "Les Demoiselles d'Avignon" (Spring, 1907). [Collection, The Museum of Modern Art, New York, acquired through the Lillie P. Bliss Bequest. Copyright © SPADEM 1965 by French Reproduction Rights Inc.]

XVI.   Johann Sebastian Bach (1685–1750). *The Well-Tempered Clavier,* Fugue I (before 1722). The first thirteen of twenty-seven bars. The double curved lines indicate the subject.

light. The other is just the opposite. Further modal discontinuity emerges from the movement from the darkness at the left to the brightness in the center, within the great implied rectangle to the darkness at the right.

The background of discontinuity against which Watteau worked was considerably different from what this painting offered, as his earlier paintings showed. Perhaps because this was an academy piece, painted in 1717 as one of the requirements for admission to L'Académie Royale de Peinture et de Sculpture, although he had been elected in 1712, Watteau made it as elaborate as he could, but the same external discontinuity is found in most of his works of these years. The external discontinuity lies in the use of three dominating implied forms and in the modal discontinuity between figures and background. Previous paintings had tended to use but one major implicit form or two at the most. It is apparent that there is a similarity between what Watteau, born in 1684, was doing and what Pope and Bach were doing at the same time: all three created external discontinuity by controlling their behavior by a greater number of formal rules than the immediate tradition from which they emerged. It remains to be seen whether this was a revolution in external discontinuity from what had been done in the seventeenth century or whether it was a continuation of the same kind of external discontinuity.

7. ARCHITECTURE

From what was said in the preceding section and at the end of the preceding chapter, architecture offers both the kind of experience emerging from the transactions with poetry and music and that emerging from painting. In proceeding through an architectural complex one experiences a sequence of spaces alternating with solids. When the wall of the solid is penetrated, the perceiver emerges into either another space or into a hollow. A solid is a solid until it is penetrated or until the perceiver is given information that it contains a hollow even though he may not enter into it. Furthermore, each face of a solid visible on the line of approach offers the kind of formal experience offered by an abstract, or non-iconic, painting. Initially, or as the perceiver approaches, iconic signs may emerge from the facade; these are iconic decoration, like Corinthian capitals, sculpture, mosaics, and murals. The custom of painting the facades of buildings is still followed in southern Germany and in Switzerland, and in the fifteenth and sixteenth centuries many of the facades of the palaces on the Grand Canal of Venice were painted by the greatest masters. A pitiful wreck of a nude by Giorgione is still preserved in the Accademia in Venice. Interior walls are, of course, commonly treated in the same way, either with non-iconic decoration or iconic signs. Architecture, then, offers two kinds of formal experience; one is dictated by the architect; the other is much more at the discretion of the perceiver, who may examine the formal information in any order he chooses, as in a painting, or ignore it entirely.

But even if he ignores it, or just glances at it, its formal function is still effective. The formal manipulation of facade or interior wall is to break up the wall plane, to create implied discontinuities. Let us go back, then, to the beginning of the architectural experience, the point at which the building first becomes visible and takes possession of the site. By "building" is not necessarily meant the central building or the most important building, which is the conclusion of the process. A mere wall, a garden wall, for example, is enough to imply a solid which further and closer inspection may or may not reveal as a screen. The first spatial experience offered by architecture, then, is that of the site, the landscape with all its features, many of them functioning as primary signs, and the dome of the sky above. The only discontinuity here is the horizon line, which may vary from the absolutely smooth, as on a vast plain, to the craggy and irregular, as in a mountain valley. As soon as the first screen is penetrated, however, the space is defined by much narrower limits; it is reduced to what lies between the screen just penetrated and that still to be penetrated. Except in enormus sites, it is also defined laterally.

At this point it is time to observe that solids are always implied. One cannot see an architectural solid from all four sides at once, or indeed from more than two. Space, however, can be both explicit and implicit. A courtyard, for example, can be a completely defined space, or it can be open on either side of the next screen, thus implying a space, not defining one. It is apparent that the architect thus has at his disposal a source for implicit discontinuity. As the solid is entered it may not turn out to contain the space its external facade implies. In fact, ordinarily it does not. The Baroque architects were particularly interested in designing street facades for churches which turned out to give quite unreliable information about the interior organization of the space. The contention of many modern architects that the exterior should always enable one to predict the interior is a mere value statement, a prescriptive statement for their own architecture. If it were taken seriously it would be necessary to reject many of the greatest buildings ever built. It is exactly in that failure of prediction that the architect has a source for internal discontinuity.

But he has, as far as solids and screens are concerned and spaces as well, still further resources. He can so break up the walls and the organization of space that he can make it difficult to read correctly exactly what kind of space one is in, or what kind of solid one is perceiving. With solids, for example, the outline may be considerably distant from the implied form of a cube or a projected rectangle. The exterior of the dome of the Pantheon, for example, implies a half sphere, but this implication is interrupted by the walls, which are a highly explicit drum interrupted by only a few bands of projecting cornice. From a position before the facade, however, even that drum is only implied. The implication of a solid, then, may be one of the basic three-dimensional configurations, or it may be any combination of these. Further, they may be combined in such a way that their relation is not additive but interpenetrational. That is, if each were complete, the other could not exist.

The same thing is true of interiors, or hollows. A hollow may be organized in terms of completely self-contained three-dimensional units, or these units may intersect. Again, an ambiguity or implied discontinuity is the result. Another source of discontinuity is the presentation of a series of similar hollows, each separated by a screen, followed by a hollow of quite different configuration: three rectangular rooms, for example, leading to a round room. Further, modal discontinuity may be achieved; and the round room may be made highly discontinuous from its implicit form. Since architecture in its semantic aspect is uniquely an art of transition, it is not surprising that modal discontinuity should be one of the most valuable devices for discontinuity the architect has.

The architect, then, achieves his discontinuities by violating implied solids, implied spaces and hollows, and implied planes. He can create internal discontinuity by establishing a formal expectancy along the line of approach and then frustrating the consequent prediction. And he can create modal discontinuity by changing the scale of his elements and the degree and manner in which the implicit discontinuities are achieved, as concluding a series of richly decorated rooms with an extremely plain and severe one. One of the sad things about so much architecture in the nineteenth and twentieth centuries is that it is urban building, offering the architect only a facade to work with. This is one of the reasons why the modern street is filled with the clamor of facades each screaming at the spectator for attention. Perhaps what we need for cities is invisible architecture for all commercial and domestic building, confining the urban architect to creating interesting street spaces and the architect of the building to creating interesting interiors. The tendency of architects to think of architecture as beginning only with the facade, or skin, of the building has been disastrous.

It remains to examine a building contemporary with Bach, Pope, and Watteau to show what architecture was doing at that time. The first twenty years of the eighteenth century have almost an embarrassment of architectural riches, but the most innovative and unusual building was the Palace of Blenheim, designed and partially built not far from Oxford for the Duke of Marlborough by Sir John Vanbrugh, assisted by Nicholas Hawksmore, who superseded him after the Duchess had dismissed Sir John, who was never permitted thereafter even to enter the gates. He never saw his unfinished masterpiece again. The various building campaigns extended from 1710 to 1724. I shall offer a brief description of the line of approach as it was designed by Vanbrugh, though never fully executed, followed by a formal analysis of some of the details of the interior courtyard (see Plates II, III, IV, and V).

As one turns into a monumental gate one enters a great avenue of trees, the trunks of which, like columns, flank the drive in a number of rows. The approach gently ascends over the brow of a hill, at the top of which a gigantic victory column in the center of the drive makes it at first impossible to see the palace. From then on, the center of it is visible, the two wings extending beyond the ends of the lines of trees, which terminate, shortly after the approach begins to descend, in a square space defined by trees. Now the whole vast extent of the palace facade is visible. In the center is a huge and extremely deep courtyard with a grand entrance at the end. On either side of the screen (never built) enclosing the courtyard, extend the enormous walls of the kitchen and stable wings. Above these walls rise in confusion innumerable towers of the most complex configuration, most, but not all, implying pyramids, and the general shape of the mass as a whole implies a low pyramid. The impression is that of a city, surrounded by military walls, and containing within it numerous churches, each with its elaborate spire or tower. The implication is that one is seeing the facade of an immense square, penetrable only through the screen. As it turns out, this is a delusion which achieves an internal discontinuity: for one is actually seeing three separate buildings, the hollow stable and kitchen wings and, far to the rear, the palace itself, connected with the two wings, however, by screens which appear to be walls of buildings, whether one examines them from within the courtyard or from the gardens beyond the stable and kitchen wings. But all this is still to come. For the moment, one seems to be before a city which shows an extraordinary modal discontinuity, for it is in part derived from the classical tradition and in part from the medieval. The profile, for example, is medieval, though the details of the noniconic and iconic ornament of those spires and towers are classical, or, occasionally, entirely original. This mixture of medieval and classical Renaissance-Baroque styles of manipulating solids, configurations, walls, and profiles is unique to Vanbrugh and Hawksmore.

The approach now descends fairly sharply towards a bridge and the palace virtually disappears, except for its violently discontinuous roofline. As one climbs the hill from the bridge, the towers disappear and one is no longer before a city but before the grand entrance of a palace. The screen is made of paired columns, so that, as one approaches, the still mysterious facade of the palace disappears as the columns glide together to create the effect of a wall. This increases the experience of transition into the courtyard, at the end of which now appears the palace facade.

The interior of the courtyard is so rich in implied, internal and modal discontinuities that it would take dozens of pages to present them all. Fortunately, such extensive analysis is not necessary. Only a few will bring out the peculiar character of the building. From the entrance to the courtyard the floor slopes up gently to a low terrace on top of which sits the main palace, nine bays wide, or so it seems at first glance. It is flanked by lower wings which project down the courtyard and are interrupted by towers almost as high as the main building; and then the wall of the courtyard is continued by still lower colonnades. These are the screens connecting the three separate buildings, but they look like facades of separate palaces. Towards the front of the courtyard are the entrance facades of the kitchen and stable wings, each with a vast portico surmounted by an immense and contortedly configured tower.

Further inspection discloses, however, that the theme of the fortified town is continued. The main entrance facade of the palace projects forward from the body of it and in fact is presented as an entirely separate building, not attached to the front but penetrating through it. This extraordinary implicit discontinuity is equalled only by the towers. Those at the kitchen and stable entrances and those halfway up the courtyard are each crowned with elaborate spires, implying cubes or projected rectangles. But in addition there are visible four more tower crowns, each of which, therefore, also implies a tower underneath it. But there are only two towers on the garden front. The other two tower crowns sit on the roofs of the L-shaped wings flanking the central structure. The implication is that beyond the visible interior wall of the courtyard lies a whole other series of palaces, but this expectation is entirely violated as one penetrates through the palace into the garden and walks around it. Actually, the interior wall of the courtyard is so handled that at least some sixteen buildings are implied, though there are really only three.

One final device will be enough. The screens connecting the palace with the service buildings are fronted by colonnades. These turn and form quadrants in front of the L-shaped wings, terminating just short of the main palace and on a line between it and the extreme front of the entrance porch, thus making a bay for the palace facade from which the porch projects. On the interior face of this bay the quadrant colonnade is incorporated into the wing, so that on one face it is part of that wing, and on the other, the quadrant, it is an entirely separate building with a facade of engaged columns, although when it is on the front of the wings the columns are free-standing. But the most powerful discontinuity is the fact that the screen-line of this facade is interrupted by an immense tower in a completely different mode, quasi-medieval, quasi-late provincial Roman. The colonnade is seen to enter this tower and emerge on the adjacent face. The implication is that it has made a right angle in the middle of the tower. This extraordinary implicit discontinuity, created by ambiguity, is exceeded only by the cornice line of the colonnade, which not only penetrates the tower, follows the quadrant, continues along the interior face of the L-shaped wing, but in addition is carried right across the facade not only of the main palace but also of the porch, which, it will be remembered, is presented not as the porch of the palace but as the porch of a completely separate building penetrating through the body of the palace, and by implication emerging the same distance on the other or garden face of it, as, in fact, it does not.

The garden facade presents almost none of this architectural hurly-burly. What happens to the colonnade is an example of internal discontinuity, the presentation of a theme and then its violation or variation, and the intrusion of the strange square and brutal towers into its course creates not only implicit discontinuity but modal discontinuity, contrasting as they do with the elegance and refinement of the colonnade.

These are but a few examples of the rich discontinuities offered by Blenheim. As one might expect, some have judged it a most ugly building, but others, including myself, have seen it as an architectural masterpiece. Indeed, I know of no work which shows such a thorough mastery of discontinuity and such an extraordinary ability to make a building problematic. It is evident, also, that what we see governing Vanbrugh is highly similar to what we saw governing Pope, Watteau, and Bach; the discontinuities are the reward for imposing on themselves an extraordinary number of rules, many in conflict, but all of which had to be obeyed so that they might be violated. Each of them exposed himself to an extremely difficult problem. Each arrived at solutions filled not only with discontinuities but also with ambiguities. Those of Vanbrugh are obvious. The ambiguities of Watteau lie in the domination of his major paintings by two or more large implicit forms, none of which bear hierarchical relation to any other. The ambiguities of Bach appear in contrapuntal music that sounds like sequences of harmonic blocks and in melodies that slip seamlessly from one voice to another. Those of Pope are syntactical; one of his most striking devices is to offer a misleading syntactical sequence which appears to violate the caesura, but which actually makes sense only if the caesura is observed.

Each of these artists created masterpieces, but masterpieces of what style? Pope is usually asserted to be Rococo, mostly because of the delicate charm of parts of *The Rape of the Lock*, on semantic grounds, then, not formal ones. Watteau has been variously called Rococo and Baroque, but Rococo principally because his subject matter was very popular with subsequent Rococo painters, such as Fragonard, again on semantic not formal grounds. Bach is always recognized as Baroque, if this term is applicable to the history of music at all. Vanbrugh is sometimes called Baroque, English Baroque, or *sui generis*, neither Baroque, nor Rococo, nor anything else. We are then, face to face, at last, with the crucial problem of this book. I have offered an explanation of the peculiar phenomenon of nonfunctional stylistic dynamism in art. My explanation is that the distinguishing attribute of the artist's role is to create occasions for disorientation, and of the perceiver's role to experience it. The distinguishing mark of the perceiver's transaction with the work of art is discontinuity of experience, not continuity; disorder, not order; emotional disturbance, not emotional catharsis, even though some works of art have a cadential close, or the explicit presentation of the implied form. This is true even of Blenheim, for the perceiver's field, as he mounts the last steps of the porch entrance, is filled with the powerful almost explicit rectangle of the high porch surmounted by the most explicit form of the entire building, the triangular pediment. But a work of art need not have closure or cadence; it can be open, unresolved, ending in discord and confusion. Certainly modern art has taught us that, if nothing else. Cadence seems to be, really, merely a sign that the experience has now come to an end. The cathartic effect is merely the relief from the disorientation and disturbance and powerful emotional affect which has preceded it. It feels so good when it stops.

Nonfunctional dynamism, then, is accounted for by the general theory of artistic discontinuity. Two questions remain. The first is, "What keeps discontinuity from being random? Why are stylistic continua recognizable? Why do the boundaries of such continua have a revolutionary character?" When this is answered, it will be possible to propose an answer for the final question, the question of questions, "Why has artistic behavior been established as a social role? Why do people look at works of art? Why do they bother? Why has man been willing to make the enormous economic investment that art requires? Does art have an adaptational function? If it does, what is it?"

SIX:
THE RELATIONSHIP
OF THE ARTS

1. A HYPOTHESIS

When an artist innovates a new device for internal, implicit, or modal discontinuity, he has not necessarily established an external discontinuity. That can be achieved only if he repeats that device. He can also work the other way: in a series of works he can abandon an established device. The effect is the same. An explanation for this has been offered in the discussion of style above. It takes two works of art to reveal a stylistic trait. It takes two experiences of a category of identity, an individual human being, for instance, to perceive the style of that category. In this sense, and in this sense only, can it be said that a single work of art has style. But when we apply the term "style" to the historical dimension, when we arrange similar works of art along a chronological line, style emerges only when two or more objects are found to have a trait in common. The semantic aspect of art certainly exhibits style, but it is, as we have seen, a functional style, responding to non-artistic demands from the other faces of the cultural pyramid. Non-functional style is to be located in the external discontinuities of a work of art. Why is it, then, that an external discontinuity can be established? Clearly, not all of them necessarily are.

Artists frequently try out various kinds of discontinuity, sometimes in works of art which leave their studios and are offered as occasions for public artistic perception. Others are discarded; the evidence that they were tried is to be found in notebooks, sketchbooks, diaries, journals, letters to friends. This seems to account for the fact that it is not uncommon to find in such documents, and sometimes in completed works, "anticipations" of subsequent formal, or non-functional, style.

Such anticipations have been the subject of awe-struck commentary by critics and stylistic historians; the artist is praised for seeing so far into the future, for having, it would seem, predicted the direction that style would take. This in turn leads to the notion that there is something not exactly fated or predestined—we are much too sophisticated to use such words to-day—about stylistic continuity, but rather that there is an internal logic to stylistic development. At this point the distinction between semantic structures and semantic packages is exceedingly useful. Logic is the extraction, analysis, and manipulation of the structural signs of arbitrary verbal compound signs. Such structural signs are not to be found in configurational semiosis or in primary semiosis. That is why such semiosis can use natural configurations for semantic functions, but arbitrary signs can do so only by the conventionalization of emblems, or derived signs. Certainly, there is no structure to discontinuities. They are clearly packages, not structures. Furthermore, since they offer disorientation rather than orientation, they are not signs at all, because signs require a conventionalized link between interpretant (orientation, weighted average), sign configuration, and referent (categorial range). Discontinuities are signs only to an interpreter not engaged in performing the role of perceiver but in constructing the history of stylistic continua. The stylistic historian is not engaged in using an already established referent for discontinuities but in innovating such a referential link, one he hopes will be sufficiently well-grounded to be accepted and conventionalized for others than himself.

This is where I cannot agree with Leonard B. Meyer, much as I admire his work.[1] He thinks that expectancy frustrations in art are signs of chance. He does not mean that they are a sign that the artist has taken a chance, permitted himself random innovation; he means that they are signs of metaphysical chance.

---

[1] See Chapter V, note 12.

Chance is an uncompromising fact which permeates all the realms of being: the physical, the biological, the social, the personal, and the aesthetic. It is but chance that there is a solar system; but chance that life developed on this planet; but the chance of a series of fortuitous mutations that there is human life as we know it; but chance that any particular human consciousness comes into being; and, once living, both past and present chance events continually condition and modify the course and tenor of our lives.

Thus it is that music, mirroring the essential shape and substance of human experience, from time to time contains sudden shocking clashes with unpredictable chance. . . .

The pedants have piously attempted to explain away the inexplicable in order to make their analyses jibe with their mechanistic misconceptions of what constitutes the basis for musical unity, logic, and inevitability. But chance will not be denied.[2]

The artist and the perceiver both expose themselves to chance when they experience discontinuity; but it does not follow that the devices for discontinuity are anything more than signs that the artist has exposed himself to chance or randomness. To make music—or art in general—a sign of chance is to do two things. First, it is to hypostatize the word "chance" and make it refer to an entity. But words cannot do this; they can only refer to categories of perception. Meyer has made a series of what I have called middle statements, the kind of statement logical positivists refer to as a metaphysical statement and which they think of as nonsense or meaningless. As we have seen, this position is now rather old-fashioned; for following the line of more recent studies of a language, such statements, as suggested above, may be translated into theoretical constructs from which operational or instrumental constructs can be derived. What "chance" means, as Meyer uses the term, is that there are a good many things in man's experience of "himself" and the "world"—categories of perceptual configurations—for which he has not yet been able to construct theories from which may be derived predictive statements capable of being operationally verified. Second, such hypostatization means therefore that musical discontinuity—or any kind of discontinuity in art—is a conventionalized term for such a proposition, and that, since music is only the deposit of behavior, composers consciously or unconsciously use discontinuities as emblems of the verbal sign, "chance."

For this reason I find Meyer's explanation of discontinuity unacceptable. On the other hand he has certainly demonstrated beyond

[2] *Emotion and Meaning in Music* by Leonard B. Meyer, Chicago, 1956, pp. 195–196. Copyright The University of Chicago Press. Used by permission of The University of Chicago Press.

the shadow of a doubt that what he calls "deviation from an ideal type"—or discontinuity—is offered by music and is equivalent to what in other realms of human perception is called chance. Strictly speaking, then, it is not true that a work of art is a sign-package of discontinuities. It is only the stylistic historian who assembles such sign packages. Works of art may be packages of discontinuities, in the sense they are not structured by structural signs, but they are not *sign* packages. In preparing to execute a work of art, therefore, the artist performs a series of random experiments with discontinuities, either overtly or covertly. When the practice of making overt sketches began we can scarcely know, but there is evidence that it existed in ancient Egypt and it certainly has been established as part of the artist's role for some millennia. Further examples may be found in the extraordinary collection of poetic sketches and drafts in the University of Buffalo Library. This kind of activity accounts for anticipations. Within a given culture, the artists in any media are bound to hit on stylistic devices which other artists, hundreds of years later, also hit upon. This is exactly the same problem as that explored under "novelty" and "originality." Just as some mechanical inventions have been innovated over and over by individuals who did not know they had already been innovated and even culturally established, so with artists. Their experimentation with randomness is readily explainable by the notion of discontinuity. The problem is to offer some explanation as to why the artist rejects some random innovations and incorporates others into his finished product.

A couple of examples will perhaps illuminate the problem. Dürer painted a number of watercolors in a style which had no subsequent influence, which did not become established; in particular he painted one of a dream image, which, even more than the others, has an extraordinarily modern look. To find anything like it in established style we must turn to the Expressionism of the early decades of this century, and to find parallels to some of the other watercolors we must turn to watercolors by Turner and the style of the Impressionists. These watercolors are not anticipations; they are experiments in innovation which Dürer decided not to incorporate into the paintings he did for public use. He kept them for his private delectation. He, and no doubt some of his friends and pupils, were the only perceivers of these works. Had he made them public, would their external discontinuities have been established in sixteenth-century German style? Who can tell? The only thing of importance is that he made no attempt to conventionalize them into his culture. Another example comes from the career of Gustave Moreau, the late nineteenth-century French painter in whom recently there has been a revival of interest. But the interest is not so much in his highly finished and highly iconistic paintings which he exhibited to the public but in certain sketches in oil in which he worked out the color schemes of finished paintings. These, now, look exactly like the abstract Expressionism of the 1950's. That, of course, is precisely why they have been revived, and there has been the usual awe-struck and fatuous comment about his powerful and extraordinary "anticipations" of modern art. But the point is not that he made them; the point is that he did not exhibit them or sell them. To him they were sketches; there is no reason why to-day we cannot look at them as examples of abstract expressionism, and indeed every reason why we should, if we want to. But this is quite a different matter from the claim that they are anticipations and the implication that therefore there is a certain logic of style which is preordained, or fated, or something of that sort. Such statements are middle or metaphysical statements.

The key word in the preceding paragraph is "decide." That the artist experiments with various kinds of randomness can be deduced from the general theory of discontinuity, and this deduction is supported by the actual evidence of random experimentation, of self-exposure to chance, provided by sketchbooks and other documents and artifacts. But the artist not only creates a series of possible devices for discontinuity: he also *decides* which ones he is going to incorporate in the finished work, the completion and exposure of which consummate the artist's role, even though the only person to play the perceiver's role is himself. Actually, of course, in making the work the artist is constantly shifting back and forth between the two roles. The question, then, resolves itself into the form, "What makes the artist decide as he does?" And this is a central question, because only in the similarity of successive decisions can external discontinuities accumulate into stylistic continua, bounded by stylistic revolutions. Thus the experimentation is random, but the decision is not.

At this point a word is necessary about the behavior and logic which lie behind the establishment of stylistic continua. It is not merely the "discovery" or construction of such continua by simple observation. Nothing, if transactionalism or the directive-state theory or modern philosophy have any validity, happens that way. If these continua are more than illusions they must rest on predictive behavior and they must be confirmed by such behavior. The simple fact is that an individual experienced in the art of a particular medium of any large historical segment of a culture can successfully predict when a particular work of art was done, and this prediction can be verified by documentary research. I once predicted that an unsigned series of watercolor illustrations for Milton had been done between 1790 and 1800 as the basis for an edition of *Paradise Lost* illustrated with copper engravings. Ten minutes research in the excellent Milton collection of the Princeton University Library discovered the edition, which was published in 1795.[3] This sort of thing has been repeated thousands and thousands of times by amateurs and professionals. Stylistic continua are arrived at by the process of creating weighted averages which then serve as orientations or hypotheses for the ensuing search behavior. This is the firm rock on which constructs of stylistic continua rest. The revolutionary boundaries of such continua have been established by the same process, in all the arts. Thus the chronological congruence, uncertain as it often is, among the historical location of stylistic boundaries by investigators in different media of art can be reduced to predictive behavior. And, to repeat a point made before, this congruence cannot be the consequence of a defining attribute of each art, for the rules of each media are inescapably bound up with the media themselves, since such rules are prescriptive statements about how the artist's behavior should be controlled when he is manipulating his medium. Since the continuity of style and stylistic revolutions are the result of certain decisions the artist makes, and since these factors are common to at least the four arts examined here, and since randomness or rule violation is inseparable from the medium, it appears to follow that the decision is separable from the medium, that, in fact, it has nothing to do with the medium at all. But if it is not derived from the medium it is separable from exposure to discontinuity, since discontinuity is not separable from the medium. And being separable from discontinuity, the decision about which discontinuity to use in the completed work is separable from the defining attribute of art, which is non-functional stylistic dynamism, or discontinuity. The basis for the decision, therefore, must lie outside of the defining attribute of the artist's behavior. The particular decision made must be in response to non-artistic demands, demands emanating from the other faces of the

---

[3] Morse Peckham, "Blake, Milton, and Edward Burney," *The Princeton University Library Chronicle*, XI, 1950, pp. 107–126.

cultural pyramid. Finally, since the only evidence for the history of those other faces is composed of documentary and other artificial sign structures and packages, there must be some connection between the semantic aspect and the formal aspect.

But this last point is only of slight importance, indeed, frequently of no importance at all. Since the formal aspect varies independently of the semantic aspect, it is perfectly possible that the decisions responsible for the stylistic continuum of a period are responses to quite different demands from those which are signified in the semantic aspect. The stylistic historian is engaged in an effort which requires him to perceive a stylistic continuum as the sign of the response of a series of artists to demands emanating from non-artistic fields of the culture in which the artist works. He innovates that link and hopes to conventionalize it. But he need not assume that the semantic functions and the stylistic continuum are signs of the artist's response to demands emanating from the same cultural level. In fact, it would be a profound error so to assume, and it has been. It is the error responsible for the unsatisfactory and unacceptable results achieved by the tradition examined in Chapter I. The functional style—the semantic style—can be in response to demands emanating from a low cultural level while the nonfunctional style—the formal aspect—can be the result of responding to demands emanating from the highest cultural level. Or vice versa; numerous artists with something to say at the highest cultural level have presented in their works an utterly out-of-date formal aspect which had sunk from the highest cultural level, where it had originated, to a middle or even lower cultural level. Much more common, however, especially in periods when art was situationally determined by the demands of church and state and other forms of great economic power, is the first kind of semantic-formal incongruity. The semantic aspect of Egyptian art and architecture changed scarcely at all from the First Dynasty to the Ptolemaic dynasties, and even then it did not change much. The same millennia, however, saw numerous stylistic revolutions. The eternal sameness of Egyptian art and architecture is a myth. The experienced archaeologist and stylistic analyst can date Egyptian works on the basis of non-functional style just as well as their fellows can in Greek, Roman, Medieval, or Modern European culture.

It is now possible to put the problem in the form of a hypothesis: *The arts are related because the decisions responsible for non-functional stylistic*

*continua at any cultural level are controlled by semantic behavior currently
existing at the same level; when that semantic behavior changes radically, there
is a stylistic revolution.* In practice, this hypothesis refers to the behavior
of the artist. His role requires him to innovate external discontinuities
in each work of art he creates. The higher he is on the cultural pyramid,
the greater the pressure of that requirement. There is nothing in the
artistic medium itself or in the culturally conventionalized rules governing its manipulation which either requires him to create a discon-
continuity or directs him in how to decide about the degree and kind
of the external discontinuity. We are to conceive of him as faced with
a practical infinity of choices; to create at all, he must make a decision.
Like all decisions, this one is determined by the values, both explicit
and implicit, of his cultural environment. If he is a New York artist
of the 1960's, those values tell him that, to be a successful artist, he
must make a great innovative leap; if he can, he must start a whole new
artistic fashion. If that is beyond him, he must make as much of a discontinuity as he can in the current fashion. On the other hand, if he
is a producer of Hollywood horror movies for children, his values tell
him that he must make only enough of a discontinuity to differentiate
the new picture from the old ones. Or if he is a popular singer of what
is currently known as folk songs, he knows that his popularity depends
in part on keeping quite close to certain styles in melody, harmony,
and rhythm. It is worth emphasizing that formal discontinuity is controlled by the values of the same level, but it does not follow that the
semantic aspect of the work presents the values of the same level; they
may be from a lower level or a higher.

The practical problem is this: Can that semantic behavior be stated
in a proposition or series of propositions that can be conceived as controlling the decisions of artists in various media so as to produce
parallel stylistic continua and revolutions?

The operant word here is "conceived." It is not required that the
propositions should be identical with or even closely related to the
propositions actually current at the time. The propositions are themselves signs of attitudes, or assumptions, or orientations. The artist may
very well be under the control of such orientations, even though he has
no corresponding propositions and though the orientation shows up
only in his decision. The reasons for this are two: orientations may be
signified in both natural and artificial signs of all sorts, or they may
not be signified in the culture at all. Ordinarily in fact, an orientation
precedes the innovation of a sign; hence metaphor. It is not meaning-

less to say, "I know what I think but I don't know how to say it." It is not true that all orientations, or hypotheses, or assumptions, or weighted averages are categorized by signs. Finally, and most important, language is not isomorphic with the world, nor are any signs, nor any explicit categories. It cannot, therefore, be isomorphic with categories of perception which, from the point of view of language, are part of the world. Further, a great many orientations, most of them in fact, are signified verbally in hypostatized metaphysical or middle statements. For these reasons, therefore, cultural history is full of statements about what Plato, or Shakespeare, or Milton, or Bernini, or Descartes, or Tennyson, or Kandinsky, or Wittgenstein really meant. The translation of such middle statements into assumptive, hypothetical (in the Bruner sense) or orientative statements can then be applied to the artist's non-functional stylistic decision-making behavior.

The next step is to suggest reasons for accepting the probability of the proposed hypothesis. What we need is a series of propositions about the arts of several successive stylistic continua, and these propositions must respond adequately to the requirements for such propositions as set up by the hypothesis. For this purpose, I shall limit myself to poetry, painting, architecture, and music. These are the arts which for centuries have been most intensively cultivated at the European cultural apex. They are the "high arts." Consequently, all the discontinuities will be highly visible. (Sculpture, of course, could be added, but it has become separate from architecture only fairly recently and so resembles painting, at least in our culture, that it can be omitted for the sake of simplifying a complex situation.) The periods I have chosen are the Baroque (1600–1720), the Enlightenment (1720–1790), and the Early Romantic (1790–1830). These dates, of course, are only approximate; for one thing, they differ for each of the arts, but ordinarily within the range of only about a decade. Some of the reasons for taking my material from this period have been indicated at the beginning of Chapter IV, but there is a further reason. In the past four decades there has been intensive study in the history of ideas from the late sixteenth century to the present. It is now possible to speak with some assurance about both the explicit and implicit assumptions of the semantic behavior at the cultural apex since 1600. In short, there has been enough research to make it possible to present those ideas in fairly simple terms; in other periods it is still hard to see the woods for the trees. Such simplicity is essential if one is to present those assumptions in the form of pervasive values. That is, we can now see the assumptions *behind* the philosophical, scientific, ethical, and critical statements. We can now recover the general and pervasive orientation which could influence an artist, although he might have no technical competence in the various disciplines in which the assumptions of his times are worked out in detail. The assumptions in earlier periods of European cultures and in other cultures do not have as yet this ready availability.

2. BAROQUE

The movement to develop appropriate propositions in the effort to make the hypothesis acceptable is necessarily dialectical, a movement back and forth between two constructs, one, of the stylistic continuum, the other, of the semantic evidence at the same cultural level. But the complete verbal exposition of such a movement would be tedious and probably impossible. Rather, I shall first discuss with some brevity a hypothesis about Baroque style, then in more detail Enlightenment style, and finally, again, quite briefly, the early Romantic style.

We have seen that the four early eighteenth-century artists we examined—Bach, Pope, Watteau, and Vanbrugh—are all characterized by an external discontinuity consequent upon the self-imposition of increase in the number of rules, a good many of them in conflict. The result was a very high level of discontinuity. This is one reason I chose to use these works as examples of the various kinds of discontinuity: the high level makes discontinuities very easy to spot. Now the exposure to a large number of very demanding rules, particularly when some of those rules are inconsistent with each other, means a high level of exposure to problems, which are the forms in which awareness of the gap between behavior and situational requirement is perceived. The general reliability of this proposition can be seen in any number of situations. Chess, involving so many very stringent rules, offers more problems than tag; an evening in a lower class bar, though such places have their etiquette, their rules, is less productive of problems than the meeting of heads of state, an occasion governed by a multitude of protocols, which are also rules. The more modern science has governed itself by rules the more productive its efforts have been, simply because more problems are exposed.

If problem-exposure is the attribute which justifies placing the work of these four artists in a stylistic category, then to assert that they are Baroque means that the decisions of all Baroque artists were governed by an orientation that gave a high value to problem-exposure and that to give a similar value to the same experience is the characteristic of the non-artistic activity of the high level culture during the seventeenth and early eighteenth centuries.

Here a couple of side-issues need to be met. Is it not true that all discontinuity involves problem awareness, since it is the result of the experience of the disparity between the formal expectancy and the perceptual configuration? No, it is not. Here the game metaphor helps again. Disparity may be experienced without the emergence of the perception of a problem. Normally, of course, disparities are ignored; if the individual feels any disorientation he gets rid of it by suppressing his awareness of the disparity. In art, disparity awareness is not suppressed: neither does it result in the perception of a problem. It is merely experienced. The artists concerned made their decisions in order to increase their problems: this does not mean that their art offered problems, but it does mean that their art showed an unusually high level of discontinuity, and that, if they were Baroque artists, previous artists in the Baroque style also produced art which moved, through the approximately century and a quarter involved, to an increasing level of discontinuity.

The other issue is also relatively minor but needs a word or two of attention. Whenever a new orientation is responsible for a stylistic revolution, that revolution may be concurrent with the appearance of that innovation in non-artistic semantic evidence, or it may precede it, or it may follow it. It is a matter of whether the revolutionary artist himself was also a member of the non-artistic high-level cultural community, or was in close contact with some member, or came under the influence of that community only after the new orientation had been fairly well established.

Nevertheless, it is true that the individual who wishes to expose himself to problems must train himself to a high degree of sensitivity to perception of the disparity between the pattern he is using as a hypothesis for his behavior and the actual data offered. The artist, as artist, values such sensitivity; that is why he experiments in sketches and other preliminaries. However, if the high-level culture of his time also gives a high value to disparity awareness, he has two reasons for choosing among his possibilities the one that gives the greatest amount of discontinuity. In other cultural situations in which, for whatever reason, disparity awareness is given a low value, he will select among the possibilities for discontinuity he has made available to himself one close to the lower end of the range. On the whole, scientific culture ascribes a high value to disparity awareness, giving its highest rewards to scientists who are most capable of responding to disparities and formulating problems. The greatest thing a great scientist can do is to offer the scientific community a great problem; this is far more important than offering a great solution to an existent problem or even to solving the great problem he himself has formulated. And over and over again, great scientists have reported that their first step towards discovering the great problem was a feeling that something was wrong, that something, they knew not what, was unaccounted for by the theories they were using in their investigations. This feeling may be called *cognitive tension.*

> One characteristic of cognitive activity, whether at the level of instrumental activity or in the playful realms of chess, is that it has associated with it some rather unique affective states. The sense of tension that occurs when we cannot "place" somebody, the frustration we have been able to induce in subjects serving in tachistoscopic experiments when exposure levels were too low, the malaise of the trained mind with a seemingly causeless effect—all of these are as characteristic of frustrated cognitive activity as desire is of blocked sexual activity.[4]

Now all of this may seem to be somewhat remote from the problem of Baroque style, but it is in fact very much to the point, for it was in the seventeenth century that what we can recognize as modern science actually was founded. In *Science and the Modern World* Whitehead asserts that all of modern science is an investigation of the scientific problems uncovered during that century. A few examples will suffice.

> Contrary to the popular belief that genius breaks radically with its age, three of the greatest seventeenth-century minds, Pierre Fermat, Isaac Newton, and Gottfried Wilhelm Leibniz, each working independently of the other, became absorbed in the problems of the calculus.[5]

Descartes undertook to reduce all knowledge to the single proposition "Cogito, ergo sum" and to recreate the world on this ground alone, governing his subsequent behavior by the most stringent rules he could arrive at. That they turned out to be not quite stringent

---

[4] Jerome S. Bruner, *A Study of Thinking*, New York, 1956, pp. 16–17. A tachistoscope is a device for exposing visual stimuli very briefly.
[5] Morris Kline, *Mathematics in Western Culture*, New York, 1953, p. 214.

enough is beside the point. Locke, similarly, undertook to do without any information for the mind except what might be derived from experience. For obvious reasons, he too did not achieve complete success. But for our purposes it again is of no consequence. Both of these men selected strategies which insured the maximum amount of cognitive tension, the maximum amount of the tension that comes from disparity awareness, and the maximum amount of problem exposure. In the history of thought, it is doubtful if anyone had done the like. Neither could have done what he did had not Bacon, early in the century, separated natural philosophy, or science, from super-natural philosophy, or theology. He undertook to do without

> the idols of the tribe, the cave, the market place, and the theater: that is, the illusions that man suffers from because he is a human being, because he is a unique cultural product, because he uses unanalyzed language, and because he has been intellectually amused and deceived by all preceding philosophies.[6]

Bacon's was a singularly drastic attempt to do without conventional-ized orientations and to see the world afresh, to expose oneself to the maximum of problems, to believe nothing that cannot be experimen-tally verified. To be sure, his theory of experimentation turned out to be useless, but all modern science depends upon his effort to create such a theory.

Coming a little closer to artistic behavior, consider what happened to English prose style. There is now some doubt as to whether the simplification of English prose in the last forty years of the seventeenth century was a direct response to the demands emanating from the Royal Society of London for Improving Natural Knowledge, but it was certainly responsive to the values controlling the members of that Society. The plain simple style, which attempted a purely descriptive, or more properly, predictive prose was the result of prose writers imposing on themselves a number of limiting rules. Heretofore, the prose writer could use the full resources of the language, metaphor, rhetorical figures of speech, primary signs, even a certain amount of discontinuity. Primarily informational prose was frequently written by someone who was also playing the artist's role. Sir Thomas Browne's *Hydriotaphia, Urne-Buriall, or, A discourse of the sepulchrall urnes lately found in Norfolk* is an excellent example. But the new prose obeyed rules which forbade the writer to use anything but the simplest prose

---

[6] Peckham, *Beyond the Tragic Vision*, p. 70.

necessary to do the job. It was a purely functional prose, and it was designed to cut away everything that might hinder exposure to the problem at hand or reduce tension by displaying cathartic terms and figures of speech. All of these efforts—and this is but a tiny sampling of the innumerable instances that could be cited—are marked by a determination to get rid of that accumulation of verbal patterns which make it so easy to plug the dike, to throw in another troop of soldiers, when the individual experiences cognitive tension. The key to the high level culture of the astonishingly creative seventeenth century is in its self-imposition of rules which achieved on the one hand a radical simplification and on the other a radical stringency of rule-controlled behavior. The highest value was given to the capacity to endure cognitive tension.

If we glance for a moment at some of the themes found in the art of men who were operating at the highest cultural level both semantically and formally, we find similar phenomena. The semantic aspect takes the form of constructing the work around a problem. In Milton it is the attempt to justify God's ways to man with the least theological paraphernalia possible, to think through the problem from scratch. In Dryden's heroic tragedies it is the problem of love and duty, the conflict between the private role of the aristocrat and his public role, and this was also the problem Racine worked with. As we have seen, Pope's "Eloisa to Abelard" dramatized a similar problem, the ambiguity of religious and erotic emotion. It was above all a great age of satire, which attacks humanity because of the difference between what man says he values and what his behavior shows he really values. Swift's *Gulliver's Travels* semantically, at least, is a Baroque work; and formally also, because it is written according to very strict rules derived from travel literature. It violently frustrates the expectations raised by its format and its opening. And it is written in the new plain style, in which the most fantastic events are discussed as if they were no more remarkable than the adventures one might have walking along London's Strand. In his epitaph Swift said that his heart was lacerated by savage indignation; his fury was directed at man's ability to deceive himself. His determination to see the world and human life as they really are puts him, in spite of his political and religious conservatism, in the company of Bacon, Descartes, Newton, and Locke. He focussed upon the intellectual consequences of original sin and the fall from grace, and Pope did the same thing in *The Dunciad*, published in 1728, only two years after *Gulliver's Travels*.

In music the same forces can be seen at work. The early seventeenth century saw the rise of the *concertato* style.

> The *concertato* style . . . is one in which different musical elements are engaged not on a completely cooperative basis, as in counterpoint or monody, but in a manner which deliberately emphasizes the contrast of one voice or instrument against another, or of one group against another, or of a group against a solo.[7]

This manner of writing was developed by accumulated discontinuities into the concerto grosso, in which a group of solo instruments alternately struggles against and cooperates with the orchestra. And the fugue is almost an emblem of Baroque music, with its strict rules and its maximization of discontinuity. The fugue emerged by cumulative external discontinuities from the *ricercare*, a word that in modern Italian means "research." A ricercare was a searching out of the possibilities of what one can do with a musical theme in contrapuntal music. And like science and prose style, music was subjected to a radical simplification, a reduction of modes to two scales, really one, and the vertical-horizontal integration of harmony and melody. The same forces of radical simplification and multiplication of rules can be seen in painting; hence what has so often been called Baroque unity. But it is not really unity. It is the reduction of the major implicit forms of the painting to one and its presentation in terms of an implicit discontinuity which increases steadily through the work of Watteau; it is true that he returned to the simultaneous presentation of major implied forms, but they were superimposed, not, as in the sixteenth century, juxtaposed. In the semantic aspect, the primary signs show the same forces at work. The plunge into depth of the Baroque landscape is not only a sign of demand; it is exposure without the defenses of recession in planes and successive reduction of color iconicity. The extreme distance is as pressing on the perceiver as the foreground. Likewise the striking increase in iconicity which began at the end of the sixteenth century was governed by the same desire for exposure to reality which lay behind the science and the new prose style. The essence of Baroque architecture is spatial disorientation and the dissolution of solids and screens.

Daniells' location of the Baroque spirit in the desire to assert the predominance of the will is not, then, entirely meaningless;[8] his error

---

[7] Donald Jay Grout, *A History of Western Music*, New York, 1960.
[8] Chapter I, Section 1, above.

comes from associating it with the desire for political power, which was certainly nothing novel and was certainly not at the cultural apex; and also from interpreting certain preselected primary signs instead of attempting to account for non-functional stylistic dynamism and continuity. Politically, the equivalence of the orientation that accounts for the accumulated external discontinuity of the Baroque, its formal continuum, are the innovative politics of the time, some of a conservative cast, some characterized by what we would to-day call liberalism. The desire for a simplified mode of political organization, more consonant with the actual demands of man's interaction with the environment, whether the actual state was unified by central power or whether the power was dispersed into cooperative and independently responsible units—this was the seventeenth-century political spirit. Hence the emphasis on finding a natural basis for political and social organization, not a divinely revealed and theological basis.

The proposed hypothesis has led then, to this conclusion about the values dominant at the highest cultural level from the late sixteenth century to approximately the third decade of the eighteenth century, insofar as they affected both innovative semantic behavior and the innovative formal behavior of art: What controlled the innovative artists' decisions which resulted in external discontinuity and the semantic behavior of innovative philosophers, scientists, and valuators—all at the highest cultural level—was (1) the determination to endure as much cognitive tension as possible, and (2) the maximization of problem exposure by (a) initial reduction of all rules and gradual multiplication of derived rules, and (b) increasing the stringency of all rules. In no period of modern European culture have philosophy, science, valuation, and art been so deliberately designed to be exciting. To be utterly dogmatic, anyone who does not find Pope's poems exciting does not know how to read poetry.

3. ENLIGHTENMENT

The discussion of Baroque style began with certain statements about the formal aspect of the work of four early eighteenth-century artists. An attempt was then made to discover those ruling values at the highest cultural level of the seventeenth century which could conceivably provide a basis for the decisions made by various artists of the time; their accumulated external discontinuities provided the foundation or starting line for the four artists we began with. It is apparent that there is little or nothing in common to the style of Donne and Pope, or Herrick and Pope, but it is conceivable that the formal decisions of all three were controlled by the same values. Thus the poetry of Donne began as a revolutionary external discontinuity from what had preceded him and what the vast majority of poets continued to do for some time. It is instructive that among his first efforts were satires, and the reasons why the seventeenth and early eighteenth centuries formed an age of satire we have already seen. But more to the point is what was asserted about the Donne conceit above: the importation of a term extremely remote from the local terms, and the development of a metaphor by stringent logical rules, the essence of which was to apply as many of the attributes of the imported category as possible to the local situation, to establish a novel but logically convincing emergent category. The same decisional values were applied by the somewhat later Herrick in a completely different manner. The rules he imposed upon himself involved an extreme reduction in available poetic diction, an extreme reduction in scale—he is the English master of the poetic miniature—and the incongruent confrontation of the classical-Renaissance pastoral tradition with the actual folk practices of the farmers and farm workers of his parish in southwest England. His diction in some ways already shows the characteristics of the subsequent plain prose style, and his statements are highly "realistic," that is, predictive. Herbert combined Donne's conceit with a Herrick-like plainness of diction and added his own concern with the psychological realities of religious experience. Thus emerges the extremely important probability already suggested above in the discussion of "style," that a style is properly thought of as a dynamic continuum, not a category all members of which must display the same attributes. This is extremely important for comprehending what happened to the formal aspect of the arts between the 1720's and the 1790's.

For this period a number of styles have been distinguished, just as Early, Middle, and Late Baroque have been somewhat uselessly discriminated. The subsequent period has been classified under the headings of Rococo, "Romanticism," Sentimentalism, *Sturm-und-Drang*, Classicism and Neo-Classicism, and Revolutionary, referring to the styles current in France during the French Revolution. Certainly, at first glance, the style of Tiepolo in the 1730's seems to have little in common with the style of David in the 1790's. Yet, as we have seen, this does not necessarily mean that the paintings of both men do not belong to the same stylistic continuum, or that all the paintings of either belong to the same stylistic continuum: the early work of Tiepolo is quite clearly Baroque. Instead, however, of beginning with analyses of their styles and those of artists in other media, in discussing these styles I shall begin with some account of a value system quite different from that of the seventeenth century and then attempt to show how it is conceivable that it was in response to these new values that the artists of the last three-quarters of the eighteenth century made their decisions about the kind of external discontinuity they wished to achieve. All these styles may be logically included under Enlightenment styles, just as it would be more accurate to use the term "Baroque styles" rather than the singular form.

As we have seen, the highest cultural level from the 1590's to the 1720's was intensely interested in problem exposure and cognitive tension. The Enlightenment moved in exactly the opposite direction: it was interested in, and became steadily more interested in, the resolution of tension, or to use Bruner's earlier term, affective congruence, the *feeling* that the situation matches the expectation or directive state.

> While this is a special case of test by consistency, it merits treatment on its own. It is best described as an act of categorizing or identifying an event that carries with it a feeling of subjective certainty or even necessity. Such subjective certainty may also characterize an act whose validation rests on other forms of validating test. But we refer to the pure case: the unjustifiable intuitive leap buttressed by a sense of conviction. One infers the existence of God, for example, from the overwhelming beauty of a mountain scene: "Such beauty could be produced neither by man nor by the random force of nature." God's presence is thereafter inferred from the experience of beauty. There is buttressing both by consistency and by consensus, but what provides the basic validating criterion is the affective component in the act of categorizing. . . .
>
> . . . In its most extreme pathological form, validation by affective congruence makes it possible for the paranoid to construct a pseudo environment in which the random noises about him are categorized as words being spoken against him. At the level of normal functioning, it permits the acceptance of such unknowable absolutes as God, the Dignity of Man, or Hell.[9]

And even the scientist uses validation by affective congruence for heuristic purposes; that is, such validation is the basis on which he undertakes to use a promising hypothesis. The hypothesis *feels* right.

---

[9] Bruner, *A Study of Thinking*, pp. 20–21. In the second sentence of this passage Bruner's language is a little unclear. The clause "that carries with it . . . necessity" modifies "act of categorizing . . . " *not* "event."

Just as he begins to doubt his theories when he feels that something is wrong, so he will try out a new theory if it feels right. He proceeds, as so many scientists have said, by hunches, which are experiences of affective congruence. For this feeling I shall use the term *cognitive harmony*, to mark it as an antithesis to *cognitive tension*.

It would have been impossible for Bruner to have given a better example for our purposes than inferring the existence of God from the overwhelming beauty of a mountain scene; for this kind of behavior is intensely typical of the Enlightenment. In England the most conspicuous founder of this tradition was Anthony Ashley Cooper, Third Earl of Shaftesbury (1671–1713), whose most important works were published between 1708 and 1711. *A Letter Concerning Enthusiasm* is concerned with the rescue of an affect which the highest cultural level of the seventeenth century had rejected; Shaftesbury dragged it up from lower cultural levels and justified it at the highest. The Enlightenment has been called the Age of Reason, and such a term is justified so long as it is realized that Enlightenment man put logical manipulation to the service of cognitive harmony, instead of, as with men of the seventeenth century, cognitive tension. Enlightenment man focussed on problem solving, not problem exposure, not on the awareness of the gap between behavioral pattern and environmental demand but on the closing of that gap. Hence the emergence of sentimentalism, the awe-struck posture before the natural sublime, the melting of the soul before natural beauty, and the increasing interest in the primitive, the irrational, and, ultimately, the irrationally terrible. Another quotation from Bruner is very much to the point:

> The more basic the confirmation of a hypothesis is to the carrying out of goal-striving activity, the greater will be its strength. It will be more readily aroused, more easily confirmed, less readily infirmed.[10]

This is why the notion of adaptation of organism to the environment became the dominating value of the eighteenth century and why its political and social behavior was aimed at the perfect adaptation of organism to environment. The seventeenth century was interested in enduring the tension consequent upon problem exposure; therefore it rejected enthusiasm. The Enlightenment was interested in reducing that tension in order to achieve cognitive harmony; it embraced enthusiasm and sentimentalism. At the highest cultural level of the

---

[10] Bruner, "Personality Dynamics . . . ," p. 127.

Enlightenment, in an area in which economic power and social status intersected with innovative culture to form the social center, two highly instructive innovations were the development of upholstered furniture and the innovation of a large range of kinds of dishes, each appropriate to a particular food or category of food. Psychic and physical comfort and perfect adaptation were the values that lay behind its search behavior and the logical manipulations of its terminology.

All of this comes out so well in one of the first documents clearly announcing the new evangel that it is worth quoting at some length. The passage will doubtlessly seem, in fact, excessively long, but if the reader can endure it, I advise him to read all of it. Only length can indicate how the Enlightenment suppresses possible objections to a position by repeating the same idea in different words, over and over again, until the effect of the words blots out any threatening cognitive tension by a heavily reinforced cognitive harmony. It is the apostrophe to nature from Shaftesbury's *The Moralists: A Philosophical Rhapsody*.

> Ye fields and woods, my refuge from the toilsome world of business, receive me in your quiet sanctuaries, and favour my retreat and thoughtful solitude! Ye verdant plains, how gladly I salute ye! Hail all ye blissful mansions! known seats! delightful prospects! Majestic beauties of this earth, and all ye rural powers and graces! Blessed be ye chaste abodes of happiest mortals, who here in peaceful innocence enjoy a life unenvied, though divine; whilst with its blessed tranquillity it affords a happy leisure and retreat for man, who, made for contemplation and to search his own and other natures, may here best meditate the causes of things, and, placed amidst the various scenes of Nature, may nearer view her works.
>
> O glorious nature! supremely fair and sovereignly good! all loving and all lovely, all divine! whose looks are so becoming and of such infinite grace; whose study brings such wisdom, and whose contemplation such delight; whose every single work affords an ampler scene, and is a nobler spectacle than all which ever art presented! O mighty Nature! wise substitute of Providence! impowered creatress! Or thou impowering Deity, supreme creator! Thee I invoke and thee alone adore. To thee this solitude, this place, these rural meditations are sacred; whilst thus inspired with harmony of thought, though unconfined by words, and in loose numbers, I sing of Nature's order in created beings, and celebrate the beauties which resolve in thee, the source and principle of all beauty and perfection.
>
> Thy being is boundless, unsearchable, impenetrable. In thy immensity all thought is lost, fancy gives over its flight, and wearied imagination spends itself in vain, finding no coast nor limit of this ocean, nor, in the widest tract through which it soars, one point yet nearer the circumference than the first centre whence it parted. Thus having oft essayed, thus sallied forth into the wide expanse, when I return again within myself, struck with the sense of this so narrow being and of the fulness of that immense one, I dare no more behold the amazing depths nor sound the abyss of Deity.

Yet since by thee, O sovereign mind, I have been formed such as I am, intelligent and rational, since the peculiar dignity of my nature is to know and contemplate thee, permit that with due freedom I exert those faculties with which thou has adorned me. Bear with my venturous and bold approach. And since nor vain curiosity, nor fond conceit, nor love of aught save thee alone inspires me with such thoughts as these, be thou my assistant and guide me in this pursuit, whilst I venture thus to tread the labyrinth of wide Nature and endeavor to trace thee in thy works.

When artists make their discontinuity decisions in response to such an attitude, the accumulated external discontinuities should show a steady reduction in internal, implicit, and modal discontinuity. What should happen is that the implicit forms become increasingly explicit, that what in the Baroque styles of music and poetry is characteristic of cadential endings becomes, in the course of the century, increasingly characteristic of the entire work of art. Focussing on the behavior of the artist, one should find that he chooses the device showing least discontinuity from among the random range of discontinuities of his sketches and experiments. I shall offer a few examples from each of the four arts in turn to show that this is exactly what happened.

In architecture two lines of external discontinuity may be easily traced: the reemergence of the implicit regular solids from the shattered and violently discontinuous solid and profile of the last stage of the Baroque as seen in Blenheim; and the reemergence of the wall as a plane from the highly discontinuous wall of the late Baroque.

Filippo Iuvara (?1676–1736), older than Bach, Pope, and Watteau, of the same generation as Vanbrugh, spent the earlier part of his career designing buildings for the royal court at Turin in a typically very late, or terminal Baroque style. By "terminal" I do not mean that by internal stylistic logic Baroque came to an end and that its stylistic possibilities were exhausted. The term refers merely to the fact that this was the last innovative Baroque style. The new style emerged not only in Iuvara's last buildings. He was one of the masters who brought it about. From 1729 to 1733 he built for the King of Sardinia, who was also the Duke of Savoy, a hunting lodge southwest of Turin, Stupinigi (see Plate VI). The approach is along what at first seems to be a typical Baroque axis, like those of Versailles and Blenheim, but in fact it is quite different, for it is broken up into a series of large well-defined spaces in each of which the perceiver feels firmly oriented. The lodge itself is a new departure, for it is clearly assembled out of elements which may be grasped with great ease. Each element is self-contained, and the articulation of the whole complex is firmly established. It offers very little in the way of ambi-guity. The main block which terminates the axis is just as clearly separated from the wings, which join it at an angle. It is entirely self-contained and could be lifted out of the complex as neatly as a hat out of a box. There is some trace of the interpenetrating solids so characteristic of Blenheim and other Baroque buildings, and which are also evident in Iuvara's own mountain pilgrimage church near Turin, the Superga; but it is greatly reduced, and the high wings at right angles could be read as elements attached to the central drum were it not for their roofs. The implication of a rectangular building penetrating through a circular building is greatly reduced. The wall treatment also shows a notable reduction from the discontinuity of Baroque walls. They were designed to imply a kind of fake functional architecture. It was conceived as a screen, the openings of which contained smaller screens. If it were removed, there would be no wall. But in Stupinigi the wall is reemerging in its own right. If the pilasters and cornices were removed there would still be a wall. The pilaster-cornice articulation is presented as a grid placed on the wall for decorative purposes rather than as an apparently self-contained archi-tecture without which there would be no wall. Further, the articula-tory penetration into the wall from the plane of the face of the pilasters is extremely shallow: it has almost none of the Baroque deep pene-tration. And, except on the main building, the pilasters have neither capitals nor bases. Thus the articulation is a screen with large holes punched in it attached to a solid wall. Finally, the whole building is painted white; even the shadows are not dark but only a pale gray. The Baroque spectrum from deep shadow to light is disappearing.

Balthasar Neumann (1687–1753) was contemporary with Bach, Watteau, and Pope, but he too moved into the new style when from 1742 to 1744 he designed the great pilgrimage church of Vierzehn-heiligen in northern Bavaria (see Plates VII and VIII). At first glance the exterior is Baroque, but a little more inspection reveals that external discontinuity has occurred. The windows are no longer ex-plained by pseudo-architecture but are quite clearly holes punched through the wall. To be sure, something like this is observable in Kloster Banz on the other side of the valley, built by Johann Dient-zendorfer from 1710 to 1719. But the articulation of the facade of Banz suggests that the pseudo-architecture is holding itself up and that the wall would fall down without it. The facade of Vierzehnheiligen, obviously modeled on Banz, is quite different, for here the columns and pilasters are quite clearly decorative elements applied to a self-sustaining wall. It is in the interiors of the two buildings, however, that the differences between late Baroque and Rococo are plain. Unlike Banz, Vierzehnheiligen is filled with light and the most delicate colors. Its completion extends into the 1770's and in some details even into the 1780's. By contrast, the exterior is still at the best only a mild reversal of the Baroque stylistic direction. The interior colors are white and delicate green, soft gold and pink and lavender. Again, unlike the Baroque churches, it is filled with light. Enormous windows filled with clear glass deprive it of all the modal discontinuity of light and shadow which is so remarkable a feature of Baroque churches. In fact, although it is a church, it is like nothing so much as a vast boudoir. None of the terrible mystery of religion is here, only the consolations of tension-reducing sentimentality. But the most striking effect of all is the way the interior space is so precisely defined by smooth, flowing walls. There is almost no ambiguity of space, and what spatial ambiguity Neumann designed has been minimized by the decorators of the interior who carried on the work after his death. It is a hollow even more easily perceived than the central solid of Stupinigi.

By the time Vierzehnheiligen could be called complete, it was already out of date. In 1768 Jacques Ange Gabriel (1698–1782) designed the Petit Trianon at Versailles (see Plate IX). France, of course, was at this time the cultural center of Europe, and the Petit Trianon is highly illuminating as to the values controlling the architect. In the works we have already examined, the solid of the building is discerned only after the fake architecture articulating the wall has been perceived and understood. At Vierzehnheiligen the facade gives little information about the solid and not much more about the interior organization of space, though the side walls and the transept exteriors do. At the Petit Trianon, the opposite happens to a perceiver with the Rococo expectations of the 1760's. The building is clearly a regular projected rectangle. Unlike Baroque buildings or earlier Rococo buildings it offers no pilasters or columns at the corners. Thus the window openings are even more clearly holes in the wall, and the columned porch on one facade and the similarly arranged pilasters on the others are obviously elements which have been tacked onto the wall. The articulation is all in front of the wall plane. Only the reveals of the windows open through it. And the cornice seems like a ribbon wrapped around the top of a rectangular box. The wall and the solid are becoming increasingly explicit. The interior continues the same external discontinuity. Like the earlier buildings of the Rococo period there are numerous exquisitely carved decorations above and around doors, along dados, on ceilings, around fireplaces, and so on. But these are either in the same stone as the walls or in the same white plaster. That is, they have not been gilded, as they were in the Amalienburg at the Nymphenburg in Munich, a building built for much the same social function, privacy for the royal family away from the etiquette of court life. The Amalienburg precedes the Petit Trianon by some decades, and its Rococo ornament almost completely covers walls and ceilings, instead of being presented in patches, as in the Petit Trianon. The walls are painted blue, or orange, or green, and the Rococo plaster work is silvered. It is not surprising that some stylistic historians have not been able to decide whether the Petit Trianon is late Rococo or early Neo-Classic.

A clearly Neo-Classic style emerged in the next decade, but this can be skipped over to bring us to the final stage of this steady reemergence of solid and wall in the work of a group of late eighteenth-century French architects, of whom the principal figures were Étienne-Louis Boulée (1728–1799) and Claude-Nicolas Ledoux (1736–1806). Each of them designed vast building projects which remained unbuilt. They have in common a total restoration of explicit wall and solid and hollow. Boulée planned a cenotaph for Isaac Newton, who, with Locke, was a saint for Enlightenment secularists, principally because they misunderstood both of them (see Plate X). Boulée designed a perfect sphere set in a perfect low drum set on top of another perfect low drum, cut away to reveal the sphere within. The sphere is like a ball in a socket. There is no articulation to speak of, and only a slight modal discontinuity in the planting of trees on the drum terraces and in the use of a different surface for the lower drum. The implicit forms of architecture are made almost completely explicit, and in the design for an entrance to a cemetery, Boulée went even beyond this, for the implicit form, a triangle, is absolutely explicit and is presented twice. Only in the inverted and truncated triangle of the entrance gate itself is there any suggestion of discontinuity. Further than this it would be impossible to go, except in presenting explicit projected rectangles and cubes, and this is exactly what Ledoux did. Almost no discontinuity is left except for external discontinuity. That the series of decisions that led to this outcome were in response to the value demands so evident in Shaftesbury, who was translated and discussed in France, is to me irresistible.

The stylistic continuity from buildings which lie on the boundary between Baroque and Rococo to works which, no matter how different in appearance, were the consequence of artists' decision-making in response to the same value scheme is precisely parallel to the continuum from Herrick or Inigo Jones to the profoundly different Pope and Vanbrugh. With this continuity established as conceivable in architecture, the similar continuities in the other arts may be more briefly presented.

In music the new attitudes were strikingly signaled by the innovation of the *style galant* and the *style bourgeois,* both of which abandoned counterpoint. The one was the style of the aristocracy, the other of the middle classes, but these terms merely indicate that music was still situationally controlled. The *style galant* in particular was uninterested in the excitement of J. S. Bach. Its melodies, presented against a discreet background of simplified harmony which reduced sharply the continuous harmonic dynamism of Baroque music, had themselves few internal discontinuities and were highly repetitious. The middle-class style was more "expressive." It used greater implicit discontinuity in the melodic line. And this brought out what was to be an increasing characteristic not only of Enlightenment music but also of painting, architecture, and poetry, the increasing dependency for affect upon the presentation of primary signs. The late works of Boulée and Ledoux and their school showed simple verticality and horizontality, and the music contemporary with them reduced the implicit discontinuity of melody and depended for its affect upon an easy motion up and down, simple and very obvious transitions back and forth from major to minor, and an unvarying speed and rhythm for each movement. This isolation of the primary signs in cultural fields other than the arts is obviously directly consonant with the corresponding semantic emphasis on sentimentality and the irrational, on the easy and sensuous beautiful and the awe-inspiring sublime, but divested of the various discontinuities with which the sublime was accompanied during the seventeenth century. It is this isolation of the primary signs that is responsible for musicologists' calling Enlightenment music "expressive." It was, of course, no more expressive than Baroque music, and in fact considerably less, but the accumulation of external discontinuities based on the steady reduction of implicit, internal, and modal discontinuity meant that as the century wore on, music became increasingly dependent for affect upon the simple presentation of primary signs. Thus in Mozart's *The Magic Flute* (1791) the chorus "O

Isis and Osiris" consists principally of chorus and orchestra making big sounds in simple and long-sustained C major chords.

This in itself is enough to show what was happening, but a few other examples may serve to sustain this position a little better. The most striking innovation in musical types of the century was the emergence, through an accumulation of external discontinuity, of the sonata, whether in one, two, or three, or four movements, or even more, for Mozart's divertimentos and cassations belong to the same type. The first movement rule for the Baroque concerto grosso and sonata called for the presentation of a melody followed by continuous free or fantasia variation, concluding with a restatement of the theme. Sometimes the theme was repeated; sometimes the variations were interrupted by cadenzas on the harmonies of the movement. In Bach's Brandenburg Concertos, written in a terminal Baroque style, the theme is presented but once and then varied for a considerable period of time. They thus offer far more internal discontinuity than the *concerti grossi* of Vivaldi, which were the base line for Bach's external discontinuities in this type. For this rule, the Enlightenment came to substitute one calling for two melodies, each, in terms of primary signs, contrasting with the other. But by the end of the century these melodies were actually made up of short chains of very common melodic sequences, close to the scale or triad pattern, of which perhaps only the initial one had sufficient character to be called a "melody" in the narrower sense, something you can remember and whistle. Frequently, towards the end of the century, there were three such melodic chains. The third, in particular, had so little individual character that it is easily confused with a transitional passage, although often enough it was close to the first of the three, or developed harmonically and melodically out of the last element of the second melodic chain. In short, a great many things could happen, and the notion of "the sonata-allegro form" is as mythical as the notion of a fugal form, in the sense that it consisted of rules about what must be presented and in what order.

This presentation of three melodic chains instead of one highly individual melody involves the same principle as the reduction of the Medieval modes to one major-minor scale at the beginning of Baroque music, only backwards. The principle is simple. The less frequently an expectation is reinforced the less a frustration or violation of that expectation is likely to cause an affect in the perceiver. Hence the development sections of the sonata-allegro type, or sonata first-movement type, were variations on melodic configurations without much character or on melodic configurations without any, that is, making explicit the forms of expectations. The parallel to late eighteenth-century architecture is obvious. This may have been the reason for the innovation of repeating the exposition, that part of the movement which presented the two or three melodic chains. Unless the melodic chains were repeated there would be very little affect derivable from the few patches of characteristic melody. On the other hand the repetition merely multiplied the reinforcement of nearly explicit melody, and in innumerable development sections of Enlightenment first-movement types the fantasia is not based on the melodies of the exposition at all, but rather consists of a cadenza-like fantasy on scales and triads. This, of course, enormously reduced the affect of the work. The second movement, therefore, was the one particularly important for affect. Derived from operatic arias, it was the movement in which there was the greatest dependence on primary signs. The last two movements, if there were two more, were usually a minuet and a rondo, both of which call for an enormous amount of repetition. If all the repeats in some Mozart minuets are performed, it is possible to hear the same four-bar melody sixteen times. This reference to bar phrases brings in another characteristic of Enlightenment music which steadily became more prominent, the organization of all melodies and melodic chains in multiples of four bars, each of which was marked by a cadence or a semi-cadence. This increased very considerably the predictability of phrase and length over Baroque music, in which, especially towards the end, phrase length was highly unpredictable and steadily longer. It also put great emphasis upon the phrase as a primary sign of smoothness of impulse.

A number of studies have been written about the "evolution" of the sonata, referring both to the sonata type and the sonata first-movement type. Musical types, of course, do not evolve, but the evolutionary metaphor is peculiarly appropriate, though thoroughly misleading, when it is applied to the stabilization of the sonata. In the biological world a species is only gradually stabilized, only breeds true after a long period of time—according to Sir Charles Darwin, a million years. Of course, a sub-species can be selected to breed true in a fairly short time. Variations can be accumulated in a particular direction by artificial, or human, selection. Thus most recognized breeds of dogs are of fairly recent origin. The peculiarity of the sonata in the eighteenth century was the striking analogy of its emergence to the emergence of a biological breed. The two phenomena seem remarkably alike. The explanation lies in the fact that breeding, let us say, a Weimaraner, and stabilizing the sonata type, are both activated by the desire to increase predictability. What the "evolution of the sonata" refers to is the fact that as the century drew to its close, the musical perceiver could be more and more successful in predicting what he was going to get when he encountered the type-title "sonata." The implicit form of the type became increasingly explicit.

One final example will bring out the same principle. If the opening melodies of the keyboard sonatas of Carl Philip Emanuel Bach (1714–1788), Haydn (1732–1809), and Mozart (1756–1791) are arranged in chronological order, a striking phenomenon is at once apparent: the melodic contour grows steadily smoother. The melodies of Bach in the 1740's are jagged, but those of Mozart ripple up and down the scale or triad. The principal implicit discontinuity is change of direction, and the principal modal discontinuity is the shift from scale to triad melodies. The same phenomenon can be seen in the rhythm. In Bach the rhythmic pattern is highly irregular, so much so that to-day it is by no means easy to play the notes with their correct time value. But Mozart's melodies are rhythmically very smooth. They are easy to play, but not easy to play well. Mozart's piano music, and indeed all of his music, is hard to play, for one mistake is obvious. In many of J. S. Bach's fugues a wrong note makes surprisingly little difference to one who does not know the music well. Further, Mozart can sound mechanical and wooden, and usually does. Mozartean performance depends upon the most delicate and subtle *rubato*, a continuous flow of minimal rhythmic discontinuity, so minimal that it was impossible to notate it. Rhythmic discontinuity had been reduced to the point where it had to be left to the decisions of the performer. It is worth, noting, however, that in the last year or so before his death, Mozart's music began to show external discontinuities from his own style which suggest that had he lived he would have become a Romantic composer, would have participated, like Beethoven, but earlier, in the stylistic revolution against Enlightenment music. One of the most important indications is his sudden late interest in the counterpoint of Bach. Many of the artists of that Romantic stylistic revolution turned to Baroque art, primarily for models of how to restore discontinuity to art and to turn away from a kind of style in which the explicit is nearly identical with the implicit. One historian of German Romanticism has even gone so far as to suggest—and he is by no means unconvincing—that German Romanticism resulted from the impact of the still Baroque culture of southern Germany on a group of young northern Germans who had become discontented with the limitations of Enlightenment thought.[11]

When it comes to painting, the same stylistic continuum is so obviously at work that the demonstration can be brief. Giovanni Battista Tiepolo (1696–1770) spent his early career as a clearly terminal Baroque painter, but in the late 1720's it became evident that his work was going through a stylistic revolution, of which it is enough to refer to two features. At about this time there began to be significant reduction in chiaroscuro, which by the late 1740's, or even earlier, had almost entirely vanished, particularly in his ceiling paintings. As in architecture, the disappearance of the primary sign of inadequacy is in itself highly significant. The possibility of human inadequacy was precisely the quality in experience which the Enlightenment was uninterested in seeing against adequacy. As we have seen, a work of art can be a construct not of existent values but of desired or "ideal" values. This does not mean that darkness disappeared from Enlightenment painting or architecture. A good many painters, particularly of the increasingly irrational later Enlightenment, specialized in darkness. Fuseli is an excellent example, and the Boulée school of architecture often designed buildings the hollows of which were to be filled with a sublime gloom. It is rather that the beautiful and the sublime were separated; Baroque architecture and painting, as in the work of Salvator Rosa, preferred to put them into the same work for the violence of the contrast between adequacy and inadequacy. Now, the disappearance of chiaroscuro from Tiepolo's work also means the disappearance of one source of modal discontinuity, and at the same time his colors became increasingly bright, clear, and radiant, all of one tonal value. Tiepolo's ceiling paintings particularly show the new tendencies, for instead of the intertwining and overlapping implicit forms of such a late Baroque ceiling painter as Cortona, he separates his figures and his groups of figures into patches which he sows broadcast all over the ceiling, usually arranged at distances equal enough to suggest a rhythmic regularity (see Plate XI). The background of the painting is simply blue sky with radiant clouds, and the proportion of figures to sky becomes steadily smaller.

---

[11] Richard Benz, *Die Deutsche Romantik: Geschichte einer Geistigen Bewegung*, Stuttgart, 1956.

In the final series in the Royal Palace at Madrid, relatively small figures drift about enormous expanses of open sky, variegated only with great patches of cloud. This scattering of groups of figures over enormous spaces reduces the internal discontinuity that comes from placing similar implicit forms in close proximinity, as in Watteau's "Pilgrimage." These great and beautiful empty spaces not only are consonant with the architecture in emphasizing the wall, but are also like so many passages in the music of the time; it is beautiful, but not much is going on. The same device also reduces implicit discontinuity, for, as he paints on during the century, less and less are his ceiling paintings dominated by any single implied form.

Richard Wilson (1714–1782), almost from his earliest paintings, shows Enlightenment values behind his decisions. One of his most instructive paintings is the view of Mt. Snowdon, now in the Walker Art Gallery in Liverpool (see Plate XII). (Nottingham also has a version.) This painting was done perhaps as early as 1765, but certainly no later than 1775.[12] In the foreground is a large almost circular lake. Almost exactly in the center of the picture is a low pyramidal hill, flanked on the left by an almost perfectly smooth line of hillside, on the right by a more disturbed line with two pyramidal peaks. In the background is the low pyramid of the peak of Snowdon, placed against the low pyramid of the bulk of the mountain. The foreground is entirely in shades of brown and greenish brown. Snowdon is blue. The sky, with a few white clouds, is a paler blue. The implicit forms are quite separate one from the other, a flattened oval (not allowing for the perspective, which implies a circle) and the slightly flattened triangle, which is offered in a form close to explicitness three times, and twice more in configurations not very far from the implicit form. It is truly sublime. It was meant to be sublime. Almost the entire affect comes from the primary signs and the iconic signs of highly regular natural features. The internal discontinuity from triangle to triangle, for example, is considerably less than that of "White on White."

It would be difficult to come closer to presenting explicit forms and still have an iconic painting, but Jacques Louis David (1774–1825) succeeded in doing so in his famous "The Death of Marat," painted

---

[12] Arno Schönberger and Halldor Soehner, with Theodor Müller, tr. by Daphne Woodward, *The Rococo Age: Art and Civilization of the 18th Century*, New York, 1960, p. 385.

in 1793 immediately after the revolutionary leader had been assassinated by Charlotte Corday (see Plate XIII). The picture depends for its affect almost entirely on its function as an emblem of martyrdom of the champions of liberty to the representatives of *l'Ancien Régime*. It consists almost solely of rectangles: the packing box which Marat was using for a bath-side writing stand (itself an emblem of his revolutionary simplicity and love of the people, from whom he had sprung), the bath covered with a blanket which makes it consist of two quite clear rectangles, the rectangle of the sheet over which his arm hangs, and the rectangle of the area of sheet against which his murdered head rests. The background is entirely without articulation, a vast rectangle occupying more than half of the painting, completely explicit except for the line of Marat's letter, arm, shoulder, and head at the bottom. There is, then, some internal discontinuity, of which the basic theme is established by the almost perfect rectangle of the side of the box facing the perceiver. This is further simplified since only the top shows, but neither of the sides. Each variation on the basic implied form is itself almost as close to being an explicit presentation of the implication as the box itself. It is almost as stripped of discontinuity as the architecture of Boulée and Ledoux, and as stripped as the great choruses of *The Magic Flute*, an opera the libretto of which is devoted to a presentation of Enlightenment values in terms of emblems, both verbal and visual. Virtually the only remaining step would be to get rid of configurational signs by eliminating iconicity, but that, of course, did not happen until Malevich. The task of the first wave of Romantic painters was to restore discontinuity to painting. It was a task, as we shall see, that Ingres assumed.

No modern European nation has so continuous a history of poetry operating superbly at the highest cultural level as England. But one of the great mysteries in that tradition was the near disappearance in the second half of the eighteenth century of new poets who have survived in the canon. Goldsmith wrote little poetry, though *The Deserted Village* lasted a long time. A few bits of Chatterton's tiny output have lasted, and some of Cowper, notably *The Task*. But none of these are read much to-day except by scholars. Blake alone has a great twentieth-century reputation, but aside from the *Songs of Innocence and Experience*, it is generally admitted that most of the rest of his voluminous output, no matter how interesting semantically, is formally barely readable. And this external discontinuity, which is to us a decline in poetic quality, is only less notable in other European cultures because the decline was not from such heights. It has been called the Age of Prose, but in fact rarely has so much poetry been written and published and widely read. One extremely popular form, topographical poetry, which was devoted to landscape description of particular locations in England, has virtually disappeared. To find examples is difficult even in excellent libraries, yet it was enormously popular in its day.

From the point of view of this book, the reason for what we judge a decline—though there is no evidence that the Enlightenment public felt it so—is not difficult to comprehend. Of all the arts, music suffered least from Enlightenment values; but music has the greatest number of rules, and these rules are highly arbitrary. Further, since it uses few situational signs, and those rarely, except when words are simultaneously presented, the new dependency of the other arts on primary signs for affect was not noticeable, except for the fact that serious music became increasingly independent of words and performance situation. The sublime entered types and situation of music closed to it before the 1740's or in a way even the 1760's, particularly the orchestral sonata (symphonies), the orchestral sonata with one solo instrument (piano and violin and other instrumental concerti), and the chamber sonata (keyboard sonatas, piano-violin sonatas, trios, quartets). But of course the convergence of these instrumental combinations on the sonata type is a further instance of the increasing demand for predictability. The arbitrary rule complexity of music and the increasing seriousness of instrumental music have kept the music of the last fifteen years of the century alive, for the earlier work of Haydn and Mozart, not to speak of all of the work of C. P. E. Bach, has disappeared entirely from the active orchestral repertoire and is only now beginning to be revived under the impact of the long-playing record. To be sure, Haydn and Mozart were geniuses, but geniuses can be geniuses only when they are working in favorable cultural situations. Further, when music is completely stripped of discontinuity one is left with nothing but scales running from inaudibility in the bass to inaudibility in the treble, and back again, without rhythm, phrase, or change in speed or volume—or with a simple unmodulated drumming. The domestic architecture of the late eighteenth century survived because, fulfilling as it did Enlightenment demands for physical and psychological comfort, it established a standard for pleasant homes against which all subsequent domestic architecture has been measured, and usually found wanting. And certainly for a century and more, the painting of the late eighteenth century has been more or less ignored, except for the fashionable and elegant portrait.

Poetry was bound to suffer most, because it has the fewest resources both in discontinuity and in primary significance. The first stylistic revolution away from Baroque poetry was James Thomson's *The Seasons*, published from 1726 to 1730 and frequently revised and published throughout the century. It is difficult to believe now that this work, well into the middle of the nineteenth century, was one of the most popular and admired and loved poems in the history of English literature. By the middle of the century it had been translated into French and German, and in both countries it was highly admired at the highest and most innovative cultural levels. It continued in verse what Shaftesbury had begun in prose. Its sharp reduction in available discontinuity is particularly notable in two devices. First, Thomson abandoned the Popean couplet and returned to blank verse, roughly modeled on Milton. This alone, as we have seen, would have meant some reduction in discontinuity. But Thomson also enormously reduced Milton's level of syntactical discontinuity and of junctural discontinuity, both at the caesura within the line and at the end of the line. This meant that syntactical elements usually coincided with the end of the line, but not, as in Pope, with self-contained syntactical elements. Thomson ended sentences wherever it was convenient to do so, except at the end of the verse paragraph. A few lines will make this clear, and to make the external discontinuity obvious, I shall first quote a few lines from Pope's *Windsor Forest* (1713).

> The groves of Eden, vanish'd now so long,
> Live in description, and look green in song:
> These, were my breast inspir'd with equal flame,
> Like them in beauty, should be like in fame.
> Here hills and vales, the woodland and the plain,
> Here earth and water seem to strive again:

Contrast this with the following. It is the opening of "Spring," the first part of *The Seasons*, published in 1726, though the text here is from the final revision of twenty years later.

> Come, gentle Spring,—ethereal mildness, come;
> And from the bosom of yon dropping cloud,
> While music wakes around, veil'd in a shower
> Of shadowing roses, on our plains descend.

• • • • • • • • • • • • • • • •

Forth fly the tepid Airs; and unconfin'd,
Unbinding earth, the moving softness strays.
Joyous th'impatient husbandman perceives
Relenting nature, and his lusty steers
Drives from their stalls to where the well-us'd plough
Lies in the furrow, loosen'd from the frost.

Even the practiced reader of Pope feels syntactical difficulties in *Windsor Forest*, difficulties which he must overcome, and he feels himself struggling with them. But Thomson offers a striking reduction in such problems and can be read with comprehension much more readily.

What Thomson (1700–1748) began, Thomas Gray (1716–1771) and William Collins (1721–1759) continued. To the poetry of Collins and the earlier poetry of Gray the appellation of Rococo is peculiarly appropriate. Both specialized in the "beautiful"; though from the middle 1740's Gray became more and more interested in the sublime; his later poems inspired a good many sublime painters. Gray and Collins restored the stanza to serious innovative poetry, a field in which it had scarcely been seen since the early seventeenth century. The stanzas tended to be rather short, frequently of only four lines, and offered therefore a notable increase in predictability. Further, the syntactic structure of both shows even less discontinuity than Thomson's, consisting for the most part of what is commonly known in Freshman English as the "run-on sentence," which tacks parallel modifying elements to one major element, or offers a whole string of subjects or objects or complements. A couple of examples will serve to show these principles. The first is from Collins' "Ode to Evening," published in 1746.

For when thy folding Star arising shews
His paly Circlet, at his warning Lamp
    The fragrant *Hours*, and *Elves*
    Who slept in Buds the Day,
And many a *Nymph* who wreaths her Brows with Sedge,
And sheds the fresh'ning Dew, and lovelier still,
    The *Pensive Pleasures* sweet
    Prepare thy shadowy Car.

The second is the opening to Gray's famous "Elegy Written in a Country Churchyard," published in 1751.

The Curfew tolls the knell of parting day,
The lowing herd wind slowly o'er the lea,
The plowman homeward plods his weary way,
And leaves the world to darkness and to me.

Now fades the glimmering landscape on the sight,
And all the air a solemn stillness holds,
Save where the beetle wheels his droning flight,
And drowsy tinklings lull the distant folds;

With slight changes, these eight lines could be arranged in any order at all, and the order of the two stanzas as written could be perfectly well reversed, without the slightest damage to sense, or, it must be admitted, to their charm.

When Oliver Goldsmith (1730–1774) published in 1770 *The Deserted Village*, he continued these tendencies. To be sure, he used the couplet, but is far from the heroic or closed couplet, utterly different from Pope's. In fact, it is little more than a two-line stanza, and the rule is simply that when the sentence does end, it ends at the end of a line. A sample will sum up all these tendencies:

How often have I paus'd on ev'ry charm,
The shelter'd cot, the cultivated farm,
The never-failing brook, the busy mill,
The decent church that topp'd the neighb'ring hill,
The hawthorn bush, with seats beneath the shade,
For talking age and whisp'ring lovers made!
How often have I bless'd the coming day,
When toil remitting lent its turn to play,
And all the village train, from labour free,
Led up their sports beneath the spreading tree;
While many a pastime circled in the shade,
The young contending as the old survey'd;

And so on. The sense that writing in English presents a problem in that it requires a linear presentation of a two-dimensional structure has almost entirely evaporated. To put this passage into prose would require only minimal changes.

Cowper continued along the same lines, except that he returned to blank verse and increased to a somewhat higher level syntactical discontinuity; but even that was dissociated from the discontinuity of the English poetic tradition in that it was used ironically, with a faint effect of parody. A device that had traditionally worked to support situational and primary signs of considerable affect was now applied to the trivia of domestic life. This shows the other side of the coin which in the 1760's James Macpherson passed throughout Europe as genuine primitive currency, the poems he asserted he had discovered in the Scotch highlands and had translated from the Gaelic. These were the once-famous Ossianic poems which were received throughout Europe with a most violent enthusiasm, by the young Goethe, among others. This is poetry because it was offered as poetry, but Macpherson abandons virtually the entire resources for poetic discontinuity. Almost the only rhythmic devices are brief patches of regular triple rhythm, and less frequently of duple. This gives the work some modal discontinuity, but, since the work is printed as prose, no implicit discontinuity is possible. Only a sample can do it justice. This is from *Fingal*.

> They flew sudden across the heath. He slowly moved, like a cloud of thunder, when the sultry plain of summer is silent and dark; his sword is before him as a sunbeam; terrible as the streaming meteor of night. He came toward a chief of Lochlin. He spoke to the son of the wave. "Who is that so dark and sad, at the rock of the roaring stream? He cannot bound over its course. How stately is the chief! his bossy shield is on his side; his spear like the tree of the desert! Youth of the dark-red hair, art thou of the foes of Fingal?"

This is the pure late Enlightenment sublime; and for some decades passionate enthusiasm for Ossian marked the audience at the highest cultural level. It is obvious that what Macpherson has done is to have presented verbal signs of natural and configurational embodiments of primary signs, and to have used as his stylistic base the King James English Bible, with a touch of Homer. The style of Ossian became the point of departure for Blake, who, in his prophetic books, created the last Enlightenment style to emerge in English poetry. Blake arranges his verse in lines, but his lines are so long, his caesuras so frequent and so irregular, even random, and his syntactical structure so additive, with virtually no discontinuity, that when his poetry is printed as prose, the loss is minimal. But Blake was not at the cultural apex. He was a man of genius, but also something of a crackpot. Formally, neither his poetry nor his painting have much of the truly innovative about them. They are still, though for the most part created well within the nineteenth century, controlled by decisions derived from Enlightenment values. And scholarship tends increasingly to show that the semantic aspect of his poetry was much more traditional than was once supposed, dependent more on an old and culturally submerged, or lower-level, religious tradition, not truly innovative. Even while he was forging his ideas and creating his style, a formal revolution against the Enlightenment was under way. The first of the Romantic styles was already emerging.

4. ROMANTIC

The formal decisions of Romantic artists were controlled by a wholly novel set of values. Perhaps nothing so novel and so profoundly revolutionary had emerged in human culture since the early neolithic period, or perhaps even before. It can be put in several ways. One is to recast slightly what has been said about the men of the seventeenth century and the Enlightenment. The seventeenth-century innovators were intensely interested in cognitive tension and problem exposure, in the gap between the pattern and the environmental demand. Nevertheless, that interest was ultimately motivated by a faith, religious in origin, that the gap could be closed. In Paradise, before the Fall, there was no gap. Enlightenment innovators were convinced that the gap was not the result of the Fall of Man but of his errors and the consequent political and religious tyranny which terrorized him and prevented him from closing the gap; they were motivated by an intense desire to do so, to create patterns of behavior which were exactly respondent to the demands of interaction with the environment. But Romantic innovators, both on philosophical grounds and on the pragmatic grounds of the transmutation of the revolutionary effort of France into a bloody tyranny, were convinced that the gap could not be closed, ever, that there would always be a disparity between the hypotheses and interests of man and the demands of interacting with the environment, that man's very mode of thinking—his categorial construction of the world—was not derived from the world but from himself, that the world, the environment, as contrasted with the interpreted situation, was forever inaccessible, that, in the Kantian phrase, the *Ding-an-sich*, the object-in-and-of-itself, as a self-existent entity, could never be known.

This is why Coleridge could arrive at the structure of transactionalism or directive-state theory as early as the 1820's and why Schopenhauer could say even earlier that the way we represent the world to ourselves is determined by our will, our interests, our intentions. It is why such theories, together with modern philosophy, and in particular the contemporary philosophy of science—in short, the point of view from which this book is written—is but a development and refinement of the Romantic tradition. Cognitive tension, therefore, became once again a central value, but with a difference from the superficially similar seventeenth-century valuation. In that century the motivation arose from the conviction that problem exposure led to problem solving. Cognitive tension and problem exposure were means to an end. To the Romantic, cognitive tension and problem exposure are an end in themselves. To the Romantic, as to the modern scientist, the most important thing one can do is not to find an answer, it is to ask a question; a problem is successfully solved only if it leads to a question which logically includes both the original question and the answer. This is the essence of the Hegelian mode, which is still culturally valid, although so much of Hegel's metaphysical baggage—his middle statements—has had to be abandoned. When such a vision began to control artists' decisions about discontinuity—and many of them arrived at it independently of philosophers, playing, as they were, the philosopher's role themselves—the result was at once a striking, even violent, increase in discontinuity.

Another way of putting it is to say that the Romantics for the first time distinguished the self from the role. The role thus became the mere instrument for realizing the self, as well as the instrument with which society blocked self-realization. This created the Romantic paradox: the Romantic could participate in human life only by playing a role: but if he did, he ran the risk of obliterating the distinction between role and self, of losing self. How a man could be at once an existent self and a successful role player was the Romantic psychic problem, and still is. The cultural history of the Romantic tradition can be written in terms of the various strategies made to solve this problem, and such an attempt is to be found in my *Beyond the Tragic Vision.* This way of looking at the situation had the same effect as the philosophical way. If the problem could be solved, it could be done so only by breaking through man's current ways of thinking about himself and the world. But the only way to do that was first to expose those ways as illusions. This necessarily involved a profound disorientation. A violent increase in formal discontinuity was the consequence.

Still another way of presenting the problem is to examine briefly what the Romantic did with primary signs, which as we have seen, had emerged so prominently with the steady Enlightenment reduction in formal discontinuity. The confusion between the Enlightenment terrible sublime and Romanticism arises from three factors: the failure to realize that the semantic aspect of art varies independently from the formal aspect; the failure to realize why the Romantics were as interested in primary signs as the late Enlightenment artists; and the failure to realize how differently the Romantics categorized them and why they did so.

The distinction between self and role is clear enough if one thinks of, say, Tom Jones, an Enlightenment hero who is rewarded when he learns to play properly a role which is devoted to environmental adaptation, and such a Romantic hero as Byron's Don Juan or Stendhal's Julien Sorel, or Wordsworth's "I" in *The Prelude*, whose rewards come when they have dissociated themselves from role and society and who reap a second reward when they have discovered a *modus vivendi* which enables them to live in society but keep apart from it, to use a role as an instrument for self-realization and not for social control of the self. Nevertheless, terms like "self" and "society" can be, and usually have been, hypostatizations, and role is but one element of the dramatic metaphor applied to human behavior. Clearly "self" can only refer to attributes of human behavior still remaining after role behavior is eliminated. They can, then, refer to those pervasive attributes of human behavior which are signified by primary signs. To be sure, each individual consists of a different package of such attributes. In that sense it can be said that a self is unique. To experience the sense of selfhood, therefore, it is necessary to perceive the world only in terms of these pervasive attributes, uniquely packaged in one's own personality. One perceives the situation, but one ignores all its clues to role behavior. The simultaneous perception of primary sign and configurational sign, which had been the perceptual mode as far back as evidence can be gathered, was split into two. Situational signs were separated from primary signs.

This is analogous to, though utterly different from, the perception of the schizoid or the paranoid, who sees situational clues only as primary signs. This is why it is often said that the Romantics discovered the "unconscious," another unfortunate hypostatization, the consequence, as Whitehead would say, of the fallacy of misplaced concreteness. There was nothing unconscious about primary signs. They had been there throughout human history. What the Romantics did was to perceive the world in such a way that they interpreted only primary signs, and to learn to manipulate the semantic aspect of art in such a way that they could do with the primary signs as they wished, to make them, for example, particularly in the first Romantic styles, signs of their own uniquely packaged pervasive attributes or selves. This mode of Romantic perception may be properly called, I think, "trans-situational" perception" (or non-situational or primary). They called it transcendental perception. Historically, it is probably true that this new mode of perception and primary sign manipulation arose because the Enlightenment, by draining away discontinuity, had isolated and put into high relief the signs of pervasive behavioral attributes.

In order to have a word which could refer to a primary sign so perceived and so presented in a structure of arbitrary signs, many Romantics, quite independently, began to use the word "symbol." I am sure the reader has wondered why I have not used this vexing term before. It would seem clear that when I use "primary sign" I am signifying the same category other people refer to when they use the word "symbol." One reason I have not used it is that the word has so many semantic functions. What I have called here "structural signs," "empty signs," "verbal signs," "written signs of phonic categories," and, especially, "emblems" have all been called "symbols." Like "form" it is a word with so many semantic functions that in a given situation one scarcely knows how to interpret it: interpretational variability is frustrated and suspended. But there are better reasons. One explanation for the striking instability of "symbol" is, of course, that the more frequently used a word is, the greater the probability of its developing manifold semantic functions, especially because it is very handy for metaphor. I. A. Richards, for example, has distinguished eight functions for "to be," and these are by no means all of them.[13] But another reason is considerably more significant. The usual assumption is that a "sign" is somehow different from a "symbol." This can only mean that the perceptual configuration of a symbol is different from the perceptual configuration of a sign. If this were the case, there would be fewer arguments about whether a configuration is a sign or a symbol; but such arguments are constant. The fact is that everything in the world is a sign, and that everything in the world is also a symbol. "Sign" and "symbol" are not categories of objects, nor of perceptual configurations, nor two different categories of a more inclusive category of "sign" in the sense that some signs are signs but some signs are symbols; "sign" and "symbol" are categories of perception. They refer, as the Romantics discovered, to

---

[13] See his *How to Read a Page,* London, 1943, pp. 162–163.

two different modes of perception. This is why they used the term "symbol," which previously had been equivalent to "emblem," as it was then used, referring to an allegorical emblem, rather than as used here, to any derived sign. They were saying, "What we mean by a symbol is something like an emblem. It refers to some human characteristic. But as far as we are concerned, it is an unconscious characteristic. That is, what a visual emblem refers to can also be referred to by language. But this is not true of a symbol, because there is no language to talk about it with. The only language available is metaphorical language." This has led to a vast confusion between "symbol" and "metaphor"; but that the Romantics had a point is obvious if it is recalled that one occasion for metaphor is the non-existence of a local term capable of referring to the category or categories the speaker wants to refer to. He discovers a blank in the language and has to plug it with a metaphor as a bridge to his next categories. The Romantics discovered blanks for pervasive attributes, and they had to bridge them with metaphors.

But just as "emblem" can be extended—justifiably, I believe—into "derived sign," so the Romantic use of "symbol" can be and has been extended. Such an extension is particularly important in the writings of Freud, who himself emerged from the Romantic tradition, unhappily ‚somewhat confused with the Enlightenment tradition, which is still the principal intellectual tradition for the middle and even some elements of the lower cultural levels in twentieth-century Europe and America. In the narrow sense, "symbolic perception" means interpreting a configuration as a sign of a pervasive attribute; extended, it means, as a sign of one's unique package of such attributes; further extended, as a sign of the uniqueness of that package as a sign of the self; still further extended, as a sign of one's unique interests; then, as a sign of interests; then, in its ultimate extension, as a sign of an orientation, an expectancy, a set, a directive state.

One can say of a lover, "He sees his beloved as a symbol of his erotic orientation." This kind of statement is appropriate, as the Romantics insisted, to situations in which the lover has no language with which to categorize and locate and predict the consequences of his erotic interests in the beloved, which, of course, can be all sorts of combinations of interests, from sexual to religious. But one can also say, "He sees his beloved as a sign of his erotic orientation." Such a statement is appropriate when the lover has at his disposal verbal signs with which he can talk about his erotic orientation or interests. Or an orthodox

Freudian psychoanalyst can say, "The lover's perception of his beloved as a symbol of his erotic orientation is a sign that the lad has an unresolved Oedipus complex." In this instance the speaker proposes to use his interpretation of the lover's behavior, the lover's symbolic perception, as a predictive sign of the lover's future behavior. What the therapist tries to do, of course, is to break up the symbolic perception by giving—or teaching the patient to develop—a language with which to talk about orientations for which he has no language and which are damaging to his environmental interaction, whether that environment is natural or social. Sometimes he succeeds.

A further extension of the semantic functioning of "symbol" is possible without loss of precision, and with some gain. We can interpret any sign in two ways, just as it can be perceived in two modes. We can interpret the interpreter's mode of perception as *predictive*, referring "forward from the sign," or as *orientative*, referring "backward from the sign" to the interpretation, the set, the directive state. Thus when we call a sign a "symbol" we merely mean that we are directing our attention to the orientative aspect of the transaction, rather than to the environmental aspect. Thus, just as a compound sign is a construct of the environment, it can also be interpreted as a construct of an orientation. This makes it possible to account for the claim that all art is symbolic. Such a statement appears to have several meanings.

One meaning is that the perceiver's role involves directing attention to the orientative aspect and perceiving it in the symbolic mode of perception. This is undoubtedly true, but I think it has been already taken care of in Chapter II in the application of the audience element of the dramatic metaphor to the perceiver's role. As Shakespeare said, "the lunatic, the lover, and the poet" are engaged in symbol perception, and he could well have added, "the poet's (or artist's) audience." This is the phenomenon that makes the various projective tests possible, Rorschach, Thematic Apperception, and so on. In such situations the sense of the self as other is suspended and the situation is interpreted only for its orientative aspect, the sign or predictive aspect being neglected. This is what Coleridge was talking about in his famous phrase, "the willing suspension of disbelief." It seems clear, also, that the discontinuity of art facilitates such perception, for, as we have seen several times, in a disorienting situation the individual falls back on familiar modes of perception and categorization. Unable to interpret the disorienting configuration as a sign, he perceives it as a symbol. Thus the lunatic, who uses orientative sets inappropriate to the situation, who is disoriented to any situation, interprets the situation as symbolic of his compulsive orientations. In the old expression for madness, he is "possessed," just as old and familiar lovers are possessed when they hear "our song" and melt into a very pure erotic orientation. Such symbolic perception is "willing" before art, rather than "unwilling," as it is with the lunatic, only in the sense that it is appropriate to the artistic situation. It is "willing" because it is part of a socially established and sanctified role, that of art perceiver. This is what we mean when we say, "The play was so interesting I lost myself in it." What has been lost is the self-perception which makes the distinction between self and other possible. Symbol perception, then, may be thought of as the audience aspect of the role of art perceiver, but, as Shakespeare knew better than Coleridge, it is not a defining aspect. Since such neglect of the sign aspect of any transaction is dangerous, this is a further explanation of the psychic insulation so characteristic of the art situation.

The other possible meaning to the statement that all art is symbolic, or that it is an orientative construct, is that this is an exclusive property of art. This appears to be what the New Critics are talking about when they assert that poetry's semantic function is unique.[14] It may also be what they are talking about when they speak of "organic unity," since they appear to connect the two. For example, "*The Waste Land* is an assertion that European culture is disintegrating." This interpretation moves forward from the sign. Or "*The Waste Land* is a symbol of that state of mind which is responsible for the assertion that European culture is disintegrating." This interpretation moves backward from the sign. Which does poetry do? Which interpretation is moving along the right path for the interpretation of poetry? Or any work of art?

Obviously it depends on the interests of the interpreter. For what is true of poetry, that it moves both forward from the sign and backward, is true of all statements, and of all signs. Thus it is true that poetry is symbolic, but the reason is that all semiosis is symbolic as well as predictive. All signs are also symbols. This fact is what makes the technique of verbal psychotherapy possible, as well as psychotherapy by visual signs, that practised by Margaret Naumburg.[15]

---

[14] I mean such critics as Robert Penn Warren, Cleanth Brooks, W. K. Wimsatt, Jr., Murray Krieger, and their host of followers. The position is beginning to be known as "Contextualism."

[15] See Note 25 to Chapter IV, above.

Nevertheless, it is true that the Romantics were interested in moving backward from the sign, specifically to themselves. This was a new interest for man. It meant a discovery of "the unconscious." The cultural background to psychoanalysis is this Romantic interest, and so is the background of the New Critics, who developed their theory from poets in the Romantic tradition who were interested in moving backward from the sign. There is little doubt that though Eliot may have wished to assert that European culture is disintegrating, such a statement was important to him only so far as he could construct an orientation from which such a statement would necessarily flow. This is, it would appear, what he meant by the "objective correlative," the "formula for the feeling."

Claims that poetry (or all art, like Suzanne Langer's)[16] is symbolic or expressive form are not, then, derived from poetry and art, but are merely statements of the demands of the extra-artistic aspect of Romantic culture. Clearly a work of art, like any semiotic structure or package, can be looked at in one of two ways, as a model for the perceiver's behavior or as a model of the orientation of the individual offering the sign field. Its function for the interpreter can be behavioral control over interaction with the environment or behavioral control over orientative activity. It can be interpreted as prescriptive or symptomatic.

Here it is necessary to make a distinction a little more precisely than has heretofor been necessary. Earlier a distinction was made between descriptive (or predictive) statements and prescriptive statements. The first kind of statement refers to the way the world is, the second to the way one ought to behave towards it. It is generally believed that these are two radically different kinds of statements, with no way of getting from one to the other, except by illegitimate metaphysical propositions. This is the famous distinction between "fact" and "value," which has been so praised and so blamed in the last few decades. But if transactionalism or the modern philosophy of science, if any form of pragmatism, instrumentalism, or operationalism, has any validity, then a predictive (descriptive) statement is not merely a statement about the way the world is; it is rather a recommendation that the world ought to be looked at in a given way, a recommendation generally implicit in the situation in which the statement is made. It says, "*If* you look at the world in such and such a way, *then* this is

---

[16] See Note 5 to Chapter III, above.

what you will see." It does not presume to make assertions about what is really there, but only assertions about what will be found if the world is perceived in a particular way. Thus descriptive (or predictive) statements are also, by implication, prescriptive statements. Hence, there are two kinds of prescriptive statements, indirectly prescriptive (predictive or descriptive) and directly prescriptive (moral, didactic, or value) statements. But if this is the case, it would seem that movements from indirectly to directly prescriptive statements (from descriptive to value statements) are not illegitimate, for this reason: The indirect or implicit prescriptions of predictive statements may be called "metaphysical" statements when they are made explicit. Such metaphysical statements are also behind directly prescriptive statements. Consequently to move from an indirectly prescriptive statement to a directly prescriptive statement is legitimate if the movement is through an implicit metaphysic (or orientation) common to both. The shortened version of such a movement is, "This is the way the world is and *therefore* this is the way you ought to behave towards it"; it is not necessarily illegitimate but can be subjected to the same logical control that can control any other movement from statement to statement, such as a movement from one scientific statement to another. If this is so, then value statements can be logically deduced from descriptive statements. After all, logical deduction does not move by itself, but only because some particular human individual with particular interests wants it to move, has decided that it shall move.[17] In any case, the interpreter with symbolic interests can regard both directly and indirectly prescriptive statements as either prescriptive or symptomatic, as either telling us the world is and what we ought to do about it, or revelatory of the implicit orientation or metaphysic behind them.

Any semiotic structure or package, then, is a prescriptive construct for organizing behavior. It is a model. One can use it as a model for controlling environmental interaction, or as a model for separating orientation from environment and manipulating orientative behavior in terms of constructed situations abstracted from environment. This appears to be what fiction does, though such activity is not exclusive

---

[17] The logical foundation for such a conclusion may be found in Morton White's *Toward Reunion in Philosophy*, Cambridge, Mass., 1956, although I do not know if White would agree with this conclusion, which also appears to be congruent with Stephen C. Pepper's results, as set forth in *World Hypotheses*, Berkeley, 1942, and *The Basis of Criticism in the Arts*, Cambridge, Mass., 1946.

to fiction but is found as a constant in human verbal behavior, as suggested above. It is obvious that the Romantic tradition rejected didactic poetry, poetry of direct prescription, because it was interested not in morality but in "insight," that is, insight into the foundations from which one proceeds, insight into one's metaphysic or orientation. But this is true not merely of Romantic art but of all Romantic culture. The psychoanalyst does not ask, "Is this statement of the patient's true or false, right or wrong?" but, "Of what pervasive orientation is this statement a symptom, that is, a symbol? If I can make a verbal construct of the patient's pervasive and harmful orientation, I will have defined a syndrome."

To-day, the Freudian, the artist like Malevich and Kandinsky, aestheticians like Langer, and other claimants, like Eliot himself, for art as significant or expressive form are clearly interested in art as symptom, not in art as prescription, whether predictive or morally didactic, that is, commendatory of particular values. Thomas Kuhn in his investigation of scientists' behavior is doing the same thing, evincing the same interests in behavior as symptomatic. In this the New Critics are exactly like their predecessors and antagonists, the old intentionalists. The only difference is that the New Critics discovered that the symptomatic aspect of the poem was not necessarily symptomatic of the poet's orientation but of that of an invented spokesman, that the poet does what a liar does: he implies an orientation which he does not hold, an orientation which is the proper basis for the interpretation of the statement, whether poet's or liar's. In short, they discovered that poetry is an orientative construct. But so is all language, all sign behavior. It is not a question of whether art should or should not be prescriptive, whether it should or should not give us moral "truth" or "truth" about the environment; or whether it should give us symptomatic orientative "truth." It is, on the contrary, a question of which is the interpreter's interest. Is it directed to interpreting the semantic aspect of the work of art as prescriptive sign or as orientative symbol? And it is also a question of which the artist is interested in. By responding to the demands of his culture he will present works which are more readily and appropriately interpreted one way or the other. Clearly, from the evidence offered here, and from the works themselves, for the past fifty years the artists' interests have been directed toward constructing symptomatic semiotic fields, rather than prescriptive, and they have signified their interests by distorting the structure and packaging aspects of art which conform to the rules which govern non-artistic semiotic behavior. Modern theorists of art have simply done the same thing. Believing themselves to be making statements of universal validity about art-as-symbol, they have merely been carrying on the Romantic tradition.

This is what is properly meant, therefore, when it is asserted that the Romantics' art is symbolic: they found a mode of perception which separates sign perception from symbol perception. Heretofore the two modes had been simultaneous. Heretofore symbol perception had been linked to situations; even the symbolic perception of the primary signs of music had been situational, for music was situationally controlled. But the Romantics learned to apply symbol perception to any situation, more or less at will, depending on the individual's psychophysical condition. When Beethoven "freed music," he freed primary signs from situational control. And by metaphor, the Romantics innovated new signs to locate these non-situational attributes of human behavior, and particularly to be signs of selfhood, of the sense that one is a unique package of such attributes. Eventually this function developed into "a unique package of orientations or perceptually directive interests." But at the same time they also increased strikingly the level of iconicity in art. Briefly, this was the result of (a) the desire to see the world so intensely that the role clues would disappear, and (b) the desire to break through to new orientations, a motivation the satisfaction for which depended upon the awareness of the disparity between, on the one hand, the current categories of organizing perceptions and judgments and interpretations, and on the other, the perceptual data offered. Hence the extraordinary dynamism of Romantic culture, whether in art, in philosophy, in science, or in valuation. Never had innovation been valued so highly.

The revolution from Enlightenment style, therefore, led to a new style in both the formal aspect of art and in the semantic aspect. To be sure, as we have seen, there cannot be a non-functional stylistic revolution unless there is a previous or concurrent semantic revolution at the same cultural level. But never before had both aspects of the artistic revolution had such a congruent intensity, even in the shift from Medieval to Renaissance styles. Enlightenment orientations and values are far closer to Medieval attitudes than they are to Romantic. In some ways, indeed, the semantic aspect of the Romantic artistic revolution was even greater than the formal, for the Romantic artist's problem of how to get discontinuity back into art was highly frustrating. For two reasons, therefore, the history of Romantic art is characterized by historical revivalism. Only with the emergence in the 1860's of what is generally called Aestheticism and what, in *Beyond the Tragic Vision,* I have called Stylism, did the Romantic tradition begin to create a series of styles which were not revivalistic; and only with the emergence of the first of the modern styles in the first decade of the twentieth century did it succeed.

One reason for the historicism of Romantic art can be derived from the self-role problem. Since all human interaction can be carried on only in socially established roles, including artistic behavior, the only way to signify the self is to play unique packages of roles and to manipulate them in strikingly unusual ways. It is either that or creating new roles. Romanticism did create several new roles, the Bohemian, the Dandy, the Demonic Virtuoso, which was the specialty of performing artists like Liszt and Paganini. But even a new role can be discernible as such only if it combines elements of old roles in a new way. For the artist, therefore, faced with the problem of the depleted formal style of the Enlightenment, the obvious, and indeed the only thing to do, was to adopt the roles of artists from the past and play them in a new way. It is not accidental that the modern conception of the problem of artistic style emerges at this time. The architect, for example, lumped all Gothic architecture into one stylistic category, derived sets of attributes, and then manipulated those stylistic attributes in such a way that it was evident that a unique sensibility was at work. He did the same thing with Greek architecture; skirting the Renaissance categorization of Classic architecture derived from Vitruvius, he turned instead to reports of archaeological excavations and travelers to Greece and manipulated Greek architecture as no Greek ever would have. To blame the architects of the nineteenth century for their revivalism is pointless. On the one hand, they had no choice. A new style cannot be made up from nothing. Even the first modern architectural style, Art Nouveau, was a synthesis of Medieval, Baroque, and Rococo elements. On the other hand, they behaved as they did because such behavior fulfilled their interests of establishing a sign of unique selfhood.

The same process can be seen in all the other arts. Wordsworth revived the Miltonic sonnet and the Baroque pindaric ode, as well as Thomsonian blank verse, and handled them in a strikingly new way, so that it was apparent that though a tradition was being used it was also being violated and freely manipulated. Keats used the Elizabethan sonnet as the basis for the unique stanzaic structure in his odes.

Coleridge used the traditional ballad as the medium for the first important effort to manipulate freely verbal emblems of primary signs and to create signs of selfhood and alienation of self from role, of artist from society. This was the extraordinarily innovative *Ancient Mariner*. Beethoven likewise turned to Baroque types, incorporating the fugue into the piano sonata and the string quartet. As might be expected, he manipulated it so freely that pedants ever since have said that they are bad fugues, reasonably enough, when one remembers that a late nineteenth-century conservatory instructor in composition insisted and taught that all Bach's fugues, since he violated the "laws" of the fugue, were shockingly bad fugues and should be assiduously avoided by all students who wished to write proper fugues. Fugal "laws" of course are entirely a myth. And Beethoven further introduced extreme external discontinuity into the tradition of composing the sonata-type. Ingres turned to Raphael; Delacroix turned to Rubens, just as Constable turned to Rubens' landscapes. But all three, consistent with another non-artistic demand already examined, increased the level of iconicity beyond what any of their predecessors in the Baroque or Enlightenment styles had achieved.

It is obvious, also, that the same practice not only created powerful external discontinuities from the styles they were using as models to violate. It also gave these artists paradigms for increasing enormously the level of internal, modal, and implicit discontinuity. Thus the chronological pattern of Beethoven's melodies reversed the direction which melody had followed during the Enlightenment, moving not toward predictable melody but away from it. In the same way he made long and sustained melodies the themes of his sonata-allegro movements, instead of the Enlightenment chains of melodic platitudes. In the same way he dissolved the late Enlightenment predictable sonata type, both the first movement type and the type as a whole. By the end of his career he was writing quartets in more movements than had been stabilized in the last years of the preceding century. Similarly, Constable dissolved the surface of the painting into loose strokes, establishing an external discontinuity that was eventually to lead to French Impressionism fifty years later (see Plate XIV). The German painter, Caspar David Friedrich, composed many of his paintings in such rigid implied symmetry that any violation was more powerful than it had ever been in the days of the Enlightenment; and at the same time he developed rich devices of internal discontinuity. Both he and Constable raised color intensity to new levels; like all of the artists of the period, they were interested in putting together once again the beautiful and the sublime, which the Enlightenment had separated, not only to signify the struggle between adequacy and inadequacy but also to create new sources for modal discontinuity in place of the modal continuity of the late eighteenth century. One of Wordsworth's most striking innovations, one which set him off from all previous English poets, was a technique of modal discontinuity which enabled him to shift from the prosaic to the sublime in a couple of lines. In the famous sonnet, "The world is too much with us," he innovates implicit discontinuity by carrying over into the ninth line the sentence which traditionally should end with the termination of the eighth. In *Christabel* Coleridge innovated a striking external discontinuity by returning to a principle of early Medieval poetry, though apparently without knowing it. He kept the number of stresses stable at four and varied the number of syllables to as many as twelve or more. And then he created internal discontinuity by violating that rule. It was some years before architects turned to the Baroque; initially the Gothic was their great instrument for disintegrating the explicitness of implied solids, screens, profiles, and walls to which the late Enlightenment had reduced architecture. Even when they used the Classic styles, they violated the canons of proportion of the Renaissance tradition, and synthesized Greek and Roman and Gothic rules of formal combination with the utmost abandon.

Finally, almost all the artists, to the degree it was possible, separated the type of art from its traditional situation. Insofar as the fugue was used in the Enlightenment at all, it was virtually confined to ecclesiastical situations; but Beethoven introduced it into the Third Symphony, the keyboard sonata, and the chamber sonata. In the same way, the poets broke the rules that had hitherto governed the genres, the rules that prescribed the verbal behavior for particular kinds of attitudes. In this sense, instead of, like Pope, pushing at the boundaries of decorum, they broke through those boundaries. Architects did the same: hence the use of Classic styles for churches and Gothic and Romanesque styles for banks. The Bohemian, the Dandy, and the Virtuoso can be identified because their behavior is inappropriate, but as far as situational rules were concerned, all the Romantic artists, throughout the century, were intensely interested in inappropriate behavior, whether they were leading a lobster on a pink ribbon or making a railroad station look like a cathedral. It is exactly the inappropriate which makes others recognize the existence of a self to be distinguished from the role. That tradition of the inappropriate is still the motivating force behind much of the behavior of Pop artists to-day. The artist is not really so interested in shocking the middle classes as he is in displaying behavioral attributes that make it impossible for anyone to categorize him as a member of the middle classes. It is always fun to be rude to the bourgeois, but the Romantic artist's serious interest is in signifying the self and in breaking down those illusory attitudes so popular with the middle classes which keep him from experiencing to the full the disparity between pattern and environmental demand, which prevent him from grasping perceptually more of reality, though reality itself he can never reach, which deny him the agony and the epiphany of cognitive tensions, and a wholly new mode of resolving such tension into cognitive harmony.

Finally, this cultural demand for defining and symbolizing the self will be our last example of how non-artistic cultural demands upon the artist are responsible for external discontinuity and for stylistic continua. When the various styles of the Romantic tradition are compared with other stylistic periods, one obvious phenomenon leaps out: in the sense that there are Gothic styles, and a High Renaissance style—in the sense that there is Mannerism, and Baroque and Rococo, there is no Romantic style. There is only a sequence of styles, each of which is strikingly discontinuous from its predecessor or predecessors. Indeed, it is true that each artist creates a unique style. To be sure, he builds upon and departs from his predecessor, as Tennyson built upon and departed from Wordsworth and Keats, or Wagner built upon and departed from Beethoven and Weber. But the obvious stylistic continuum that obtains from Dryden to Pope or from Heinrich Schütz to J. S. Bach is absent. Further, at the time, an artist was valued to the degree he succeeded in establishing a new style. Compared with preceding periods, a stylistic anarchy reigned. And this situation, of course, is still very true to-day, a virtually irrefutable proof that we are still, in our most advanced creations, Romantics. The reason for this novel kind of stylistic continuum was the demand that the artist symbolize the pure self in his work. His style was to be his and uniquely his. If it could be confused with anyone else's, or if the external discontinuity were not sufficiently powerful and striking, he was not and could not be admitted to a place at the apex of the cultural pyramid. Stylistic originality became the test of excellence. The Romantic tradition is marked by an extraordinary speed-up in the rate of non-functional stylistic dynamism. The stylistic distance traveled from Wordsworth to T. S. Eliot, from Ingres to Picasso, from Beethoven to Schönberg, is greater than the stylistic distance traversed from the Romanesque of the eleventh century to the last Enlightenment styles of Mozart, Blake, and David. The symmetrical front of a Romanesque cathedral is closer to Boulée than Boulée is to the asymmetry of Frank Lloyd Wright. And this central problem of the Romantic artists yields yet another explanation for the historicism or revivalism of the nineteenth-century Romantic arts. The terrible demand that each artist create a unique style meant that in desperation he ransacked the past for stylistic ideas as well as for styles which he could manipulate in a novel way to symbolize the uniqueness of his self. And finally, this is perhaps why, in the first decade of this century, all of the arts made the striking breakthrough into what we still call Modern Style. The nineteenth-century had pillaged the past and learned from it, and in so doing earned a profounder comprehension of the formal aspect of art than had any group of artists before them. That great knowledge of the formal possibilities of art coupled with the non-formal or semantic demands to realize the self in art and to exploit cognitive tension in order to break through to a new vision culminated in the extraordinary cultural convergence of the early twentieth-century arts into a wholly new artistic vision—that cultural convergence which, as we saw in Chapter I, is our primary evidence for the relation of the arts (see Plate XV).

The role of the artist, then, demands that he create external discontinuity by offering the perceiver implicit, internal, and modal discontinuity. The various arts are related not because they offer signs of orientations, but because the decisions for external discontinuity, for non-functional stylistic dynamism, create historically concurrent non-functional stylistic continua, since those decisions are in response to demands made upon the artist not by any defining attribute of his art but by the extra-artistic demands of his cultural level. And this, for example, is why folk art, which is derived from the highest cultural levels, descends to the lower levels by a steady decrease of discontinuity, by a steady reemergence of the implicit forms, and by the establishment of a slower and slower rate of non-functional stylistic dynamism. The further the individual is from the cultural apex and the social center, the less interested he is in innovation.

If all this is true, that is, if it is a valid explanation of why educated, cultivated, perceptive, and sensitive individuals like Sypher and Daniells are convinced that the arts are related, even though they have been able to convince no qualified person not already prepared to agree with them, if all that has been offered in this book so far is an acceptable construct, then it should be possible to offer some answer to the last remaining unanswered question: What is the function of art as a biological adaptation? Why has man spent on it such an enormous innovative effort and such treasures of energy and economic resource? Could not all this wealth be disbursed to some better, some more desirable, some more human purpose, some end that takes pity on the sufferings of men? Does not the arrogance and indifference of the roles of art, of artist and perceiver, so perplexing, so shocking, so monstrous—does not the *cruelty* of art violate man's only decencies?

SEVEN:
RAGE FOR CHAOS

The basic trouble with the stimulus-response theory is that it is incapable of explaining the dynamic character of human behavior, the human capacity for change. Ultimately it is a mechanical metaphor. At the physiological level it has its uses, and that is the level at which it first appeared in the seventeenth century. One is tempted to guess that it emerged from Descartes' hypothesis that animals feel no pain; since, apparently, they cannot say, "Cogito, ergo sum," they have no minds and therefore no souls. That the S-R model was enormously valuable for a long time is undeniable; there is no need to imply anything to the contrary. As a model it performed a very great task, and for some purposes it still can; by applying Newtonian mechanics to behavior it enabled the psychologist to make all kinds of enormously valuable observations and theoretical and operational constructs because it circumvented the problem of mind. By the late 1930's, however, something of a scandal was developing, and it was necessary to introduce the notion of *intervening variable*, to acknowledge that something happened between the stimulus and response that covered variation in response when the human organism actually interacted with the environment and which did not show up where the behaviorists wanted it to, at the physiological level.[1] It was at this point that the

---

[1] Kenneth McCorquodale and Paul E. Meehl, "Hypothetical Constructs and Intervening Variables," *Psychological Review*, LV, 1948, reprinted in *Readings in the Philosophy of Science*, ed. Herbert Feigl and May Brodbeck, New York, 1953, pp. 596–611.

transactionalists began to move in and that Bruner's problem emerged. Working at the level of social psychology, he found the S-R model virtually unusable, as did all workers, ultimately, who attempted to use it at the level of analysis which undertakes to give reference to the term "personality" or at the level at which cultural anthropologists work. Students of literature and the other arts found it useless and, in the desperate effort to find some psychological theory which helped to account for artistic phenomena, turned to Freudianism, which at least provided some kind of explanation for and account of interpretational variability.

Yet oddly enough the theory of aestheticians and critics showed the same weakness as S-R theory. The notion that aesthetic object is necessarily linked to aesthetic experience was precisely the same as that a given stimulus necessarily elicits a given response in a demonstrably normal organism. This continued in spite of the fact that the very small amount of experimental research done on the matter had almost totally negative results. Just as S-R theory could not account for the historicity of behavioral dynamics, so traditional aesthetics had really no way of explaining why mankind needs more than one aesthetic object, or at the best, one for each of the senses. If art is the search for perfect order, surely man would have found it by this time, or would have given up the search as a bad job; but in fact, aestheticians and critics have insisted that man has created that perfect aesthetic order over and over again. Why, then, should he keep on doing it? Thus one looks in vain, for an adequate explanation of the dynamic aspect of art. It is not enough to say that an attitude is symbolized by a work, and that when attitudes change, style changes. As we have seen, the formal aspect of style varies independently from the semantic aspect; and if the work of art is defined as a compound sign of a complex attitude—as indeed it is, though not an isomorphic sign, only an anamorphic construct—only the semantic aspect of art is taken care of; and, further, art can signify attitudes no better than any other sign structure, and on the whole not so well as psychology, philosophy, and cultural history. When the Wölfflin school are talking about aesthetic symbols they are merely talking about primary signs or configurational signs functioning as emblems of verbal signs.

Actually the only explanation ever offered is "creativity," but this is merely a sign for a category the range of which they are trying to explain. To hypostatize such a term is to say nothing. It only provides a term for the dynamism of art; it merely means, "The history of art is dynamic because the history of art is dynamic." "Creativity" or "the creative imagination" merely perpetrates a grotesque fallacy of misplaced concreteness. The psychologists who postulated intervening variables, knew what they were doing and why they were doing it; they were in trouble; they had permitted themselves to become aware of a problem, and they did not attempt to hide under a word of great status and such numerous semantic functions that nobody could possibly locate empirically what its users are talking about. "Intervening variable" is jargon, and it is infinitely preferable to something like "creative" or the "creative imagination" which, among aestheticians and art historians and literary critics, only serves to elicit validation by affective congruence. In the humanistic tradition "creative" gives one such a warm and expansive feeling that it seems impossible that it is but a name for what it purports to describe and explain. Terms like "order" and "unity" are terms of the same sort. They make the members of the cultural group who use them have the *affective experience of meaning* without forcing them to go to the trouble of finding out whether they have understood anything or not. These words are the totems of in-groups at the higher cultural levels. They are the equivalent of the insignia of the Masonic Shriners.

The one phenomenon to be explained about artistic behavior, in artist and perceiver alike, is non-functional stylistic dynamism, not "creativity." If this is explained, it is scarcely true that everything about art is explained, but because the essential is explained, a ground appears on which an explanation of the perceiver's and the artist's behavior can be constructed; and works of art themselves can be explained as the deposits of the artist's behavior, not as artifacts but as perceptual configurations. The central thing that needs explaining is why the artist is compelled to create more works of art, noticeably different from those already existing, and why the perceiver wearies of the art he has and wants something new. Such an explanation this book has attempted to offer. Only two matters remain: to explain this phenomenon from the point of view of biological adaptation and to explain the phenomenon of artistic valuation. The second is a minor matter and may be disposed of first.

Artistic value is a minor matter in spite of the fact that most aestheticians insist that it is the central matter of all, the problem on the solution of which any aesthetic theory must stand or fall. They all fall. The principal difficulty with statements about whether this work of art or that is good or bad is that they are all so excruciatingly uninteresting. If we want to know something about a work of art, if we want to know better how to perceive it, if we want to raise ourselves to the cultural level at which we can respond adequately to a work of art, value statements give us no help whatever, except in one way, and one way only. They create a canon, an unstable, constantly shifting canon, a canon for which we can find no justification whatever, except verbal myths, but nevertheless a canon. They tell us that men whom we can respect have valued this work; they tell us that it has been valued at the highest cultural level; and the study of the history of the canon shows that any work of art that has been valued at that level, even though it has been cast down the face of the pyramid, will be so valued again.

Why do people make value statements about works of art? The answer is a triviality; they do so because they make value statements about everything else in the world. Seventy-five percent of conversation consists of value statements. One has only to eavesdrop on a conversation in a bus, or merely listen to oneself talking to somebody else, to realize this. Seventy-five percent is probably too conservative. Perhaps not more than five percent of human verbal effort is devoted to making predictive statements. Perhaps this is why ninety-five percent of human effort is wasted. What, then, could be the function of value statements? And again the answer is close at hand. Value statements can all be resolved to moral prescriptive statements. "You ought to do this. You ought not to do that." Value statements and value attitudes are human efforts to create a predictable world by stabilizing categories, that is, by limiting the acceptable range of "ought to" statements. This, as we have seen, is another fool's errand, though it appears to be absolutely impossible for human beings to operate otherwise. Values function by controlling behavior, the behavior of others and the behavior of oneself. Value statements about art are merely efforts to stabilize the world of art so that one can know in advance that whatever the task of artistic perception may be, this particular work of art will, or will not, perform it.

But since value statements cannot be derived from works of art, but only applied to them, they are derived from other and extra-artistic sources, morality, philosophy, various sciences. Consequently they reflect the instability of such areas at the high innovative level. Nothing, not even women's clothes, is so unstable as fashions in value judgments at this higher cultural level. The result is that if one takes fashionable valuations seriously, vast areas of art are made inaccessible. Artistic valuations are the greatest hindrance imaginable to the adequate response to a work of art, particularly if it is out of fashion; and if it is in fashion, valuations can limit the perception of what can be responded to, since like all statements they are prescriptive statements, behavior-controlling models. They are in fact truly useful only as a means of discovering and focusing on what they do *not* select for positive valuation.

I have spoken frequently of the valuator's face of the pyramid of cultural innovation, but I have said little about it. I refer to the assertion of what, currently, at the various levels of culture, in the fields of philosophy, science, and art, is worth paying attention to. The valuator is not an individual but a role. It is often said that the humanist is a valuator, but the scholar, the historian of poetic meanings, the art historian whose field is iconography, like Panofsky, the interpreter of art, are all special forms of cultural historian. Their activities lie not on the valuator's face of the pyramid but on the scientific face. Their activity, like the activity of the historian of the formal aspect of art, is ultimately based on confirmed predictive statements, and they are engaged in making constructs based on such statements, constructs which are unstable, as all scientific constructs are, and must be. The role of valuator, rather, is the role of gatekeeper and cleaner of Augean stables. His task is to admit, or to refuse to admit, to preserve or to toss out, whatever in science, philosophy, or art, is, on the basis of current innovative values, to be admitted or excluded or thrown away. And because when this role operates at the highest cultural level, it operates at the highest level of innovation; its canon of philosophic and scientific propositions and works of art is, therefore, unstable. Evaluation is continuously dismantling that canon and rebuilding it.

Of what use, then, is that canon, that consequence of evaluation's effort to create instability masked as an effort to create stability? Of very great use indeed. It tells anyone at the lower levels of culture in whatever scientific or artistic or philosophical endeavor he may be interested in, what he must know to enter the gates. It informs him what, at the present time, is considered to be capable of performing adequately the tasks of science, art, and philosophy. And it offers him a fair and noble and ordered world beyond the gates. To be sure, when he is at last admitted, as the result of years of hard work and the presentation of the proper credentials, if only to himself, he finds instead a wild jungle, filled with savage beasts who will rend apart anyone who presumes to disagree with them, filled with booby traps and swamps of decaying and rotten values, which nobody has gotten around to cleaning up. The gatekeeper is the cleaner of Augean stables; but he is not Hercules. His task is never finished, or even adequately begun, and it is unending. But to the initiate who has been admitted through the gates, it is no matter. After a few startled moments he soon feels perfectly at home and becomes a rending beast himself. That is the game inside the gates of the apex of the cultural pyramid; it is a murderous jungle; and sometimes it is as beautiful as paradise. Sometimes the weather changes, and the skies clear, and one is in the Garden of the Lord, and the Lord walks beside.

Value statements about works of art, then, tell you what is currently believed to be best capable of performing the function of art. Once an individual is inside high-level culture, he can decide for himself, but mostly he does it by affective congruence, because it feels right, because for some reason it gives him an experience which he knows will help him if he uses it correctly. What, then, is the function of art that makes us live better, that adapts us better to the biological-perceptual situation we find ourselves in?

Man desires above all a predictable and ordered world, a world to which he is oriented, and this is the motivation behind the role of the scientist. But because man desires such a world so passionately, he is very much inclined to ignore anything that intimates that he does not have it. And to anything that disorients him, anything that requires him to experience cognitive tension he ascribes negative value. Only in protected situations, characterized by high walls of psychic insulation, can he afford to let himself be aware of the disparity between his interests, that is, his expectancy or set or orientation, and the data his interaction with the environment actually produces. That art offers precisely this kind of experience has, I hope, been adequately demonstrated. But to understand the perceiver's role better, let us once more consider the various ways of categorizing human behavior which the dramatic metaphor offers.

It is clear that art is useless, that perceiver and artist are arrogant and indifferent. It is their psychic insulation which makes such cruelty possible. Art tells us nothing about the world that we cannot find elsewhere and more reliably. Art does not make us better citizens, or more moral, or more honest. It may conceivably make us worse. It is easy to become addicted to art; it can be as dangerous as any drug. Art is something of a nuisance; it has certainly ruined the teakettle and, on the whole, the house. The great poetry of the past, if we take it too seriously, is capable of teaching us the most revolting nonsense. Dante is a prime example. Clearly the perception of art and the affective response to its signs and its discontinuities prepare us for no mode of behavior, no role, no pattern, no style. But it *is* preparation. Of the various possibilities of the dramatic metaphor, art fits most easily into rehearsal.

We rehearse for various roles all our lives, and for various patterns of behavior. We rehearse our national, our local, and our personal styles. These things we rehearse so that we may participate in a predictable world of social and environmental interaction. But we also must rehearse the power to perceive the failure, the necessary failure, of all those patterns of behavior. Art, as an adaptational mechanism, is reinforcement of the ability to be aware of the disparity between behavioral pattern and the demands consequent upon the interaction with the environment. Art is rehearsal for those real situations in which it is vital for our survival to endure cognitive tension, to refuse the comforts of validation by affective congruence when such validation is inappropriate because too vital interests are at stake; art is the reinforcement of the capacity to endure disorientation so that a real and significant problem may emerge. Art is the exposure to the tensions and problems of a false world so that man may endure exposing himself to the tensions and problems of the real world.

Did man create art in order to satisfy a physiologic need for a more stimulating environment than the order-directed social environment offers? It is conceivable. Certainly evolutionary history offers many far more complex, subtle, and highly selective adaptations. And such a notion is perfectly consonant with the explanation offered here of the function of artistic behavior in biologic adaptation.

Art is not reality, it is not truth, it is not value. It is nothing but a construct, because it is nothing but signs, and signs can only be constructs. But art is not even a reliable prescriptive construct, for its semantic character is subordinate to its disorientative function. Art offers man an entry into a fraudulent and deceiving world, but it is necessary. Art is an expensive nuisance, but it is necessary. It is a biological adaptation which serves to keep man alive, aware, capable of perceiving that he is neither adequate nor inadequate but a perilous mixture of the two, capable of innovation. Art is rehearsal for the orientation which makes innovation possible. Because it is fraudulent, deceiving, and enticing, it is a Circe; it can turn men into beasts. The only moral justification for the study of the highest level of art of the present and of the past, and for the years of difficult self-discipline and training necessary to make one capable of responding adequately to it, is to take what it can give so seriously, so passionately, with such conviction that one can learn to do without it. Of all man's burdens, art is one of the most terrible and certainly the most necessary. Without it he would not, he could not be human. But of that burden, with effort, with skill, with intelligence, and above all with luck, it is perhaps possible—at least for the very old—to be free.

APPENDIX

APPENDIX

A Possible Physiological Explanation of the Rage for Order

For some years Dr. Bernard Rimland, Director of the Personnel Measurement Research Department, U.S. Naval Personnel Research Laboratory, San Diego, California, has been engaged in the study of infantile autism. This is an "exceedingly rare behavior disorder in children," first established by Dr. Leo Kanner of Johns Hopkins. In 1964, Dr. Rimland published the result of his work in *Infantile Autism: The Syndrome and Its Implications for a Neural Theory of Behavior* (New York, Appleton-Century-Crofts). His studies have led him to a theory of the physiological basis of behavior which is of the greatest interest to anyone disposed to consider favorably my theories on artistic behavior, or, indeed, to anyone interested in human behavior; for Dr. Rimland's book is fascinating and his hypothesis is of the highest interest. I shall present here a brief and, of course, inadequate discussion of Dr. Rimland's ideas. Only his book can do them full justice.

Autistic children are not only rare; they are also characterized by unusually intelligent and achieving parents, and their family backgrounds have a strikingly low incidence of psychosis. It is as if nature intended them to be very superior individuals, but that something went wrong. They have often been classified as schizophrenics, but this is an error. The most important thing about them is their inability to "conceptualize," and by this Dr. Rimland means exactly what I have described as "categorizing" in Chapter III. Let us imagine a spectrum of human behavior, extending from manic-depressive psychosis at one end to schizophrenia at the other. Within the non-psychotic spectrum the range would be from schizoid types to cycloid (manic-depressive cycle) types. At the extreme cycloid end would be autistic psychosis. At the extreme schizoid end is schizophrenia. Schizophrenia is characterized by over-categorization, by responses which are irrelevant to the situation. That is, the schizophrenic jumbles up conventionalized categories; one attribute is enough for him to establish an identity between two conventionally separate ranges. That is why schizophrenic language is so extraordinarily metaphorical. The infantile autist, on the other hand, shows no powers of categorization whatever. For example, if he discovers that one block of several dozen randomly arranged blocks has been changed in his absence, he will fly into a rage. As Dr. Rimland puts it, whatever is fed into the sensory system comes out again virtually unchanged, when the appropriate stimulus is presented.

Using the work of other psychologists, Dr. Rimland defines intelligence as "the degree of availability of one's experiences for the solution of immediate problems and the anticipation of future ones"; and "the ability to see relationships and meanings by having access to as many alternatives as possible at approximately the same instant of time." He thinks that the brain's Arousal Mechanism, also called the Ascending Reticular Formation, is the place where sensation is linked to memory, although he feels that his theory does not depend upon this hypothesis. In any case, that linkage, he believes, is done in terms of patterns; that is, we think not logically but analogically, not by deductive steps but by observing similarities and dissimilarities between remembered patterns and new ones. This, of course, is perfectly consistent with and provides a ready explanation for the theory of discontinuity presented in this book. He also agrees that "emotion is the resultant of a discrepancy between expectation and actuality," which is precisely the definition I have offered. And creativity he explains as the drive "to fill the gaps in knowledge, to bring order to the content of mind, to *create* new coherences." At the root of intelligence, emotion, and creativity lies what he believes to be "neuron entelechy." "Entelechy" probably comes from the Greek "to be complete." He proposes, then, that "the brain contains neurons which are particularly responsive to certain specific patterns of stimulation, and that an experience of 'pleasure,' 'reward,' 'satisfaction,' or 'realization' for the organism occurs when a neuron is stimulated by an appropriately patterned pulse of coded sensory input. The degree of 'satisfaction' would be in part a function of the number of neurons responding. *For lack of better terminology*, we may say the neurons 'want' to discharge, and that they 'resonate' when stimulated by their appropriate pattern, or by patterns similar to it. The neuron would have previously been conditioned or tuned to respond to its critical stimulant pattern by genetic and/or experiential factors, usually acting jointly."

It hardly is necessary for me to underline how well this supports my general position and that of the various transactionalists, directive-state theorists, and expectancy theorists on whom I have depended to support my thesis. Even some of the language, as for example "tuned," is identical with that in the passages quoted in my Chapter V.

The brain, then, filters experience on the basis of past experience, and it does so by applying analogies from past experience. As Dr. Rimland says so exceedingly well, "If the brain operates as we here propose, in terms of analogies and perceived similarities rather than analytically, as has heretofore been believed, it would be instances of rational behavior which could be called aberrant. This is perhaps the more realistic view." The schizoid-cycloid spectrum, then, is a consequence of the over-functioning or the under-functioning of this filter, which in turn is dependent upon the neurons' "will" to find "satisfaction" in patterned resonation with other neurons. This is quite consistent with biological theory, which asserts that a population group includes a range or spectrum of each genetically transmitted characteristic. What Dr. Rimland proposes, then, is nothing less than a genetic explanation of behavior which heretofore has been considered entirely a matter of cultural transmission. As he says, instinct, which for decades has been swept under the rug, has suddenly reappeared. Not that innate ideas have reappeared, but the disposition to over-pattern or to under-pattern behavior appears to be innate.

Autism is virtually incurable. Certain schizophrenics are incurable. Other schizophrenics, or extreme schizoids, and some manic-depressives, or extreme cylcoids, can be helped by psychotherapy, though at the present time there is much evidence that such cases may be self-correcting; after a certain lapse of time, they would return from psychosis whether or not they received psychotherapy. Indeed, there is so much evidence that a massive research effort has been launched to find out if psychotherapy is of any use at all. Again, it is instructive that many psychiatrists believe that only neurotics and psychotics with high intelligence and high achievement can profit from any kind of psychotherapy, and that the kind does not make much difference. For my purposes, all this is enough to suggest that although the individual may be *innately placed* at some point in the spectrum, he is able to move one way or another along the spectrum; he is not *innately fixed* at one point. Experience can improve his placement, or damage it. (Yet it is to be noted that some modern psychiatrists are beginning to think that neurosis and psychosis are not dysfunctional but actually functional; they serve some purpose of the organism or of the personality.) I think it is just to consider the individual flexible in this matter. Even a few autistic children have been improved, and certain drugs can help.

From this point of view it would appear that my theory of the function of artistic behavior is questionable. That is, cycloids need to be moved towards the schizoid end, and schizoids need to be moved in the opposite direction, toward cycloid behavior. Art, then, would be helpful to cycloids but damaging to schizoids. But an important factor argues against this conclusion. Discontinuities are not categorial; they are not signs. Neither schizoids nor cycloids can endure cognitive tension; the one responds by too loose a categorizing behavior; the other, by too tight. Faced with cognitive tension, the schizoid seeks order by a frantic summoning up of all the categorizes available; the cycloid by a depressed reduction of available categories. A psychiatrist has told me that he is terribly bored by manic-depressives; they say the same thing over and over again. And my own experience includes an individual who may have been precipitated into psychosis by intense intellectual experience with poetry characterized by a high and very difficult metaphorical content.

Moreover, the theory of neuron entelechy suggests that this spectrum is not in fact symmetrical, that there is a bias towards order, that is, towards the cycloid end. High intelligence is characterized by an unusual degree of filtering. The highly intelligent person can often create his own psychic insulation, at least up to a point; Dr. Rimland thinks that the folk legend of the absent-minded professor bears out this theory of intelligence and high filtering power. As he says, at first the autistic child appears to be unusually intelligent. His inability to categorize emerges only after several years, and it marks his use of language as well as everything else. He never uses metaphors, and he cannot create a category of identify for himself. Many such children never learn the function of "I." And as my theory of the cultural pyramid and its apex suggests, highly intelligent people who like innovation (or creativity) in philosophy, science, and evaluation, also like highly innovative art, that is, art marked by the current extreme of external discontinuity. In short, I find

Dr. Rimland's suggestions about creativity biased in the direction of problem solving, and not sufficiently appreciative of the fact that cognitive tension must be felt before a problem can be defined, and that it must be categorized and made explicit before it can be solved. "The common element in creativity in both the arts and sciences is that the creative person is able to see similarities and relationships that are new and unique," he asserts. But it seems to me that first the creative person must be able to see dissimilarities where before only similarities had been seen, and the absence of relationships in areas in which by tradition relationships are to be found. He must be able to see that the emperor has no clothes. The creative person gets started by seeing an absurdity in conventional wisdom, as Dr. Rimland has.

Intelligence, Dr. Rimland says, is a necessary but not a sufficient prerequisite to creativity. I cannot see that he has sufficiently differentiated between creativity and intelligence. By his account, creativity (the seeing of new relationships) is only a higher power of intelligence (the ability to see relationships). As I suggested in the Preface, the human ability to create order (to see relationships) both qualifies man and disqualifies him in his adaptive efforts. If the neurons "feel" "pleasure," "satisfaction" and the rest, when their "will" to order is "gratified," the human tendency to suppress reality for the sake of order is certainly accounted for. (It will be observed that Dr. Rimland is quite aware he is using a metaphor in order to talk about neurons.) But in that case, clearly some kind of activity is necessary to work against that tendency, to resist the pleasure the organism gets from neuron entelechy. It is my belief that the formal aspect of art serves the function of providing education in that resistance, that capacity to endure cognitive tension. Dr. Rimland's statement about creativity in art works perfectly well for the semantic aspect of art, which is not a distinguishing attribute of art anyway, but it does not work at all for the formal aspect, if my explanation of that aspect has even a grain of truth in it. But if I am right, my assertion that art is a necessity for man, that his astounding evolutionary and cultural development would not have been possible without it, seems to be well founded.

From all this, it is possible to ask questions which would be capable, I think, of being studied by extensive research. Is there any correlation between the intelligent person who is creative and the richness and extent of his experience with the various arts at the cultural apex? My own experience in the academic world suggests that there is. And again, is there any correlation between the degree of successful recovery from neurosis and psychosis suffered by intelligent creative people and the richness and extent of their experience in such art? And again, my own experience and reading in such matters suggests to me that there might very well be such a correlation.

A final point is, I think, worth making. Dr. Rimland's theory puts Schopenhauer's ideas about the world as will and representation in an entirely new light. It has long been rejected from serious philosophical consideration; in one course I teach Schopenhauer because the Department of Philosophy does not think him worth bothering with. They are probably right that he is a negligible philosopher, but as a psychologist he seems to have had something important to say after all, in his assertion that the world, as man knows it, is nothing but the will to organized individuation. Further, Dr. Rimland's theory serves as a wonderful substantiation for Nietzsche's assertion that the proudest pleasure of the human mind is the creation of the world. For "mind" here, perhaps, we can now substitute "brain," or even "neurons of the brain."

BIBLIOGRAPHY

BIBLIOGRAPHY

Ackerman, James S. *The Architecture of Michelangelo*. N.Y.: Viking Press, 1961.

Allport, Floyd H. *Theories of Perception and the Concept of Structure*. N.Y.: John Wiley & Sons, 1955.

Arnheim, Rudolf. *Art and Visual Perception: A Psychology of the Creative Eye*. Berkeley: U. of California Press, 1957.

Barnett, H. G. *Innovation: The Basis of Cultural Change*. N.Y.: McGraw-Hill, 1953.

Beardsley, Monroe. *Aesthetics*. N.Y.: Harcourt, Brace & World, 1958.

Benz, Richard. *Die Deutsche Romantik: Geschichte einer Geistigen Bewegung*. Stuttgart: Reclam-Verlag, 1956.

Bouleau, Charles. *The Painter's Secret Geometry*. N.Y.: Harcourt, Brace, & World, 1963.

Boulger, James D. *Coleridge as Religious Thinker*. New Haven: Yale U. Press, 1961.

Bridgman, Percy. *The Way Things Are*. Cambridge: Harvard U. Press, 1959.

Bruner, Jerome S., and Cecile C. Goodman. "Value and Need as Organizing Factors in Perception," *Journal of Abnormal and Social Psychology*, 1947, pp. 33–44.

Bruner, Jerome S. "Personality Dynamics and the Process of Perceiving," in Robert R. Blake and Glenn V. Ramsey, *Perception: An Approach to Personality*. N.Y.: Ronald Press, 1951, pp. 121–147.

Bruner, Jerome S., Jacqueline J. Goodnow, and George A. Austin. *A Study of Thinking*, with an Appendix on Language, by Roger W. Brown. N.Y.: John Wiley & Sons, 1956.

Brunius, Teddy. "The Uses of Works of Art," *The Journal of Aesthetics and Art Criticism*, XXII, 1963, pp. 123–133.

Bukofzer, Manfred F. *Music in the Baroque Era: From Monteverdi to Bach*. N.Y.: W. W. Norton, 1947.

Chapple, Elliot D., and Carleton S. Coon. *Principles of Anthropology*. N.Y.: Henry Holt, 1942.

Cles-Reden, Sibylle von. *The Realm of the Great Goddess: The Story of the Megalith Builders*. N.Y.: Prentice-Hall, 1962.

Cooke, Deryck. *The Language of Music*. London: Oxford U. Press, 1959.

Daniells, Roy. *Milton, Mannerism, and Baroque.* U. of Toronto Press, 1963.

Empson, William. *Seven Types of Ambiguity.* New Directions, 1947.

Engelberg, Edward. *The Vast Design: Patterns in W. B. Yeats's Aesthetic.* U. of Toronto Press, 1964.

Fantz, Robert L. "The Origin of Form Perception," *Scientific American,* Vol. 204, May, 1961, pp. 66–72.

Foster, Richard. *The New Romantics: A Reappraisal of the New Criticism.* Bloomington: Indiana U. Press, 1962.

Frankfort, Henri. *The Art and Architecture of the Ancient Orient.* Baltimore: Penguin Books, 1955.

Giedion, Siegfried. *The Eternal Present: A Contribution on Constancy and Change.* N.Y.: Pantheon Books.

Vol. I: *The Beginnings of Art,* 1957.

Vol. II: *The Beginnings of Architecture,* 1964.

Goffman, Erving. *The Presentation of Self in Everyday Life.* N.Y.: Doubleday, 1959.

Gombrich, E. H. *Art and Illusion: A Study in the Psychology of Pictorial Representation.* N.Y.: Pantheon Books, 1960.

Goodman, Nelson. "The Way the World Is," *The Review of Metaphysics,* XIV, 1960, pp. 48–56.

Griaule, Marcel, and Germaine Dieterlin. "The Dogon," *African Worlds.* London: Oxford U. Press for UNESCO, 1954.

Grout, Donald Jay. *A History of Western Music.* N.Y.: W. W. Norton, 1960.

Haftmann, Werner. *Painting in the 20th Century.* N.Y.: Frederick A. Praeger, 1960.

Haskell, Douglas. *Patrons and Painters: A Study in the Relations between Art and Society, in the Age of the Baroque.* N.Y.: Alfred A. Knopf, 1963.

Hess, Eckhard H. "Shadows and Depth Perception," *Scientific American,* Vol. 204, March, 1961, pp. 138–148.

Hoijer, Harry, ed. *Language in Culture.* Chicago: U. of Chicago Press, 1954.

Jackson, Laura [Riding]. "Further on Poetry," *Chelsea,* No. 14, 1964, pp. 38–47.

Kennick, William E. "Does Traditional Aesthetic Rest on a Mistake?" *Mind,* LXVII, 1958, pp. 317–334.

Kilpatrick, Franklin P. "Introduction," *Explorations in Transactional Psychology,* ed., Kilpatrick. N.Y.: N.Y.U. Press, 1961.

Kline, Morris. *Mathematics in Western Culture.* N.Y.: Oxford U. Press, 1953.

Kluckhohn, Clyde, and W. H. Kelley. "The Concept of Culture," in *The Science of Man in the World Crisis,* ed. R. Linton. N.Y.: Columbia U. Press, 1945, p. 97.

Kubler, George. *The Shape of Time: Remarks on the History of Things.* New Haven: Yale U. Press, 1962.

Kuhn, Thomas S. *The Structure of Scientific Revolutions.* U. of Chicago Press, 1962.

Lane, Robert E. *The Liberties of Wit: Humanism, Criticism, and the Civic Mind.* New Haven: Yale U. Press, 1961.

Lang, Paul Henry. *Music in Western Civilization.* N.Y.: W. W. Norton, 1941.

Langer, Susanne K. *Philosophy in a New Key.* Cambridge: Harvard U. Press, 1951.

———. *Feeling and Form.* N.Y.: Charles Scribner's Sons, 1953.

———. *Problems of Art: Ten Philosophical Lectures.* N.Y.: Charles Scribner's Sons, 1957.

Levi, Albert William. *Literature, Philosophy, & the Imagination.* Bloomington: Indiana U. Press, 1962.

Levy, Gertrude Rachel. *The Gate of Horn*. London: Faber, 1949.

Lewis, Warren H. *The Splendid Century*. N.Y.: Wm. Sloane Ass., 1953.

London *Times Literary Supplement*, review of Elizabeth Jennings, *Recoveries*, June 11, 1964, p. 512.

Malevich, Kasimir. *The Non-Objective World*, tr. by Howard Dearstyne. Chicago: Paul Theobald, 1959.

Manson, Grant Carpenter. *Frank Lloyd Wright to 1910: The First Golden Age*. N.Y.: Reinhold, 1958.

Margenau, Henry. *Open Vistas: Philosophical Perspectives of Modern Science*. New Haven: Yale U. Press, 1961.

McCorquodale, Kenneth, and Paul E. Meehl. "Hypothetical Constructs and Intervening Variables," *Psychological Review*, LV, 1948, reprinted in *Readings in the Philosophy of Science*, ed. Herbert Feigl and May Brodbeck. N.Y.: Appleton-Century-Crofts, 1953, pp. 596–611.

Mead, George Herbert. *Mind, Self, and Society*. Chicago: U. of Chicago Press, 1934.

Menninger, Karl, with Martin Mayman and Paul Pruyser. *The Vital Balance: The Process in Mental Health and Illness*. N.Y.: Viking Press, 1963.

Meyer, Leonard B. *Emotion and Meaning in Music*. Chicago: U. of Chicago Press, 1956.

Michel, Édouard, Mme. Robert Aulanier, and Hélène de Vallée. *Watteau: "L'Embarquement pour l'Ile de Cythère,"* Monographies des Peintures du Musée du Louvre, II, Éditions des Musées Nationaux. Paris [?1939].

Mises, Richard Von. *Positivism: A Study in Human Understanding*. Cambridge, Harvard U. Press, 1951.

Morris, Charles W. "Foundations of the Theory of Signs," *International Encyclopedia of Unified Science*, I, No. 2, pp. 77–137, Chicago, 1955.

———. *Signs, Language, and Behavior*. N.J.: Prentice-Hall, 1946.

Naumburg, Margaret. "Expanding Non-Verbal Aspects of Art Education on the University Level," *Journal of Aesthetics and Art Criticism*, XIX, 1961, pp. 439–451.

Peckham, Morse. "Blake, Milton, and Edward Burney," *The Princeton University Library Chronicle*, XI, 1950, pp. 107–126.

———. *Beyond the Tragic Vision*. N.Y.: George Braziller, 1962.

Pepper, Stephen C. *World Hypotheses*. Berkeley and Los Angeles: U. of California Press, 1942.

———. *The Basis of Criticism in the Arts*. Cambridge: Harvard U. Press, 1946.

Richards, I. A. *How to Read a Page*. London: Kegan Paul, Trench, Trubner & Co., Ltd., 1943.

Robb, David M. *The Harper History of Painting: The Occidental Tradition*. N.Y.: Harper, 1951.

Schönberg, Arnold. "Verklärte Nacht," *The Music of Arnold Schönberg*, Vol. II, Columbia Records, 1962.

Schönberger, Arno, and Halldor Soehner, with Theodor Müller, tr. by Daphne Woodward. *The Rococo Age: Art and Civilization of the 18th Century*. N.Y.: McGraw-Hill, 1960.

Scully, Vincent. *The Earth, the Temples and the Gods*. New Haven: Yale U. Press, 1962.

Simson, Otto Von. *The Gothic Cathedral*. N.Y.: Pantheon Books, 1953.

Skinner, B. F. *Verbal Behavior*, Appleton-Century-Crofts, 1957.

Stillman, Edmund, and William Pfaff. *The Politics of Hysteria: The Sources of Twentieth-Century Conflict*. N.Y.: Harper & Row, 1964.

Sypher, Wylie. *Four Stages of Renaissance Style*. N.Y.: Doubleday, 1952.

——. *Rococo to Cubism in Art and Literature*. N.Y.: Random House, 1960.

Szasz, Thomas S. *The Myth of Mental Illness: Foundations of a Theory of Conduct*. N.Y.: Hoeber-Harper, 1961.

Tapié, Victor L. *The Age of Grandeur*, tr. by A. Ross Williamson. N.Y.: Frederick A. Praeger, 1960.

Time, "Education," March 9, 1962, pp. 62, 65.

——, "Religion," July 10, 1964, p. 64.

Turbayne, Colin Murray. *The Myth of Metaphor*. New Haven: Yale U. Press, 1962.

Weitz, Morris. "The Role of Theory in Aesthetics," *Problems in Aesthetics*, ed. Weitz. N.Y.: Macmillan, 1959.

White, Morton. *Toward Reunion in Philosophy*. Cambridge: Harvard U. Press, 1956.

Whitehead, Alfred North. *Science and the Modern World*. N.Y.: Macmillan, 1948.

Ziff, Paul. *Semantic Analysis*. Ithaca: Cornell U. Press, 1960.

INDEX OF SPECIAL TERMS

INDEX OF SPECIAL TERMS

[*Note:* This is not an index of all occurrences, but rather of the most important. It is designed to serve as a glossary.]

INDEX OF PROPER NAMES

INDEX OF PROPER NAMES